FPCC

SEP 1 8 2000

 St. Louis Community College

Forest Park
Florissant Valley
Meramec

Instructional Resources
St. Louis, Missouri

CONTEMPORARY
Black
Biography

ISSN-1058-1316

CONTEMPORARY

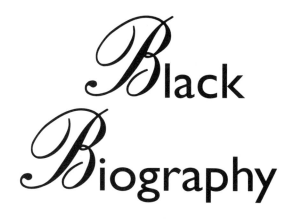

Black

Biography

Profiles from the International Black Community

Volume 25

David G. Oblender, Editor

GALE GROUP

Detroit
New York
San Francisco
London
Boston
Woodbridge, CT

STAFF

David G. Oblender, *Editor*

Shirelle Phelps, *Contributing Editor*

Shelly Dickey, *Managing Editor, Multicultural Department*
Maria Franklin, *Permissions Manager*
Margaret Chamberlain, *Permissions Specialist*

Dorothy Maki, *Manufacturing Manager*
Stacy Melson, *Buyer*
Cynthia Baldwin, *Product Design Manager*
Michael Logusz, *Graphic Artist*
Randy Bassett, *Image Database Supervisor*
Pamela A. Reed, *Imaging Coordinator*
Robyn V. Young, *Senior Editor, Imaging and Multimedia Content*
Robert Duncan, *Imaging Specialist*

Victoria B. Cariappa, *Research Manager*
Barbara McNeil, *Research Specialist*
Ron Morelli, *Research Assistant*

Mary Beth Trimper, *Manager, Composition and Electronic Prepress*
Gary Leach, *Compostion Specialist*

ISBN 0-7876-3249-X
ISSN 1058-1316

10 9 8 7 6 5 4 3 2 1

Contemporary Black Biography
Advisory Board

Contents

Introduction ix

Photo Credits xi

Cumulative Nationality Index 191

Cumulative Occupation Index 199

Cumulative Subject Index 215

Cumulative Name Index 251

Introduction

Contemporary Black Biography provides informative biographical profiles of the important and influential persons of African heritage who form the international black community: men and women who have changed today's world and are shaping tomorrow's.

Contemporary Black Biography covers persons of various nationalities in a wide variety of fields, including architecture, art, business, dance, education, fashion, film, industry, journalism, law, literature, medicine, music, politics and government, publishing, religion, science and technology, social issues, sports, television, theater, and others.

In addition to in-depth coverage of names found in today's headlines,*Contemporary Black Biography* provides coverage of selected individuals from earlier in this century whose influence continues to impact on contemporary life. *Contemporary Black Biography* also provides coverage of important and influential persons who are not yet household names and are therefore likely to be ignored by other biographical reference series. Each volume also includes listee updates on names previously appearing in CBB.

Designed for Quick Research and Interesting Reading

- **Attractive page design** incorporates textual subheads, making it easy to find the information you're looking for.

- **Easy-to-locate data sections** provide quick access to vital personal statistics, career informa- tion, major awards, and mailing addresses, when available.

- **Informative biographical essays** trace the subject's personal and professional life with the kind of in-depth analysis you need.

- **To further enhance your appreciation** of the subject, most entries include photographic portraits.

- **Sources for additional information** direct the user to selected books, magazines, and news- papers where more information on the individuals can be obtained.

Helpful Indexes Make It Easy to Find the Information You Need

Contemporary Black Biography includes cumulative Nationality, Occupation, Subject, and Name indexes that make it easy to locate entries in a variety of useful ways.

Available in Electronic Formats

Diskette/Magnetic Tape. *Contemporary Black Biography* is available for licensing on magnetic tape or diskette in a fielded format. Either the complete database or a custom selection of entries may be ordered. The database is available for internal data processing and nonpublishing purposes only. For more information, call (800) 877-GALE.

Online. *Contemporary Black Biography* is available online through Mead Data Central's NEXIS Service in the NEXIS, PEOPLE and SPORTS Libraries in the GALBIO file.

We Welcome Your Suggestions

The editors welcome your comments and suggestions for enhancing and improving *Contemporary Black Biography.* If you would like to suggest persons for inclusion in the series, please submit these names to the editors. Mail comments or suggestions to:

The Editor
Contemporary Black Biography
Gale Group
27500 Drake Rd.
Farmington Hills, MI 48331-3535
Phone: (800) 347-4253

Photo Credits

PHOTOGRAPHS AND ILLUSTRATIONS APPEARING IN *CONTEMPORARY BLACK BIOGRAPHY*, VOLUME 25, WERE RECEIVED FROM THE FOLLOWING SOURCES:

All Reproduced by Permission:**Adams, Sheila,**photograph. Courtesy of the Urban League of Greater Cincinnati. **Anderson, Elmer,** photograph. Courtesy of the World of Sports First International Afro-American Sports Hall of Fame and Gallery. **Anthony, Wendell,** photograph. Courtesy of the NAACP, Detroit Branch. Reproduced by permission. **Baisden, Michael,** photograph. Courtesy of Legacy Publishing. **Beverly, Frankie,** photograph. AP/Wide World Photos. **Bolton, Terrell,** photograph by L.M. Otero. AP/Wide World Photos. **Brazile, Donna,** photograph by Mark Humphrey. AP/Wide World Photos. **Brown, Foxy,** photograph by Laura Walters. The Gamma Liaison Network. **Brown, Joyce F.,** photograph by John Senzeer. Courtesy of Fashion Institute of Technology (FIT). **Bullins, Ed,** photograph by Marva Rae. Helen Merrill Ltd. **Burris, Roland W.,** photograph. Fisk University Library. **Campanella, Roy,** photograph. Archive Photos. **de Passe, Suzanne,** photograph by Charles Arrigo. AP/World Wide Photos. **Diggs, Taye,** photograph by Fred Prouser. Archive Photos. **Elder, Larry,** photograph. KABC Radio. **Ferguson, Roger W.,** photograph by Brooks/Glogau Studio. **Fields, C. Virginia,** photograph by Ed Bailey. AP/Wide World Photos. **Givens, Robin,** photograph. AP/Wide World Photos. **Gordon, Dexter,** photograph. AP/Wide World Photos. **Griffith, Yolanda,** photograph by Rich Pedroncelli. AP/Wide World Photos. **Heard, Gar,** photograph by Susan Walsh. AP/Wide World Photos. **Higginbotham, A. Leon,** photograph. Corbis-Bettmann. **Hillard, Terry,** photograph. Courtesy of the Chicago Police Department. **Isley, Ronald,** photograph by Nick Ut. AP/Wide World Photos. **Jackson, Millie,** photograph. Corbis. **Jefferson, William J.,** photograph by Judi Bottoni. AP/Wide World Photos. **Lee, Barbara,** photograph by Dennis Magee. AP/Wide World Photos. **Meeks, Gregory,** photograph. Courtesy of the office of Gregory Meeks. **Mosley, Walter,** photograph by Jerry Bauer. **Mutebi, Ronald,** photograph by Kris Snibbe. AP/Wide World Photos. **Nakhid, David,** photograph by Denis Poroy. AP/Wide World Photos. **Patterson, Louise,** photograph. AP/Wide World Photos. **Payton, Walter,** photograph. AP/Wide World Photos. **Quarles, Norma,** photograph. AP/Wide World Photos. **Rivers, Glenn "Doc",** photograph by Scott Audette. AP/Wide World Photos **Sklarek, Norma,** photograph by Mark Schurer. **St. John, Kristoff,** photograph. AP/Wide World Photos. **Summer, Donna,** photograph. AP/Wide World Photos. **Taylor, Lawrence,** photograph by Mark Duncan. AP/Wide World Photos. **Thomas, Derrick,** photograph. AP/Wide World Photos. **Thompson, Tina,** photograph. AP/Wide World Photos. **Watson, Bob,** photograph by Marty Lederhandler. AP/Wide World Photos. **Williams, Joe,** photograph by Jack Vartoogian. **Wright, Deborah C.,** photograph. Courtesy of Carver Federal Savings Bank, New York **Wynn, Albert,** photograph by Joe Marquette. AP/Wide World Photos.

Sheila J. Adams

1943—

Organization president

Sheila Adams has made it her life's work to bring greater economic opportunity to those people who have yet to realize the American dream. For over a decade, she has served as president and chief executive officer of the Urban League of Greater Cincinnati, overseeing a broad range of services designed to strengthen the African American community. In her view, it is a fitting legacy for the great-granddaughter of a slave who escaped to Canada through Ohio's Underground Railroad to teach other African Americans how to escape economic hardship by developing marketable skills. "It's that old adage about if you give a person a fish, he'll eat for a day, but if you teach a person to fish, he'll eat for a lifetime," Adams told *Contemporary Black Biography (CBB)*.

Born in Cincinnati in 1943, Adams was the youngest of seven children in the Thompson family. She was educated at local schools, but it was her father's example that set the tenor for her life. Adams's father owned a well-regarded plaster contracting company. His motto—"If it's up to me, excellent it will be"—soon became his daughter's work ethic as she strove to excel. After graduating from Withrow High School, she attended Central State College for a year before transferring to the University of Cincinnati. In 1964, Adams earned a bachelor's degree in sociology. She recalled in an interview with *CBB*, "I wanted to do all this great stuff for the world, but I eventually realized that economic improvements were what would really help people."

Kept the Home Fires Burning

During her junior year of college, Adams married a professional basketball player. After earning her bachelor's degree, she opted to raise a family while her husband lived the life of a professional athlete. Adams raised two sons and a daughter, putting her homemaking skills to the test when her sons were young. She highly valued the roles of wife and homemaker. According to Adams, American culture does a disservice when it devalues women's work in the home. "The most important work for a mother at home is home life," she said emphatically in her interview with CBB. "Whenever I speak to women, I make sure they know that motherhood is valuable and they should value their contributions to society by being good mothers and homemakers."

Adams eventually divorced her husband, and entered the workforce. She served for nine years as a personnel officer and chief planner for the Employment and

At a Glance . . .

Born in Cincinnati, OH, on June 1, 1943; married, 1963 (later divorced), married Alexander Adams (retired college professor), 1992; children: Derek, Brian, Ariana (from first marriage). *Education:* University of Cincinnati, B.A. (sociology), 1964.

Career: City of Cincinnati, Employment and Training Division, personnel officer andchief planner, 1971-81; Private Industry Council, president, 1982-89; Urban League of GreaterCincinnati, president and chief executive officer, 1990-.

Selected awards: YWCA Career Woman of Achievement, 1988; Withrow High SchoolHall of Fame, 1991; *Cincinnati Enquirer* Woman of the Year, 1993; Delta Sigma Theta Economic Empowerment Award, 1995; Enterprise Award—Individual of the Year, 1996;YMCA Character Award, 1997; Black Career Women, Inc. Legacy Messenger, 1997; Dr. MartinL King J. "Dream Keeper Award" for Individual and Corporate Achievement, theArts Consortium of Cincinnati and the City of Cincinnati, 1998; Distinguished Black Women Award, Black Women in Sisterhood for Action, 1999; Cincinnati Bell Building Bridges Award,2000.

Selected memberships: Ohio Council of Urban League (chair); The Cincinnati Youth Collaborative; Family and Children First Executive Committee; Black Career Women;Cincinnati Links; Alpha Kappa Alpha Sorority; delegate for the President Clinton Summit forAmerica's Future, 1997.

Addresses: *Office* —Urban League of Greater Cincinnati, 3458 ReadingRd., Cincinnati, OH 45229-3128.

emergencies that come with family life."

Led League to New Heights

In 1990, Adams took the helm of the Urban League of Greater Cincinnati. This organization, founded in 1949, strives through training and development programs to promote self-sufficiency. Among its many programs, the Urban League runs after-school educational support programs where students receive tutoring, homework assistance, and access to computer-based learning. The educational programs are staffed by volunteers drawn from the African American church and the larger community. Other programs help urban youth to develop academically, personally, and socially. Several programs teach youths about the risks of contracting the human immunodeficiency virus (HIV), the virus that causes AIDS, and the need for sexual abstinence. For parents, teachers, and community leaders, the League offers parent empowerment training and violence-resistance training. It also offers a welcome program for new members of the Cincinnati community. In the workforce development arena, the Urban League provides computer training, high school equivalence diploma courses, job counseling, resume and interview classes, and job referrals. Its YouthWorks jobs-readiness program helps 14 to 17-year-old students prepare themselves to enter the workforce for the first time. Adams's role involved overseeing all of these programs.

Adams is a graduate of Leadership Cincinnati X. This program helps prepare participants for future leadership roles by bringing aspiring leaders together to consider community needs and how they might be met. Since less than a fourth of the participants were members of minority groups, Adams decided to create a similar program. She founded the African American Leadership Development Program in 1993, with the goal of nurturing leaders who would then make a direct and positive impact on the African American community. Businesses and organizations in the Cincinnati area sponsor participants in this popular ten-month development program.

In 1995, Adams launched a capital campaign to build a 23,000 square foot facility which would serve as headquarters for Urban League programs. When the facility opened two years later, it was equipped to serve thousands of families. The 4.4 million facility stood as a testament to the partnerships between business people, civic leaders, and philanthropists who funded its construction and support Urban League programs. It also reflected Adams's vision and skillful leadership. Although Adams noted some improvement in employment and education prospects for African Americans, "things just aren't there yet," she told *CBB*. "Until the playing field is level, there will always be a need for the Urban League to speak for people and lift them up." Adams confirmed her long-term commitment to the

Training Division of the City of Cincinnati before becoming president of the Private Industry Council in 1982. In these positions, Adams gained important knowledge of the business world, and realized her goal of "making a difference" by promoting economic opportunities for some 30,000 greater Cincinnati area residents. She also learned to balance her family and work roles. As she told *CBB*, "I knew that I had to juggle family and my job, so I put support systems in place. I've always been fortunate enough to have jobs where my family responsibilities were understood. And I was able to do my job well despite the occasional

Urban League and its goals. "I can't afford to give up," Adams remarked to *CBB*. "I see little babies coming out of school, passing my office everyday. I cannot afford to get discouraged. I cannot give up. Every time I look in the eyes of little children, I think of how they deserve a future. That's not to say I don't get discouraged sometimes. I do, but not for long. All of us deserve what society has to offer."

Sources

Periodicals

Essence, September, 1998.
Opportunity Journal, August, 1998.

Other

Additional material for this profile was obtained from The Urban League of Greater Cincinnati's site on the World Wide Web, at http:\\www.gcul.org\; and from an interview with Sheila Adams on April 27, 2000.

—Jeanne M. Lesinski

Elmer Anderson

1941—

Museum founder

Elmer Anderson is proud of his accomplishments. It is a pride which fills his voice with emotion and which holds his head high. From the fields in his Detroit neighborhood to the sandlot fields of the semi-professional leagues, Anderson's life has been dominated by the game of baseball. When his playing days were over, he turned his energies and his passions towards ensuring that the contributions of African American baseball players – and athletes in general – to the world of American sports would be heralded forever.

Anderson was born on August 21, 1941 in Detroit, Michigan. As a youngster, he remained close to his parents and to his sister, Sharon Marie, who was several years his junior. As he reflected on his early years in an interview with *Contemporary Black Biography,* Anderson noted that his childhood fantasies forever revolved around sports, and particularly around baseball. In fact, pick-up baseball games with his friends in the neighborhood fields constitute some of his fondest memories. Using sticks because they could not afford bats, Anderson and his friends went to the baseball diamond and spent hour upon hour reenacting the plays of their heroes, baseball greats such as Joe Dimaggio, Jackie Robinson, and Josh Gibson.

Anderson idolized Willie Mays and Mickey Mantle, for he loved, as he told *CBB,* to "hit the long ball." The homeowners surrounding the fields where Anderson played were less impressed with his drive and style, for rarely a day passed when he did not break a window. Chuckling, Anderson told *CBB* that after each crash, he would dash home, feign illness in front of his mother, and then hide in his bedroom. When not actually playing in a game, Anderson devoted still more hours to the sport, amusing himself by throwing balls against outdoor walls and then chasing them, outfielder-style.

Began Semi-Professional Baseball Career

In 1959, after graduating from Northeastern High School in Detroit, Anderson took the first step towards realizing his childhood dream of playing professional baseball when he signed with the semi-professional Detroit Motor City Redcaps, who were a part of the Jacksonville, Florida Redcaps of the then Negro League. As the *Michigan Chronicle* reported, Anderson is remembered for "his high-leaping, belly-sliding, dipsy-doodle catches in the outfield," as well as for his power hitting. Sam Davis, who played with Anderson in several old-timers games and later served as the president and on the Board of Trustees of Anderson's Hall of Fame, vividly remembers Anderson's daring athleticism. In a discussion with *CBB,* Davis recalls Anderson leaping over an open manhole in the outfield to catch a ball and, in another instance, chasing down a drive in foul territory and snaring it, a catch no one in the park thought could be made. Anderson's skill was later captured for a national audience when he played an outfielder in a made-for-television film in 1983 entitled Tiger Town.

Throughout his baseball career, Anderson worked for several companies as a block fitter for automotive frames. When the Red Caps folded in 1967, Anderson joined Detroit Diesel, a division of General Motors, in a similar capacity. In 1970 Detroit Diesel recognized Anderson's dedication and accomplishments, awarding him with an engine trophy and a savings bond for an assembly line he had designed. As he explained to *CBB,* "I always liked to create something."

Detroit Diesel proved to be far more than a simple place of employment for Anderson. During his early years at the plant, as the Negro leagues continued to disband, many former baseball players flocked to Detroit, and specifically into job openings at the major automotive factories. Anderson realized the wealth of sports history which his fellow assembly line workers possessed, and he wanted to ensure that it was captured before it was lost forever. In December of 1977 he approached Art Finney, then the newspaper editor of UAW Local 163, with the idea of writing articles in the union newspapers about former African American athletes. Finney capitalized on Anderson's idea and started to write one story each month for his newspapers, stories drawn not only from the annals of baseball, but from football, basketball, and boxing, too.

Envisioned Creation of Hall of Fame

As the number of published stories began to mount, the list of potential biographies grew exponentially. Initially Finney and Anderson had envisioned that the interviews would ultimately be compiled into a book entitled *For the Love of the Game,* a book which would remind its readership of the times when, as Leslie Smith reflected, "men played for the love of the game and fans watched them for the same reason." However, Anderson and Finney soon discovered that there was far too much history for the confines of one book, and thus together they conceived of the idea of an African American sports hall of fame museum.

With the assistance of the Museum of African American History, Anderson and Finney worked to chronicle the history of African Americans in sports from the mid-1800s until 1960. Frank Saunders, a sports writer for the *Michigan Chronicle,* supported the efforts of Anderson and Finney and, through the *Chronicle,* began to gather stories nationwide that helped to generate interest in an African American sports museum. According to Finney, he and Anderson planned to target people "of all ages, colors, and creeds who accomplished something outstanding in any and all fields of endeavor, but never quite made it in the so-called big-time."

In 1981, the museum concept received an even bigger boost when Anderson and Finney were invited to attend the Negro Baseball Reunion in Ashland, KY. There, the two men met Leroy "Satchel" Paige and James "Cool Papa" Bell. As Anderson recounted to *CBB,* it was at these meetings that the ideas for an organization to honor African American athletes "all started booming." Having quickly befriended Paige, Anderson was chosen as "the young godfather" of the group. Older players promised to remain with him in spirit to help bring the museum to fruition.

Although he never fulfilled his dream of playing baseball at the major league level, Anderson did fulfill his dream of an African American sports hall of fame museum. As he told Valerie Lynn Dorsey of *USA Today,* "Satchel Paige told me not to let my dream die and that I could reach all kinds of people of all ages and all races from around the world." On January 9, 1982 the National Afro-American Sports Hall of Fame and Gallery officially opened to the public. It was the first organization to honor black athletes worldwide. With Anderson publicly recognized as the founder, Ronald Teasley was selected as the first president, and James Lewis was chosen as the curator.

Oversaw Establishment of Hall of Fame

Former baseball players rallied to energize fundraising efforts for the museum. Several old-timers games were played in Detroit and Grand Rapids in August and September of 1982. In 1983, Terry Cabell organized the Afro-American All Stars, a baseball team formed to play exhibition baseball games in order to raise funds for the hall of fame. The team consisted of former players from the professional, semi-professional, sandlot, and Negro League teams. Anderson also played on the team. The Afro-American All Stars played their first game on September 24, 1983.

Not only did the old-timers games generate revenue for the museum, but they also helped to raise awareness and interest in the museum's mission. At a ceremony held at Mercy College in Detroit on September 13, 1986, the National Afro-American Sports Hall of Fame and Gallery held its first induction ceremony. Inductees included former Detroit Lion great Richard "Night Train" Lane, basketball coach William J. Robinson, and boxer Joe Louis. Anderson and Finney were also inducted. The Hall of Fame took a further step towards international recognition when it became a member of the International Association of Sports Museums and Halls of Fame in 1987. The museum officially became an international organization in 1990, and was renamed the World of Sports First International Afro-American Sports Hall of Fame and Gallery.

Under Anderson's guidance, the Hall of Fame has remained true to Anderson and Finney's initial conception. The museum recognizes African American athletes whose success, according to Dorsey, "equaled or surpassed the achievements of white athletes with whom they were not allowed to compete because of segregation." Moreover, the hall also recognizes African American sports pioneers and people of other ethnic backgrounds who helped to promote the accomplishments of African American athletes. While glorifying these athletes, the museum also seeks to educate children, especially African American youths, about their history, to delve into their struggles as well as their successes. As George C. Scott told Rob Parker of the *Michigan Chronicle,* "When we house who they were, what they did, and what they gave, it is symbolic enough for our young people to know they aren't the first person trying to do something." In 1994, Anderson was selected by the International Boxing Hall of Fame to have a gold cast fist made of his right hand. He

was the first non-boxing sports celebrity to receive this award.

By 2000, the Hall of Fame housed pictures, artifacts, old uniforms, Hall of Fame plaques, boxing trunks, and boxing gloves. Anderson continues to dream about the museum and to build upon these dreams. Of primary importance to Anderson is securing a building specifically dedicated to the museum, which remains housed on the fourth floor of the Wayne County Building in Detroit. Moreover, Anderson dreams of establishing a "walk of fame" dedicated to African American athletes. Given all the dreams that Anderson has transformed into realities, it should not be surprising when he reaches these goals – and then some.

Sources

Books

The All-Time All Stars of Black Baseball, TK Publishers, 1983.

Periodicals

Detroit Free Press, May 26, 1999.
Grand Rapids Press, September 12, 1982.
Jet, March 4, 1991, p. 50.
Michigan Chronicle, June 17, 1978; September 20, 1980; August 28, 1982; September 11, 1982; June 2, 1984; January 12, 2000; March 15-21, 2000.
Northwest Area Business Association, February 1987, p. 2.
Northwest Union News, November 1978.
USA Today, May 5, 1993, p. 11C.

Other

Additional information for this profile was obtained from an interview with *Contemporary Black Biography,* April, 2000, and from promotional materials provided by the World of Sports First International Afro-American Sports Hall of Fame & Gallery.

—Lisa S. Weitzman

Wendell Anthony

1950—

Minister, NAACP leader

When the Detroit chapter of the NAACP chose the Reverend Wendell Anthony as its president in 1993, it signified a new era for this particular branch, which has the largest membership roster in the country. An outspoken, dynamic minister whose master's thesis once discussed the church as an agent for reform and renewal inside the urban African American community, Anthony immediately set about revitalizing what some saw was a moribund local organization.

Anthony was born in St. Louis, Missouri, in 1950. When he was two years-old, his parents divorced. Anthony's mother eventually remarried, and left her young son with relatives for a time while she and her new husband established themselves in Detroit. Anthony moved to Detroit when he was eight, and grew up in a comfortable home on the city's west side. His parents both worked for the post office. Anthony's sense of justice showed itself at an early age: he claimed to have once led a walkout of his elementary school classroom over an unfair punishment. By the mid-1960s, the era of the burgeoning black power movement, Anthony used some of the movement's arguments as president of the student council at Detroit Central High School. He argued for a black history curriculum within the school system, and called for the

hiring of more teachers and administrators of color. When a favorite administrator was transferred out of Central High, Anthony organized a protest against the decision.

Witnessed Devastating Riots

During the summer of 1967, Anthony watched as Detroit was torn apart by terrible riots that devastated entire city blocks. African American Detroiters endured National Guard troops and army tanks that were stationed within their neighborhoods, and large numbers of whites fled the city in the riot's aftermath. The crisis also heralded the start of a concerted effort by the city's numerous African American social, political, and religious groups to create a positive force for change within the community. Anthony was already a part of this movement, having engaged in civil-rights actions earlier in the decade with the NAACP youth group. He also became active in his church, Fellowship Chapel, and became a protégé of its pastor, the Reverend James Wadsworth.

After graduating from Central High in 1968, Anthony enrolled at Wayne State University, where he continued his activism. In 1970, he was invited to participate

At a Glance . . .

Born 1950, in St. Louis, MO; son of James (a postal worker) and Ida (a postal worker) Patton; married Janice Germaine, 1972 (divorced, 1985); children: Tolani, Maia. *Education:* Wayne State University, B.A., 1976; Marygrove College, M.A., 1984.

Career: Broadstreet Presbyterian Church, Detroit, MI, coordinator of communityoutreach program, 1974-80; ordained minister, 1981; Holt, Rinehart, and Winston (textbookpublishers), sales representative, mid-1980s; Fellowship Chapel, Detroit, MI, associate minister, 1983-86, pastor, 1986-; head of Detroit Branch NAACP, 1993-.

Addresses: *Office*—Detroit Branch NAACP, 2990 E. Grand Blvd., Detroit, MI 48205.

in a trip to Africa sponsored in part by the Fellowship Chapel. He and other young leaders spent two months in Ghana and Liberia, a visit Anthony later called a decisive event in his life. "We saw and stayed with people from the government, the Peace Corps and just regular people," he told Joe Swickard of the *Detroit Free Press.* "It just struck me so powerfully—here were black folks running the government, the schools, everything. It was a revelation. I had never seen black folks in charge of anything like that before. It inspired me."

Almost Became a Lawyer

As a result of that trip, Anthony began a longtime association with the Pan African Congress, a group created to foster socio-political links with Africa, and he would make several subsequent trips to the continent. While taking courses at Wayne State, he found work as the coordinator of a community outreach program for a Detroit church, which allowed him to implement some of his progressive ideas about African American identity and self-reliance. Anthony oversaw a tutoring program for youths, and served as a liaison between the church and several neighborhood groups. When he graduated from Wayne State in 1976, Anthony was certified as a social worker, but never worked formally in the profession. By this time, he was also married and the father of a daughter.

During the late 1970s and early 1980s, Anthony studied for the ministry—rejecting the idea of law school, which had tempted him for a time—and worked as a school textbook salesperson. He also

became increasingly active in the church of his youth, Fellowship Chapel. Two years after his ordination, Anthony became an associate pastor at the church. He earned a master's degree in pastoral ministry from Detroit's Marygrove College in 1984. His marriage ended that year, and a bitter legal battle ensued. Anthony eventually won custody of his two daughters.

Advanced to Leadership at Church

It became evident that Rev. Wadsworth was considering Anthony as his eventual successor, but that moment was hastened when the pastor fell ill with cancer. After Wadsworth's death in 1986, Anthony became the leader of the Fellowship Chapel's congregation. He immediately began working to revitalize the church by bringing in new members and creating an atmosphere of devoutness mingled with social activism. He founded the Isuthu Institute (Coming into Manhood Program), one of oldest such male mentoring programs in the United States; its female counterpart, the Intonjane Institute, also developed in time. "With Anthony at the helm, Fellowship became a church noted for having an unusually large number of men in its congregation and its programs for young black males," wrote *Detroit Free Press* reporter Dori J. Maynard.

Anthony's reputation as one of Detroit's most dynamic African American pastors continued to develop. In the spring of 1990, he was invited to join a 21-person delegation of American church leaders who met with recently freed South African civil rights leader Nelson Mandela. Later that year, Anthony co-chaired the leg of a Freedom Tour that brought Mandela to Detroit. Also in 1990, he became involved in a boycott of one of the city's two newspapers, the *Detroit Free Press,* as well as the local ABC television affiliate. At the time, race relations in Detroit were tense, and the media was considered partly to blame. Corporate-run media such as the *Detroit Free Press* and the ABC affiliate seemed to focus on the more sensational stories and problems revolving around the city and its predominantly African American leadership.

High-Profile Local Minister

Anthony announced the boycott from his pulpit at the Fellowship Chapel. The boycott, which was instigated by the Inter-Faith Council of Religious and Civic Leaders, was a turning point in race relations in Detroit. Several months later, an executive of the boycotted television station told the *Detroit Free Press,* "I think probably it has made everybody a little more sensitive. Has it totally changed the way we do things? No, but there have probably been some little changes here and there."

Anthony continued to lead an annual pilgrimage of Detroiters to African countries in an itinerary that included Ghana, Senegal, and Benin, and expanded the congregation and social-service programs at his Fellowship Chapel. Membership at the chapel would eventually quadruple during Anthony's tenure as pastor. Since the mid-1980s, the Isuthu and Intonjane Institutes were joined by job-training programs, ACT and SAT preparation courses, and even the establishment of a health clinic in Ghana. Anthony continued to lead Sunday services. "When I'm preaching, I'm in a different world," Anthony told the *Detroit Free Press*'s Shawn D. Lewis. "That's like total energy, ecstasy ... It's like a sponge. And you wring yourself out to drain yourself so that the people can absorb you."

In 1993, Anthony led a march of 250,000 people in Detroit to commemorate the 30th anniversary of a similar demonstration led by the late Reverend Martin Luther King Jr. through the city in June of 1963. He became active in fundraising and relief efforts for the growing number of refugees of the Rwandan civil war. In 1995, Anthony was co-chair of the Detroit committee for the Million Man March.

Elected Head of Detroit NAACP

In 1993, after a rather contentious election that pitted the old guard against a more progressive faction, Anthony was elected chair of the Detroit NAACP branch. The largest NAACP chapter in the United States since its founding in 1912—three years after national organization was chartered—the Detroit NAACP had a long, distinguished record of local activism and positive impact upon the city's political scene. The contentious leadership battle in 1993, however, reflected certain latent divisions among the branch's 51,000 members. Anthony ran against the handpicked successor to the branch's esteemed outgoing president. Anthony's supporters urged members to cast their votes for him based on his extensive record of achievement within the city of Detroit, and felt that the NAACP needed to take on a more active, outspoken role in the city.

More conservative members of the NAACP worried that Anthony was perhaps too militant, and might alienate corporate donors. As pastor of Fellowship Chapel, he once turned down a 10,000 grant to his church from the parent company of a large Detroit-area department store that had no stores left within the city. Despite these reservations, Anthony won the election. His success as NAACP chairman was resoundingly affirmed when he continued to be re-elected chairman every two years, often by wide margins.

"Just Join Something!"

Not surprisingly, Anthony was impervious to criticism that the NAACP had grown moribund in recent years. "People often want to belittle, criticize and denigrate,

but I say take a look at yourself," Anthony told the *Detroit Free Press*. "If you don't like the NAACP, join SCLC]Southern Christian Leadership Conference]. If you don't like that, join your local church. If you don't like that, join the Girl Scouts. Just join something! There is enough hell burning in Detroit for everybody to get their own individual bucket and put out a fire."

Under Anthony's leadership, the Detroit branch of the NAACP began an important "Buy in Detroit" campaign to promote economic activity within the city. He also played a crucial role in negotiating a settlement with the state's largest insurer, the American Automobile Association, over an NAACP suit that charged bias in its setting of insurance rates for Detroiters. Anthony also became active in calling for minority ownership in the city's planned casinos after voters approved a gambling referendum in the mid-1990s. He received national attention in 1998 when he was arrested in a protest outside the U.S. Supreme Court building in Washington D.C. The demonstration was ignited by the Supreme Court's failure to hire African American law clerks during a two-year span. "For how long can the court judge diversity and equity," Anthony told the *Detroit Free Press*, "if in fact it lacks the diversity and equity it claims to judge?"

Sources

Detroit Free Press, January 6, 1991, p. 1F; June 20, 1993, p. 12; November 7, 1994, p. A1; October 20, 1999.

Other

Additional information for this profile was provided by the Detroit Branch NAACP.

—Carol Brennan

Michael Baisden

1963—

Author

At one point in Michael Baisden's life, success seemed to elude him. A Chicago small-business owner and public-transit employee, he had written a nonfiction book on the subject of infidelity in relationships. Several major publishers refused to publish his book. Undaunted, Baisden borrowed the funds to publish it himself. That book, *Never Satisfied: How and Why Men Cheat,* touched a chord with readers, and his success story has become one of the most remarkable in the African American book-publishing industry.

Baisden was a route driver for the Chicago Transit Authority in the early 1990s, and the owner of a faltering small business. Moved by the tales of heartache and duplicity that were told to him by his friends, he decided to begin collecting their stories for a book that would provide some insight into modern relationships. In order to get his book published, Baisden sold his car, borrowed money, and founded Legacy Publishing. Legacy's debut book was *Never Satisfied,* which was issued in 1995. *Never Satisfied* is a collection of interviews with men and women who relate their experiences in deceitful relationships. Baisden writes extensively about the common perception that men seem to be commitment-phobic. He rejects several

theories, and argues that women behave unconscionably as well—especially women who knowingly date married or otherwise involved men, or turn a blind eye to the infidelities of their partner. Through anecdotes and his own conjectures, Baisden constructs a scenario in which these situations occur. "Most cheating men, especially the married ones, will come right out and tell her the details of his situation," he writes in *Never Satisfied.* "This will allow her to make a judgment as to whether or not she can go along with the program. Respect and consideration for his wife or girlfriend is absolutely necessary if the relationship has any chance at longevity."

A Fresh Approach

In *Never Satisfied,* Baisden focuses on how an unfaithful man is forced to construct a world of lies, and how the contemporary dance-club scene helps to foster infidelity. "Just as the animal hunter relies on guns, traps, and camouflage to capture his prey, the cheating man depends on smooth talk, good looks, and the low morals of his victims to accomplish his goals," Baisden writes. In the book's introduction, he remarks, "What I

At a Glance . . .

Born in 1963; single; children: one daughter.

Career: Chicago Department of Transit, route driver, early 1990s; author of *NeverSatisfied: How and Why Men Cheat,* 1995, *Men Cry in the Dark,* 1997, *The Maintenance Man: It's Midnight, Do You Know Where Your Woman Is?,* 1999; founder of Legacy Publishing.

Addresses: *Home*—Atlanta, GA. *Office*—Legacy Publishing, P.O. Box 49644, Atlanta, GA 30359.

am attempting to do, at the very least, is to expose the games that are quite seriously destroying our relationships with our women, and as a direct result, affecting our ability to maintain healthy relationships which could be beneficial to both ourselves and the children that are unsuspecting players in too many of those very games."

Baisden embarked on a series of exhaustive tours to promote his book. He promoted *Never Satisfied* in bookstores, nightclubs, and even hair salons, and it became a phenomenal success. *Never Satisfied* sold nearly 50,000 copies. Baisden used the profits to pay back the money he had borrowed and to write his first novel, *Men Cry in the Dark.* Published in 1997, it sold more than 30,000 copies in hardcover alone. The plot revolves around four friends from Chicago's South Side, and touches upon their attempts at financial entrepreneurship, relationships, single parenthood, and interracial dating.

Hunger for Love

In *Men Cry in the Dark,* Baisden created a group of characters whose economic situations and social quandaries reflected issues within affluent, urban African American life in the 1990s. One of the characters, Derrick, is a former computer-industry associate who left the corporate world to launch his own magazine. Although he is sometimes arrogant in his interpersonal relationships, he seeks a committed partnership with a woman. Derrick is forced to reassess his attitude when he meets Angela, a woman who is a genuine match for him. Derrick's friend, Tony, is the classic Romeo, but also a single parent who is devoted to his daughter. When Tony decides that he wants to settle down and marry his girlfriend, the mother of his young daughter begins to make trouble. Ben is a successful Chicago florist who is consistently railroaded by uncaring women. His friends often remind him that he only dates women who are too young for him, and eager to

take advantage of his generosity. Mark, the fourth male in the novel, is frequently criticized by his friends for refusing to date African American women.

Part of the success of *Men Cry in the Dark* came from what *Publishers Weekly* writer Carol Taylor described as its collective appeal. "Black readers, like all readers, want recognizable and realistic images of themselves and their lives, not stereotypes endlessly replayed in the same venues, neighborhoods, relationships and careers," noted Taylor. Baisden is often compared with other newly successful African American male authors who explore black life in fiction, such as Eric Jerome Dickey and Omar Tyree. "These writers deal thoughtfully with the male side of relationship issues while doling out a healthy dose of sexy escapism," asserted Taylor. She also noted Baisden's remarkable ability to publish his own works, citing industry "reports that he]Baisden] has declined offers to join a traditional publisher."

A Popular Motivational Speaker

The success of his first two books, combined with his attractive looks, made Baisden a popular figure on the book-signing circuit. Thousands of women often attended his book signings to hear his forthright, but firm, relationship advice. The audiences grew so large that Baisden began a series of seminars, Love, Lust and Lies, in which he discussed some of the problems in contemporary relationships and how both men and women might begin to create a healthier pattern of love within their relationships. His 1999 novel, *The Maintenance Man: It's Midnight, Do You Know Where Your Woman Is?,* addressed similar themes. One of the novel's lead characters is Malcolm Tremell, a handsome, successful male escort who is desperate to find a more respectable job. This desire grows increasingly stronger after he meets a wonderful woman, and is unable to reveal his true profession to her. Malcolm's best friend, Simon, owns an Atlanta nightclub, and learns that his fiancée is possibly involved with a handsome pastor. Another character is Teddy, a male stripper who has no qualms about taking advantage of women. One of the novel's female characters, Ariel, works as the nightclub's manager. She would like to leave her job at the nightclub and become a wife and mother. However, Ariel's family and friends constantly remind her that her dating standards are much too high.

The *Publishers Weekly* article called *Maintenance Man* "a steamy bad-boy novel full of the stuff readers crave—love, sex, betrayal and money." Taylor described Baisden as part of the wave of what has been termed the "Brotherman" genre—the counterpart of the resoundingly successful "Sistergirl" fiction exemplified by female African American writers like Terry McMillan. Baisden is single and lives in Atlanta.

Selected writings

Never Satisfied: How and Why Men Cheat, Legacy
   Publishing, 1995.
Men Cry in the Dark, Legacy Publishing, 1997.
*The Maintenance Man: It's Midnight, Do You Know
   Where Your Woman Is?,* Legacy Publishing, 1999.

Sources

Publishers Weekly, December 13, 1999, p. 37.

Other

Additional information for this profile was provided by
http:\\www.michaelbaisden.com.

—Carol Brennan

Shirley Bassey

1937—

Singer

British singer Shirley Bassey won an entirely new generation of fans when she guested on a 1997 song from British techno act, the Propellerheads. "History Repeating" charted in both Europe and North America, and appeared on the soundtrack to the popular 1998 film *There's Something About Mary.* Yet Bassey had enjoyed a long, four-decade career as a performer before this point, recording a string of hit singles in the 1960s and garnering a devoted cult following for her torchy, often slightly risqué songs, glamorous looks, and compelling stage presence. Sometimes called "Bassey the Belter" for her strong alto voice, Bassey had previously enjoyed a huge international hit when she performed the title song to the 1964 James Bond film *Goldfinger.* She remains one of the one of the top-performing female singers in the history of the British charts. Don Heckman, writing for the *Los Angeles Times,* called Bassey "an extraordinarily powerful live entertainer with one of the most instantly recognizable voices in popular music."

Born Shirley Veronica Bassey in Tiger Bay, a dockside neighborhood of Cardiff, Wales, on January 8, 1937, the future songstress was the last of seven children born to Henry and Eliza Bassey, an interracial couple. Her father was a seaman from Nigeria who left the family when his youngest child was just two, and was never heard from again. Interviewed by Deborah Ross of the British London newspaper *The Independent* in 1997, Bassey said that "I never even asked my mother about him. I didn't want to carry that baggage through my life. I just let it go."

Worked in Factory

When her mother remarried, the children moved to an all-white neighborhood in Cardiff, where Bassey began singing, though she was, by nature, a shy child. After dropping out of school at the age of 14, Bassey found work as a packer in a Cardiff enamelware factory for wages of nine dollars a week. On the weekends, she sang for extra income in local clubs. Her first real performance came in 1953 at the Grand Theatre in Luton, Bedfordshire, England, and from there she went on to appear in a number of black-themed musicals and revues, including a production called Memories of Jolson and Hot From Harlem, which toured the United Kingdom. Homesick, she returned to Cardiff and found a job waiting tables, but the stage soon lured her back.

In 1955, a popular British comedian invited Bassey to appear in his Christmas show, *Such Is Life,* in one of London's West End theaters. She recorded her first single, "Burn My Candle," around this time, and her voice soon attracted major industry interest; critics and fans were also enchanted, and Bassey was quickly likened to Eartha Kitt, Lena Horne, and even Judy Garland. Her first chart success, the "Banana Boat Song," debuted in early 1957 and quickly reached No. 8 on the British charts. Bassey went on to record a string of hit singles over the next few years. She also packed concert halls, earned and spent lavish amounts on show-stopping stage gowns that highlighted her svelte, but well-endowed figure, and became a household name in Britain. Yet Bassey was also forced to endure her share of attention from the tabloid press,

At a Glance . . .

Born January 8, 1937, in Cardiff, Wales, United Kingdom; daughter of Henry (a seaman) and Eliza Bassey; married Kenneth Hume (a television producer), 1961 (marriage ended); married Sergio Novak; children: Sharon, Samantha (deceased, 1985), Mark.

Career: Worked in an enamelware factory as a packer, Cardiff, Wales, early 1950s;began singing career at clubs in Cardiff; appeared on the London stage in musical revues thatincluded *Hot From Harlem*, mid-1950s; recorded first single, "Burn MyCandle," 1955; recorded first LP, *The Bewitching Miss Bassey*, 1959.

Awards: Named Commander of the British Empire, 1994, and Dame of the British Empire, c. 1999.

especially after a dejected former boyfriend held her at gunpoint in a hotel in London.

Success and Tragedy

Bassey's debut album, *The Bewitching Miss Bassey*, was released on EMI\Columbia. She moved to New York and enjoyed great success with her cabaret act, and then expanded her audience with shows in Las Vegas. Her name was even romantically linked with that of Frank Sinatra, one of the biggest stars of the era. Bassey once again suffered some salacious publicity during this era as well, when the British press revealed that she had become a mother at the age of 18. One of Bassey's sisters had been raising the daughter, named Sharon, but the singer then took custody of her.

Bassey's personal life would be marked by a series of tragedies. In 1961, she wed television producer Kenneth Hume, but he committed suicide after their divorce. A second husband, Sergio Novak, an Italian producer, served a stint as her manager, as Hume had done as well. Bassey told Ross in the *Independent* interview that both decisions revealed poor judgment on her part. "I've always been the breadwinner and men don't like that. They turn on you," Bassey declared. "They bite the hand that feeds them. Eventually, too, they become very jealous of the love one has with an audience."

The Most Enduring Bond Girl

That audience even included President John F. Kennedy at a White House performance, but it was Bassey's surprising rendition of the theme song to the popular James Bond film, "Goldfinger," that made her a huge international star in 1964. She would go on to record two other theme songs for Bond films, *Diamonds Are Forever* in 1971 and *Moonraker*, released eight years later. She continued to enjoy several other hit songs, even during the rock era when such torchy pop songs seemed rather out of step with the times. Both "Big Spender" from 1967 and a 1969 tune, "This Is My Life," were impressive hits for the singer.

In 1969, Bassey and her family—which would include two other children, Samantha and Mark—moved to Switzerland. Still in great demand as a performer, Bassey continued to perform around the globe, and was a frequent presence on British television for many years. She later admitted on more than one occasion that her performing career did not make her the best mother, and that her children would often begin crying when they saw suitcases appear in the hallway as she prepared to tour again.

History Repeated

After a 1978 album, *The Magic Is You*, Bassey retreated to Switzerland and semiretirement. Again, family tragedy struck when her daughter Samantha was found dead, a probable suicide, at the foot of a bridge in Bristol, England, in 1985. Despite her semiretired status, Bassey found it difficult to resist the lure of offers to record and perform, and enjoyed surprising success when she appeared on a 1987 track from the Swiss electronic band, Yello. But it was the efforts a decade later of another alternative act, two British sound engineers who recorded under the name Propellerheads, that revived Bassey's unique appeal. "The two Propellerhead boys sent the song to me, and though I loved the music I thought it was more something for Tina Turner than for me," she told *San Francisco Chronicle* writer Neva Chonin. They persevered, however, and convinced Bassey to record with them. "History Repeating" became the standout track on the album, and a hit on both sides of the Atlantic. *New Musical Express*'s Sylvia Patterson reviewed *Decksanddrumsandrockandroll* and called the single with Bassey "unsurpassingly mighty."

The singer, who has received two honorifics from the Queen Elizabeth and is formally known as Dame Shirley Bassey, eventually relocated to the French Riviera enclave of Monte Carlo. Well into her sixties, she continued to perform, and her shows are packed with devoted fans. Her voice remained the same strong, enigmatic alto, which she has credited to her serious commitment to vocal exercise. As to her physical stamina, she confessed to Heckman in the *Los Angeles Times* article, "my two secrets are drinking lots of water and working out every day before the show. I go to the gym, I do the treadmill and I lift tiny weights. I exercise my voice, and I watch what I eat.

And it's not a chore for me because I like the results."

Bassey, who turned 63 in 2000, seemed uninterested in permanent retirement. "Maybe when I'm 70 I'll think, I've done it all. Now what?," she told Chonin in the *San Francisco Chronicle*. "That's when I'll go explore the pyramids and all the places I've wanted to visit but haven't had the time to. I'm a gypsy, you see. I love a good adventure."

Selected discography

Solo albums

The Bewitching Miss Bassey, EMI\Columbia, 1959.
Fabulous Shirley Bassey, EMI\Columbia, 1960.
Shirley, EMI\Columbia, 1961.
Let's Face the Music, EMI\Columbia, 1962.
Shirley Bassey at the Pigalle, EMI\Columbia, 1965.
Shirley Bassey Belts the Best!, EMI\Columbia, 1965.
I've Got a Song for You, EMI\Columbia, 1966.
Live at the Talk of the Town, EMI\Columbia, 1970.
Something, United Artists, 1970.
Something Else, United Artists, 1971.
Big Spender, United Artists, 1971.
I Capricorn, United Artists, 1972.
Never, Never, Never, United Artists, 1973.
Live at Carnegie Hall, United Artists, 1973.
Nobody Does It Like Me, United Artists, 1974.
Love, Life and Feelings, United Artists, 1976.
You Take My Heart Away, United Artists, 1977.
The Magic Is You, United Artists, 1978.
This Is My Life, United Artists, 1979.
Love Songs, 1982.
All By Myself, 1984.

I Am What I Am, 1984.
I've Got You Under My Skin, 1985.
Born to Sing the Blues, 1987.
Let Me Sing and I'm Happy, 1988.
La Mujer, 1989.
Keep The Music Playing, 1991.
Shirley Bassey Sings The Songs Of Andrew Lloyd Webber, 1993.
The Show Must Go On, Polygram, 1996.

Other

(With Yello) *The Rhythm Divine,* Mercury, 1987.
(With Propellerheads), *Decksanddrumsandrockandroll,* Wall of Sound, 1997.

Sources

Books

Gammond, Peter, *Oxford Companion to Popular Music,* Oxford University Press. 1991.

Periodicals

Ebony, March 1963.
Independent (London), September 15, 1997.
Los Angeles Times, October 16, 1998.
New Musical Express, January 24, 1998.
Observer, September 11, 1994.
San Francisco Chronicle, October 21, 1998.

—Carol Brennan

Frankie Beverly

1946—

Rhythm and blues singer

Most musicians are lucky to get one shot at stardom, and even then it doesn't last long. Frankie Beverly, who formed Maze Featuring Frankie Beverly over 30 years ago, is even more fortunate. After over three decades in the music business, nearly 30 hit singles, nine Top Ten hits, and eight gold records, he is still going strong. His music doesn't get air play on the popular radio stations, and he doesn't sell millions of albums or win Grammy awards. But, despite all that, Beverly and Maze is one of the most consistently popular R&B bands.

Beverly was inspired to sing as a child in the church choir. "Like most black artists," he said in an *iMusic-.com* profile, "I was influenced by going to church. You know, it was like anyone that could sing was featured in a Sunday program! So I did a lot of solos in church . . . a lot of singing!" When he was about eight or nine-years-old, the first record he can remember hearing was Lloyd Price's "Lawdy Miss Clowdy." He loved it, but then heard Frankie Lymon and the Teenagers, which really inspired him. Beverly even changed his first name from Howard to Frankie. He became a huge fan of the group's hit singles, such as "I Want You to be My Girl," "Who Can Explain?," and "The ABC's of Love." Every time that Frankie Lymon and the Teen-

agers appeared on "The Ed Sullivan Show," he watched the program. Every time they played a concert in town, Beverly was in the audience. He credits Frankie Lymon and the Teenagers for being a catalyst that helped foster his interest in music.

Joined The Silhouettes

While still in junior high school, Beverly was recruited into a vocal group called The Silhouettes. The group had just lost its singer, and word on the street was that Beverly could sing just like Frankie Lymon. "Little Frankie," as he was known around Philadelphia, played his first professional concert at the age of 12. Beverly's father could've cared less about his son's musical career. He wanted him to get a job, and follow more "serious" pursuits. "We clashed as I was growing up," Beverly told iMusic.com. In retrospect, Beverly credited his family for standing behind him. He stayed with The Silhouettes for about a year, but began to feel out of touch with his bandmates, who were older. Beverly left The Silhouettes to form his own band.

Beverly's first group was called The Blenders, an a cappella (voices only, no instruments) and doo-wop

At a Glance . . .

Born Howard Beverly in 1946, raised in Philadelphia, PA.

Career: Lead singer, Frankie Beverly and Maze, 1977-; recorded the albums: *MazeFeaturing Frankie Beverly,* 1977; *Golden Time of Day,* 1978; *Inspiration,* 1979; *Joy and Pain,* 1980; *Live in New Orleans,* 1980; *We Are One,* 1983; *Can't Stop the Love,* 1985; *Maze Featuring Frankie Beverly Live inL.A.,* 1986; *Silky Soul,* 1989; *Back to Basics,* 1993; *Southern Girl,* 1996; *Rebel for Life,* 1998.

Awards: Eight gold albums for sales of over 100,000 each.

Addresses: *Office*—Capitol Records, 1750 N. Vine St., Hollywood CA90028.

group. He found it difficult to find bandmates who were as serious about music as he was. After The Blenders broke up, Beverly formed The Butlers, and started recording. The Butlers' sound was in the vein of the traditional vocal harmony groups of the time. The Butlers recorded on local Philadelphia record labels from 1963 to 1968. As the 1960s drew on, Beverly and his band were more influenced by groups like Sly and the Family Stone, and developed a new sound and a new name, Raw Soul.

Raw Soul Headed West

A future member of Maze, percussionist McKinley "Bug" Williams, was an original member of The Butlers, and stayed with Beverly in Raw Soul. The group played shows in and around Philadelphia, but Beverly knew that they had to move west to achieve more wide-spread success. "Philly wasn't going to be the place for what we wanted to do," he said on *iMusic-.com.* In 1971, the group headed out to the San Francisco Bay Area. Other bands that Beverly respected, such as Sly and the Family Stone, Santana, and Cold Blood, were also based there.

Raw Soul had an eventful cross-country road trip, and arrived in Oakland, California. At first, things were tough for the group. They slept in their bus, and couldn't get paid shows. One day, they met a girl who was crazy about the band's sound, and she promised to set up concert dates for them. Within a month, the band landed a job through her at a San Francisco club called The Scene. They played at the club for a year.

Ultimately, the club's owner decided to invest in Beverly and Raw Soul, and paid for them to record a whole album's worth of songs. They sent those demo recordings around to record companies, but found no interest. Those recordings, however, became the basis for the first Maze album.

Raw Soul received their big break when Marvin Gaye's sister-in-law saw them perform live. She was impressed with the group's sound and notified Gaye, who was looking for a backup band to tour with. Within a week, Gaye was in the audience, watching a live Raw Soul show. "I can't describe how I felt," Beverly told *iMusic.com,* "because he was an idol of mine . . . and I couldn't believe he was checking us out!" Soon, Raw Soul was not only Gaye's backup band on tour, but also the opening band. They also had the opportunity to perform original material. Gaye took the band under his wing, helped them financially, and used his influence in the music industry to open doors for the group. They sent out their demo recordings again, and received a phone call from Capitol Records executive Larkin Arnold. About a week after he received the tape, Arnold signed Raw Soul to their first record deal. The band changed its name to Maze Featuring Frankie Beverly and released its first record, *Maze Featuring Frankie Beverly,* in 1977.

Enjoyed Consistent Success

From their first release, the group enjoyed consistent success. They had nearly 30 hit singles from 1977 to 1993—nine of which were Top 10 R&B singles—and eight of its ten releases went gold. Maze's most notable Top 10 hits include "Running Away," "Love is the Key," "Back in Stride," "Too Many Games," "Can't Get Over You," and "Silky Soul." When the band first toured Europe in 1981, Beverly was shocked by the overwhelmingly positive response they received. He was even more surprised by the racial makeup of the audience. "I was looking for black folks to be at the shows," Beverly told *iMusic.com,* "because that's basically who makes up our audiences]in the United States]—and when I looked out there, I saw a crowd that was 99-percent white, grooving, digging our music."

Beverly credits his struggles during the early years of his career for helping him to deal well with success. Ever humble, he is thrilled that he's been able to share some of Maze's success by bringing young talent into the spotlight. Opening acts for Maze have included Anita Baker, Regina Belle, and Toni Braxton, all of whom went on to achieve great success.

Remained Popular

As noteworthy as the band's longevity is it's ability to play before sellout crowds. Music industry analysts compare Maze to Neil Diamond or the Grateful Dead, in that their modest record sales don't affect concert ticket sales. "There isn't a one-to-one correlation between record sales and ticket sales, Gary Bongiovanni, editor of *Pollstar,* the concert-industry magazine, told the *Dallas Morning News.* Thomas Bacote, a program director for KRBV-FM in Dallas, told the *Dallas Morning News* that the group's success is due to "the uplifting, almost spiritual vibe they have at . . .concerts." Even Beverly can't explain the group's tremendous concert appeal. "I have no idea why we're so much bigger live than we are with our records," he told the *Dallas Morning News.* "I just call it the Maze Craze."

Beverly noted that Maze stays together by sticking to its "organic" formula, which was developed in the 1960s. "It's not like we come out with dancers and we're swinging from the rafters," he said in the *Dallas Morning News.* "I've got nothing against the hip-hop thing," he continued. "but there's too many people going in and pushing buttons on some machine for five or ten minutes—ding, ding, dong, dong, boom, boom—and they think they've written a classic. It takes blood, sweat, and tears to write a classic."

Selected discography

Maze Featuring Frankie Beverly, Capitol,1977.
Inspiration, Razor & Tie,1979.
Joy and Pain, Razor & Tie,1980.
Live in New Orleans, Capitol,1980.
We Are One, Capitol, 1983.
Can't Stop the Love, Razor & Tie,1985.
Maze Featuring Frankie Beverly Live in L.A., Capitol, 1986.
Silky Soul, Warner Bros.,1989.
Back to Basics, Warner Bros.,1993.
Southern Girl, Capitol,1996.
Rebel 4 Life, Sony International, 1998.

Sources

Periodicals

Dallas Morning News, September 26, 1996, p. 5C.
Knight-Ridder\Tribune News Service, February 2, 1994.
St. Louis Post Dispatch, November 21, 1997, p. E4.

Other

Additional information for this profile was obtained from "Maze Featuring Frankie Beverly," *iMusic.com,* at http:\\www.imusic.com (February 24, 2000).

—Brenna Sanchez

Terrell D. Bolton

1959(?)—

Police chief

Terrell Bolton made history in 1999 when he was named police chief of Dallas, Texas. Not only was he the city's first African American chief, but he was also selected from within the department's ranks. The poor, African American child from segregation-era Mississippi had grown up to assume leadership of a police department that is sworn to protect the citizens of Dallas. Bolton faced rising crime and festering racial problems in the city, and the public had high expectations of him. He wasted no time in earning their support.

Drank from White Fountain

It's a testament to his upbringing that Bolton would become the first African American police chief of Dallas. He grew up in a four-room, cinder-block house on the poor side of a rural southeast Mississippi town called Richton. His neighborhood was separated from the richer white neighborhood by shabby storefronts. Bolton watched the Ku Klux Klan march down Main Street and, until integration efforts swept the south, went to a segregated school. He also snuck drinks from the town's whites-only drinking fountains. "When nobody was looking, I'd take a little swig," he told the

Dallas Morning News. "Let me tell you, it tasted all the same."

Bolton's father was a "junkman" who salvaged scrap metal, and his mother cleaned houses to supplement the government assistance that the family of ten received. The Boltons were the poorest family in Richton. However, the family was very close-knit. "We were raised in a Christian home with very good work ethics," Dr. Vickie Bolton Neal, the chief's sister and a Dallas Public Schools psychologist told the *Dallas Morning News.* "My mother constantly motivated us. She would tell us we could do anything." The children had chores to do and got good grades. Their parent's motivation paid off. All of the Bolton children became overachievers—they grew up to include two health care executives, a psychologist, and four law enforcement leaders. "Public service was another thing," Neal continued in the *Dallas Morning News.* "My parents and my grandmother taught us to always help others."

Shot in the Head

Bolton decided to pursue a career in law enforcement

At a Glance . . .

Born c. 1959 in Richton, MS; divorced 1980; married to Glenda, 1983; children: Terrell Jr., two daughters. *Education:* Jackson State University, bachelor's degree in criminal justice, 1980; graduate, Federal Bureau of Investigations National Academy, Quantico, Virginia.

Career: Dallas Police Department; patrol officer, 1980-84; sergeant 1984-88; deputychief, 1988-91, assistant chief, 1991-99; police chief, 1999-.

Addresses: *Office*—Dallas Police Department, 2014 Main St., Rm. 506, Dallas, TX 75201.

at a young age. At the age of six, while riding in the back of his father's truck, he was shot in the head by someone firing a pellet gun. Bolton's father went straight to the police department to file a report. However, as an African American in the south, his report fell on deaf ears. No one was arrested or charged for the shooting. "I told myself that day that if I ever went into law enforcement, I would treat everyone equally," Bolton told the *Dallas Morning News.* "And that's what I have done throughout my career." He "could've gone the other way," he continued, "But I'm a testimony to the strong influences of love, family, and hard work." Bolton's coworkers agree. "He treats everybody like they're his equal," Deborah Joseph, the chief's secretary, said in the *Dallas Morning News.* "He's not a big chief."

Known for his talents as a drummer and basketball player in high school, and for his "robot dance" at school football games, Bolton went on to Jackson State University in nearby Hattiesburg. While still in college, Bolton was recruited by the Dallas Police Department. He took the job in 1980, leaving his wife of two years and an infant son, Terrell Jr., behind. Although Bolton divorced his wife, he maintained a relationship with his son. In 1983, he married his second wife, Glenda, and they had two daughters.

Bolton rose quickly through the ranks in the Dallas Police Department. He was made sergeant within four years, deputy chief in four more, and assistant chief three years after that, in 1991. He was offered a position as police chief in Jackson, Mississippi, but turned it down. He also established a strong bond with the former chief, Ben Click. Click believed that Bolton was the right choice as his replacement. He told the *Dallas Morning News,* "Because of the black-white issues that have plagued Dallas throughout its history, this is a great move. Yet there are other qualities he

[Bolton] brings."

Quick Replacement, Easy Choice

Chief Click announced his retirement in August of 1999. Two weeks later, Dallas City Manager Ted Benavides named Bolton to the position. There were rumblings that Benavides had made a hasty decision. Also, there were three higher-ranking officers who were bypassed, as well as a deputy chief. "I totally respect the manager's decision," Chief Robert Jackson, one of the higher-ranking officers, said in the *Dallas Morning News.*

Crime statistics were beginning to rise before Bolton was named chief. About a decade before he took office, race relations in Dallas were at an all-time low. After a series of controversial police shootings of African Americans, police supporters and community activists were pitted against each other. It came to a head when, during an incident in downtown Dallas, a crowd was accused of inciting a mentally unstable African American to shoot a police officer in 1998. In addition to his crime fighting responsibilities, Bolton was charged with calming racial tensions within the city.

Brought Positive Changes

Almost immediately after his appointment, Bolton made drastic changes to his command staff. These changes drew strong public criticism. "What I did initially with the administration, I had to do that early and get that over with," Bolton said in the *Dallas Morning News.* "I knew I had a department that was responding slowly to calls for service, and I knew we had property crime increases throughout the city. I have to not worry about my popularity from day to day and do what I was sworn to do—to make this city as safe as I can make it." Despite the criticism, department response times improved 20 percent. By March of 2000, crime in Dallas was down three percent from the same time in 1999. Bolton assigned an ongoing police presence to a community that had complained about the crime problems associated with the topless dance clubs in their neighborhood. After demands to the Dallas police to do something about the situation had gone unheeded for years, Bolton's quick action was applauded. Linda Neal, a resident in one of the affected areas, told the *Dallas Morning News* that Bolton "responded very well. Not just with the words that people want to hear, but by fulfilling what they told us. That impresses people in the long run."

In January of 2000, Bolton launched a crime-fighting plan called Initiative 2000. The plan assigned specific patrol divisions to particular beats. These patrols targeted teen curfew violators, prostitution, drug transactions, gangs, car break-ins, and apartment-complex burglaries, among other problems. When officers weren't on a case, they were encouraged to talk to residents and shop owners in order to better understand neighborhood concerns. When a particular problem was reported—a rash of car break-ins in a neighborhood, for example—a team was assigned immediately to address the matter. "We are going to keep focused and sustain our momentum," Bolton said about Initiative 2000 in the *Dallas Morning News.* "We want the criminal element to know that we have more officers out there and we're going to make a difference." Although his predecessor was chief for only six years, Bolton planned to remain on the job for 20 years. "I plan to buy burial plots in Dallas," he told the *Dallas Morning News.*

Sources

Periodicals

Dallas Morning News, August 21, 1999, p. 1A; August 25, 1999, p. 19A; August 29, 1999, p. 1A; March 16, 2000, p. 21A; April 16, 2000, p. 1A.

—Brenna Sanchez

Kelvin E. Boston

1955(?)—

Television host, author

Personal-finance expert Kelvin E. Boston is the host of a syndicated financial-advice program aimed at African American audiences. Since 1991, *The Color of Money* has aired on several dozen public television stations, and Boston has become a leading financial guru in a field seemingly glutted with the type. Yet Boston's approach, which he describes fully in his 1996 book *Smart Money Moves for African-Americans,* is termed a "holistic" one: a wealth-creation strategy that takes into account African American attitudes about money, spending, and saving. "Have you been taught to live a life of poverty or prosperity?" Boston posits in his book. "A lot of us are taught that to be righteous is to be poor, and a lot of us take it literally."

Born in the mid-1950s, Boston grew up in a public-housing project in Wilmington, Delaware; he returned to the area after earning a degree in English literature from Lincoln University in Pennsylvania. Back in Wilmington, he worked for an agency that helped first-time home buyers. In the early 1980s, he relocated to the Toledo, Ohio area, where he worked as a financial advisor at for IDS\American Express Financial Services. By the late 1980s, he had moved an hour north, to Detroit, where he became involved in a number of ventures. He served as president of Polaris Communications, which in the early 1990s was involved in an effort to save an empty downtown Detroit department store from demolition; the plans by Boston and his partners to create a hotel complex for the multistory building were one of many failed attempts by various investor groups to rescue the landmark building.

Boston also created Boston Media, a Detroit company, and served as director of Calvert New Africa Mutual Fund, which boasted 8.3 million in assets invested in African companies or with foreign firms doing business there. With a partner, he purchased *Corporate Detroit,* a successful local magazine, and ran that for some time. His syndicated television show, *The Color of Money,* was launched in 1991. It aired on Black Entertainment Network (BET) and then began to be picked up by an increasing number of public television stations. Boston said that he realized the potential for financial advising services targeted to the African American community through his work for IDS; furthermore, the proliferation of money-management advice programs that began airing during this era seemed, to Boston, to lack a crucial element. "Millions of middle-income Americans, especially minorities, weren't getting what they needed from these shows," he said in an interview with *Success* magazine—"sound financial advice and inspiration. I decided to give them that. I knew the power of a dollar and a dream."

Boston's approach is one that he describes as "holistic," or taking into account cultural attitudes and esteem issues. He recalled that once, as a financial advisor, a client of his with children to support had come into a sum of insurance money after her husband died. He urged her to invest it soundly, which she did for a time, but then began to convert the investments back into cash. "It wasn't until she cashed in her last investment that I realized what was going on—the money made her uncomfortable," Boston explained in the interview with *Success.* "Before her husband's passing, she was

At a Glance . . .

Born c. 1955, in Wilmington, DE. *Education:* Lincoln University, B.A.

Career: Co-founder of a housing counseling service in Wilmington, DE; IDS\American Express Financial Services, Toledo, OH, financial advisor, c. early 1980s; PolarisCommunications, Detroit, MI, president; Boston Media, Detroit, president; Calvert New AfricaMutual Fund, director; *Corporate Detroit* magazine, Detroit, co-owner until 1995; *The Color of Money* (syndicated television program), host, 1991-.

Addresses: *Office*—Boston Media, Inc., 3011 W. Grand Blvd., Detroit, MI 48202-3016.

used to living from paycheck to paycheck . . .. At that moment, I knew I had a new mission: to help my clients understand and correct their attitudes toward wealth."

In 1996, Boston wrote his first book, *Smart Money Moves for African-Americans,* published by Putnam. In it, he sets forth many of the ideas and strategies from *The Color of Money* episodes, but in far greater detail. Early chapters discuss the economic history of African Americans, and how the past has shaped present attitudes. Before the omnibus U.S. civil rights legislation in 1964, for instance, equal employment and pay opportunities were not the law of the land, and as a result, blacks often earned far less money than their white co-workers; furthermore, they rarely attained a job level that offered solid retirement benefit plans.

Boston also points out the great disparities in present-day saving and investing statistics between black and white Americans: the average net worth among African Americans is 11,000, while for whites, it is 51,000; interest income averages also vary dramatically: 872 versus 7,308 annually. "Businesses finally respect African American purchasing power, but not our economic clout," Boston told *Detroit Free Press* reporter Rachel Konrad. "We have little net worth in banks, mutual funds, real estate and businesses. As America's No. 1 minority, we have the opportunity to put our financial house in order."

In *Smart Money Moves,* Boston critiques the institutions that have shaped a role in the success of African-Americans: the church, the civil rights movement, and the public-school system. These three, he argues, have not educated blacks about how to create wealth, or why creating wealth is so vital to the achievements of the group as a whole. "]M]any of us can't name one black entrepreneur or millionaire," he told Konrad in the

Detroit Free Press interview. "By not knowing who our financial heroes are, we tell others that we don't have any."

Smart Money Moves features chapters that explore such topics as making a budget, how to buy a car, the pitfalls of home mortgages, how start a business, investing in the stock market, and planning for retirement. Boston shows how careful strategies can help households with an income of just 30,000 considerably improve their balance sheet. He counsels readers to avoid credit-card debt, and advocates a plan he calls "The Power of 10"—investing ten percent of one's income in opportunities likely to bring a 10 percent return for ten years. He discusses the paucity of African American entrepreneurs, and urges readers to consider working for themselves as the ultimate achievement of financial—and personal—freedom. An appendix guide lists further sources for guidance, including minority-owned CPA firms and mutual funds. "He has a special chapter for women and ends with an inspiration admonishment that spiritual, physical, intellectual, and financial success all go hand in hand," remarked a *Booklist* review by David Rouse.

Selected writings

Smart Money Moves for African Americans, foreword by Dennis Kimbro, Putnam, 1996.

Sources

Black Enterprise, March 1996, p. 49.
Booklist, January 1, 1996, p. 765; February 15, 1996, p. 972.
Detroit Free Press, January 3, 1996, p. 1E.
Detroit News, January 21, 1996, p. 1A.
Essence, March, 1996, p. 38.
New York Times, February 18, 1996, p. F7.
Success, November 1993, p. 32.

—Carol Brennan

Donna Brazile

1959—

Campaign manager

In the fall of 1999, Vice President Al Gore named veteran Democratic Party organizer Donna Brazile as his campaign manager for the 2000 presidential campaign. She became the first African American woman to achieve such a prestigious—and difficult—position in national party politics. Brazile, however, had long been a fixture in Democratic circles, known for her formidable grass-roots organizing skills. In 1987, the *Wall Street Journal* named her one of "the powers that (might) be" in national politics in the year 2000. "I'm obsessed with the thought of making things happen. . . . Ultimately, I do it because I'm scared," confessed Brazile about her career choice to *Washington Post* reporter Donna Britt. "I don't ever, ever, ever want to be poor again. And the best way to insure that won't happen is to organize, to fight for our lives."

Brazile was born in a New Orleans charity hospital on December 15, 1959, and grew up in nearby Kenner, Louisiana. Her father, Lionel, was a Korean War veteran who, at various points in his life, had been run over by a truck, suffered a broken back, and even had a heart attack while riding on a city bus. On that occasion, he simply got off and checked himself into a hospital. There were nine children in the Brazile family,

and their father's income as a janitor was not always sufficient, so he often moonlighted or worked double shifts. Brazile's mother also worked as a domestic servant, and the children's grandmother lived with them as well. Brazile used to read the morning paper to her, which helped to foster her interest in politics.

Became a Youthful Activist

Brazile has often stressed that she grew up in an impoverished household, and remembering the hardships from her youth inspired her to become active in politics. "There still are poor people," Brazile told Robin Givhan in the *Washington Post* about her long commitment to Democratic politics. "There still are people struggling to live off 5.15 an hour." Federal minimum-wage laws, civil-rights bills, affirmative action programs, Medicare, Head Start preschool funding, and numerous other pieces of social legislation have all originated with Democratic legislators and were signed into law by Democratic presidents.

In Brazile's childhood neighborhood, there were no playground facilities. At the age of nine, Brazile learned that a candidate for city council was promising to have

At a Glance . . .

Born December 15, 1959, in New Orleans, LA; daughter of a Lionel (a janitor) and Jean (a domestic worker) Brazile. *Education:* Earned degree in industrial psychology from Louisiana State University. *Politics:* Democrat. *Religion:* Roman Catholic.

Career: National Student Education Fund, Washington, D.C., lobbyist, early 1980s; 20thAnniversary March on Washington, national director, 1983; worked for the Rev. JesseJackson's presidential campaign, and for the (Walter) Mondale-(Geraldine) FerraroDemocratic ticket, both 1984; Gephardt for President, national field director, 1987; MichaelDukakis for President campaign, national field director, 1988; affiliated with Community for Creative Non-Violence (an advocate group for the homeless), Washington, D.C., 1989; chief ofstaff for Eleanor Holmes Norton (delegate from the District of Columbia in the U.S. House ofRepresentatives), 1990-99; head of Voter\Campaign Assessment Program for the Democrati Congressional Campaign Committee, 1998; Al Gore for President 2000 Campaign, began asdeputy campaign manager and national political director, May, 1999, became campaign manager,October, 1999. Also an adjunct professor of political science, University of Maryland, CollegePark, MD.

Member: National Political Congress of Black Women, co-founder, first executivedirector.

Addresses: *Office*—GORE2000, 2410 Charlotte Ave., Nashville, TN37203.

one built. She volunteered for the campaign and passed out leaflets in her neighborhood. The candidate won the election and Brazile's neighborhood received a new playground. She later organized the first female baseball team in her community.

In 1975, Brazile's grandmother suffered a stroke and became disabled. She still lived with the family, and Brazile and her sisters helped to take care of her. Brazile would forever associate the smell of roses—her grandmother's favorite scent—with a premonition of death. In 1976, although she was not yet old enough to vote, she volunteered for the Democratic presidential campaign of Georgia governor Jimmy Carter. Brazile stuffed envelopes at her local headquarters for the Carter-Mondale ticket.

Became a D.C. Lobbyist

Brazile financed her college education at Louisiana State University with student loans and financial aid. After earning a degree in industrial psychology, she found work as a lobbyist for the National Student Education Fund in Washington, D.C. From there, she was hired by Coretta Scott King to work on the planning and re-enactment of Martin Luther King Jr.'s famous 1963 civil rights march on the nation's capital. Brazile's work for the King foundation coincided with the successful drive to make the slain civil-rights leader's birthday a national holiday.

In 1984, Brazile became involved with the Rev. Jesse Jackson's presidential campaign, serving as mobilization director and director of the Rainbow Coalition. In both cases, however, she was replaced by a white associate. That same year, Brazile worked on Walter Mondale's unsuccessful campaign for the White House. In 1987, she was hired as National Field Director for a Missouri senator making a bid for the Democratic Party nomination, Dick Gephardt. Brazile made history by becoming the first African American to hold such a post for a mainstream white candidate. "She has the ability to walk into a room of southern white male politicians and get results," a colleague in the Gephardt campaign office told the *Wall Street Journal.* When Gephardt won the Iowa caucuses early in 1988, Brazile's organizational skills were cited as a primary reason for the victory.

The Dukakis Debacle

When Massachusetts governor Michael Dukakis defeated Gephardt for the Democratic presidential nomination in the summer of 1988, Brazile was hired by his campaign organization for the same post that she had held on Gephardt's senior staff: organizing the "field," which involved marshaling votes by setting up and running efficient, dedicated local efforts, such as phone banks. However, Republican front-runner George Bush waged a bitter, divisive campaign against Dukakis that reached its lowest point with the airing of a notorious television campaign ad featuring the face of an angry-looking African American male. The man in the ad was Willie Horton, a Massachusetts resident who was convicted of a crime and then released from prison on a furlough that had been signed by Dukakis. Following his release from prison, Horton committed rape and murder. The campaign ad was both offensive and effective, and many African American leaders strongly protested. For her part, Brazile was incensed that the Dukakis staff had failed to effectively counter the attack.

Dukakis's campaign was also hindered by the fact that

Dukakis rarely campaigned in African American neighborhoods. Strategies and statements released from the Dukakis camp alienated Brazile and other prominent African Americans within the Democratic party. Brazile grew increasingly dismayed, and even endured racism herself on one occasion. As Brazile recounted to Britt, a Midwestern farmer walked up to her during a campaign stop and announced, "You're a Willie Horton n———." Not one to shrink from a fight, she strongly chastised the farmer before heading back to the campaign bus.

The tension between the Bush and Dukakis camps continued to build. One day, while speaking with reporters, Brazile mentioned the oft-repeated rumors that Bush had committed adultery. She urged the reporters to investigate the charges against the Republican candidate. Later, Brazile publicly denounced the Bush campaign's racist tactics, and denounced him as a philanderer. Realizing that the frustrations of her job had sparked her inflammatory words, she submitted her resignation. The campaign manager to whom Brazile's resignation was submitted, Susan Estrich, told Givhan in the *Washington Post* interview that she herself had joked with Brazile that "if I could have figured out a way to get fired, I'd have done it, too." Dukakis went on to lose the election after fielding one of the most poorly organized presidential campaigns in history.

Endured More Hardship

Following her resignation from the Dukakis campaign, Brazile found herself without a job. She was also certain that her career in politics was over. To make matters worse, her mother was admitted to a charity hospital. "I kept telling myself, 'She's okay, she's okay,'" Brazile said in the *Post* interview with Britt in 1989. "This was the most intense period of my life. I was trying to figure out, ''What did I say?' I needed time to become a human being again, to withdraw. Then I smelled the roses and I froze." Brazile's mother died soon after at the age of 53. Because her mother did not have health insurance, Brazile used her last paycheck from the Dukakis campaign to pay for the funeral costs.

During her late twenties, Brazile reevaluated her life. She gave up smoking and red meat, began exercising, and quickly shed 45 pounds. She contemplated attending law school, and landed a new job in Washington as an associate for Mitch Snyder, a well-known advocate for the homeless. For almost a year, Brazile lived at Snyder's Community for Creative Non-Violence, the shelter where her office was located. Under Brazile's direction, the Community for Creative Non-Violence coordinated Washington, D.C.'s Housing Now! march in the fall of 1989.

Signed on with Gore 2000

In 1990, Brazile became chief of staff for Eleanor Holmes Norton, who represents the District of Columbia as a non-voting member of the U.S. House of Representatives, and held the job for the next several years. She also continued working within the Democratic Party. In 1996, Brazile served as local director for the District of Columbia during the Clinton\Gore presidential campaign. During the 1998 midterm elections, she ran the Voter\Campaign Assessment Program, an effort organized by the Democratic Congressional Campaign Committee to bring more African Americans to the polls. The program was a great success, and a solid number of Democratic candidates was elected to Congress that year.

Brazile began working for the Gore for President campaign in the spring of 1999 when its offices were still on K Street, also called "Lobbyists' Row," in the heart of Washington, D.C. Initially, she served as Gore's national political director and deputy campaign manager. In October of 1999, Brazile was late for a staff meeting at which Gore was scheduled to make an important announcement. When the elevator doors opened, her colleagues accosted her, and she learned that Gore wanted to meet with her privately. She assumed she was about the be fired again. However, Gore offered her a promotion to campaign manager. By accepting the position, Brazile became the first African American woman to head a presidential campaign.

Received a Historic Promotion

"She is the heart of grassroots activism and political leadership and she'll be a great leader for our national campaign," Gore said in announcing the appointment, which also coincided with the revelation that his campaign headquarters would relocate to his home state of Tennessee. "Her more than twenty years of experience in local and national campaigns across the country is a terrific benefit to our effort. I look forward to working with her in her new capacity and I know she will fight hard to bring this campaign closer to the working families of America," Gore remarked. Upon learning of Brazile's promotion, the press was quick to point out that Brazile had been fired from the Dukakis campaign several years earlier. However, as Katharine E. Seelye wrote in the *New York Times,* "Gore's appointment of her indicates he has little concern about it [the 1988 firing over the George Bush fracas]. As one aide back in Washington put it: 'Spreading rumors? Holy smokes! In this town?'"

The appointment of Brazile as campaign manager was viewed as a positive development. It also sent the message that Gore—unlike some of his predecessors—realized that what is termed "the black vote" does not automatically go to the Democratic candidate. "Brazile has been important in shoring up Gore's support among the Democrats' traditional constituencies," noted James Bennet in the *New York Times,* referring to the working poor, African Americans, and organized labor.

Brazile was also charged with the task of cutting campaign spending. One of her first duties as campaign manager was "an examination of what she called 'Goreworld,'" explained Bennet in the *New York Times,* "the results of which revolted her. Consultants were getting paid as much as 15,000 monthly; paid advisers were rendering opinions on what kind of paper the headquarters should use." Brazile immediately slashed the salaries of some staffers, a move that was based , in part, on the fact that living expenses in Tennessee were far more reasonable than in the District of Columbia.

Tackled a Tough Job

The principal focus of Brazile's job was to develop strategies that would help Gore win the White House. To help accomplish this task, she worked closely with campaign chairman Tony Coelho and Gore 2000 media advisors Carter Eskew and Bob Shrum. In the *New York Times* report, Bennet explained the nature of Brazile's job: she had sketched for the reporter a triangle diagram: three phrases on each point read "proven leader," "principled fighter," and "experience that matters." She then explained to Bennet that every statement made by Gore or his campaign staff, in the effort to win voters, needed to touch upon those points. "Every conversation—no matter how it starts off— it's got to go into this box," she told Bennet.

During her first months on the job in Nashville, Brazile continued to commute back and forth to the Washington D.C. area to teach a class, "African American Participation in American Politics," at University of Maryland's College Park campus. It is Brazile's contention that the current state of political campaigns, with their reliance on polls and highly paid consultants, is ineffective in bringing together voters on the issues. Brazile's wealth of field experience at the grassroots level helped to make her the ideal person to train staffers and volunteers for Gore. "I put my energy, voice and spirit into fighting for anybody who wants to speak their voice," she told Givhan. "I don't care what the right wing, the left wing or the chicken wing has to say."

Sources

Black Enterprise, February 1996, p. 22.
National Review, February 7, 2000, pp. 17-18.
New York Times, October 7, 1999; October 11, 1999; January 7, 2000;
New York Times Magazine, December 12, 1999; January 23, 2000.
Wall Street Journal, December 4, 1987.
Washington Post, October 7, 1989, p. C1; November 16, 1999, p. C1.

Other

Additional information for this profile was provided by http:\\www.algore2000.org.

—Carol Brennan

Foxy Brown

1979—

Rap artist

At the age of 16, rapper Foxy Brown was a star. She sold over one million copies of her first record, *Ill Na Na.* With her second album, *Chyna Doll,* Brown did what only one other female rapper, superstar Lauren Hill, had done: She premiered in the No. 1 position on The Billboard 200 list of the best-selling albums in the United States. However, she also received criticism for her sexually explicit lyrics and her image as an obscenity-throwing, vulgar, underdressed sexpot. Brown, whose real name is Inga Marchand, allegedly attacked the editor of *Vibe* magazine on a New York street. She was lumped together with other bad-girl rappers like Lil' Kim and Da Brat, and got very little respect on the street. "I was gonna be a sex symbol," Brown told *Essence.* "That was my gimmick. I thought being a sex symbol was what I had to do to make it work." Although her bad-girl image increased her record sales, it devastated her mother and family. In 1999, she vowed to revamp her image.

Middle-Class Ghetto Princess

Although her lyrics paint the portrait of a hardened ghetto goddess, Brown was raised with her two older brothers in the middle-class neighborhood of Park Slope in Brooklyn. Brown's parents divorced when she was four, and she didn't see much of her dad after that. The family then moved in with Brown's grandfather. Her mother cared for her aging father, and taught elementary school. Brown attended high school at Brooklyn College Academy. The family attended Baptist church, and were very close-knit. In an interview with *Essence,* Brown said, "In our family, we said 'I love you' every night. . . .That's the love we had."

Brown's mother wasn't surprised that her daughter would end up on stage. She told *Essence,* "Inga used to dress up in my high heels and put my pearls on." Brown's teachers commended her for her high grades and hard work, but told her mother that she was a chatterbox. Brown's wild side emerged at an early age. While working part time at a local beauty salon, she would come home with gold sprayed in her hair. Brown started rapping in the school lunchroom, reciting the rhymes of Heavy D and Queen Latifah, among others. She went on to gain attention as a talented MC at city rap competitions. Brown's mother thought her daughter was simply a fast talker. "I didn't know that Inga

At a Glance . . .

Born Inga Marchand on September 9, 1979, raised in Park Slope, Brooklyn, NY.

Career: Rapper for Def Jam Recordings, 1996-; appeared with Total, Lil Kim, and DaBrat on the song "No One Else," 1995; rapped on the song "I ShotYa," with L.L. Cool J, 1995; recorded her debut solo album *Ill Na Na*, 1996;appeared on the song "You're Makin' Me High," with Toni Braxton,1996; appeared with Case on the song "Touch Me, Tease Me," 1996; released thealbum *Chyna Girl*, 1998; founded Ill Na Na Entertainment, 1999.

Addresses: *Office*—Def Jam Recordings, 160 Varick St., 12th Floor, NewYork, NY 10013.

could rap," she told *Essence.* "I didn't even know what rap was. I just knew that Inga was talking real fast, but she'd always talked fast, so it wasn't anything new."

Tough as Foxy Brown

In 1995, soon-to-be-megastar rapper and producer Jay-Z discovered Brown and used her on *The Nutty Professor* soundtrack. She then appeared on LL Cool J's song "I Shot Ya," and Toni Braxton's "You're Makin' Me High." *Rolling Stone* magazine said she had a rhyming style "as badass as the boys while putting a femme touch on it." After being involved in a major-label bidding war, Brown signed with Def Jam Records. She took the name Foxy Brown from the blaxploitation film of the same name. The film starred her hero, the sexy, no-nonsense actress Pam Grier.

Brown released her first album, *Ill Na Na*, in 1996. Although many interpreted the title as lewd, Brown really got it by adding Ill, meaning good, to Na Na, her childhood nickname. *Rolling Stone* said the album showed that Brown had "the powerful voice and expert rhyme skills that belie her age." The article also noted that her "come hither looks, exposed flesh, and abundantly sexual lyrics" were inappropriate for some listeners. At the tender age of 16, Brown was a platinum-selling rapper, and a star with a notorious reputation. Because her music career kept her too busy to attend class, Brown finished high school by taking correspondence courses. Her second album, *Chyna Doll*, was released in 1998 and featured sexually explicit lyrics. *Entertainment Weekly* called the album "as glossy and hard as Foxy Brown's exquisitely manicured nails."

Dirty Words Earned Dirty Looks

Although her lewd persona sold records, it didn't earn Brown much respect. In public places, she was routinely groped by men, and women would roll their eyes in disgust when they saw her. Brown and other female rappers were seen by some as lacking knowledge about the true meaning of sex, feminism, and power. *Essence* contributor Joan Morgan described these female rappers as "creatures of their own design who exercise the same creative rights as their male counterparts—coupling highly materialistic, violent and lewd personas with deliciously infectious rhythms and rhymes." Shortly before the release of *Chyna Doll*, Brown appeared on the cover of *Vibe* in a bikini, while grabbing her breast and crotch. Her mother was devastated. Although Brown said that the photo was used against her wishes, the resulting controversy helped to fuel sales of *Chyna Doll*. Angered by the use of the photograph, Brown allegedly attacked the editor of *Vibe* on a New York City sidewalk. Many record stores wouldn't display the poster for *Chyna Doll* because it featured another revealing photograph.

Faced with the disapproval of her mother, Brown vowed to clean up her act. In 1999, she told the media she'd be "sexy but classy" and that she'd "gradually" tone down her lyrics. However, she seemed torn between pleasing her mother and pleasing her fans. Brown was quoted as saying in *Essence,* "I want women to be proud of me as a whole—grandmothers, mothers—and I want to change the way I am perceived." Moments later, in the same interview, she remarked, "I'm not even going to say that I'm going to change my lyrics, because I'll be going against everything I stand for. And I won't have any of the fans that loved me and supported me through the first four years of my career. My two-plus million fans would be like, "This isn't Foxy.'"

Brown did make some attempts to branch out and revamp her image. She hired an African American female publicist, who wanted to promote a more sophisticated Foxy Brown, and teamed up with a stylist who dressed her in designer business suits rather than lingerie and bikinis. She also got a job modeling jeans for Calvin Klein. Brown also sought credibility as a business woman. At the age of 20, she started her own record label, Ill Na Na Entertainment. Brown told *Rolling Stone,* "I just want to be accepted, not for a female or male, just accepted, period. For being me."

Selected discography

Ill Na Na, Def Jam, 1996.
Chyna Girl, Def Jam, 1998.

Sources

Periodicals

Entertainment Weekly, February 5, 1999, p.69.
Essence, March 1997, p. 76; August 1999, p.72.

Other

Additional information for this profile was obtained from "Foxy Brown," RollingStone.com, http:\\www.rollingstone.tunes.com (February 24, 2000); and "Foxy Brown," UBL.com - Music's Homepage, http:\\www.ubl.com (February 24, 2000).

—Brenna Sanchez

Joyce F. Brown

1946—

Educator, administrator, psychologist

Joyce F. Brown was raised to believe in herself and that, if she worked hard, she would be able to achieve her goals. Armed with these principles, this postman's daughter from Harlem became a professor and vice-chancellor at a major university, a deputy mayor for the city of New York, and the president of the Fashion Institute of Technology (FIT), the first woman and the first African American to serve in that post. Presiding over an enrollment of 12,000 students, it has become Brown's mandate to lead FIT into the next century with an investment in technology and an expanded campus in New York's garment district.

Born in New York City to Robert E. Brown, a postal clerk, and Joyce Brown, a clerk with the New York City Housing Authority, Brown was raised in the Harlem section of the city and attended Catholic schools. Her parents set firm guidelines for Brown and her older sister. "It was always a given that we would go to college and be the best we could be in whatever we chose to do," she told Monte Williams of the *New York Times*. "There was a strong work ethic and the belief that if we worked hard and did not expect that it would be easy and we kept at it, it would work."

Following graduation from high school, Brown attended Marymount College in Tarrytown, New York, then returned to New York City to take graduate courses at New York University. As a clinical psychology graduate student, Brown was also working full time as a financial aid counselor at the university. "I'm the 'mail room' story,'" she told Phaedra Brotherton of *Black Enterprise*. "I enjoyed the administrative work I did early on, so I stayed."

A Life in Public Education

Over the next decade, Brown held a variety of other administrative and faculty positions at a number of New York institutions. In 1983, she accepted a position at Bernard Baruch College of the City University of New York (CUNY). As dean of urban affairs, Brown directed a number of initiatives, including the Urban Summit of Big City Mayors and ongoing programs between the New York City Board of Education and the university that are designed to improve academic preparation and retention in secondary schools.

In 1990, Brown was named acting president of Baruch

At a Glance . . .

Born Joyce F. Brown on July 7, 1946 in New York, NY; daughter of Robert E. Brown, a postal clerk, and Joyce Cappie Brown, a clerk with the New York City Housing Authority; married H. Carl McCall, New York State comptroller, August 13, 1983. *Education:* Marymount College, B.A., 1968; New York University, M.A., 1970, Ph.D, 1980; Institute for Educational Management, Harvard University, 1990.

Career: Financial aid counselor, New York University, 1969-70; dean of urban affairs,Bernard Baruch College of the City University of New York (CUNY), 1983-90, acting president,1990, vice chancellor for urban affairs and development, 1990-93; deputy mayor for public andcommunity affairs, 1993; professor of clinical psychology at the Graduate School and UniversityCenter of CUNY, 1994-98; president, Fashion Institute of Technology and chief executiveofficer of the Educational Foundation for the Fashion Industries, 1998-.

Addresses: *Office*—Fashion Institute of Technology, President'sOffice, Seventh Avenue at 27th Street, New York, NY 10001.

College. She was later named vice chancellor for urban affairs and development. In that role, Brown led a South African education development program in conjunction with corporate agencies and other educational institutions. The goal of the program was to strengthen and increase the skills and professional experience of black South Africans through exposure to educational and professional placements.

The South African program was noticed by then-New York City Mayor David Dinkins. In 1993, Mayor Dinkins named Brown deputy mayor for public and community affairs. "In my administration *everyone* had a voice," the former mayor told Monte Williams of the *New York Times.* "Joyce was somebody whose opinion I respected." The following year, Brown accepted a professorship of clinical psychology at the Graduate School and University Center of CUNY.

Named FIT President

In 1998, following a year-long nationwide search and 89 interviews, a ten-member board appointed Brown as president of the Fashion Institute of Technology, a college of the State University of New York (SUNY)

system. "FIT is a unique New York City institution which contributes significantly to the economic vitality of the region," Brown said at the time of her appointment. "The college provides both national and international opportunities for our many talented and creative students to realize their potential. I look forward to leading FIT as we continue to invigorate our academic programs and participate in the global marketplace." Brown was also named chief executive officer of the Educational Foundation for the Fashion Industries, an advisory and support body of FIT.

As the president of a high profile institution such as FIT, Brown faced the added pressure of being the first woman and first African American to hold the post. Her concern about such matters was eclipsed by her pride. "Being black is never incidental," she told Monte Williams of the *New York Times.* "It's central to who I am. But I don't think FIT set out to make a statement about gender or ethnicity. They wanted to find the best person to lead the institution."

Brown recognizes the importance of being a role model to young women of all races. As the keynote speaker at a Women's History Month event which honored Brown and six other talented women, she remarked, "We must tell our story—to set the record straight, to recognize the brave, bold, and brilliant women whose achievements have been overlooked, and most importantly, to give women and girls everywhere role models, a sense of their own worth, and the confidence to pursue their dreams and goals."

Looking Forward

While FIT may have focused on fashion when it was founded in 1956, it has since expanded into a broader educational experience. In addition to fashion, FIT offers 30 majors including interior design, advertising and marketing communications, photography, toy design, cosmetics and fragrance marketing. "I think FIT exemplifies so much of what is New York—it's dynamic, it's creative and it's always moving and out there on the cutting edge," Brown told Arthur Friedman of *WWD.* "When visitors come to the city and they think of the museums and other great institutions that are integral to New York, we want them to think of FIT."

To that end, Brown has embarked on a capital campaign to expand the campus and update the school's technological capabilities. "We have to make sure we're ahead of the curve in technology and I don't think that's easy," Brown admitted to Friedman. "It takes money and it takes talent and it takes time, and you have to find all three of those things if you're going to keep developing." Additionally, Brown planned to expand the school's facilities to include a courtyard, new classrooms and lounges, and a hall for fashion shows and presentations. "I'm very anxious to get moving on that expansion," she told Friedman. "We need to start so people will be able to see things moving."

Although Brown's plans for FIT were ambitious, she had a built-in support system when she arrived at the school. "I've been really pleased by the core of optimism," she told Friedman. "Many people have been here for many years and are very devoted and committed to the institution. They live with the belief and the hope that we will revitalize and make whatever organization or structural changes we need to make to really present ourselves as a coherent, cohesive, integrated community. . . . It's a lot easier to appeal to the community when you have a natural constituency. It keeps us sharp and shows us the directions in which we need to grow."

Brown arrived at FIT with more than 30 years of experience in public higher education and a simple mandate. "Just lead with a certain level of confidence," she told Phaedra Brotherton of *Black Enterprise,* "and trust in your abilities and experience." Brown also believes in remaining open to new possibilities. As she told Friedman in *WWD,* "What I've learned so far is that the industry has a great deal of goodwill toward the institution and wants it to succeed. There's a great opportunity to create a growth path and develop in ways we probably can't even imagine right now."

Sources

Daily News Record, May 6, 1998, p. 2.
Jet, May 18, 1998, p. 34.
New York Times, April 29, 1998, p. B-6; December 2, 1998, p. B-19.
WWD, April 28, 1998, p. 19; September 8, 1998, p.8.

Other

Additional information for this profile was provided by the Office of College Relations at the Fashion Institute of Technology.

—Brian Escamilla

Ed Bullins

1935—

Playwright

Beginning his career in the politically turbulent San Francisco Bay area of the 1960s, Ed Bullins created plays that often reflected the militant spirit of the times. Viewed as a whole, however, his body of work embodies more universal themes. His violent dramas of individuals enmeshed in spirals of destruction and self-destruction have resonated with theatergoers of all races, for they explore the feelings of people trapped in a hostile society that offers no wider sense of community. Bullins, the angry young playwright of the 1960s and 1970s, saw his work take on near-classic longevity by the end of the century, with the appearance of new productions and a book-length study of his writings.

Born July 2, 1935, Bullins grew up in a tough neighborhood in north Philadelphia. His mother was a government worker, and for the most part his childhood was a peaceful one; he excelled as a student in a mostly white grade school, and the family took vacations in rural Maryland. However, Bullins attended an inner-city junior high school, where he became involved with a street gang. In one confrontation he was stabbed, and his heart temporarily stopped. Bullins later wrote about this near-death experience in his sole novel, *The Reluctant Rapist*; though few of his dramas

were overtly autobiographical, they often take violence as a subject.

Bullins dropped out of high school and entered the U.S. Navy in 1952, remaining in the service until 1955 and continuing his education through avid reading. He was also a formidable lighweight boxer. After leaving the Navy he returned to Philadelphia, married, and had several children, but he was restless, and in 1958 lit out for Los Angeles, leaving his family behind. He finished a high school equivalency degree and enrolled at Los Angeles City College, where he studied for several years and began to write short stories, briefly editing a campus literary magazine. Some of Bullins's stories were collected in the volume *The Hungered One: Early Writings,* published in 1971.

Realizing that the African American audience he hoped to reach did not have a strong tradition of reading fiction, Bullins turned instead to drama in the early 1960s. At first, his tumultuous works were too far out of the decorous mainstream of the day to even get a hearing. "Nobody would produce my work," he later told *The New Yorker.* "Some people said my language was too obscene, and others said the stuff I was writing was not theatre in the traditional sense." Bullins per-

At a Glance . . .

Born July 2, 1935, in Philadelphia, PA; son of Edward and Bertha Marie (Queen) Bullins. *Education:* Attended Los Angeles City College, San Francisco State College (now University), B.A., Antioch University, 1989; M.F.A., San Francisco State University, 1994. Has written under pseudonym Kingsley B. Bass, Jr.

Career: Playwright. First play produced, *Clara's Ole Man,* 1965; involvedwith Black Panther party, 1965-67; served briefly as Black Panther Minister of Culture; joinedNew Lafayette Theatre, New York, 1967; became playwright-in-residence, 1968, and associatedirector, 1971; became playwright-in-residence, American Place Theatre, 1973; guest instructor,various colleges and universities, 1970s; instructor in playwriting and dramatic performance,City College of San Francisco, 1984-88; lecturer, Sonoma State University and University ofCalifornia at Berkeley, 1988-95; Professor of Theater, Northeastern University, Boston, 1995-.

Selected awards: Rockefeller Foundation grants, 1968, 1970, and 1973; Obie awards fordistinguished playwriting, 1971 and 1975; Black Arts Alliance award, 1971; Guggenheimfellowships for playwriting, 1971 and 1976; National Endowment for the Arts playwritinggrants, 1972 and 1989; New York Drama Critics Circle award (for *The Taking of MissJanie*), 1975.

Addresses: *Home*—2128A Fifth St., Berkeley, CA 94710;*Agent*—c\o Helen Merrill, 435 W. 23rd St., 1A, New York, NY 10011

man who goes to visit a woman in her apartment, thinking that her "ole man" is away. The "ole man," however, turns out to be a lesbian named Big Girl; the protagonist encounters various grotesque characters and is finally beaten severely by members of a street gang. The work anticipated Bullins's characteristic creation of an atmosphere of simmering, senseless, almost random violence.

In San Francisco Bullins was closely associated with a group of militant black intellectuals, including Huey Newton and Bobby Seale, that soon took shape as the Black Panthers. Bullins even served for a time as the organization's Minister of Culture, and wrote several plays that embodied black nationalist aims, explicitly directed at blacks and shunning any attempt to appeal to white audiences. In 1970's *The Gentleman Caller,* a maid murders her mistress and her visitor, and then answers the mistress's phone with apocalyptic pronouncements: "It is time for Black people to come together . . . to form a nation that will rise from our enslaved mass and meet the oppressor . . . meet the devil and conquer and destroy him."

But Bullins always maintained a certain distance from revolutionary rhetoric, and even parodied it at times. Despite his rejection of the validity of their judgments of his work, Bullins's plays appealed to many white critics, who praised the raw power of his ghetto dramas, finding in them elemental examples of the tragic power of theater at its best. Bullins moved to New York, where in 1968 he became involved with the New Lafayette Theatre, an organization based in the Harlem neighborhood that attempted to build a solid tradition of theatrical repertory in a black urban setting. It was a major institution of the so-called "black arts" movement. The theatre closed in 1973, but not before Bullins had written a dozen plays for it, often considered the greatest among his more than fifty works.

In the early 1970s Bullins reached what was probably the high-water mark of his career in terms of popular success. He won numerous awards, including three Obie awards, a New York Drama Critics Circle award, and a Guggenheim Foundation fellowship—something that would have been anathema to the Black Panther adherent of just a few years earlier. Bullins became playwright-in-residence at New York's American Place Theatre, and the drama departments of prominent Eastern educational institutions began to seek him out for guest lectureships.

In the late 1970s, Bullins suffered a decline in the frequency with which his plays were produced in New York, resulting in part from attacks on his work by feminist critics dismayed at the aspect of sexual violence that they often contained. Bullins entered a prolonged period of what seemed to be creative silence, although he continued to teach, for a time at prestigious Amherst College, Columbia University, and Dartmouth College. He returned to school himself,

sisted, inspired in part by the pioneering short dramas of playwright LeRoi Jones (now Amiri Baraka), then just beginning to transform black theater with their heated intensity. He moved to San Francisco in 1964 and enrolled in a writing program at San Francisco State College.

The wide-open cultural atmosphere of the Bay Area in the middle 1960s proved congenial for Bullins, and it was there that one of his plays was first produced in 1965. That play, *Clara's Ole Man,* actually went on to gain wide acclaim for Bullins after a 1968 New York production. Like many of Bullins's plays, it is set in a slum area in the 1950s. Its main character is a young finally earning a B.A. degree from Antioch University in 1989, and going on for a Master of Fine Arts degree at San Francisco State University, granted in 1994.

In the 1990s it emerged that Bullins, though occupying the spotlight less than before, had continued to write and to live a creative life. Some of his earlier dramas had been conceived as a large group that Bullins called the Twentieth-Century Cycle; he continued work on the cycle, which centered loosely on a group of core characters. (The first cycle play was Bullins's very first full-length play, 1968's *In the Wine Time*.) In 1993 he issued a printed collection of his works, *New\Lost Plays by Ed Bullins*, and in 1997 his play *Boy x Man* ("Boy Times Man"), was produced. His eventful life itself also came full circle: in 1994 he was involved in an auto crash that once again brought him to the brink of death.

Selected works

Clara's Ole Man, 1965.
The Theme Is Blackness, 1966.
In the Wine Time, 1968.
The Gentleman Caller, 1969.
Street Sounds, 1970.
The Duplex: A Black Love Fable in Four Movements, 1971.
The Reluctant Rapist (novel), 1973.
The Taking of Miss Janie, 1975.
The Mystery of Phyllis Wheatley, 1976.
Boy x Man, 1997.

Sources

Books

Bowman, John S., *The Cambridge Dictionary of American Biography,* Cambridge University Press, 1995.
Contemporary Authors, New Revision Series, volume 73, Gale, 1999.
Hay, Samuel A., *Ed Bullins: A Literary Biography,* Wayne State University Press, 1997.
Riggs, Thomas, *Contemporary Dramatists,* sixth ed., St. James Press, 1999.
Smith, Jessie Carney, ed., *Notable Black American Men,* Gale, 1999.
Valade, Roger, ed., *The Schomburg Center Guide to Black Literature from the Eighteenth Century to the Present,* Gale, 1996.

Periodicals

New Yorker, June 16, 1973.

—James M. Manheim

Roland W. Burris

1937—

Politician

Roland W. Burris first ran for political office in Illinois in 1968, and since the 1970s has held two of the state's highest elected posts. He was Illinois's first African American comptroller, or treasurer, as well as its first African American attorney general. Yet Burris has also made unsuccessful bids for the governorship of Illinois—a state that has elected more African Americans to its top offices than any other in the union—but he failed to win the necessary political support among the powerful Chicago-Springfield Democratic Party organization. "Some politicians are easy to pigeonhole," remarked *Chicago* magazine writer Greg Hinz. "Roland Burris is not one of them . . . .. His most visible side is that of the fighter, a man determined to succeed by dint of persistence and guile and hard work."

Burris was born in 1937 in Centralia, Illinois, in the south-central part of the state, where his father, Earl, ran a small grocery store to supplement his income as a laborer for the Illinois Central Gulf Railroad. The Burrises had lived in Centralia for four generations, and Burris inherited a strong sense of community, a Baptist faith, and desire to eradicate injustice. He cited the summer of 1953 as a significant one in his life, for it began on Memorial Day with his dive into Centralia's

municipal swimming pool. The city had unofficially barred the town's African American residents from using the facility, until Earl Burris decided that it should be otherwise. Burris's father even hired a lawyer to meet them at the pool that day, in case of trouble, but the attorney failed to appear. "All summer long, I heard my dad saying, 'If we as a race of people are going to get anywhere, we need lawyers and elected officials who are responsive and responsible,'" Burris recalled in the *Chicago* magazine interview. By the end of that summer, the 16-year-old Burris had decided to pursue a career in politics.

Pursued a Political Career

Burris studied political science at Southern Illinois University in Carbondale, and became a politically active student as well. He headed a group that exposed discriminatory practices among Carbondale merchants toward African American students, and spent a year in Hamburg, Germany, studying international law. In 1963, Burris earned his law degree from Howard University, and worked for a short time as a federal bank examiner. In 1964, he was hired by Continental

At a Glance . . .

Born August 3, 1937, in Centralia, IL; son of Earl (a railroad laborer and grocery-store proprietor) and Emma Burris; married to Berlean Miller (a college administrator); children: Rolanda Sue, Roland II. *Education:* Southern Illinois University, B.A., 1959; earned law degree from Howard University, 1963. *Religion:* Baptist.

Career: Federal bank examiner, c. 1963-64; began at Continental Illinois National Bank,Chicago, IL, 1964, left in 1973 as vice president; Illinois State Department of General Services,director, 1973-76; elected state comptroller for Illinois, 1978, re-elected twice; elected Illinoisattorney general, 1990-94; Jones, Ware & Grenard (law firm), Chicago, managing partner;Buford & Peters (law firm), Chicago, of counsel; adjunct professor, Southern IllinoisUniversity, Carbondale, IL, 1995-.

Awards: African American Hall of Fame; Howard University Alumni of the Year;Distinguished Public Service Award, Anti-Defamation League of B'nai B'rith.

Member: Democratic National Committee; National Association for the Advancementof Colored People; Boy Scouts of America; Southern Illinois University Alumni Association;Financial Accounting Foundation (trustee, 1992-95), Howard University, School of Law Boardof Directors; Mental Health Association of Greater Chicago; Chicago Urban League; CookCounty Bar Association.

Addresses: *Office*—Buford & Peters, LLC, 111 W. Washington St.,Suite 1861, Chicago, IL 60602 .

Illinois National Bank, where he rose to the post of vice president in less than a decade. In his management position, Burris worked to help more minority businesses obtain loans at a time when financial institutions practiced unofficial discrimination in their commercial lending policies.

Burris ran for a seat in the Illinois state legislature in 1968, but finished in last place among the five candidates. "That was the best thing that ever happened to me," he later told the *Chicago Tribune* about his unsuccessful campaign. "I'm very religious, so I figure it was divine intervention that I lost. The Lord not only

saw to it that I lost, but that I came in last." He vowed to work harder at cultivating a base of political support. After working at Continental Illinois National Bank during the day, Burris would devote his evenings to political activities, becoming involved in several local organizations on Chicago's South Side.

Won Historic Victories

Illinois politics, at both the state and local level, is dominated by the Democratic Party organization. Dissatisfaction with this state of affairs led Burris to campaign for Dan Walker, who successfully ran for governor as an independent Democrat in 1973. In return, Walker named Burris to head the state's Department of General Services. When Walker ran again in 1976, Burris ran for comptroller on the same ticket, but lost. Two years later, Burris won election to the comptroller's office, and became the first African American to achieve a statewide electoral victory in Illinois.

Burris was reelected comptroller twice, and for a time even served as national executive director for the Reverend Jesse Jackson's influential Chicago-based organization, Operation PUSH. In 1984 Burris decided to run for one of Illinois's seats in U.S. Senate. He came in second in the Democratic primary to Paul Simon, who would make a bid for the White House several years later. In 1990, Burris became Illinois's first African American attorney general. During his four years in office, he enjoyed a high public profile and oversaw an aggressive office that meted out pollution fines, investigated consumer fraud cases, battled nursing-home problems, and used a grand jury law to prosecute drug dealers.

In the 1980s, Burris's name was discussed as a possible candidate for Chicago mayor, but he initially shied away from entering into this particularly contentious arena of political combat. In 1993, however, he announced his bid for the governorship of Illinois as a Democrat. Early reports predicted that Burris, with his extensive public-service background, had an excellent chance to win the job. The Reverend Jesse Jackson called Burris "a sturdy, non-flashy bridge-builder," according to a *Chicago Tribune* report by Thomas Hardy. "He has a comfort level with all groups because he has pretty much found the common denominator," Jackson told the newspaper. "In political life, if you can find middle C on the piano, it is the same note in all languages and in all places."

Burris lost the Democratic primary by less than 100,000 votes. In 1995, he made a bid for Chicago mayor, but ran against popular incumbent Democrat Richard Daley, who some political analysts noted may have alienated some members of the Democratic Party. Burris once again entered the governor's race in 1998, but once more faced formidable challenges from fellow

Democratic candidates. Although he had solid support among African American voters, "downstate" Democrats around his native Centralia, and wide name recognition, Burris did not have enough in his campaign coffers to buy even one television ad. Had he won, it "would have marked the first time any state had nominated a black candidate for governor and U.S. senator," observed *New York Times* writer Dirk Johnson. But as Johnson also noted, "it had been no secret that some Democratic leaders were fearful that a victory by Burris would convey the impression of an almost all-black Democratic ticket."

Burris, who became a partner with the Chicago law firm Jones, Ware & Grenard before joining the downtown Chicago attorneys' offices of Buford & Peters, also teaches at his alma mater, Southern Illinois University, as an adjunct professor. He and his wife live in a South Side home that was once owned by gospel singer Mahalia Jackson. His long career in public service is not likely at an end, although Burris rejects the race-politics connection. "I don't run as a black man," he told Hardy in the *Chicago Tribune* in 1993. "I run for office as an individual with an answer to the problems of all citizens. Certainly there is a degree of sensitivity to the plight of my people because of the racist structure of society, but I have been able to bridge that because of my upbringing and ability to interact with people."

Sources

Chicago, February 1994, p. 74.
Chicago Tribune, November 8, 1993.
Jet, April 4, 1994, p. 5.
New York Times, March 13, 1998, p. A13; March 19, 1998.
Washington Post, March 17, 1998, p. A4.

—Carol Brennan

Roy Campanella

1921–1993

Professional baseball player

Arguably the greatest catcher in the history of baseball, and certainly one of the game's best all-around players, Roy Campanella's raw talent was so singular as a youth that he began his career at the age of 15. He learned the ins and outs of catching from one of the very best: the great Biz Mackey, catcher for the Negro League's Baltimore Elite (pronounced "E-light") Giants. Barred from regular major league baseball because of his color, Campanella played the first ten years of his career in the Negro Leagues, from 1936 through 1945. He was the fourth African American to be signed to a professional contract in 1946, and the first to integrate the American Association of the Major Leagues, in 1948. Following two years in the minors, Campanella joined the parent Brooklyn Dodgers, where he became a full-fledged star on a team full of stars, including Jackie Robinson, Duke Snider, and Pee Wee Reese.

In the course of his career, Campanella played in All-Star games three times in the Negro League, and played on All-Star teams eight consecutive years in the majors, from 1949 through 1956. He played on five National League pennant teams and helped lead the Dodgers to their World Series win in 1955 over the New York Yankees. He was voted MVP in 1951, 1953, and 1955. He was a remarkable player.

Campanella's brilliant career in baseball ended abruptly in January, 1958, on the eve of the Dodgers' move to California. His car skidded off the road and overturned, pinning him in the wreckage and breaking his neck. His spinal cord was irreparably damaged. A quadriplegic overnight, he would spend the rest of his life in a motorized wheelchair. But Campanella's indomitable spirit and zest for life would not allow him to give up. Although he would never walk again or play the game he so loved, he did return to the world, working as a pitching and catching coach for the Dodgers during spring training, as well as serving as a community relations ambassador for the organization.

Roy Campanella was born November 19, 1921 in Philadelphia, Pennsylvania. He was the youngest of four children born to Ida Mercer Campanella, a black woman, and John Campanella, a white Italian American who worked in the fresh produce trade. He would eventually own his own fruit and vegetable market. When Roy was seven, the family moved to Kerbaugh Street in the Nicetown section of Philadelphia, where he grew up. The Campanellas were strict parents, although not unkind. Roy played stickball and baseball as a youth. By the time he finished ninth grade at Gillespie Junior High, he was thinking more about playing professional baseball than spending the next three years at Simon Gratz High. During the summer of 1936, just before he turned 15, Campanella was approached to play semi-pro ball with the Bacharach Giants, a Philadelphia team. Although Ida Campanella

resisted, wanting her son to finish school, she was gradually persuaded by the amounts of money Roy was being promised. Thirty-five dollars to catch two weekend games was a lot of money in the midst of the Depression.

Quit School to Play Baseball

Before long Roy was taking time off from school to travel with the Bacharach Giants, and by his junior year he decided to quit altogether. When he met Biz Mackey, the great catcher was looking for an understudy to train. Taking a pay cut, Campanella jumped at the chance to play for the Baltimore Elite Giants, a highly respected professional team in the Negro National League. He joined the Elite Giants in 1937 and began to learn the finer points of catching from a master.

Campanella played for Tom Wilson's Elite Giants from 1937 to 1942. He played in the All-Star East-West game in 1941 and was named MVP of that game. He married for the first time in 1939. The first Mrs. Campanella was a Philadelphia girl named Bernice Ray, and the couple had two daughters: Joyce in 1940, and Beverly in 1941. Campanella's long absences strained the marriage, however, and they agreed to separate. They divorced a few years later. Campanella received his draft notice in April, 1941, but received a deferment that allowed him to continue to play ball. After Pearl Harbor he was playing winter ball down in Puerto Rico when he was notified he had been reclassified and had to return to the States immediately. He assembled tank parts until the spring of 1942, when he rejoined the Elites.

Campanella had been fined by owner Tom Wilson for jumping the club to play in a special benefit game. Campanella felt the fine was unfair, and when the owner of the Mexican League offered him a chance to play for more than twice what he made with the Elites, he took it. He spent 1943 playing for Monterrey, helping the team win their first league pennant. He returned to the Elites in 1944 when Wilson, desperate for a decent catcher, forgave the fine. Campanella played in the All-Star games again in 1944 and 1945. Larry Moffi and Jonathan Kronstadt noted in their book, *Crossing the Line*, "During his career with Baltimore, Campanella. . .managed twice to nudge all-time great Josh Gibson off the Negro League all-star team."

Signed with the Brooklyn Dodgers

Campanella had been scouted by the Dodger organization and they were impressed by his power and speed. Jules Tygiel wrote in the introduction to the 1995 edition of Campanella's book *It's Great to Be Alive*, "We were all in on scouting Campanella,' recalled Dodger scout Clyde Sukeforth. 'You couldn't go wrong there.'" Campanella was signed to the Dodger club in 1946. He was the fourth black to integrate major league baseball, following Jackie Robinson, John Wright, and Don Newcombe. Roy Partlow and Don Bankhead came immediately after Campanella. Tygiel wrote in 1995 that "contrary to the legend that portrays Jackie Robinson as the only man who could have withstood the rigors of baseball's 'great experiment,' Campanella could just as easily have become the focal point of baseball integration." According to Tygiel, Dodger president Branch Rickey actually considered Campanella over Robinson "and at one time planned to announce the signing of Robinson and Campanella simultaneously. But Rickey, in part due to the pressures of New York City politics, selected Robinson and chose to let him stand alone."

In 1945 Campanella had married Ruthe Wills and adopted her son David. When he was signed by the Dodgers in 1946, the family moved north. His two daughters remained in Philadelphia with their mother.

Integrated American Association

The Dodgers sent Campanella first to their Class B club in Nashua, New Hampshire, where, along with pitcher Don Newcombe, he played the 1946 season in the New England League. According to Donald Honig's *The Greatest Catchers of All Time,* "Campanella batted .290 and was voted the league's most valuable player." He was sent to the top Dodger farm club at Montreal in 1947. Expecting to play with the Dodgers in 1948, Campanella was told he needed to first integrate the American Association. Protesting that he was a baseball player, not a pioneer, Campanella nevertheless went to St. Paul and became the first black to play in the American Association in 1948. After a month, he was brought up to the Dodgers, where he became the first black catcher in the major leagues, and stayed until 1958.

Campanella was an undisputed asset to the team. He embarked on a ten-year career in the major leagues that was so dazzling that it still feels immediate today. He was a member of the all-star team for eight consecutive years–from 1949 through 1956. As Honig noted, "Playing on what was virtually an all-star team, Campanella had to share the headlines with the speed, power, or defensive splendor of one or the other of his teammates. But when it came to selecting the most critically important man on this sterling roster, three times the sportswriters went to Campanella, voting him the league's most valuable player in 1951, 1953, and 1955." His statistics were impressive. According to Riley, he batted .325 with 33 home runs and 108 RBIs for the MVP honor in 1951. In 1953 he earned it with a .312 batting average, 41 home runs, and 142 RBIs. A .318 average, 32 homers, and 107 RBIs were good for the title in 1955.

Campanella was chosen to be the catcher in four of *The Sporting News* Major League All-Star teams, in 1949, 1951, 1953, and 1955, and was named *The Sporting News* Outstanding National League Player in 1953. He helped lead the Brooklyn Dodgers to five pennant wins, in 1949, 1952, 1953, 1955, and 1956, and helped the Dodgers beat the New York Yankees for the World Championship in 1955. Campanella himself picked 1953 as his most memorable year. "Nineteen-fifty-three was the best year I ever had in baseball," he wrote in *It's Good to Be Alive.* "Free of injuries for the first time in several years, I hit everybody and everything." He added that his greatest compliment came from Ty Cobb in 1955. Campanella wrote, "He was quoted as saying that I would be remembered more than any other player of my time; that someday I would be rated with the greatest catchers of all time. I appreciated that coming from such a man."

Campanella had a temperament ideally suited to the role of catcher. Sweet, unflappable, and humble, he handled a nearly all-white pitching staff and soon earned their respect and friendship. Honig wrote, "Campanella nurtured a pitching staff that included [Don] Newcombe, Carl Erskine, Clam Labine, and left-handers Johnny Padres and Preacher Roe, all of whom extolled their great catcher." From Padres: "Just seeing him back there made you a better pitcher." From Newcombe: "He was something of the psychologist. . . . He knew that sometimes if he got me mad I'd pitch better, so out he'd come in the middle of a game. . .and give me some needling. He knew when to do it and how." Padres gave credit to Campanella for his contribution to the 1955 World Series win over the Yankees. Padres pitched a 2-0 shutout in game seven of the series. "The win was half Campy's," Honig quoted Padres as saying. "He never called a better game. He saw how my stuff was working and he seemed to know what the Yankee hitters were looking for. I don't think I shook him off but once or twice the whole game."

Accident Ended Playing Career

Campanella's glorious career came to an end in 1958. It was January, and he had stayed late at the package liquor store he had purchased as a financial hedge in 1951. He had left the store in Harlem and was close to home in Glen Cove, Long Island, when the car hit a patch of ice and skidded off the road. He was not speeding, but he was unfamiliar with the car. It was a rental; his own was in the shop. The car overturned, pinning him inside, breaking his neck. He was paralyzed from the chest down. Ron Fimrite wrote in *Sports Illustrated* in 1990 that a team of "seven doctors operated for four hours and twenty minutes to save Campanella's life." After three months in the hospital, he was transferred to the Rusk Institute in Manhattan for physical therapy and to learn to cope with the new life that lay ahead.

Campanella wrote in his autobiography, "to tell the truth, I didn't think I was going to live those first few days. . .following the accident." He was full of fears, wondering what would become of him, how he would support his family. Filled with despair, he admitted there were many times when he was close to hysterics. After a stern talk from one of his doctors, urging him to work harder at a recovery, Campanella began the long road back. "This was a challenge," he wrote, "the greatest I ever faced. I knew I would have a long, tough fight ahead of me, but I was no longer afraid." Turning to God for help, he noted, "It's quite a nice thing to have God on your side–and I know He is on mine. . . .I'm a lucky man. I thank God I'm alive."

Campanella made slow but steady progress after that, even learning to catch a ball again. In 1958 he was offered the opportunity to become a radio show host. The show was called "Campy's Corner," and it proved to be good therapy. The first shows were broadcast from his hospital room. Then he was offered a position with the Dodgers as a part-time coach and radio announcer for home games. In 1959 he returned to Vero Beach, Florida, for spring training with the Dodgers, in his new role as a coach.

Campanella's mental and physical progress following his accident was an inspiration to millions, prompting Dr. Rusk to speculate that Campanella's contribution to the world of the disabled was likely to be far more significant than those he had ever made on a baseball diamond. From 1959 until about 1990, Campanella continued to work for the Dodger organization, first as a coach, and later as a community relations man. He and his second wife separated in 1960, and following her death, he married Roxie Doles, a former nurse and neighbor. They were inseparable for the rest of his life.

In 1959 the Dodgers honored him at a preseason game designated Roy Campanella Night. According to *USA Today* in 1999, "Attendance at the Los Angeles Coliseum was 93,103, which remains the record for a big league game." Campanella was inducted on the first ballot into the Baseball Hall of Fame in 1969, and was inducted into the Black Athletes Hall of Fame in 1975. Campanella died of a heart attack in 1993 at his home in Woodland Hills, California.

When considering the storied life of Roy Campanella, it is easy to fall into pondering the "what ifs" that inevitably arise in such a discussion. What if there had been no racial barrier in major league baseball? What might he have accomplished had he spent the first ten years of his career in the majors as well? What if he, not Robinson, had been chosen to break the color line? What more might he have accomplished had he not had the tragic accident in 1958? It is tempting and easy to speculate. But the fact is that despite these obstacles, Roy Campanella accomplished amazing things any-

way. Indeed, it is probably his many awe-inspiring successes which cause us to dream of what more might have been, if only Campanella had gotten a fair shake out of life. Campanella himself, however, accepted whatever life had to offer him, with gratitude, grace, and immeasurable dignity.

Sources

Books

The African American Almanac, Eighth Edition. Edited by Jessie Carney Smith and Joseph M. Palmisano. Detroit: Gale, 2000.

Biographical Dictionary of American Sports: Baseball. Edited by David L. Potter. New York: Greenwood Press, 1987.

Campanella, Roy. *It's Good to Be Alive.* New York: Little, Brown, 1959. Reprinted, with introduction by Jules Tygiel, Lincoln: University of Nebraska Press, 1995.

Cohen, Stanley. *Dodgers! The First 100 Years.* New York: Carol Publishing Group, 1990.

Honig, Donald. *The Greatest Catchers of All Time.* Dubuque, IA: Wm. C. Brown Publishers, 1991.

Moffi, Larry, and Jonathan Kronstadt. *Crossing the Line: Black Major Leaguers, 1947-1959.* Iowa City: University of Iowa Press, 1994.

Notable Black American Men. Edited by Jessie Carney Smith. Detroit: Gale, 1999.

Peterson, Robert. *Only the Ball Was White.* New York: Oxford University Press, 1970.

Ritter, Lawrence and Donald Honig. *The 100 Greatest Baseball Players of All Time.* New York: Crown Publishers, 1981.

Periodicals

Jet, July 12, 1993, p.14; November 25, 1996, p.22.

Sports Illustrated, June 27, 1983, p.40; September 24, 1990, p.94; July 5, 1993, p.70.

People Weekly, May 19, 1986, p.141; July 12, 1993, p.97.

Time, January 15, 1990; July 12, 1993.

USA Today, January 31, 1999.

—Ellen Dennis French

Herbert Carnegie

1919—

Athlete, motivational educator

A legendary Canadian hockey player during the 1940s, Herbert Carnegie dreamed of a career in the National Hockey League. For years, he watched as teammates and competitors were drafted by NHL teams. The color barrier in professional hockey, however, would not be broken until 1957. Carnegie's dream of a career in the National Hockey League would go unfulfilled.

Carnegie was born in Toronto, Canada, in 1919, into a large family headed by Jamaican immigrant parents. They lived on the west side of city, where they were the only black household in the neighborhood. The family soon moved to the Willowdale area of North York, a rural part of Toronto, when Carnegie was still an infant. By living in North York, the Carnegies were able to have a larger home, and Carnegie's father, George, was able to supplement a meager income as a janitor for a Toronto utility company by growing produce and raising livestock.

Carnegie's father had left school as an adolescent, and strongly emphasized the value of education to his seven children. He lectured them continuously, and told them how contemptuously his white coworkers treated him at times. Occasionally, Carnegie's father hurled a broom at one of his children as a reminder of how their future boss would treat them if they didn't stay in school and prepare for a professional career. Carnegie and his siblings were well aware of the racism in Canadian society even at this early age, for they were almost always the only blacks in their neighborhood, school, and local Baptist congregation. "As coloured kids, we

were put down nearly every day by name-calling," Carnegie wrote in his autobiography, *A Fly in a Pail of Milk.*

Found Talent on the Ice

As a youngster, Carnegie became angry when his classmates called him derogatory names, and preferred to use his fists to retaliate. He earned good grades, and discovered his passion for hockey when he put on a pair of his older brother's skates around the age of eight. On the pond in Willowdale that day, he realized he was a quick, adept skater. Soon, he spent nearly all of his free time skating. Carnegie and his brother Ossie practiced endlessly, and spent hours playing pick-up hockey with the neighborhood boys. When they could not find a real hockey puck to use, they improvised by using frozen horse manure.

Like their playmates, the Carnegie brothers listened intently to National Hockey League games that were broadcast on the radio. These broadcasts were a Saturday-night staple in Canada during the 1920s. Like other Canadian boys, the Carnegies felt that playing professional hockey was their destiny. "Both Ossie and I set our sights on the National Hockey League (NHL)," Carnegie wrote in his memoirs. "We didn't spend much time talking about it. We just assumed we were the best, and soon the world would know it as well." They continued to practice passing, shooting, and dodging imaginary opponents. "Day in, day out, our goal was to be better than we were the day

Born November 8, 1919, in Toronto, Ontario, Canada; son of George Nathaniel (a janitor) and Adina Janes (Mitchell) Carnegie; married Audrey Redmon, 1940; children: Goldie, Bernice, Rochelle, Dale. *Education:* Earned degree from University of Western Ontario, 1962.

Career: Semi-professional hockey player in Ontario and Quebec, 1939-55; employee ofBuffalo Ankerite Mill, Perron, Ontario, Canada, early 1940s; machinist in mill in Timmins,Ontario, 1942-44; North York Board of Education, assessment officer, 1956; Borough of NorthYork, recreation supervisor, 1957-62; Boys Club director, Scarborough Police Youth Club,1962-64; Investors Syndicate, sales associate, 1964, became Toronto division manager.

Awards: Order of Ontario, 1996; Metropolitan Toronto Canada Day Medal; QueenSilver Jubilee Medal, 1977; Commemorative medal for the 125th anniversary of Canada; OntarioGovernment Achievement Award for Good Citizenship; Pride Black Achievement Award.

Addresses: *Office*—Herbert H. Carnegie Future Aces Foundation, Box92293, 2900 Warden Ave., Scarborough, Ontario M1W 3Y9, Canada.

before," Carnegie recalled. Both Carnegies played on the Lansing Public School team, and Herbert joined a midget team when he was 14-years-old. He and his brother were always the only black players on the team, and their father was the lone black man in the stands.

Celebrated Local Athlete

Despite his pride, George Carnegie had felt the sting of racism for much of his life, and had little delusions about an integrated Canadian society. He warned his sons, "You know they won't let any black boys into the National Hockey League!" as Carnegie recalled in *A Fly in a Pail of Milk.* Carnegie's father had hoped that his son would become a doctor instead. Undeterred, Carnegie went on to play for Earl Haig Collegiate School in North York for a year. However, he and his brother decided to transfer to a school in Toronto in the hopes of receiving more press attention for their playing abilities. Toronto newspaper reporters rarely covered high-school hockey games in places like North York. Carnegie's father agreed, and even let his sons

use his car to make the daily trip.

At Toronto's Northern Vocational School, Carnegie was a standout player who rapidly progressed through the three team levels in 1935. As an added bonus, the school's home ice was the famous Maple Leaf Gardens, home of the NHL's Toronto Maple Leafs. Despite his talent on the ice, however, Carnegie was subjected to racial slurs from both opponents and spectators.

Although Carnegie played golf, football, and ran track, hockey remained his first love. He practiced hockey for two hours each morning before attending school. On one occasion, he made the Toronto preps section headlines when he scored five goals in a single game. Carnegie was certain that he had a future in the NHL. "Sports can be an awfully seductive pursuit for a young person," he wrote in *A Fly in a Pail of Milk.* "And that's especially true for youngsters who see their horizons in the narrowest of terms. For some, sports seems the only escape from the misery around them. And professional sports may provide instant gratification—applause, adulation, and attention."

"Turn Carnegie White"

One day during a practice at Maple Leaf Gardens, Carnegie's coach pointed out the owner of the Toronto Maple Leafs, who was sitting by himself in the stands. The owner, Conn Smythe, had marveled at Carnegie's natural talents, but then stated that he wished "'he could turn Carnegie white'," as Carnegie recalled in his autobiography. "I can't remember exactly what I thought, but a little voice in the back of my head was kissing my NHL hopes goodbye."

Carnegie was irate that others would judge his hockey abilities based on his skin color. He told his parents what had happened, and they, too, were saddened. This experience marked the beginning of a period of bitterness in Carnegie's young life. Around this time, he meet a shy, well-to-do young woman named Audrey Redmon. He began working for her father's hauling company while courting her, but her family was adamant that Audrey find a more ambitious suitor.

A Rough Life

In 1939, Carnegie followed his brother Ossie north to a remote part of Ontario in order to play for team known as the Perron Flyers. The brothers lived in a tiny mining town that was full of newcomers in search of work. They were surprised to find that racism was virtually nonexistent there. Carnegie worked as a janitor in a mill, and spent four successful seasons with the team. He earned 30 a week for both jobs, and lived in a boarding house with his brother. The Flyers often defeated teams whose players went on to NHL training camps. "Although my brother and I had finished among the league's top scorers, the NHL scouts left us standing in the cold," Carnegie remembered in his autobiography. Even a dire shortage of players caused by the onset of World War II did not improve their chances. "Ossie and I talked about it and there was no doubt in our minds that our problem was colour . . . . . There was no one to speak for us and we never made a fuss with anyone," Carnegie recalled in *A Fly in a Pail of Milk*. Still, he remained hopeful. "I felt that if I continued to play hard and to excel, sooner or later, I would get my chance. Somebody out there, I continued to hope, would have a heart."

Carnegie and Audrey Redmon eloped, but her family soon forgave her. During their first year together, the couple lived in Perron and started a family. They moved to another mining town, Timmins, which was slightly larger. Generally, racism was still prevalent in Ontario. At times, restaurants refused to serve them. Carnegie was even rejected for military service during World War II. At the time, there was an unspoken policy preventing blacks from serving in the Canadian armed forces. "That realization led me to conclude that Papa was right," Carnegie recalled in his autobiography. "Race was far more significant in Canadian society than I ever could have imagined. Was this a society for which I wanted to risk my life?"

Made Canadian Hockey History

During the early 1940s, Carnegie played for the Timmins team and worked as a machinist. Over the next few years, he and his wife would have four children. The Carnegie brothers continued to attract attention as talented skaters and scorers, and word of their hockey prowess reached as far as New Brunswick. Another black hockey player, Manny McIntyre, was also creating a sensation in New Brunswick. McIntyre decided to come to Timmins to play with the Carnegie brothers in 1941—Carnegie played center wing, his brother right wing, and McIntyre left wing. They became the first all-black line in semi-professional hockey, and soon became a star attraction for the Timmins team. Local sportswriters tagged them with various names, including the Brown Bombers, Dark Destroyers, and Dusky Speedsters.

In 1944, McIntyre negotiated a better contract for himself and the Carnegie brothers in the Quebec Provincial League. They earned 75 a week playing for the Shawningan Falls Cataracts, the home team of a paper mill town southwest of Quebec City. Here, the all-black line continued to attract attention for their terrific skills. They were still subjected to racial slurs from spectators, however. McIntyre then negotiated a jump to the Sherbrooke Saints, which was considered the best team in North American semi-pro hockey. Many of the team's players rapidly advanced to careers in the NHL.

Disappointment at Rangers' Camp

Carnegie continued to excel as a player. He was named team captain in 1946, and won Most Valuable Player awards for three years running in the late 1940s. During this same era, an outstanding black baseball player named Jackie Robinson was signed to the Brooklyn Dodgers. Robinson played his first game for the Dodgers in 1947 in a much publicized, sometimes viciously debated debut. Sadly for Carnegie, no NHL owner followed the Dodgers' example.

In 1948, Carnegie was invited to the New York Rangers' training camp. "I was more than capable, after all those years, of measuring my own skills against those of others," Carnegie recalled in his autobiography. "And I skated well, checked well, taking the puck away from the stars, scored goals and set up plays." After a stellar week of practice, he was offered a contract with the Rangers' farm team. However, the move would have meant a drastic pay cut from his Sherbrooke salary, and he had a family to support. Carnegie turned down the offer, and it marked "the end of my dream to play in the NHL," Carnegie recalled in *A Fly in a Pail of Milk*.

Both Ossie Carnegie and McIntyre eventually left to play professional hockey in France. Carnegie joined the Quebec Aces in Quebec City for the 1949-50 season. He played for the Owen Sound Mercurys in the Ontario Hockey League during the 1953-54 season. This season would be his last as a hockey player. At the age of 34, Carnegie realized that he had been lucky to escape from the sport without any permanent injuries, which were common before the advent of improved safety equipment. His teeth were also intact. In the summer of 1954, he began working as a clerk at a Toronto hospital, and spent the next two years at the tedious job, which often left him free time to doodle. To combat boredom, Carnegie began sketching play formations for the young hockey team that he was coaching.

The Future Aces

Carnegie had named his team the Future Aces, but he felt that he was not a natural-born coach. Instead, he developed what he came to call the Carnegie System of Positional Hockey, and founded the Future Aces Hockey School. The school was founded after Carnegie's son Dale brought 40 friends home to learn hockey skills. Some of the boys were from poor families and could barely afford equipment, so Carnegie began raising money for them through sponsorship deals with merchants in North York. He came to consider himself a far better instructor than coach, and soon gave up the latter altogether. "Not every young player wanted to be in the NHL as I had," Carnegie wrote in *A Fly in a Pail of Milk*. "But most young boys loved hockey the way I did and they needed to be taught how to play the game or even how to watch and enjoy the game."

For a time, Carnegie worked for the North York Parks and Recreation Department as a sports director while taking college courses part-time through the University of Western Ontario. In 1962, he finally earned the college degree that his father had long anticipated for him. To support his family, Carnegie worked for the local school system and as a Boys Club director. He was then hired as an investment-services sales representative, a career in which he excelled for three decades. Early in his career in investment services, Carnegie found that his career in hockey helped him to overcome any racial barriers. Colleagues and clients remembered Carnegie and his brother fondly. He eventually became Toronto division manager and a board member with the company, Investors Syndicate.

Carnegie became an outstanding golfer in his later years,, taking several amateur golf titles and club championships. He continued his Future Aces school, which expanded into clinics in several other communities. A college scholarship fund, the Herbert H. Carnegie Future Aces Foundation, was also created. The Future Aces creed, written by Carnegie himself, stresses attitude, cooperation, sportsmanship, and motivation. In his autobiography, Carnegie reflected on the color barrier that had stifled his dream of playing in the NHL, and how the setback became a source of personal inspiration. "I had learned as my father had regretfully predicted that it was not so]racial equality in Canada]," he wrote. "Well, what I wanted was a Canada where kids could dream and dreams could become realities, and the place to start was with young people."

Sources

Carnegie, Herb, with Robert Payne, *A Fly in a Pail of Milk: The Herb Carnegie Story,* Mosaic Press, 1997.

—Carol Brennan

Suzanne de Passe

1948(?)—

Music and television executive

Suzanne de Passe remains remarkably little known in view of her impressive list of accomplishments. As an executive at Motown records during the company's second set of glory years in the 1970s, de Passe nurtured the careers of some of the greatest entertainers of the modern era, including Michael Jackson and Commodores's lead vocalist Lionel Richie. As one of Hollywood's hardest working and most respected independent television producers, she brought to fruition one of most-watched and most artistically acclaimed television miniseries of all time, the eight-hour Western epic *Lonesome Dove,* broadcast in 1989.

Suzanne Celeste de Passe was born around 1948, to West Indian parents in the Harlem neighborhood of New York City. Her parents divorced when she was three, but her father, a salesman for the Seagram liquor firm, continued to play a strong role in her life after his remarriage six years later. Ambitious from an early age, de Passe attended a private school (the New Lincoln School) in New York, and set her sights on becoming a writer. Majoring in English, she attended Syracuse University, and then transferred to Manhattan Community College.

Booked Talent for Disco

She had talents outside of school, though, and these grew so fast that they ultimately took precedence over the completion of her college education. While still in school, she had held down a job at New York's fashionable Cheetah Disco; there her ear for new music and musicians impressed the management so much that she was hired as talent coordinator, a position that gave her invaluable experience in both mechanics and the artistic side of the music business. From the Cheetah Disco, de Passe moved on to New York's Howard Stein talent agency, and at a party she met Berry Gordy, who would become her mentor and the most important inspiration behind her own creative career.

Gordy at the time was riding high as the founder and chairman of Motown Records, the pioneering Detroit label that brought black popular music to a level of nationwide success that it had never before achieved. After hiring de Passe in 1968 and bringing her to the company's new headquarters in Los Angeles, Gordy groomed her in the creative side of the business. Though known as a stern taskmaster, he was patient

At a Glance . . .

Born 1948 in New York, NY; raised in Harlem neighborhood; of West Indian descent; married actor Paul Le Mat, 1978. *Education:* Attended Manhattan Community College.

Career: Music, television, and film executive. Became assistant to Motown Recordsfounder Berry Gordy, 1968; began to work in talent acquisition for Motown, 1970; became director of West Coast creative division of Motown, 1970s; became vice president of Motown-Industries, 1970s; became president of Motown Productions, 1981; produced award-winning CBS-TV miniseries *Lonesome Dove,* 1989; founded de Passe Entertainment, 1992.

Addresses: *Office*—President, De Passe Entertainment, 5750 Wilshire Blvd., Ste 640, Los Angeles, CA 90036-3697.

with his new charge. "Gordy let me mess up a lot of things [and] spend a lot of his money," de Passe told *Forbes* magazine.

Not far into her twenties, de Passe worked to develop new talent as the vice president of Motown's West Coast creative division. One day she encountered a unique act consisting of five singing brothers—the Jackson Five—headed by an incredibly energetic youngster. "I was just knocked out," de Passe told *People.* "There was this little guy [Michael Jackson] attacking some of the most mature R&B material that existed." De Passe honed her management skills as she supervised the Jackson Five's music and choreography, and must be given considerable credit for the initial flowering of Michael Jackson's mercurial career.

Scripted Billie Holiday Film Bio

The multitalented de Passe put her writing skills to work on another major project for Motown: she was the co-writer for the 1972 Billie Holiday film biography *Lady Sings the Blues,* starring Diana Ross. She rose through the ranks at Motown, becoming vice president of Motown's West Coast division, and then vice president of Motown Industries as a whole. Some of the work was rewarding and glamorous, but some was less so: in the 1970s, one of de Passe's duties was to act as go-between for Gordy and vocal diva Diana Ross, then a much-publicized show-business pairing. "It was a highly combustible situation," de Passe recalled in a *People* interview. Despite the touchiness of the duty,

Ross and de Passe became good friends; the singer served as matron of honor at de Passe's 1978 wedding to actor Paul Le Mat.

Lending her writing and production abilities to two other Motown-generated stage productions, *Mahogany* and *The Wiz,* de Passe was rewarded for her ability to realize so many complex projects when she was named president of Motown Productions in 1981. This new division of the company was intended to broaden the music-oriented company's reach into television and movies. Starting modestly with several television movies, de Passe gained recognition for producing the Motown retrospective *Motown 25: Yesterday, Today, Forever,* the first in an ongoing series of Motown television specials that continued to bring the company revenue through associated music album releases. Even after leaving Motown, de Passe produced specials recognizing the company's 30- and 40-year landmarks.

In 1989, de Passe raised eyebrows with a daring move: she produced a CBS television network miniseries of Larry McMurtry's sprawling Western novel, *Lonesome Dove.* The odds seemed stacked heavily against the series's success: most observers thought that in those early days of video and cable competition for television, a four-night, eight-hour presentation was doomed to failure. It also seemed that de Passe, an urban-raised woman who had devoted her life to African American culture, might have been an unlikely choice to helm a project steeped in the lore of the old West.

Grabbed Rights to McMurtry Novel

But de Passe had read the Pulitzer Prize–winning novel in manuscript even before it reached publication, and, according to *Forbes,* "instantly saw in it a modern-day classic." While other studios held back, discouraged by the book's length, de Passe had cannily snapped up the television and movie rights to the book for a mere 50,000 in 1985. Her judgment was vindicated when *Lonesome Dove* won rave reviews, top ratings, and Peabody, Golden Globe, and Emmy awards. The one event that marred de Passe's triumph was the bankruptcy of a company associated with the making of the film; de Passe's own fee was among the casualties.

Yet de Passe has been known to sacrifice part of her own pay at times, in order to help bring success to projects she is committed to. There is a streak of creative idealism in de Passe's character: a writer herself, she has done what it takes to bring projects to completion, even with uncertain financial underpinnings. "In this business, if you believe in something enough, sometimes it requires a gesture to get other people involved," she told *Newsweek.*

She founded her own company, de Passe Entertainment, in 1992, but continued a close association with

Motown. She produced other successful programs based on McMurtry's novels, branched out into weekly programming with the ABC network series "Sister, Sister," and continued to created and produce projects that told parts of the always compelling Motown story. One of these, a two-part 1998 program on the career of the Motown vocal group the Temptations, had a budget of over 16 million.

A true leader, de Passe has been the focus of two studies of her personal management style, conducted by the Harvard Business School. Compared with other influential entertainment-industry figures who find their lives made the stuff of gossip columns, de Passe has gained less recognition and perhaps less remuneration. "I've made a lot more money for others than for myself," she admitted to *Newsweek* in 1998. "I can't retire." American entertainment, however, has been all the richer for her contributions.

Sources

Books

Henderson, Ashyia N., and Shirelle Phelps, eds., Who's Who Among African Americans. 12th ed. Gale, 1999.
Smith, Jessie Carney, ed., *Notable Black American Women, Book II.* Gale, 1996.

Periodicals

Forbes, January 23, 1989, p. 58.
Newsweek, November 2, 1998, p. 48.
People, March 22, 1991, p. 64.
Time, January 30, 1989, p. 51.

—James M. Manheim

Taye Diggs

1972—

Actor

A Broadway veteran best known for his role as the handsome young Jamaican in *How Stella Got Her Groove Back,* Taye Diggs is part of a new generation of African American leading men who are enjoying impressive Hollywood success—while steering clear of negative typecasting. Diggs, along with actors such as Larenz Tate and Djimon Hounsou, have benefitted from a recent spate of popular films, like *Stella,* whose themes seem to rest upon color-blind hopes, dreams, and sorrows, but just happen to feature a cast of color. Though Diggs's film debut made him a household name, he was already well-known to New York theatergoers, especially after appearing in the original cast of the acclaimed Broadway musical *Rent* in 1996. An accomplished stage actor, singer, and dancer, he has been hailed as the successor to Sidney Poitier, the first African American to win an Academy Award for Best Actor.

Bestowed with the first name of "Scott" when he was born in Rochester, New York, in 1972, Diggs was the oldest of five children in his family. "Taye" supplanted his real name following the habit of one of his uncles, who used to call him "Scot-tay." As a teenager, he was thin, awkward, and on the short side. "I was a large

geek," *Ebony* magazine reported him as saying. "I remember going home and praying to God and saying, 'I want to be good-looking. I want to have a girlfriend. I want girls to like me.'" To improve his physique, Diggs took modern dance classes and lifted weights. His mother convinced him to attend the local performing-arts high school, where, he said, "I came into my own," the *Ebony* article stated. "If you wore glasses or tight pants, you were still accepted. It was pleasant. It was not only the jocks who got the girls."

A Stint in Tokyo

After earning a degree in theater from Syracuse University, Diggs moved to New York City, where he was fortunate to land an understudy role in a major Broadway production. As an understudy, an inexperienced actor shadows a colleague, learning the lines and stage cues of the role, in the event that an emergency replacement is necessary. Diggs then took the unusual step of moving to Japan, where he found work as a performer at Tokyo Disneyland in its "Caribbeanland" shows. When he returned to the United States, he landed a role in a planned Broadway rock opera called *Rent.*

Rent debuted in early 1996, and won immediate, enthusiastic reviews for its musical portrayal of life, love, and death among a group of modern-day bohemians in New York's hip East Village neighborhood. Based in part on the Puccini opera *La Boheme, Rent* also achieved a certain tragic notoriety due to the sudden death of its creator, Jonathan Larson, just weeks before it opened. Centered around a group of struggling artists, *Rent* touched upon heroin addiction and the specter of AIDS, and won the Tony Award for best Broadway musical that year.

A Rising Star

In *Rent,* Diggs was cast as Benjamin, once a denizen of the East Village scene himself. Benny, however, turned on his friends when he achieved some measure of financial success, and is now the despised landlord of the building where many of the characters live. At one point he padlocks the building, while also trying to eject a group of homeless people squatting in the building next door. "Sparked by a young, intensely vibrant cast[00fe]and sustained by a glittering, inventive score, the work finds a transfixing brightness in characters living in the shadow of AIDS," asserted critic Ben Brantley of the *New York Times.*

Diggs's career trajectory climbed steadily after the success of *Rent.* He appeared in guest spots on *Law and Order* and *New York Undercover,* and in 1997 was cast as Adrian "Sugar" Hill in the CBS daytime drama *The Guiding Light.* But the actor was still appearing in *Rent* when he auditioned for and won his first-ever film role: the screen adaptation of the 1996

Terry McMillan novel, *How Stella Got Her Groove Back.* The upcoming project came close on the heels of *Waiting to Exhale,* the successful film version of another of McMillan's acclaimed novels. *Stella*'s plot revolved around an overworked single professional woman whose vacation romance with a much younger man evolves into something more serious. As producer of *Stella,* McMillan reportedly wanted Ralph Lauren model Tyson Beckford for the male lead, but Diggs's combination of looks and professional stage experience won him the role instead.

Made Sizzling Film Debut

As *Stella* opens, Bassett's character is lured to Jamaica by a friend for a much-needed vacation. A hardworking San Francisco stockbroker, Stella is also the divorced mother of an 11-year-old boy and thoroughly dejected by the dating scene. At the luxury resort she meets Diggs's character, the handsome, charming Winston Shakespeare. Just 20 years old, Winston is a native of the island and has vague plans to enter medical school soon. A romance develops, despite the age difference. When the vacation ends, the relationship continues, and Diggs soon moves into Stella's posh Marin County home. It becomes apparent, however, that in some ways he has more in common with Stella's son, who enjoys having a new friend to play video games with him.

"Diggs imbues Winston with an easy grace and dignity," opined Stephen Holden in the *New York Times.* "But his performance is too soft-spoken and embellished with too many vacant smiles for his character to emerge as anything more than a misty romantic fantasy. Even when he loses his temper, Winston is impossibly, reassuringly nice." Despite the flaws in the on-screen character, Diggs won notoriety for his role in the film because of a particularly revealing shower scene. "I didn't know what was going to be shown in the nude and I really didn't care," he told *Newsweek* reporter Allison Samuels. "I wanted the role so bad it didn't matter what I had to do to get it."

Offered Challenging Roles

In 1999, Diggs appeared in a number of other well-received films. He was part of the ensemble cast of *Go,* a comic and violent *Pulp Fiction*-style film. In it, he played Marcus, whom several of the characters meet on a Las Vegas jaunt that is one of three interrelated plots in the movie. The work follows the adventures of a hapless supermarket cashier who becomes involved in a drug deal; her best friend is then held hostage, and her English co-worker from the supermarket finds himself in Las Vegas, "in which the smoothly appealing Taye Diggs plays a major role," wrote *New York Times* film critic Janet Maslin, who called the film "a jaundiced comedy of manners that toys with who may or may not be gay, and has a white character tell a black one that 'color's just a state of mind."

The Wood, which opened in the summer of 1999, offered Diggs another appealing big-screen character study. The film's title is the nickname for a middle-class African American suburb of Los Angeles, Inglewood, and its plot follows the 13-year friendship of three men who meet as teens there in the mid-1980s. Told in flashback, *The Wood* opens as Diggs's character, Roland, is suffering from a case of pre-wedding jitters so severe that he flees to the home of an ex-girlfriend and becomes quite drunk. His longtime friends, played by Omar Epps and Richard T. Jones, track him down and attempt to get him to the altar.

Roland, however, becomes sick in the car, and they return to the ex-girlfriend's home to wash themselves off with a garden hose. "The desperate last-minute cleanup resonates with the threesome's adolescent adventures, none especially harrowing," wrote the *New York Times*'s Holden. "They include being stopped by the police in a car in which one person is carrying a gun, finding themselves in the back of a grocery store while it's being robbed and of course, pitching inept lines at girls who adamantly stand their ground."

Later in 1999, Diggs appeared in the title role of *The Best Man,* another African American-themed comedy, and a film produced by Spike Lee. Diggs was cast as Harper Stewart, a Chicago writer whose debut novel, *Unfinished Business,* is about to be published. Terrific sales and celebrity status are assured for the book and its author, because Oprah Winfrey has selected it as one of her book-club titles. Prior to this, however, Harper must first endure the New York City wedding of his friend, a former college athlete (Morris Chestnut) and notorious womanizer now coming to terms with the permanence of his upcoming wedding vows. In the pre-nuptial festivities, Harper rekindles a flirtation with bridesmaid Jordan, played by actress Nia Long, who was the inspiration for one of the characters in *Unfinished Business.*

Adding to this drama, Diggs's character is also trying to keep the groom from discovering that he once had a fling with the bride-to-be—also recounted in the forthcoming novel—and struggles to remain faithful to his girlfriend back in Chicago, despite Jordan's lure. Maslin, giving *The Best Man* a positive review in her *New York Times* column, called it "another demonstration that current movies about upscale black characters have much more traditional values than ones about catty white teen-agers."

Another Broadway Hit

Diggs returned to Broadway in the spring of 2000 when cast in *The Wild Party.* Set in the 1920s, the musical revolves around a group of vaudeville performers living it up during an economic boom. Toni Collette, Mandy Patinkin, and Eartha Kitt were also in Virginia Theater production. "He thus returns to the New York stage something of an established heartthrob, and audiences may be surprised to discover (again) what a beautiful voice he has, what a natural, un-Hollywood presence," wrote Jesse Green in the *New York Times Magazine.* Diggs's girlfriend, Idina Menzel, also appeared in the musical. The two met as cast members of *Rent*—at one point, Menzel's spirited character, a performance artist, moons the hated landlord Benjamin.

Diggs is scheduled to appear in several other films during the first year of the new century, including *Mary Jane's Last Dance* and *The Way of the Gun.* He rejects any form of typecasting. "They all say I'm a sex symbol. Just what the world needs, another sex symbol," the *Ebony* article quoted him as saying. "In the larger scheme of things, sex symbols come and go . . . .. I don't want to get the big head. I'd be more honored if someone said I was very intelligent or very deep, very thoughtful."

Sources

Ebony, December 1998, pp. 108-114; January 2000, p. 100.
Entertainment Weekly, April 16, 1999, p. 36.
Essence, October 1999, p. 70.
New York Times, February 14, 1996; August 14, 1998, p. B9; April 9, 1999; July 16, 1999; October 22, 1999, p. B26; March 19, 2000, p. AR13.
New York Times Magazine, February 13, 2000.
Newsweek, August 24, 1998, pp. 58-59.
People, September 7, 1998, p. 40; May 10, 1999, p. 125.

—Carol Brennan

Larry Elder

1952—

Radio talk show host

Presiding over the KABC drive time slot from three to seven p.m. in Los Angeles, the country's second-largest market, Larry Elder has made an indelible mark on the landscape of talk radio. Every weekday for four hours, Elder dispenses his own brand of radical opinion, opinion that is almost guaranteed to be at odds with wider African American views. For example, he favors school vouchers, limiting the power of the federal government, and decriminalization of both drugs and prostitution. He is a staunch opponent of affirmative action, race-based commerce, and the welfare system. He believes that racism is not nearly as prevalent as most African Americans believe. Elder routinely blasts African American leaders such as Rep. Maxine Waters (D-Los Angeles) for promoting racial victimization.

As a result of these often inflammatory views, Elder has been vilified as a traitor to his race. He has been called a bootlicking Uncle Tom, an Oreo (black on the outside, white on the inside), a White Man's Poster Boy, the Anti-Christ, and much worse. He has been stalked and has received death threats. Despite these attacks, Elder doggedly continues to challenge conventional African American viewpoints. He loves a good argument, and his positions are always backed up with

facts culled from extensive research: studies, solid statistics, logic, and common sense. Elder asks hard questions, tells the truth as he sees it, and is never afraid to defend his positions.

Parents Were Role Models

Laurence A. Elder was born in 1952, the second of Randolph and Viola Elder's three sons. At the time, the family lived in the largely Latino Pico-Union district of Los Angeles. Elder's father, Randolph, was on his own from the age of 13, and worked a variety of jobs. He enlisted in the military and served as a cook in the Philippines during World War II. Following the end of the war, he was refused employment as a short-order cook many times because he had no references. Elder's father moved to California, and worked several jobs at once to support his family. He also attended night school to earn his GED. By his early forties he had saved enough to open his own café, which he successfully owned and operated near downtown Los Angeles for 30 years. In his book *Tribute to My Father*, Elder wrote, "A tougher life I have rarely come across. Yet he never hated, he was never bitter, he never condemned his circumstances, and he always said there are very few problems that cannot be solved

At a Glance . . .

Born Laurence A. Elder in 1952 in Los Angeles, CA; son of Viola and Randolph Elder (a cafe owner); married and divorced. *Education:* Brown University, B.S., 1974; University of Michigan, J.D.,1977. *Politics:* Libertarian.

Career: Attorney, Squire, Sanders and Dempsey, Cleveland, Ohio, 1977-80; owner andoperator, Laurence A. Elder and Associates (a legal placement service), Cleveland, 1980-95; TVtalk show host, PBS, later Fox, Cleveland, 1988-94; radio talk show host, KABC, Los Angeles,1994-.

Addresses: *Businesses—* KABC, 3321 S. La Cienega Blvd., Los Angeles,CA 90016; Laurence A. Elder & Associates, Suite 803, 10061 Riverside Drive, TolucaLake, CA 91602.

through hard work." Elder told a *Reason* interviewer in 1996 that his father was his role model, "He was the hardest working man I've ever known . . . .. He had a work ethic that was beyond belief."

Elder's mother, Viola, was also a strong role model. Elder told *Reason,* "My mother had one year of college, which for a black woman of her age. . .is like having a Ph.D. from Harvard. She was an avid reader and she always worked with me. My mother told me that I was going to go to Stanford when I was in third or fourth grade." When Larry was seven, the family moved to the South-Central neighborhood where they still reside.

Elder was a studious child who was often picked on by bullies until a friend encouraged him to stand his ground. He graduated with honors from Crenshaw High School in 1970, having taken additional advanced courses at Fairfax High. He entered Brown University in the fall of 1970. While Elder readily admits that affirmative action gave him a boost to Ivy League status, he also points out that he did very well on his SATs. "I graduated number seven in a high school class of 250. . . .I certainly would've gotten into a competitive school regardless of my race. . . .What it [affirmative action] did for me was to kick me from one level into another level," he told *Reason.* "I am prepared to admit that I benefited from affirmative action. I am not prepared to admit that I would have been jobless, homeless, and illiterate had affirmative action not been in effect." Elder earned a bachelor's degree in political science from Brown University in 1974, and then obtain a Juris Doctor degree from the University

of Michigan Law School in 1977.

Following his graduation from law school, Elder took a position with the Cleveland law firm of Squire, Sanders and Dempsey, which was the ninth-largest law firm in the country at the time. He excelled there as a corporate trial lawyer, but soon tired of the regimented promotional system. "I wanted to make more money and I wanted to make it faster," he explained to *Reason.* "I thought I was more talented and should be accelerated much faster." Accepting that swift advancement was not a reality for anyone in the legal field, Elder decided to switch gears. Three years after joining Squire, Sanders and Dempsey, he left the firm and established Laurence A. Elder and Associates, an executive headhunting firm specializing in attorney placement. He would own this firm for the next 15 years. Turning day-to-day operations over to his second in command after six or seven years, Elder switched gears yet again. He began to devote his time to reading and writing, pursuits he had had little time for in the past. He read many of the literary classics, such as Ayn Rand's *The Fountainhead* and Aldous Huxley's *Brave New World.* Elder wrote op-ed pieces for local newspapers, pieces which were eventually published. He auditioned for the co-host slot of a local television show on PBS, and was hired. Elder hosted his own television talk show for the next six years.

Radio Opportunity Changed Life

The opinion pieces Elder wrote became lightning rods for outraged discussion. He was soon sought as a guest on local talk radio shows, and asked to defend his views. Eventually, Elder was asked to fill in for a vacationing talk show host for one week. His then-wife encouraged him to pursue the opportunity. The experience was liberating. "I had been reborn," Elder remarked to *Reason.* He explained to Paul Ciotti of the *Los Angeles Times Magazine* in 1995, "It was as if I had found the Holy Grail. I had never had so much fun in my life. I railed against liberals, I railed against black leadership, I railed against Democrats. . . .against. . .all the things that have hurt people in general and blacks in particular." Elder had found the perfect medium in which to express his views: talk radio.

In 1992, Elder met the man who would help him secure his broadcasting future. Dennis Prager, a liberal TV-radio talk show host in Los Angeles, was a fellow guest with Elder on a Cleveland show called *Morning Exchange.* Learning that Prager was based in Los Angeles, Elder followed up on this hometown connection. As a result, Prager invited him as a guest on his KABC radio show. During Christmas of 1992, the two men got together. Elder's promised 15 minutes of airtime stretched into two hours. The same thing happened again in December of 1993. This time, however, someone in a position to hire Elder was listening. Elder recounted the phone call from KABC station manager George Green to *Reason,* "He [Green] said, 'You have the three things we look for in a talk show host: you take a position, you can defend that position intelligently, and [you] have a sense of humor. The combination is awesome.'" Elder immediately returned to Los Angeles and was hired by KABC. Green told the *Los Angeles Times Magazine* that his primary motivation for hiring Elder was not his politics, but rather his intelligence and the strong response he always generated among listeners.

The Sage Goes to Work

Elder settled in at KABC in early 1994. His fans, many of whom are African American, are known as "Elderados." Elder refers to himself as "the Sage from South-Central," and ends his occasional monologues with "and you have just heard The Word." He is something of an anomaly in the African American community–a conservative libertarian whose views can be combustible, to say the least. Elder described himself to Ciotti as "a fiscal conservative." "I think taxes are too high," he told Ciotti, "and government is spending way. . .too much on things beyond its scope and expertise. But socially I also am extremely liberal." For example, Elder advocates same-sex marriage and permitting gays to serve openly in the U.S. military. He is pro-choice and believes drugs, gambling, and prostitution should be legalized. Elder is against farm subsidies and milk price supports, gun control, prayer in schools, and patronizing African American-owned businesses simply because they are African American. He is also against affirmative action and the tendency of many African Americans to see themselves as permanent victims of racism.

It is primarily Elder's positions on racial preferences, the welfare state, and racism and victimization that have drawn the ire of the African American community. Elder believes that the United States should have compensated the freed slaves but did not, and has tried to pay its debt with affirmative action. "And frankly," he stated in *Reason,* "that's 30 years of failing to hold blacks to the same standards of behavior as they would expect their own sons and daughters to adhere to. What America owes black people is a statement that we are going to evaluate you based on your talents. America owes the commitment not to discriminate." Elder believes that anti-discrimination legislation already in place, along with watchdog organizations such as the NAACP, the ACLU, and the Urban League, are enough to combat discrimination. He explained his optimism in a speech at the Libertarian Party's 1998 convention. "When you look at the progress of blacks following Emancipation, they went from 0% literacy to nearly 70% within decades," he said. "When you look at the data on job creation and income growth, blacks have come further ahead from further behind than any group in human history. This is well documented in an extraordinary book, *America in Black and White,*

which shows that blacks made more economic and social progress before affirmative action than after." Elder does not believe that rampant racism exists in American society, nor does he believe that the system is rigged against African Americans. He also believes that African American leaders do a disservice to their communities by blaming racism for existing problems. Elder promotes these views four hours a day, five days a week in his top-rated afternoon drive-time show. The show's controversial content has guaranteed it a prominent place in the ratings.

In 1997, the liberal Talking Drum Community Forum organized a boycott of Elder's show. The group picketed, passed out leaflets, and convinced advertisers to pull between 2 and 4 million in sponsorship. Although it is now speculated that the group consisted of no more than 30 members, advertisers were apparently persuaded that it was a much larger organization. Although the management of KABC would not admit to caving in to the boycott, it nonetheless cut Elder's airtime in half, ostensibly to make time for a new host. A 300,000 media campaign was mounted in Elder's defense. Supporters included the Center for the Study of Popular Culture, the ACLU, and Joe Hicks of Los Angeles's Multicultural Collaborative.

By February of 1998, Elder's show had been restored to its original four-hour time slot and advertisers were coming back. *Mediaweek* suggested that new station management was responsible for the restoration, and also noted that Elder had branched out into television with a five-minute segment on the daily afternoon newscast on KCAL Channel 9. There is also talk of syndication for Elder's radio show. Elder continues to publish a printed monthly newsletter called *The Elder Statement* and has his own website, larryelder.com. The archives of Elder's show can be accessed at many sites online.

Radley Balko noted in *SpinTech* in 1999 that "deviants from the black monolith are almost always excommunicated," citing Clarence Thomas and Ward Connerly in addition to Elder. However, many believe that what Elder has to say is far too critical to dismiss as the ravings of a wannabe white trying to get high ratings. He wants his race to succeed, but on its own merits. He wants the African American community to raise itself to the levels it certainly can achieve, without racial preferences or feelings of victimization.

Sources

Books

Who's Who Among African Americans, 12th Edition. Edited by Ashyia N. Henderson and Shirelle Phelps. Detroit: Gale, 1999.

Periodicals

Broadcasting & Cable, November 10, 1997, p.57.
Forbes, August 24, 1998, p.54.
Los Angeles Times, May 8, 1997, p.6, Calendar.
Los Angeles Times Magazine, March, 1995; May 31, 1998; July 12, 1998.
LPC Monthly, April 1998.
Mediaweek, November 17, 1997, p.37; March 2, 1998, p.33.
National Review, September 29, 1997, pp.29-30.
Publisher's Weekly, August 9, 1999, p.201.

Reason, April 1996, pp.44-50.
Wall Street Journal, October 20, 1997, p.A20.

Other

Additional information for this profile was obtained from http:\\www.cspc.org\elder\tribute.htm; and http:\\www.larryelder.com, October 10, 1999.

—Ellen Dennis French

Harry Evans

1956(?)—

Television show host

When Harry Evans III goes dumpster diving for thrown-away video tapes, he has only the success of his cable-access television show on his mind. Evans is the creator and host of *That Show With Those Black Guys,* a one half-hour talk show that features only successful, educated African American men. *That Show* is the only national talk show created, produced, hosted, and syndicated by an African American man. Seen by an estimated one million viewers across the country, Evans has committed himself and his show to overturning the media's negative stereotypes of African American men. "Though part of our community is made up of rappers and so-called gangsters, basketball players and such," he told the *Washington Afro-American,* "White media has no stake in portraying us as the hard-working and committed race of people that we are."

From "Dating Game" to "That Show"

Raised in Compton, California, near Los Angeles, Evans moved to Baltimore in 1978. In addition to hosting his television show, he works as a patient advocate for the Maryland Department of Mental Hygiene. Evans was deeply disappointed with the negative stereotypes of African American men that he saw on television. After winning a 200 grant from Howard County, Maryland, Evans launched *That Show.* Prior to launching his television show, his only other television experience was as a losing contestant on the 1970s game show, *The Dating Game.*

On each show, Evans, dressed in a suit and tie, interviews guests that have included congressmen Jesse Jackson Jr. and J.C. Watts, NAACP President Kweisi Mfume, musicians Stanley Turrentine and Antonio Hart, and Everett Hall, the fashion designer who dresses NBA stars such as Charles Barkley and Grant Hill. He doesn't interview troubled athletes or "gangsta rappas," only aspiring, achieving men whose stories aren't told enough. Evans started the show, he told the *Washington Post,* "because of my total disdain for the image of African-American men in the media. The brothers get a bad knock."

Dumpster Diving for Tapes

Evans runs a low-budget operation. He shoots the show on his own patio, with a skeleton crew. He uses the cable company's camera, and records the shows on donated video tapes. Evans used to get his video tapes from the Discovery Channel dumpster in nearby Bethesda, Maryland. Many television stations throw away a huge quantity of used video tapes, but the quality of the tapes was good enough for Evans. Late one night, an employee at a television station saw him hunting in the dumpster for tapes. After learning about the show, she became one of his main sources of used tapes. Evans estimates that he spends about 100 on each show. Most of that money is spent on postage, telephone bills, and tapes. "My show proves that the consuming public could care less whether we shoot]the show] at a 10 million studio in Hollywood or on my patio," he told *Emerge.*

At a Glance . . .

Born c. 1956. Raised in Compton, California; divorced.

Career: Patient advocate, Maryland Department of Mental Hygiene; host, *That Show With Those Black Guys,* 1994-.

Awards: Nominated for the George Foster Peabody Award, 1997. Cameo Award for Outstanding Cable Programming Excellence, 1998, 1999.

Member: Alpha Phi Alpha.

Addresses: *Office*—Harry Evans III, P.O. Box 52, Simpsonville, MD21150.

Evans's fraternity brothers in the Alpha Phi Alpha fraternity—whose national headquarters are in Baltimore—have supported him since the first show. Reginald Hart Jr. is the show's director, and Eric Canaday serves as production supervisor. Neither of these men receive a salary. Alpha Phi Alpha members across the United States have helped Evans secure syndication in many cities. "My brothers work the cameras, the sound, do the directing, and help with the editing," Evans told the *Washington Afro-American.* "There would be no show without them." Canaday is happy to donate his time and effort. "I do it because I believe in what Harry's doing," he told the *Washington Post.*

That Show With Those Black Guys first aired in October of 1994. After only three years, the show was seen in nearly 90 markets, including Los Angeles, Philadelphia, Washington D.C., and Atlanta. There is a lot of competition among cable-access television shows. Shows like *Hello Austria, Gay USA, Islamic Perspectives,* and *Eagerness of God* are the kinds of shows that Evans competes against. Also, most public cable-access shows are not syndicated, but stay within their home markets. Evans personally mails out almost 90 tapes every week to the stations that air his show.

Evans is not the first person to find success on public access television. For instance, former Speaker of the House Newt Gingrich was once a cable-access political show host. Talk-show host, model, and recording artist RuPaul also started out on public access television in Atlanta. "There's no reason for him not to have hope," Nantz Rickard, executive director of Public Access Corp. told the *Washington Post.* "Everything starts

somewhere, and people respond from their hearts. It's not always the media who are guessing from the top."

No Girls Allowed

Evans does not feature women as guests on his show. He believes that women receive enough attention from female African American talk show hosts like Oprah and Rolanda, and that men don't have an equal voice in television talk-show media. "Every time you turn on the television you see positive, strong black women," Evans told *UMOJA News.* "But we men are taking a strong hit."

"His show works," said David Felty, projects coordinator and program director for the New Orleans Educational Telecommunications Consortium. "We immediately started getting feedback . . . about the show and the format. People want it." Evans was nominated for a George Foster Peabody Award in 1997. He also won Cameo Awards for Outstanding Cable Programming Excellence, which are awarded by the cable television industry, in 1998 and 1999.

Although Curtis Symonds, the president of Black Entertainment Television, has been a guest on *That Show,* BET hasn't shown interest in featuring the show in its lineup. Evans would like to be a positive influence on the African American cable network, and criticized some of BET's programming. "BET is so far off from the mark," he told the *Washington Post,* "Some of the images they put on are awful. Look at the images we present to our kids." When people ask Evans why he is not on Black Entertainment Television, his standard response is "Ask BET." When Evans met Symonds at an industry convention, Symonds told him that the show would be a hard sell to the network's advertising clients. BET's lack of interest has not diminished Evans's hopes for *That Show With Those Black Guys.* His dream scenario, he told the *Washington Post,* is that, "The phone shall ring. It'll be King World. United Paramount, Oprah . . . saying, 'Come dance with us.'"

Sources

Periodicals

BET Weekend, July\August 1998, p.29.
Chicago Tribune, January 14, 1997.
City Paper (Baltimore), September 17, 1997.
Louisiana Weekly, April 11, 1999, p. 13.
UMOJA News (Bridgeport, Maryland), November 1998.
Washington Afro-American, May 27, 1995.
Washington Post, December 2, 1997, p. B1.

Other

Additional information was provided by Harry Evans III, 2000; and *That Black Guy Show, MSBET: Emerge Magazine online,* http:\\www.msbet.com (January 4, 2000).

—Brenna Sanchez

Roger W. Ferguson

1951—

Economist, attorney, federal administrator

In October of 1999, Roger W. Ferguson, Jr. assumed the vice-chairmanship of the Board of Governors of the Federal Reserve System. Established in 1913 during the administration of President Woodrow Wilson, the Federal Reserve System supervises the nation's banks and regulates the money supply and interest rates. Ferguson, who had been a member of the Board of Governors since 1997, was nominated for the vice chairman post by President Bill Clinton. "He is superbly qualified. . .I am very excited about the prospect of his service. I'm glad he's willing to do it," Clinton said of Ferguson to Richard A. Oppel, Jr. of the *New York Times*. Federal Reserve Board chairman Alan Greenspan told Oppel that Ferguson is "a person highly respected by his colleagues. . .an outstanding public servant, with broad experience and sound judgement."

Roger W. Ferguson, Jr. was born in Washington, D.C., in 1951. His father was a middle level government worker at the U.S. Army's mapmaking office. His mother taught at a District of Columbia public elementary school. Growing up in Washington's Northeast section, Ferguson attended a public elementary school. He eventually transferred to Sidwell Friends School, a private institution catering to Washington's power elite.

"I spent most of my time studying," Ferguson said of his childhood to Mark Leibovich of the *Washington Post*. Ferguson became interested in economics and finance at an early age. His father, despite a modest income, was an avid investor and would travel to the Federal Reserve Bank in Richmond to buy Treasury securities. "He didn't do it all the time, but he did it enough that it didn't seem odd to me that an individual would interact with the Federal Reserve," Ferguson told Jodie T. Allen of *U.S. News and World Report*.

Attended Harvard University

As an undergraduate at Harvard University, Ferguson studied economics and helped support himself by cleaning dormitory bathrooms. After graduating magna cum laude, Ferguson spent a year in England at Cambridge University's Pembroke College. Returning to Harvard, Ferguson earned a law degree in 1979 and a doctorate in economics in 1981. He has a strong allegiance to his alma mater and has served on the board of directors of the Harvard Alumni Association.

With his formal education completed, Ferguson began

his career by joining the prestigious New York law firm of Davis, Polk, and Wardell in 1981 as an attorney specializing in banking matters. He worked with commercial and investment banks and corporations on loans, mergers and acquisitions, and new product development. In 1984, he left Davis, Polk, and Wardell to accept a job at McKinsey and Company, an international business consulting firm. Based in New York, Ferguson managed a variety of McKinsey's management studies for financial institutions. According to David Wessel of the *Wall Street Journal*, Ferguson's clients at McKinsey included a large American bank seeking to increase revenues and cut costs and a Japanese bank interested in United States commercial banking. He also dealt with property-casualty insurers and brokerage houses. Ferguson eventually became a partner at McKinsey and director of research and information systems, a position which called for overseeing a staff of four-hundred research professionals and managing McKinsey's investments in information management technology. Ferguson's job was especially challenging since the Internet was radically changing the way information was collected, stored, and retrieved.

In order to consolidate McKinsey's research operations, Ferguson was required to travel to the firm's offices around the world. "Roger had to convince people in various offices to give up control over research and information. . . My instinct would be to go back and issue an edict but Roger would provide good counsel. He would suggest we give them a little time, and that they would come around. And they usually did," said Rajat Gupta, a McKinsey colleague of Ferguson's, to Leibovich. Although Ferguson is well versed in up to date technology, he is only partially convinced that the world economy has permanently shifted to an information and technological base. "I think we have to be open minded because we are experiencing relationships between growth, unemployment, and inflation that are probably outside of historical experience. I don't think we should be the first to assume the most radical change, because I think you risk a mistake. . .we may not know for quite a while what has changed and the degree to which that change is permanent or transitory," Ferguson explained to Allen.

Joined the Federal Reserve

Ferguson's first hand experience with banking and the private sector, as opposed to being an academic economist, was a significant factor in why he was nominated to the Federal Reserve Board of Governors in 1997. "Roger's work as a consultant will enable him to bring a solid problem-solver's perspective to the Fed," Lowell Bryan, a senior McKinsey partner and head of its financial institutions practice, told Wessel at the time of Ferguson's nomination to the Board. It was Secretary of the Treasury Lawrence Summers, then Deputy Treasury Secretary, who brought the relatively obscure Ferguson to the attention of the Clinton administration. Ferguson and Summers had been graduate students together at Harvard in the 1970s. "Roger is a thoughtful, capable, straightforward, analytical, wise person," Summers told Allen. Ferguson was one of several potential nominees interviewed by a selection committee to a fill a vacated seat on the Federal Reserve Board. The committee chose Ferguson by unanimous decision. Gene Sperling, director of the National Economic Council and member of the selection committee, told John M. Berry of the *Washington Post* that Ferguson was "very impressive on paper and very impressive in person."

Ferguson's nomination was confirmed by the Senate in October of 1997 and he took office the following month, becoming only the third African American in history to serve on the Federal Reserve Board. His predecessors were Andrew Brimmer, nominated by President Lyndon B. Johnson in 1966, and Emmett Rice, nominated by President Jimmy Carter in 1979. Ferguson grew up in comfortable middle class circumstances, and shuns any rags to riches characterization of his background. As he told Leibovich that "I don't carry a heavy mantle of representation for a group of people. . .My goal is just to be successful in any position I hold."

Members of the Federal Reserve Board of Governors are appointed to 14-year terms. Ferguson took over the unexpired term of Lawrence B. Lindsey, who resigned to join a private investment firm. As a member of the Board of Governors, Ferguson focused much of his attention on technology issues. He chaired the Joint Year 2000 Council, an organization set up by the international banking community to deal with Y2K issues (the inability of some computer systems to recognize dates beyond the 20th century). While many people feared that the start of the year 2000 would result in an information management disaster, Ferguson was not greatly worried. "Thanks to the good work of a large number of people, I think Y2K, when all is said and done, will pass relatively unnoticed," Ferguson told Allen.

Became Federal Reserve Vice Chairman

Only a few months remained in Ferguson's term on the Board of Governors when he was tapped to be the Board's new vice-chairman, replacing Alice M. Rivlin, who resigned in July of 1999. Nominated in August of 1999, Ferguson took office on October 5, 1999, beginning a four-year term that will run to October 5, 2003. Ferguson is generally seen as a moderate whose views are in accordance with those of long-time Federal Reserve Board chairman, Alan Greenspan. "I would call [Ferguson] a sensible centrist, non-ideological," said Janet Yellen, a former Federal Reserve governor, to Leibovich. Ferguson's predecessor Rivlin told Leibovich that Ferguson is "strong but not pushy."

One of Ferguson's duties as vice-chairman is heading a committee that studies ways to soften the reaction of financial markets to Federal Reserve decisions to raise or lower interest rates. A strategy Ferguson has utilized in regard to this problem is to make clearer and more informative public statements than the Federal Reserve has typically made in the past. "You know, we are in a bit of a dialogue with the market," Ferguson told Allen, adding that the Federal Reserve's aim is to "become

clearer speakers. . .and help the markets become better interpreters of what we're saying." Another of Ferguson's tasks is keeping close watch over the effects of deregulation on the banking industry. Ferguson believes that deregulation will make banks more secure by allowing them to diversify their investments but government oversight is still necessary to prevent overinvestment of the type that led to widespread savings and loan failures in the 1980s.

Ferguson's busy work schedule leaves him little time for outside interests. "I don't have any deep hobbies," he told Leibovich. A modest man who is uncomfortable talking about himself, Ferguson makes his home in the District of Columbia and spends what little free time he has with his wife, Annette, and their son and daughter. He has frequently been mentioned as a possible successor to Alan Greenspan as Federal Reserve chairman. Ferguson himself has made no predictions. As he told Allen, "The way I generally run my life is take whatever comes my way. . .and try to do the best I can."

Sources

American Banker, November 3, 1997, p. 2; August 9, 1999, p. 2.
Black Enterprise, September 1997, p. 24.
Fortune, October 25, 1999, p. 38.
Jet, July 28, 1997, p. 5; August 23, 1999, p. 4; October 18, 1999, p. 6.
New York Times, August 7, 1999, p. C2
U.S. News and World Report, December 6, 1999, p. 60.
Wall Street Journal, April 21, 1997, p. A3.
Washington Post, April 22, 1997, p. C3; August 14, 1999, p. E1

Other

Additional information for this profile was obtained from Federal Reserve Board, Office of the Chairman, and Federal Reserve website (www.federalreserve.gov).

—Mary Kalfatovic

C. Virginia Fields

1946—

Manhattan borough president

In 1997, C. Virginia Fields became the highest-ranking African American elected official in New York City when Manhattan voters chose her as their new borough president. A two-term veteran of the New York City Council, Fields was only the second African American woman in city history to win a council seat representing the city's most affluent, and most segregated borough. Since her election as Manhattan borough president, the name of this longtime Harlem community activist has been touted as a possible mayoral candidate for the 21st century.

Born in 1946 in Birmingham, Alabama, Fields is a social worker by training. She was the youngest of five children, and her seamstress mother strained to support the family after Fields's father, a steelworker, died when she was twelve. Her mother was also active in the local Baptist church pastored by the Rev. Fred L. Shuttlesworth, an associate of Rev. Martin Luther King Jr. during the civil rights struggles of the 1950s and early 1960s. Birmingham was also the site where four young African American girls died in a 1963 church bombing that was orchestrated by the Ku Klux Klan. Fields's childhood home was also near Bethel Baptist Church, which was the site of several bombings during the civil rights era.

Jailed for a Week

The city of Birmingham reacted strongly to these terrorist acts, and federal troops were brought in to keep the peace. Fields was active in Birmingham's civil-rights marches as a teenager, and even spent a week in jail in the aftermath of one march through the city that was led by Martin Luther King, Jr. After graduating from Tennessee's Knoxville College in 1967, Fields earned a social work degree from Indiana University. In 1970, she moved to New York City. During the subsequent decade, she worked for a number of social-service agencies as a social worker, administrator, and supervisor.

Fields also became increasingly active in local community groups in Harlem, where she owned a home. She eventually developed an interest in citywide politics. Partly as a result of her chairing of Harlem's Community Board 10 in the early 1980s, Fields became acquainted with some of the city's most influential African American political figures. David Dinkins, who served as president of Manhattan before becoming the city's first African American mayor, was a friend of Fields. She was also befriended by Percy Sutton, owner of the Apollo Theater and Manhattan's first cable

At a Glance . . .

Born Clara Virginia Clark, August 4, 1946, in Birmingham, AL; daughter of Peter (a steel-worker) and Lucille (a seamstress; maiden name, Chappell) Clark; married Henry Fields (a financial analyst), 1979 (divorced). *Education:* Knoxville College, B.A., 1967; Indiana University, M.S.W., 1969; graduate courses at New York University. *Politics:* Democrat.

Career: New York City-area career posts outside of politics include administrator with Children's Aid Society, and supervisor of social services for the New York City Work Release Program; National Board of the YWCA, consultant; Political career began with electionto chair of Community Board 10, New York City, 1981-83; elected New York City councilmember representing District 9, Manhattan, 1989, re-elected, 1993; elected Manhattan borough president, 1997-. Also active in the Harlem Urban Development Corporation.

Member: New York Urban League, New York State Council of Black Elected Democrats, Black and Hispanic Caucus, Alpha Kappa Alpha.

Addresses: *Office*—Municipal Building, 1 Centre St., Floor 19, NewYork, NY 10007-1602.

television system. Congressman Charles Rangel has also been cited as one of her mentors.

Elected to City Council

The Harlem Democratic Club championed Fields in her bid for a seat on the New York City Council in 1989. She won the election, and represented the district that comprised Harlem and part of the Upper West Side. Fields's victory made her the first female African American to be elected as a council representative for Manhattan, the wealthiest and least integrated of New York's boroughs. Her election also coincided with the historic election of David Dinkins as mayor. She served on the land use and budget committees within the Council, and secured funds for housing restoration in Harlem.

During her second term on the council, Fields continued to work to improve public and social services for

her Harlem constituency. Her positive reputation also helped to increase her base of support in the complicated network of New York City political alliances. As *New York Times* writer Jonathan P. Hicks noted, Fields "honed an image of herself as a conciliator who works easily with just about any group of New Yorkers—business and labor, the poor and the middle class and all of the city's racial and ethnic groups."

A Crowded Democratic Primary

Fields's fine political standing helped her to win crucial endorsements when she decided to run for Manhattan borough president in 1997, even though the preliminary race was congested with impressive contenders. "What happens during a race for an office with little power but a lot of symbolism?" inquired *Village Voice* writer James Bradley. "You get a campaign shaped by longtime neighborhood and political rivalries." Other Democrats running for a spot on the 1997 ticket were fellow council members Adam Clayton Powell IV and Antonio Pagan. However, Fields's main rival was state assemblywoman Deborah Glick.

Fields's race against Glick, an openly gay former tenant activist and longtime Greenwich Village resident, was inadvertently assisted by some old political tensions dating back to the 1960s. One prominent Democratic Club split into two competing groups; one group supported Glick's candidacy, while the other gave its endorsement to Fields. Like Glick, Fields was able to raise a substantial sum of money for her candidacy, nearly $200,000. However, Glick was criticized for not campaigning in Harlem and for not including enough minorities on her campaign staff.

Fields also won support from outside her relatively strong political base in Harlem, no easy feat in the sometimes racially divided arena of New York City politics. Two former mayors, outgoing borough president Ruth Messinger, as well as notable Manhattan residents such as Gloria Steinem and Bella Abzug, endorsed Fields in her bid for the Manhattan borough presidency. She defeated Glick and other candidates in the September primary race by winning 42 percent of vote. At her victory celebration, Fields told her supporters that she had run a campaign dedicated to "bringing people together across racial, religious, sexual-orientation lines, all of those things that tend to divide us unnecessarily," according to the *New York Times*.

A New Era for Harlem

When Fields won the November 1997 election, she became the first African American borough president in New York City since Dinkins's tenure as mayor. As the representative of a large constituency, Fields focused on school issues and housing. She created the Borough of Manhattan Parents Convention, and spoke out often on the need to improve hospital care for Manhattan residents, as well as creating a favorable climate for small businesses. Her name also became indelibly associated with a predicted turnaround for Harlem itself, a place whose former glory had faded greatly. As borough president, Fields was able to commission a study from the Columbia University Graduate School of Architecture, Planning and Preservation that investigated the possibilities for restoring Harlem's famous Frederick Douglass Boulevard.

The Columbia study, which was soon tagged the "Fields Plan," was announced in late 1999, and involved a grant of 2.5 million in city funds to redevelop this once-grand boulevard. Fields called the boulevard "the backbone of Harlem," according to the *New York Times*'s Nina Siegal, and spoke of the rehabilitation of Frederick Douglass Boulevard as a crucial step in the city's next historic shift in gentrification. "Its [Frederick Douglass Boulevard's] redevelopment will send a powerful message that the second Harlem Renaissance has deep and permanent roots in the community," Fields said at the same press conference.

Sources

New York Times, September 10, 1997, p. A1; September 13, 1997, p. 27; August 14, 1999, p. B3; December 15, 1999, p. B22.
Village Voice, April 1, 1997, p. 27; September 9, 1997, p. 30; September 30, 1997, p. 35; December 28, 1999, p. 27.

Other

Additional information for this profile was provided by http:\\www.ci.nyc.ny.us

—Carol Brennan

Robin Givens

1964—

Actress

Actress Robin Givens has played a wide range of characters throughout her career. A similar diversity marked the roles she played during the months of intense publicity surrounding her marriage to heavyweight boxing champion Mike Tyson. When their relationship began, Givens was frequently portrayed either as the cultured beauty in love with the street-hardened beast, or the ambitious starlet eager to ride his coattails to fame. When Givens sought divorce, alleging that Tyson had physically abused her, she was reviled in many media reports as a liar and a gold digger. In the aftermath of their marriage and Tyson's later conviction for rape, Givens has emerged as a courageous survivor. In her own eyes, the actress told an *Ebony* correspondent, she is simply a hard-working actress, "a good human being and incredibly sensitive and vulnerable."

Prior to her relationship with Tyson, Givens was known primarily for her work on the ABC-TV situation comedy *Head of the Class*. She played the part of Darlene, a student who embodied intelligence, beauty, and a snobby attitude. In some ways, the character's background was similar to that of Givens. Raised by her mother after her parents divorced when she was two years old, Givens attended exclusive private schools in New Rochelle, New York. On weekends, she took lessons in music, dance, and theater arts. This special schooling, along with her natural good looks, helped her to secure modeling jobs and small acting parts while still in her teens. She excelled academically as well, and entered the prestigious Sarah Lawrence College when she was 15.

Givens's years at Sarah Lawrence were marked by personal frictions as well as academic achievement. One of her classmates, Holly Robinson—who went on to star in the television series *21 Jump Street*—once knocked Givens down in retaliation for remarks Givens made about Robinson and her mother. The ensuing fight had to be broken up by a resident assistant at the dormitory. Another classmate, businesswoman Kimberly Alexander, was quoted in *Sports Illustrated* as saying that while she never clashed personally with Givens, "Robin didn't have any friends at Sarah Lawrence. She made her presence known, but she rubbed everybody the wrong way. At our graduation, they called her name and she was booed."

At a Glance . . .

Born in November 27, 1964 in New York, NY; daughter of Reuben Givens (an artist) and Ruth Roper (a business executive); married Michael Tyson (a boxer), February 7, 1988 (divorced, February 14, 1989); married Svetozar Marinkovic (a tennis player), August 22, 1997 (divorced, 1999); children: one. *Religion:* Catholic. *Education:* Sarah Lawrence College, B.A., 1984; postgraduate study at Harvard University.

Career: Actress appearing in television series, including *Head of the Class,*1992; *Angel Street,* 1992; *Courthouse,* 1995; *Sparks,* 1996-99; in television films, including *The Penthouse,* 1989; *The Women of Brewster Place,* 1989; *Dangerous Intentions,* 1995; *A Face to Die For,* 1996;*Michael Jordan: An American Hero,* 1999; and in motion pictures, including *A Rage in Harlem,* 1991, *Boomerang,* 1992; *Blankman,* 1994; *Foreign Student,* 1994; *Everything's Jake,* 2000; host of television show, *Forgiveor Forget,* 2000-. Founder of Never Blue Productions.

Addresses: *Home*—Los Angeles, CA. *Studio*—Twentieth Television, 2121 Avenue of the Stars, 21st Floor, LosAngeles, CA 90067.

Landed a Television Role

Personal difficulties aside, Givens's performance at Sarah Lawrence was good enough to earn her admission at Harvard University's graduate school of medicine. She enrolled in 1984 with the intention of taking premed courses, but dropped out before a year had passed to pursue a full-time acting career. By 1986 Givens was a familiar figure to American television viewers for her featured role in *Head of the Class,* a comedy about gifted high school students. Further attention came her way when she began dating such high-profile celebrities as comedian and actor Eddie Murphy and Chicago Bulls basketball star Michael Jordan. Tyson, the boxing champion who had spent much of his youth in reform school, was smitten with Givens the first time he saw her on television and attempted for the next four months to arrange a date with her.

"I was too scared to meet him," Givens was quoted as saying in *People.* When she finally gave in and met him for dinner in March of 1987, she brought along her mother, her sister, and two publicists. By May of that year she "was very much in love," although in hindsight she confessed, "I should have known about his violent nature the first time he took me to his apartment. . . . He just picked me up and carried me to 41st Street, where he lived. I didn't want to go. . . . When I wanted to leave, Michael hit me in the back of the head. It felt like my head would come off."

Despite such ominous warning signs, Givens continued to date Tyson. In November of 1987 Tyson gave some of his views on their relationship to the London *Sun.* The interview was later quoted by *Sports illustrated:* "She has wanted me to marry her for a long time but I ain't going to do it. . . . We fight all the time. She thinks she is so much better than me, just because she has had an education. . . . It may be true, but I hate the way she goes about telling me. I retaliate by telling her I am the heavyweight champion and she should know her place. Man, she really gets into a temper at that and comes at me. She knows she can't hurt me if she kicks me in the head so she tries to kick me in the groin."

Embroiled in a Rocky Marriage

Tyson and Givens had a spur-of-the-moment wedding on February 7, 1988, repeating their vows two days later after obtaining a marriage license. Cynics immediately pointed out that no prenuptial agreement had been signed, and that Tyson was worth an estimated 50 million. "I feel sorry for Mike Tyson because I hear he's a really nice guy," one of Givens's former classmates was quoted as saying in *People.* Her statement reflected the common perception that Tyson was the victim, and Givens the predator. "Our agreement is never to get divorced," Givens explained in the same magazine. "Michael said if I ever divorced him, he'd kill me." She added: "He's really just a huge teddy bear."

Over the next few months Givens continued to discuss her marriage in glowing terms, even extending that enthusiasm to the relationship between her husband and her mother, Ruth Roper. In May she announced that she was pregnant, but suffered a miscarriage the following month. Strange stories then began to surface: Tyson ran his car into two parked automobiles, reportedly because Givens was hitting him; he ran another car into a tree in an alleged suicide attempt; and he struck both Givens and her friend, pro tennis player Lori McNeil, while vacationing in the Bahamas. Givens's detractors suggested that she and her mother had provoked the incidents in order to set the scene for a favorable divorce settlement, but Givens continued to profess her love for the fighter.

In September of 1988, just seven months after their marriage, the couple appeared on the television program *20\20* in an interview segment with Barbara Walters. By that time, Givens had publicly stated that her husband was manic-depressive and that he had physically abused her. She repeated those allegations on *20\20* and, according to *Newsweek,* described her marriage as "torture, pure hell, worse than anything I could imagine." Meanwhile, Tyson sat passively alongside her, under the influence of the powerful antipsychotic drugs lithium and Thorazine. Two weeks later, Givens claimed she was awakened by Tyson striking her about the head and body. She fled their mansion and filed for divorce soon thereafter.

Tyson unsuccessfully attempted to have the marriage annulled. In his annulment petition, he accused his wife of coercing him into marriage by pretending to be pregnant. In an interview with the *Chicago Sun-Times* that was later quoted in *Ebony,* he stated that Givens and her family "don't like or respect Black people. They want to be White so bad. The way they talk about Black people you'd think you were living with the Ku Klux Klan. . . . Not only did she want to take my money, but she wanted to ruin me, embarrass me, take my manhood and humiliate me on television so that no woman would *ever* want me again, and that was evil." The end result of all the mudslinging, suits, and countersuits was a divorce in February of 1989 and a seven-figure financial settlement for Givens.

For nearly a year after the divorce, Givens kept a low profile. In 1989, she played the role of Kiswana Browne in Oprah Winfrey's critically acclaimed television movie, *Women of Brewster Place.* Givens was included in the general praise for *Brewster Place,* which chronicled the lives of a group of African American women living in an urban housing project and their struggle to maintain personal dignity. That same year, Givens starred in the television movie, *The Penthouse.* Based on a novel by Elleston Trevor, the film centered around Dinah St. Clair (Givens), a beautiful woman who has a chance meeting with her childhood sweetheart. This man is now a homicidal manic who is obsessed with rekindling their relationship. In March of 1990, Givens granted a lengthy interview to *Ebony.* Following the interview, she was portrayed much more sympathetically than she had been in the past. Givens described herself as being more mature and spiritual in the wake of the divorce and professed to be friendly with Tyson again. "If she is acting, she's doing a world-class job," noted writer Lynn Randolph. "There's an emotional depth that rings true and something in her eyes says this is not a performance."

Appeared in Motion Pictures

In 1991 Givens appeared in her first feature film, *A Rage in Harlem.* In this adaptation of a Chester Himes novel, she played Imabelle, a loose woman who falls for a pious young accountant and is forced to choose between a trunk of gold and her penniless new love. Givens more than held her own alongside costars Danny Glover and Gregory Hines, according to many reviewers. *Rolling Stone* critic Peter Travers singled her out as the only player to capture the spirit of Himes's novel, and praised her for adding "dimension and true grit to a film all too eager to settle for being a slick Hollywood package."

In 1992, Givens could be seen in the short-lived television series *Angel Street*—which featured two female homicide detectives fighting crime in a deteriorating city—as well as in the film *Boomerang.* She had a supporting role in *Boomerang,* which starred Eddie Murphy as a heartless playboy who more than meets his match in Givens's character, Jacqueline. Reviewers praised Givens for her deft portrayal of a high-powered executive who embodies stereotypically male attitudes toward sex, sports, and business.

In an article she contributed to *Ebony,* Givens commented at length on the paucity of parts available to African American actresses and her determination to expand the number of roles for African American women. To this end, she formed her own production company, Never Blue Productions. "As a young actress in Hollywood," she wrote, "I hope that some little girl looks at me and says: 'She's doing it. I can do it.' Often that possibility is what keeps me going when I'm tired and frustrated, when I feel like the injustices of the world have taken their toll on me. If I don't do my part, then the dream has died."

In 1994, Givens starred opposite comedian Damon Wayans in the film *Blankman.* As television newswoman Kimberly Jonz, she is the first to report on the adventures of a nerdy superhero named Blankman (Wayans). Although *Blankman* received mixed reviews, *Jet* praised Givens's contribution to the film because "it allowed her to reveal that she also has a natural flair for comedy." In a departure from her comedic turn in *Blankman,* Givens starred in the steamy 1994 film *Foreign Student.* In the role of April, a girl who falls in love with a French foreign exchange student in Virginia during the 1950s, Givens displayed "naked, raw sensuality," according to *Jet.*

Givens starred as Kaye Ferrar, an abused wife who summons the courage to leave her husband and start a new life with their young child, in the 1995 television movie *Dangerous Intentions.* That same year, she played the role of Suzanne Graham in the short-lived television series *Courthouse.* Givens also appeared on several episodes of the NBC television series *In the House.*

In 1996, Givens again had the opportunity to showcase her comedic talents in the role of Wilma Cuthbert on the UPN television comedy *Sparks.* She continued in this role until the show was canceled in 1999. In addition to *Sparks,* Givens played the role of Claudia in the 1996 television movie drama *A Face to Die For.* She also appeared in episodes of *Cosby* and *Moesha.* On August 22, 1997, Givens married Yugoslavian tennis instructor Svetozar Marinkovic. However, the couple separated on the same day. They filed for divorce on December 19, 1997, a divorced which was finalized in 1999.

Givens portrayed Juanita Jordan, the wife of basketball legend Michael Jordan, in the 1999 television movie *Michael Jordan: An American Hero*. In October of 1999, Givens and tennis player Murphy Jensen became the parents of a baby boy. After Jo Anne Hart, also known as "Mother Love," was fired as host of the syndicated television show *Forgive or Forget*, Givens debuted as her replacement in January of 2000. In addition to hosting *Forgive or Forget*, she also landed a role in the 2000 film *Everything's Jake*.

Sources

Boston Globe, May 3, 1991.
Detroit Free Press, July 1, 1992.
Ebony, January 1989; March 1990; June 1991; October 1992.
Emerge, September 1992.
Entertainment Weekly, July 10, 1992; September 11, 1992.
Jet, August 15, 1994.
Newsweek, October 17, 1988; May 13, 1991; July 6, 1992.
New York Times, May 3, 1991; May 12, 1991; July 1, 1992.
Oakland Press (Oakland County, MI), September 13, 1992; October 31, 1992.
People, February 22, 1988; June 27, 1988; October 17, 1988; October 24, 1988; March 6, 1989; March 20, 1989.
Rolling Stone, June 13, 1991.
Sports Illustrated, October 24, 1988; December 12, 1988.
Washington Post, May 11, 1991.

—Joan Goldsworthy and David G. Oblender

Dexter Gordon

1923–1990

Jazz saxophonist, actor

During the 1940s, Dexter Gordon emerged as one of the premiere instrumentalists to adapt the tenor saxophone to the bebop jazz idiom. After earning a reputation as a sideman in the bands of Lionel Hampton and Billy Eckstine during the 1940s, Gordon spent the next four decades as a solo artist. He lived in Europe from 1962 until 1976. Upon his return to the United States, he landed a major recording contract and critical acclaim for his recordings and live performances. Early in his career, Gordon absorbed the influence of tenor saxophonists Lester Young and Hershel Evans, and subsequently developed his own sound and approach. Throughout his life, Gordon continued to garner musical ideas from all over the jazz spectrum, including the saxophone style of one of his early followers, John Coltrane. Six and a half feet tall and handsome, Gordon possessed a gift for language - one that benefitted him when he starred in Jules Tavernier's 1986 film *Round Midnight,* a role which won him an Oscar nomination.

Dexter Keith Gordon was born on February 27, 1923, in Los Angeles, California. Gordon's father, who was an amateur clarinetist and the personal physician to Lionel Hampton and Duke Ellington, took his son to hear live jazz shows. Gordon listened to big band radio broadcasts as a child and, during his teenage years, purchased second-hand records from jukebox companies. At the age of 13 he studied clarinet and music theory. Two years later, he switched to alto saxophone. At Jefferson High School, Gordon fell under the musical instruction of Sam Browne. Multi-instrumentalist, Buddy Collette, recalled in the book *Central Avenue Sound* that the youthful Gordon was "a fun guy" who "seemed all tongue and cheek. . . .I heard that Sam Browne. . .used to keep him after school and tried to make him play scales. He was not an easy guy to teach. He was player who knew where he wanted to go, I guess. Later, he finally got to be serious." By the age of 17, Gordon took up the tenor saxophone and began musical instruction with Lloyd Reese, a multi-talented musician and former member of several prominent big bands. As Gordon was quoted in *Mingus: A Critical Biography,* "He taught us like we were going to be professionals, not just some kid just learning how to play an instrument in the school band and marching band. . . .He taught me about Art Tatum, and about listening to film music when you go to the movies." During this same time, Gordon attended school jam sessions and performed in nightclubs.

At a Glance . . .

Born Dexter Keith Gordon, February 27, 1923, in Los Angeles, CA; died of kidney failure on April 25, 1990, in Philadelphia, PA; son of Frank Alexander Gordon (a physician); married Frenja Gordon; children: Benjamin.

Career: Quit high school to perform in a local band and joined Lionel Hampton's band, 1940; left Hampton's band and became member of Lee Young's sextet, 1943;performed with Fletcher Henderson's band, 1944; performed with Louis Armstrong's band and then joined Billy Eckstine's big band, 1944 ; recorded with Dizzy Gillespie, 1945; played clubs along 52nd Street; recorded sides under own name for the Savoy label, 1945-47; recorded for the Dial label in Los Angeles, 1947; performed in Tadd Dameron's band, 1948; performed with Oscar Pettiford, 1949; recorded three albums during the 1950s; appeared in and scored the music for Jack Gelber's play *The Connection,* 1955; recorded seven albums, 1961-65; moved to Copenhagen, Denmark, 1962; returned to the United States, 1977; signed a recording contract with Columbia Records, 1977; starred in film *Round Midnight,* 1986.

Awards: Musician of the Year, *Down Beat* magazine readers poll, 1980; inducted into the Jazz Hall of Fame, 1980.

In 1939, Gordon skipped school to hear the Count Basie Orchestra featuring his saxophone hero, Lester Young. Years later, in the book *West Coast Jazz,* Gordon recalled how the Basie Orchestra, "opened with 'Clap Hands Here Comes Charlie,' and Lester came out soloing—and he was just fantastic. I really loved the man. He was melodic, rhythmic, had that bittersweet approach. . . .It felt so good to hear him play." Gordon's father died of a heart attack in 1940, and Dexter quit school to play in a local band known as the Harlem Collegians. That same year, he joined Lionel Hampton's band which included saxophonists Illinois Jacquet and Marshall Royal, the latter of whom furthered Gordon's musical education. In the liner notes to *Dexter Gordon Settin' the Pace,* Gordon recalled his joining Hampton's band at the age of 17, "We went right on the road without any rehearsal, cold. I was expecting to be sent home every night." Gordon was often late for performances, a habit Hampton often tolerated because the saxophonist's musicianship

and showmanship was a vital asset to his ensemble. As Hampton recalled in his autobiography, *Hamp,* "One time at the Paradise [Theatre] in Detroit, [Gordon] still wasn't there when we started, and were doing a number that he was supposed to solo on. Just as we got to his solo, he walked out of the wings blowing his horn. The crowd went wild. . . .I couldn't even be angry with him, because you couldn't believe the effect he had on that audience."

Immersing himself in swing music, Gordon was soon exposed to modern jazz. While in New York City with Hampton's band in 1941, Gordon heard Charlie Parker at the Savoy and visited Monroe's Uptown House, a Harlem after-hours spot that became one of the primary birthplaces of bebop. When he left Hampton's band Gordon returned to Los Angeles, where he recorded with pianist sideman Nat "King" Cole in 1943, and performed at the Club Alabam, one of Central Avenue's most popular venues. Because the Alabam generally relegated musicians to backing stage acts, Gordon and his bassist friend Charles Mingus attended after-hours jam sessions. In 1943, Gordon joined the Lee Young sextet, which included Mingus. After Gordon worked with Fletcher Henderson's band in April and May of 1944, he was invited to join the band of Louis Armstrong. Although he became friends with Armstrong and retained respect for his musicianship, Gordon found little inspiration in the band's dated material.

Worked In New York and Los Angeles

In late 1944, Gordon left Armstrong's employ for Billy Eckstine's big band, which included Dizzy Gillespie. During his stint with the Eckstine band, Gordon performed in an all-star reed section - dubbed the "Unholy Four" - comprised of the four saxophones of Gordon, Sonny Stitt, John Jackson, and Leo Parker. Along with featured saxophonist Gene Ammons, Gordon took part in legendary performances. Famous for their onstage saxophone battles, Gordon and Ammons can be heard On Eckstine's "Blow My Blues Away," with the bandleader calling out twice in the number, "Blow Mr. Gene, and blow Mr. Dexter too."

In early 1945, Gordon took part in a New York City recording session led by Dizzy Gillespie. This session produced the Guild label recording *Blue n' Boogie,* and an unreleased version of "Groovin' High." Gordon also played 52nd Street with a band consisting of Charlie Parker, Miles Davis, Bud Powell, and Max Roach. At the same time Gordon, caught up in the New York jazz scene, also began using heroin. In Mike Hennessey's book *Klook: The Story of Kenny Clarke,* Gordon recounted, "I started using it [heroin] around 1945 when just about all the big names were. But it was the most terrible mistake I ever made in my life." Along with his drug habit, Gordon also filled the jazz hipster image by dressing in the latest style. As Miles Davis recounted in his memoir *Miles,* "Dexter used to be super hip and dapper, with those big-shoulder suits everybody was wearing in those days. . .I always respected Dexter because I thought he was super hip - one of the hippest and cleanest young cats on the whole music scene back then."

Recorded Under Own Name

Beginning in October of 1945, Gordon recorded several sessions for the Savoy label. As Ted Gioia pointed out in the book *West Coast Jazz,* Gordon's first recordings "are still very much in a Lester Young vein, and his lead sides for Savoy in October 1945, reveal an undeniable streak of modern traditionalism." In January of 1946 Gordon recorded with young bebop innovators, pianist Bud Powell and drummer Max Roach. This Savoy session, asserted Gioia in *West Coast Jazz,* "was a major step forward" in Gordon's stylistic development. On these sides, added Gioia, "all the disparate elements of Gordon's work begin to come together in a distinctive way: the repeated figures reminiscent of Illinois Jacquet; the harmonic darings of the beboppers; the lyricism of Lester Young; the forcefulness gleaned from [Coleman] Hawkins; From now on these separate currents would flow together into a style reflecting the individuality of Dexter Gordon."

Gordon returned to Los Angeles in 1946. With his wide brimmed hat and zoot suits, Gordon became an idol to younger players, including Art Pepper and Stan Getz. Gordon attended jam sessions at venues like Jack's Basket, where he engaged in furious tenor saxophone battles with Wardell Gray and Teddy Edwards. The Basket's crowded saxophone contests usually ended with Gordon and Gray as the victors. In June of 1947 Gordon and Gray recorded a tenor-battle, "The Chase," a commercially successful recording for Ross Russell's newly established Dial label. The success of "The Chase" prompted the recording of another legendary Gordon-Gray saxophone battle, "The Hunt." Vital to the 1940s Los Angeles jazz scene, Gordon, as Gioia stressed in *West Coast Jazz,* "developed one of the first great modern sax styles, and—perhaps even more remarkably—did so by borrowing modestly from Parker and Gillespie. Instead, Dexter created a new approach to the tenor, a persuasive and immediately recognizable sound all his own."

Career Fell Into Periodic Decline

Around 1948, Gordon became a member of pianist Tadd Dameron's band, which played a nine-month engagement at the Royal Roost. In 1949, he joined bassist Oscar Pettiford's band which included Miles Davis, Bud Powell, and drummer Kenny Clarke. Gordon returned to California in 1949 and, during the following year, was reunited with Wardell Gary. The two saxophonists recorded for the Prestige and Decca labels, which released their 1952 concert at the Pasadena Civic Auditorium as the album *The Chase and Steeplechase.* That same year, Gordon's career took a downturn with his arrest for heroin possession. He subsequently spent two years at California's Chino Prison. During the 1950s, Gordon also served time in prisons in Fort Worth, Texas, and Lexington, Kentucky, and finally in Folsom Prison. Although he made only three recordings between 1952 and 1960, Thomas Owens noted in *Bebop: The Music and Its Players,* that Gordon's albums "announced clearly that he severed his ties with the swing era," and marked "the beginning of his mature style."

Following Gordon's release from prison, he recorded the 1960 album, *The Resurgence of Dexter Gordon,* produced by alto saxophonist Cannonball Adderley. Between 1961 and 1965, he recorded seven albums for Blue Note - *Go!, A Swingin' Affair, Doin' Alright, Dexter Calling, Our Man in Paris, One Flight Up,* and *Gettin' Around* -releases that, as Gary Giddins described in the book *Visions of Jazz,* "represented the apogee of his art. . . .Splendidly conceived and recorded, they are insuperable examples of the streamlined elegance of which jazz quartets and quintets are capable." Gordon spent these years experimenting with a hard bop sound and incorporating elements of John Coltrane's saxophone style into his music. "But Gordon never confined his borrowings to any one role model," observed Thomas Owens in *Bebop;* "he took what he liked from various places, adding new elements to whatever was already in place, and ingeniously preserving his musical identity with great clarity."

"Transcontinental Tenorist"

Gordon traveled to London in 1962 and, during that same year, arrived in Copenhagen where he lived until his return to United States in the 1970s. "I didn't intend on staying, it just happened," recounted Gordon in *Riding on a Blue Note.* "I was working and having a ball in this new environment. Before I realized it, a couple of years went by and I was considered an expatriate." Describing Gordon's life abroad, Dan Morganstern wrote in the liner notes to *Dexter Gordon: Settin' the Pace,* "Copenhagen became his home base, and unlike many expatriates he thrived and grew as a player abroad. . . .He became one of Copenhagen's most popular adopted sons, raising a family, learning some Danish (he had a gift for languages), teaching jazz in schools, appearing on TV, picking up flute and also adding soprano saxophone to roster of instruments, and cutting a familiar figure riding a bicycle through the streets of the friendly Danish capital."

While in Paris in May of 1963, Gordon recorded the Blue Note album *Our Man in Paris* with pianist Bud Powell, bassist Pierre Michelot, and drummer Kenny Clarke. In his book *Bebop,* Thomas Owens commented that Gordon's "best solos" on the recording "are in 'Scrapple From the Apple,' 'A Night in Tunisia,' and in the ballads 'Stairway to the Stars' and 'Willow, Weep For Me.' Gordon's rhythmic brinkmanship stands out in the latter piece; how can he lag behind so much and still play with the rhythm section?" In the liner notes to *Our Man in Paris,* Gordon commented on his continuing musical development, "I'm much more lucid and have a stronger sense of equilibrium. My musical conception is surer. I know where I'm going now."

While living in Copenhagen, Gordon often played American concert dates and music festivals. For the most part, however, his musical activities were concentrated in Europe. In an interview in *Down Beat,* Gordon related how life in Copenhagen "has been very good because my whole lifestyle is much calmer, much more relaxed. I can devote more time to music, and I think it is beginning to show. It's not an everyday scuffle, and I'm able to concentrate more on studying." His appearance at Copenhagen's Montmartre Jazzhus was captured on the 1967 Blue Note release, *Sonnymoon for Two.* Gordon earned his first number one ranking on *Down Beat's* Critics Poll in 1971, and began a four-year recording stint with the Prestige label. In 1972, Gordon recorded the Prestige album *Ca'Purange* with brothers Thad and Hank Jones, Stanley Clarke and Louis Hayes.

Triumphant Return To America

Gordon's return to the United States in 1976 began with a well-received performance at New York City's Storeyville Club. Several weeks later, he signed a contract with Columbia Records and was booked to play several weeks at the famous Village Vanguard. After attending one of Gordon's performances at the Vanguard in October of 1976, Whitney Baillett wrote in the book *Night Creature,* "Every handclap was a genuflection. . . .He [Gordon] locks together giant cubes of sound in his solos, piling one on another. . . .He builds these edifices in a determined, almost harsh fashion, rarely missing a note, and finishes each phrase so that it has a clear, sharp edge." Prompted by a major recording contract and critical acclaim for his performances, Gordon remained in America in 1977. That same year his first Columbia recording, the double album *Homecoming,* showcased a masterfully modern sound. Gordon's Columbia producer, Michael Cascuna, asserted in the liner notes to *Homecoming,* "Of all the people of his generation, Dexter has stayed the youngest. He is the most modern player to have come out of that period. . . .He is still learning and still growing."

In 1980, Gordon was named Musician of the Year by *Down Beat* magazine's readers poll, and named to the Jazz Hall of Fame. Despite his declining health, Gordon spent the mid 1980s recording and venturing into film acting. During the 1950s, Gordon appeared in several films and stage productions including the 1955 motion picture *Unchained* and Jack Gelber's successful play, *The Connection.* He appeared in Bernard Tavernier's 1985 film *Round Midnight,* which was released in 1986. Dedicated to Gordon's saxophone hero Lester Young and his friend Bud Powell, the film resulted from discussions between Tavernier and Francis Puadras, a Parisian commercial artist and author of *Dance of the Infidels: A Portrait of Bud Powell.* Largely based upon Powell's expatriate life with Puadras during the 1960s, the film portrays Dale Turner, an ailing saxophonist played by Gordon, who befriends a Parisian jazz aficionado who becomes his honorary guardian. In the scenes shot at the Blue Note club, where Gordon had often played in the 1960s, Gordon is joined by such musicians as Herbie Hancock (who scored the film's music), Wayne Shorter, Ron Carter, Tony Williams, and John McLaughlin. Gordon's moving portrayal of a dying jazzman earned him an Academy Award nomination.

Four years after his performance in *Round Midnight,* Gordon died of kidney failure on April 25, 1990, in Philadelphia, Pennsylvania. Several years before his death, Gordon stated in *Down Beat* that "jazz is such a living thing. It will never die, because it can use things from everywhere, from all kinds of music. . . ." A leading saxophonist during the 1940s and 1950s, Gordon spent the last decades of his life expanding his sound, taking up the soprano saxophone, and adding modern compositions to his repertoire. With the 1999 release of Gordon's early Savoy sides and the 1997 complete Blue Note box set, his music began embracing a new generation of listeners.

Selected Discography

with others

"Blowin' My Blues Away," Billy Eckstine, Deluxe, 1944.
"Blue 'n Boogie," Dizzy Gillespie, Guild, 1945.
The Wardell Gray Memorial Album, Prestige.
Wardell Gray and Dexter Gordon: The Chase and the Steeplechase, MCA Jazz.
Dexter with Wardell Gray, Giants of Jazz, 1999.

Solo albums

Dexter Gordon: Settin' the Pace, Savoy, (reissued material from 1945-1947), 1998.
Dexter Rides Again, Savoy, 1947.
The Resurgence of Dexter Gordon, Jazzland 1960, (reissued) Original Jazz Classics.
Dexter Calling, Blue Note, 1961.
Doin' Alright, Blue Note, 1961.
Go! Blue Note, 1962.
A Swingin' Affair, Blue Note, 1962.
Our Man in Paris, Blue Note, 1963.

One Flight Up, Blue Note, 1964.
Gettin' Around, Blue Note, 1965.
Ca'Purange, Prestige, recorded 1972.
Homecoming, Columbia, 1977.
Sophisticated Giant, Columbia, 1977.
Gotham City, Columbia, 1980.
The Best of Dexter Gordon, Columbia, 1980.
The Other Side of Round Midnight, Blue Note, 1986.
Live at the Monmartre Jazzhus, Black Lion [box set], 1996.
The Complete Blue Note Sixties Sessions, Blue Note [six CD box set], 1997.
Live at Carnegie Hall, Legacy Records, 1998.

Compilations

60 Years 1939-1999, Blue Note [box set], 1998.
Central Avenue Sounds, Jazz in Los Angeles 1927-1956, Rhino, 1999.

Sources

Books

Baillett, Whitney, *Night Creature: A Journal of Jazz, 1975-1980,* Oxford University Press, 1981.
Central Avenue Sound: Jazz in Los Angeles, ed. by Clora Bryant et al., University of California Press, 1998.

Davis, Miles, with Quincy Troupe, *Miles: The Autobiography,* Simon & Schuster, 1990.
Giddins, Gary. *Riding on a Blue Note,* Oxford University Press, 1981.
Giddins, Gary, *Visions of Jazz: The First Century,* Oxford University Press, 1998.
Gioia, Ted, *West Coast Jazz: Modern Jazz In California 1945-1960,* Oxford University Press, 1992.
Hampton, Lionel, with James Haskins, *Hamp: An Autobiography of Lionel Hampton,* Warner Books, 1989.
Hennessey, Mike, *Klook: The Story of Kenny Clarke,* University of Pittsburgh Press, 1990.
Owens, Thomas, *Bebop, The Music and Its Players,* Oxford University Press, 1995.
Priestly, Brian, *Mingus: A Critical Biography,* Da Capo, 1982.

Periodicals

Down Beat, June 22, 1972.

Other

Additional information for this profile was obtained from the liner notes by Dan Morganstern to *Dexter Gordon: Settin' the Pace,* Savoy, 1998; the liner notes by Nat Hentoff to *Our Man in Paris,* Blue Note, 1963; and the liner notes by Robert Palmer to *Homecoming,* Columbia, 1977.

—John Cohassey

Yolanda Griffith

1970—

Professional basketball player

Yolanda Griffith has become one of the WNBA's most talented and recognizable stars. Despite personal tragedy and hardship, she worked hard to achieve her goal of becoming a professional basketball player. Her efforts have led to her selection as the WNBA's Most Valuable Player, and a spot on the women's 2000 Olympic basketball team.

Griffith was born on March 1, 1970 in Chicago, Illinois. When she was 13 years-old, her mother died suddenly when a blood vessel burst in her brain. Griffith told Jerry Brewer of the *New York Times* about the effect her mother's death had on her: "It's still hard for me to talk about. She'll always be a part of my life. I smile everyday because when she was living, she always smiled. If I get a bad call or I miss a free throw, I'm still going to smile."

Griffith channeled all of her energy into playing sports. Alongside her two brothers, she regularly played against the boys on the basketball court across the street from her house. At George Washington High School in Chicago, she made All-American in softball and basketball and still holds the state record for most home runs. Because of her success on the athletic field, Griffith had her pick of Division I colleges to attend.

She chose Iowa, but was forced to sit out her first year of college because she did not meet the freshman eligibility requirements. After one semester at Iowa, Griffith became pregnant and decided to go back home to Chicago to have her baby. Griffith told Janis Carr of the *Orange County Register* about this time in her life: "A lot of people expected a lot from me when I graduated from high school. So I was sad because I didn't know what I was going to do. I got pregnant, had my daughter and put basketball aside until I decided what I wanted to do." After the birth of her daughter, Candace, Griffith rediscovered her desire to play basketball. However, she would play basketball only on her own terms. Her first priority was to be an attentive mother. Griffith was ready to attend DePaul University but, because she had spent one semester at Iowa, she was forced to sit out during another basketball season. Instead of staying close to home, she traveled south to West Palm Beach, Florida where she could play immediately.

Success in the Sunshine State

Griffith traveled south with her daughter, enrolled at

At a Glance . . .

Born Yolanda Griffith, March 1, 1970, in Chicago, IL; daughter of Harvey and Yvonne Griffith; children: Candace. *Education:* attended Florida Atlantic University.

Career: Starred in softball and basketball at George Washington High School, 1988; attended Palm Beach Junior College, 1991-92; attended Florida Atlantic University, 1993; played professional basketball in Euroleague in Germany, 1994-96; played for the ABL's Long Beach Sting Rays and Chicago Condors, 1997-98; joined the WNBA's Sacramento Monarchs, 1999-.

Awards: High School All-American in softball and basketball, 1988; Kodak Division II All-American, 1993; first overall pick of the ABL draft, ABL Defensive Player of the Year,1997; second player selected in the WNBA draft, Newcomer of the Year, Defensive Player of theYear, and WNBA Most Valuable Player, 1999; member of USA Olympic women'sbasketball team, 2000.

Addresses: *Home*—Sacramento, CA; *Business*—Sacramento Monarchs, One Sports Parkway, Sacramento, CA 95834.

Palm Beach Junior College, and found a job repossessing cars. During the day, she played basketball and led Palm Beach to two Florida Junior College State Championships. At night, she would hot wire cars with a partner and repossess them, sometimes with the angry owner of the car in hot pursuit. Griffith commented on her unique employment to Paul Zeise of the WNBA's magazine *Hoop:* "You know what? It paid the bills. My boss took a chance on me, I was young and had no experience. It was a little crazy some nights, and sometimes it was scary. I had a lot of excitement at that job as well, and like I said, at the time it put food on my table. Sometimes you have to do things that are difficult in order to reach your goals." After two years at Palm Beach, Griffith was faced with another difficult decision. She was again pursued by recruiters from all of the major college basketball programs, including perennial powerhouse Tennessee. Griffith was preparing to attend Western Kentucky, when she reassessed her situation. She enjoyed being in Florida, and had a support system there for her daughter. Instead of attending Western Kentucky, Griffith opted for Florida Atlantic University, a Division II school.

In 1993, Griffith was a dominant force in Division II women's basketball. She led the nation in scoring (28 points per game) and rebounding (16.0 per game). She was named as a Kodak Division II All-American after her junior season. After one year in college playing basketball, working at night, studying, and raising her daughter, Griffith decided that she could not continue this hectic schedule. She signed with an agent and sought a spot in the professional ranks. To secure a spot on a pro team, Griffith traveled overseas to Germany.

Made Professional Progress

Griffith went to Germany, and stayed for three years. She lived there with her daughter, who learned to speak German fluently, and her friend Charlene Littles, who took care of her daughter when Griffith was away. Griffith dominated the Euroleague, averaging 24.7 points and 26 rebounds a game. After three seasons overseas, she heard about two new women's professional basketball leagues that were being formed in the United States and decided to return home.

Upon returning to the United States, Griffith had to choose between playing for the American Basketball League (ABL) or the WNBA. She told Carr of the *Orange County Register* about the factors in her decision: "Playing in the WNBA crossed my mind, but I decided on the ABL because it is its own league, not somebody else's. The WNBA is just the NBA, which, yes, has a lot of money. But the ABL is doing it for themselves." The ABL's schedule was an important incentive for Griffith. Because the ABL played their games during the winter months, Griffith could spend the summers with her daughter. In addition, the ABL paid almost three times the salary of the WNBA. Griffith attended an ABL tryout camp in San Francisco, and impressed the scouts so much that she was made the first overall pick in the 1997 ABL draft by the expansion Long Beach Sting Rays. Griffith played two years in the ABL, leading Long Beach to the 1997-98 championship series. Before the league folded in December of 1998, she played briefly for the Chicago Condors.

Although the ABL did not survive, Griffith used her experience in the league to establish a name for herself. In her two years in the ABL, she averaged 18.4 points and 11.4 rebounds. Griffith was the ABL Defensive Player of the Year in 1997, and finished second in the balloting for MVP honors in 1997 and 1998. She was even invited to try out for the United States national team, but quit after three days because she did not want to be apart from her daughter.

Earned Most Valuable Player Honors

Griffith was the second player selected in the 1999

WNBA draft by the Sacramento Monarchs. Unlike other rookies, Griffith stepped into the spotlight and quickly became a dominant force. She announced her presence during her second game in the WNBA, scoring 31 points and grabbing nine rebounds against the Phoenix Mercury. Griffith also recorded 19 rebounds in one game, one more than the entire opposing team. Monarchs' point guard Ticha Penicheiro told Zeise of *Hoop* about her new teammate: "Yolanda is a special player. I've played with a lot of great players, but she is the best. She is so quick, so athletic, so strong. She is a force, nobody can stop her when she is on her game. She makes my job so much easier. She is also a great teammate and a special person." By the end of the season, Griffith had led the Monarchs to the third–best record in the Western Conference at 19-13, an improvement of eight wins over the previous season. With three games remaining in her first WNBA season, Griffith suffered a partial tear of the medial meniscus in her right knee. She underwent surgery immediately after the injury, and was forced to watch from the bench as the Monarchs lost their last three games of the season. The Monarchs were then bounced from the playoffs by the Los Angeles Sparks.

Griffith, who was named to the Western Conference All-Star Team, finished the season second in the league in scoring (18.8 points per game), first in rebounds (11.3 per game), first in steals (2.52 per game), and third in blocked shots (1.86 per game). Because of her brilliant play and impressive statistics, she became the first WNBA player to win three individual awards in the same year. She was the league's Most Valuable Player, for which she received 25,000 and a new car, Newcomer of the Year, and the Defensive Player of the Year. In addition to these awards, Griffith was named to the women's Olympic Dream Team, which will compete in the 2000 Olympics in Sydney, Australia. She told David Steele of the *San Francisco Chronicle* about the pressure to follow up the 1996 team's gold medal: "It's a challenge. They kept a lot of the core players from the '96 team on this team. There's a lot of pressure—not only for them, but for the new players. We have to protect what we've got . . .. It has to be gold. We can't take home anything less than gold."

Griffith traveled a long and difficult road to WNBA stardom. Despite the death of her mother, her unintended pregnancy at the age of 19, and her hardscrabble existence in Florida, she overcame these obstacles and achieved excellence. As Griffith's father, Harvey, told Don Bosley of the *Sacramento Bee:* "The average person, I would go so far as to say, wouldn't have made it through all of that. But Yolanda's determined."

Sources

New York Times, July 6, 1999.
Orange County Register, December 5, 1997.
Sacramento Bee, September 2, 1999.
San Francisco Chronicle, September 15, 1999.

Other

Additional information for this profile was obtained from http:\\www.wnba.com\features\yo_hoop_feature.html

—Michael J. Watkins

Gar Heard

1948—

Professional basketball coach

Gar Heard has always displayed a quiet, old-school work ethic in his career, first as a player and later as a coach in the NBA. Drafted by Seattle in 1970 out of the University of Oklahoma, Heard was once considered one of the NBA's best rebounders. Representing five different franchises in his 11-year playing career, the 6'7" forward was a formidable defender who took pride in his special ability to block shots without getting into foul trouble. Although he was not an exceptional scorer, Heard was the author of what has come to be known as "The Shot Heard 'Round the World," a buzzer-beating, high-arching, 20-foot jumpshot for the Phoenix Suns in Game Five of the 1976 NBA Finals against the Boston Celtics. The shot sent the game into triple overtime, and is considered both a shining moment in the annals of NBA history and the high point of Heard's career.

Heard has been an NBA coach for many seasons, assisting in Dallas, Indiana, Philadelphia, and Detroit. He was appointed interim head coach in Dallas midway through the 1992-93 season and was hired in June of 1999 as the head coach of the Washington Wizards franchise. Seven months later Michael Jordan, the new manager of basketball operations for the Washington Wizards, fired Heard when the lackluster Wizards failed to respond to his leadership. Former Detroit Pistons coach Alvin Gentry echoed popular opinion when he praised Heard to *The Washington Times* in 1999: "I think his best quality is that he commands instant respect," Gentry stated. "Not because he's intimidating or anything, but more his personality. I think he has an air of fairness about him."

The youngest of four children, Garfield Heard was born May 3, 1948 in Hogansville, Georgia. Hogansville is a small farming town of about 4,000 in western Georgia, midway between Columbus and Atlanta. He was raised there by his mother, Charlie Mae Heard, a housekeeper, and his grandparents. His father, Preston Martin, was not involved in Heard's upbringing. "We didn't have a lot of money," Heard told *The Washington Times* of his childhood, "but we never went hungry, we always had clothes. My mom and my grandparents saw to it that we always went to school. We appreciated what we had."

Heard was a quiet, but well-liked student at Ethel W. Kight High School. One of Heard's teachers told Bob Cohn of *The Washington Times* that Heard "was

At a Glance . . .

Born Garfield Heard on May 3, 1948, in Hogan-sville, GA; son of Charlie Mae Heard (a house-keeper) and Preston Martin; married Kathleen Cline, divorced; children: Kim, Jaasmeen, Gyasi, Avery. *Education:* Oklahoma University, B.S., 1970.

Career: Professional basketball player; forward, Seattle SuperSonics, 1970-72; Chicago Bulls, 1972-73; Buffalo Braves, 1973-76; Phoenix Suns, 1976-80; San Diego Clippers, 1980-81; volunteer assistant basketball coach, Arizona State University, 1982-83; realtor, Phoenix, Arizona, c. 1984-87; assistant coach, Dallas Mavericks, 1987-93; interim head coach, Dallas Mavericks, 1993; assistant coach, Indiana Pacers, 1993-97; assistant coach, Philadelphia 76ers,1997-98; assistant coach, Detroit Pistons, 1998-99; head coach, Washington Wizards,1999-2000.

Awards: All Big Eight Conference; MVP in the Big Eight, 1970; MVP in MarshallUniversity Tournament, 1970.

loved by everybody. All he had to do was smile." Cohn noted that Heard was "known for speaking directly, when he did speak," and added that he was "never loud or rowdy." Heard was athletic, and played both football and baseball. He was also a champion sprinter in track while in high school. Heard, however, was a standout in basketball. He played at Kight for Coach Harold Pearson, averaging 29 points and 25 rebounds per game. By his senior year, Heard was drawing the attention of college recruiters. Upon his graduation from Kight in 1966, he accepted a basketball scholarship from the University of Oklahoma in Norman.

While at Oklahoma, Heard was one of only about 300 African American students on campus. Coming from an entirely African American community, this was something of a shock. Heard adjusted to the new environment, however, and enjoyed his time there. "It was a great experience," he told Cohn. "I wouldn't mind living through it again." Under Coach John MacLeod, Heard demonstrated the work ethic at Oklahoma that would help form the basis of his ongoing reputation. According to the *Washington Post,* "Heard averaged 15.7 points and 10.6 rebounds for the Sooners, leading them in scoring (21.8) and rebounding (12.5) as a senior, when he made All-Big Eight." Heard was named MVP of the Big Eight during his senior year. In 1970, he became the first in his family to graduate from college.

Drafted into NBA

Heard was drafted in the third round by the Seattle SuperSonics in 1970. He did not play much during his rookie season, but averaged 7.9 points and 7.6 rebounds in his second year with Seattle. He was traded to Chicago early in the 1972-73 season, where his game continued to improve. He averaged 10.1 points and 5.6 rebounds per game during his lone season with the Bulls. At the end of that season, Heard was traded to the Buffalo Braves. In Buffalo, he became a starter for the first time. According to his NBA coaching bio, Heard achieved career highs in almost every category during his first season with Buffalo. He posted an average of 15.3 points and 11.7 rebounds per game. He also had 136 steals and 230 blocked shots. Heard was ranked tenth in the NBA in rebounding and sixth in blocked shots, and helped to lead the Braves to their first-ever playoff appearance. The Braves would go on to lose to the Boston Celtics in the Eastern Conference semifinals. Heard's second season with Buffalo was successful as well, and the Braves reached the playoffs again. The Braves reached the semifinals, but fell to the Washington Bullets in seven games.

The Shot Heard 'Round the World

Midway through the 1975-76 season, Heard was traded to the Phoenix Suns. As a result of that trade and some odd scheduling, Heard ended up appearing in a total of 86 games that season. He played in 50 games for Buffalo and in another 36 for Phoenix. Only two other players in NBA history have played in more games in a single season. The 1975-76 season was also memorable because it produced the play that is considered the highlight of Heard's NBA career. The play, known as "The Shot Heard 'Round the World," is also one of the finest moments in NBA history.

Phoenix finished the 1975-76 season with a 42-40 record, which was good for third place in the Pacific Division. The Suns then upset several teams to reach the NBA Finals against the Boston Celtics. During Game Five in Boston, time was running out in the second overtime. With the Suns leading by one point, John Havlicek made a 15-foot shot to put the Celtics ahead by one point, with one second remaining. A technical foul pushed the Celtics lead to two, but the referees allowed the ball to be inbounded by Phoenix at half-court. The ball was then passed to Heard, who netted a 20-foot turnaround jumper, tying the game and forcing a third overtime. Boston went on to win the game and the series, but Heard's shot stunned the crowd and has since stood as one of the finest clutch shots ever made in the NBA. It was chosen by Phoenix fans in 1999 as The Most Memorable Moment in the 30-year history of the Suns. It also figures as a critical factor when many basketball fans argue that Game Five of that series was "The Greatest Game Ever."

Heard remembered the moment as "not so much wondering if the ball was going in, but did I get the shot off in time." He told writer Joe Gilmartin in 1998, "It was really a catch-and-shoot situation." "I did make a few other plays in my career," he told Gilmartin modestly, "and I don't really want to be remembered for just one. But if that's the way it has to be, that's a good one to be remembered by." Cohn noted in *The Washington Times* in 1999 that what Heard himself considers the high point of his career was another moment altogether, "What became the defining moment in his career wasn't even the defining moment of the playoffs that year. Instead, . . .[Heard] singles out the prior series against Golden State, when he blocked Jamal Wilkes' potential game-winning, series-clinching shot to save a victory against the Warriors and keep the Suns alive. 'If he makes that shot,' Heard said, 'there is no Boston series.'"

Heard's playing career started its decline beginning with the 1976-77 season. He continued to play for Phoenix until 1980, when he signed as a free agent with the San Diego Clippers. At the end of the 1980-81 season, Heard retired from the NBA. He had played in 787 games spanning 11 seasons and posted career averages of 8.7 points per game and 7.5 rebounds per game. He had played on seven playoff teams, and in 59 playoff games. Writer Dave D'Alessandro described Heard in *The Sporting News* in 1999 as "a player's player, the kind that Jack Ramsay or John MacLeod knew they could always depend on, and . . .[he] went about his job with an unflashy gameness—tough, smart, determined, prepared and intimidating."

Embarked on Coaching Career

For a few years after his retirement, Heard concentrated on other pursuits. He volunteered as an assistant coach for the 1982-83 season at Arizona State University. He worked in real estate in Phoenix and put together a video games business. Heard found that he missed basketball, however, and accepted a position as assistant coach with the Dallas Mavericks in 1987. He was happy to work again with Coach John MacLeod, who had been his coach at Oklahoma and again in Phoenix. Heard immediately helped MacLeod guide the Mavericks to the best postseason in their history. Ritchie Adubato became head coach of the club in 1989, and Heard remained as an assistant. When Adubato was fired during the middle of the 1992-93 season, Heard was named interim head coach. The team finished the year a dismal 9-44. When Quinn Buckner took over in Dallas, Heard moved to the Indiana Pacers for the 1993-94 season, serving as assistant to Larry Brown. He helped coach the Pacers to the Eastern Conference Finals. Remaining with the Pacers for the next four seasons, Heard then rejoined Larry Brown in Philadelphia as an assistant coach to the Philadelphia 76ers in 1997-98. He spent the

1998-99 season with the Detroit Pistons as an to Pistons head coach Alvin Gentry. In mid-1999, Heard accepted the head coaching position with the Washington Wizards.

No Wizardry in Washington

During the course of his many seasons as an assistant coach, Heard was frequently considered, and then passed over, for head coaching positions. Along with Heard, former NBA greats Isiah Thomas, Kareem Abdul-Jabbar, and Glenn "Doc" Rivers were also being considered for the Washington job. Despite this stiff competition, Heard prevailed. Wizards owner Abe Pollen was very impressed with Heard during his interview, and general manager Wes Unseld stated that Heard's known strength in communicating with players was a key factor in his selection. On June 15, 1999, Heard signed a three-year contract with an annual payout, according to various reports, of between 1 and 3 million. He replaced coach Bernie Bickerstaff, who had been fired that April. Heard became the 16th head coach in team history, and faced a steep uphill climb with the Wizards. The franchise had not won a playoff game in 11 years.

The Wizards roster included several talented players, including Juwan Howard, Mitch Richmond, and Rod Strickland. However, the team lacked cohesiveness, drive, and chemistry, and was wildly inconsistent. *Sports Illustrated* noted in January of 2000 that Washington had comfortably established itself as "the league's most underachieving franchise."

Despite Heard's best efforts, the Wizards continued to lose. In addition, the Wizards allowed other teams to break losing streaks against them, prompting Heard to comment to the *Washington Post* that one of the team's biggest problems was "the relative ease with which it accepts defeat." By early January of 2000, the team had lost more than two-thirds of its games. *Washington Post* sportswriter Steve Wyche noted on January 11 that Heard understood and accepted the risks as an NBA coach. "The coach is going to be the scapegoat most of the time," Heard said. He added, "When you take a job as a coach you know that at some point you're going to get fired. It happens to everyone. . . .But I've never taken that approach. I came at this job wanting to establish a winning attitude with these guys, to make them competitive every night."

On January 19, 2000, retired basketball superstar Michael Jordan bought 10 percent of the franchise and became the Wizards' director of basketball operations. Heard was dismissed as head coach ten days later. Although the decision to fire Heard was Jordan's, he left the actual announcement to Unseld, who had hired Heard, prompting many to call the dismissal "heartless."

Heard accepted his termination as part of the job. He commented to the Associated Press on January 30, "You never have a chance to show what you can do. . . .Unfortunately, that's the nature of the business. I think they had their mind made up when. . .]Jordan] got here. I never got an opportunity to talk to him. When you come in you want to bring your own people. Next time things will work better."

With his strong work ethic and respect for professional basketball, Heard will undoubtedly receive another head coaching opportunity. *Washington Post* columnist Michael Wilbon noted in 1999, "Heard played. He stuck for more than a decade despite being drafted in the third round. He went to the playoffs seven times, played on bad teams, played on a couple of really good teams, played with stiffs and superstars. He's been there."

Sources

Books

The Official NBA Basketball Encyclopedia, 2nd Edition. Edited by Alex Sachare. New York: Villard Books, 1994.
Who's Who Among African Americans, 12 Edition. Edited by Ashyia N. Henderson and Shirelle Phelps. Detroit: Gale, 1999.
Who's Who Among Black Americans, 6th Edition. Edited by Iris Cloyd. Detroit: Gale, 1990.

Periodicals

Buffalo News, January 30, 2000.
Sports Illustrated, January 24, 2000, p.66; February 7, 2000, p.52.
The Sporting News, November 8, 1999, p.4.
The Washington Times, June 17, 1999, p.1; October 31, 1999, p.1.
Washington Post, June 16, 1999, p.D1; June 17, 1999, p.D1, p.D4; January 7, 2000, p.D8; January 11, 2000, p.D1; January 25, 2000, p.A1; January 31, 2000, p.D1.

Other

Additional information for this profile was obtained from http:\\www.nba.com\suns\00651687.html 1999; http:\\www.nba.com\wizards\bios\ coach.html 1999; http:\\www.nba.com\wizards\heard_000129.html 1999; and http:\\www.nba.com\suns\00651975.html 1999.

—Ellen Dennis French

A. Leon Higginbotham, Jr.

1928–1998

Retired federal judge

A. Leon Higginbotham rose from humble beginnings to the bench of a federal court because he refused to be thwarted by the obstacles he faced. He fought to acquire an education, earning a place in an all-white high school that no African American student had ever attended. He left his first university because it would not heat the dormitory where African American students were housed. And despite being a Yale Law School graduate, groomed for the privileged life of a lawyer, he began his career as a public servant, working as a district attorney when white law firms rejected him.

Despite these difficulties, Higginbotham won political appointments that eventually made him chief judge of the U.S. Court of Appeals for the Third Circuit. He has been praised by Guido Calabresi, dean of Yale Law School, in the *New York Times* as "a first-rate judge, a sensitive judge, who is powerful in style and analytically strong.'" The late Thurgood Marshall, former Supreme Court Justice, told the *Times,* "I think he is a great lawyer and a very great judge. Period."

Born in Trenton, New Jersey, on February 25, 1928, Aloyisus Leon Higginbotham, Jr., attended Ewing Park, a segregated public elementary school. His mother, a domestic worker, was determined to change things, however. "She knew that education was the sole passport to a better life," Higginbotham told the *New York Times.* She set her sights on the city's all-white academic high school, which required its students to have studied a year of Latin before they could be admitted. The course was not offered in African American elementary schools, however.

Although the school had never admitted an African American student, Leon's mother refused to give up, hounding the principal until he agreed to enroll him. The school's kindly Latin teacher volunteered to tutor Leon during the summer break. Looking back, Higginbotham realized how great an opportunity this was: "When I see students who went to Ewing Park with me now working as elevator operators or on street maintenance," he continued in the *New York Times,* "I often wonder what their future would have been if the school had offered Latin."

Weathered Racism

Graduating from high school at the age of 16, Higginbotham entered Purdue University, intending to be-

At a Glance . . .

Born February 25, 1928, in Trenton, NJ; died December 14, 1998, in Boston, MA; married Evelyn Brooks; children: Stephen, Karen, Kenneth, Nia. *Education:* Attended Purdue University, 1944-46. Antioch College, B.A. 1949; Yale University, LL.B., 1952.

Career: Assistant district attorney Philadelphia County 1953-54; partner Norris,Green, Harris & Higginbotham, Philadelphia, 1954-62; special hearing officer for conscientious objectors, U.S. Justice Department, 1960-62; commissioner of the Federal Trade Commission, 1962-64; commissioner of the Pennsylvania Human Relations Commission,1961-62; judge, U.S. District Court for the East District, 1964-77; judge, U.S. Court ofAppeals Third Circuit, 1977-93; counsel to Paul, Weiss, Rifkind, Wharton, 1993-98; professorat Harvard University's John F. Kennedy School of Government, 1993-98; international mediator of first South African election in which blacks were allowed to vote, 1994; testified before the House Judiciary Committee against the impeachment of President Bill Clinton,1998.

Selected awards: Raoul Wallenberg Humanitarian Award, 1994; Presidential Medalof Freedom, 1995; Spingarn Medal, 1996; numerous honorary degrees.

come an engineer. He was one of only 12 African American students on campus, all of whom were housed in an unheated attic called International House. As fall turned to winter and temperatures plummeted, conditions in the dormitory became almost unbearable. "After December and January, going to bed every night with earmuffs on, sometimes wearing shoes and several pairs of socks, I decided to go and talk to President Elliot," Higginbotham recalled in the *New York Times.*

Higginbotham intended to ask for nothing more than rooms in a heated dormitory, but the university president was unmoved. "If he had communicated to me, with some kind word or gesture, or even a sigh, that I had caused him to review his own commitment to things as they were," Higginbotham continued in the *Times,* "I might have felt that I had won a small victory and could go back in the attic and sleep." The president, however, was adamant. "'Higginbotham,'" he said, "'the law doesn't require us to let colored students in the dorm, and you either accept things as they are or

leave the university immediately.'"

The memory of that confrontation rankled Higginbotham years later. "How could it be that the law would not permit 12 good kids to sleep in a warm dormitory?' he asked indignantly in the *Times.* But Higginbotham did more than complain. He decided to abandon his engineering studies and pursue a law degree instead. He left Purdue and went to Antioch College in Ohio, where he earned a B.A. degree in sociology in 1949. Higginbotham went on to Yale Law School, graduating with an LL.B. degree in 1952. Finding work in law firms, however, proved more difficult than passing the bar exam.

Wearing a new suit purchased with money from a supportive professor and carrying letters of recommendation, Higginbotham interviewed at a Philadelphia law office where a fellow Yale grad, now a partner in the firm, was hiring. When he arrived at the office and announced that he was there for an appointment, however, the secretary was incredulous. They had not been expecting an African American man. When Higginbotham met with the Yale alumnus, he was told his credentials were impressive, but "of course, you know there's nothing I can do for you, " Higginbotham recalled ruefully in the *New York Times.* The partner named a few African American law firms and suggested he try them. This was too much for Higginbotham and he stormed out, furious. His anger turned to tears in the lobby.

With help from his law professors, Higginbotham secured a year-long clerkship with a Pennsylvania Supreme Court justice, and returned to Philadelphia in 1953 to work as an assistant district attorney for Richardson Dilworth, the city's prosecutor and another Yale graduate. He left in 1954 to become a partner in the African American law firm of Norris, Green, Harris, & Higginbotham, a group that handled civil rights cases as well as more mundane matters. During his ten years with the firm, Higginbotham also served the U.S. Justice Department as a special hearing officer for conscientious objectors, became a member of the Federal Trade Commission, and sat on the Pennsylvania Human Relations Commission—a group formed to improve race relations.

Youngest Federal Judge in 30 Years

In 1964, Higginbotham was appointed U.S. district judge for the Eastern District of Pennsylvania by President Lyndon Johnson. He was only 35-years-old, the youngest federal judge in 30 years, and at that time the only African American judge in a district court. Four years later, Higginbotham began his long association with the University of Pennsylvania Law School, where he eventually became a senior fellow. His political star still rising, he was briefly considered for the post of U.S. attorney general by President Jimmy Carter in 1976, and finally named to the U.S. Court of Appeals Third Circuit one year later. The appointment made Higginbotham the first African American member at the commission level of any federal regulatory agency. He became chief judge of the court in 1989, and chief judge emeritus, with a reduced caseload, in 1991.

Higginbotham was a prolific author during his legal career, writing over 100 articles. In 1978 he published his first book, *In the Matter of Color: Race and the American Legal Process; The Colonial Period,* an acclaimed treatise on the history of race and law in the United States. He was also the recipient of many honorary degrees.

In 1982, Higginbotham and other African American jurists were invited to visit South Africa and give a series of lectures. The country's brutal apartheid system was very much in evidence, and the group was frequently followed, questioned, and even detained as they tried to visit different sites. "It was shocking and incredible to believe that in 1982 you can have the kind of repressiveness you think of Germany having in 1930," Higginbotham told the *Philadelphia Inquirer.* "There are some analogies to pre-Civil War times. Every black had to have a pass [to travel] then, just as they do in South Africa."

Defender of Affirmative Action

Not surprisingly, Higginbotham strongly favored aggressive government enforcement of civil rights and affirmative action, issues he had spoken and written passionately about. In a 1987 panel discussion on minorities and the Constitution, he deplored the Constitution's failure to protect the rights of African Americans during most of the nation's existence. "Under the original Constitution," Higginbotham was quoted as saying in the *New York Times,* "blacks were not people." He decried the hypocrisy of slave owners writing a document that defined freedom, calling the original Constitution "an exercise in nondisclosure" because it did not address the problem of slavery.

The painful climb of African Americans from servitude to freedom has been made possible by those who refused to accept injustice, Higginbotham asserted in a 1995 New York University speaking engagement that was quoted in the *Wall Street Journal:* "[Black people] are where we are [today] because of a level of protest which has gone on for more than a century." Higginbotham has not been above registering protests of his own, as he did in 1990, when he pointedly declined to preside over a collegiate moot court competition because, as he told the *New York Times,* the University of Chicago Law School, which sponsored the event, "for two decades has not had even one black professor in either a tenured position or tenure-track position."

Perhaps it was inevitable that when the conservative

Clarence Thomas was appointed to the Supreme Court in 1991, Higginbotham openly voiced his opposition. In a scathing *University of Pennsylvania Law Review* article entitled "An Open Letter to Justice Clarence Thomas from a Federal Judicial Colleague," reprinted in the *Philadelphia Inquirer,* he took Thomas on a verbal trip to the woodshed, berating the Justice for his supposedly "stunted knowledge of history and . . . unformed judicial philosophy." Higginbotham compared his and Thomas's careers to those of their grandfathers, whose lives were severely circumscribed by Jim Crow laws. Without the changes brought about by the civil rights movement, Higginbotham wrote, "probably neither you nor I would be federal judges today." He cast Thomas as an ignorant and ungrateful beneficiary of the government programs he has opposed. Higginbotham wrote that in all of Thomas's judicial career "I could not find one shred of evidence suggesting an insightful understanding on your part of how the evolutionary movement of the Constitution and the work of the civil rights organizations have benefitted you."

The article soon received a flurry of media attention not usually given to law school reviews. The *Chicago Tribune, Los Angeles Times, Wall Street Journal,* and *New York Times* all ran articles, giving Higginbotham an even wider audience. The letter and its condescending tenor were privately criticized by other federal judges, who disapproved of Higginbotham's public rebuke, especially since Thomas, as a Supreme Court Justice, was Higginbotham's superior. Thomas Sowell, an economist with the conservative Hoover Institution and someone Thomas has publicly admired, deplored Higginbotham's inability to find the moral and ethical standards behind Thomas's opinions. "On every page," Sowell told *Facts on File,* "Higginbotham's article drips with the moral conceit that no one could possibly have differed from him for any honest or principled reason." The letter, Sowell concluded was "a long, ugly, cheap attack."

However, Higginbotham's letter struck a chord with many others, particularly Anita Hill, whom some saw as a victim of both Thomas and hearings process. The letter was reprinted later in 1992, when it became the first chapter in the book *Race-ing Justice, Engendering Power,* a series of essays written in reaction to the Hill-Thomas issue. Higginbotham befriended Anita Hill, negotiated a million-dollar publishing deal for her with Doubleday in 1993 and coauthored a book, *Race, Gender, and Power in America: The Legacy of the Hill- Thomas Hearings,* with her and Emma Coleman Jordan in 1995.

On March 5, 1993, two weeks after his 65th birthday, Higginbotham retired from the federal bench. A few months earlier, his name had once again been mentioned as a possible nominee for U.S. attorney general, but he quickly quashed the notion, saying that he wanted time to pursue other interests. In his resignation letter to President Clinton, Higginbotham wrote "[I am] deeply grateful for the privilege to have served our country," quoted the *Philadelphia Inquirer*. "In the years to come, in different venues and in different ways, I hope to continue to act to the benefit of our nation."

Upon leaving the Third Circuit Court in 1993, Higginbotham became counsel to the international law firm of Paul, Weiss, Rifkind & Wharton. He also became a public service professor of jurisprudence at Harvard University's John F. Kennedy School of Government. In 1994, at the request of Nelson Mandela, Higginbotham served as an international mediator during South Africa's first election in which blacks were allowed to vote. He also provided counsel to the Congressional Black Caucus in a series of voting rights cases before the U.S. Supreme Court. Higginbotham also received the Raoul Wallenberg Humanitarian Award in 1994.

In 1995, Higginbotham delivered the keynote address at Purdue University on the anniversary of the birth of Martin Luther King, Jr. The address focused on how the Contract with America, an initiative passed by Republican legislators, would adversely affect race relations within the United States. Higginbotham delivered his address as an imaginary letter from Martin Luther King to then Speaker of the House Newt Gingrich. As reported in MIT's school newspaper, *The Tech*, Higginbotham called the Contract with America "one of the most tragic hopes and potential cruelties in American politics." He remarked further that the Contract with America disturbed him because "not once do you]Republican legislators] say that you want to eradicate racial discrimination. Not once do you say that you want to eradicate gender discrimination." *The Tech* also noted that Higginbotham implored Gingrich to use his power for the benefit of all Americans, "It is within your power to make our nation more fair than it has been in decades, or to make it more mean."

President Bill Clinton appointed Higginbotham as commissioner of the U.S. Commission on Civil Rights in October of 1995. That same year, his years of judicial service were recognized when President Clinton awarded him the Presidential Medal of Freedom, the nation's highest civilian honor. Upon receiving the award, Higginbotham told the *Philadelphia Inquirer,* "Some people look at 65 as a time when they can get their main pension, sleep late, and have a few cocktails. While I'm in good health, I really want to work on trying to implement what Martin Luther King's goal was when he said, 'I have the temerity to believe that people everywhere can have three meals a day for the body, education for their minds, and dignity for their spirit.'"

Higginbotham was hired by Texaco Inc. in 1996 to advise the company on diversity and personnel matters. Texaco had been sued two years earlier for racial discrimination after a tape, which allegedly contained the voices of white executives making disparaging comments about African Americans, was released to the public. As reported in *Jet,* Texaco chairman and CEO Peter I. Bijur welcomed Higginbotham's appointment, "I want to ensure that Texaco's policies prohibiting discrimination in the workplace are not mere rhetoric. As we move forward, Judge Higginbotham will evaluate our practices and make recommendations as to what our programs should be in the future."

Higginbotham continued his passionate defense of affirmative action. In 1996, he addressed the U.S. Senate Judiciary Committee on the importance of maintaining affirmative action programs. *Jet* reported that "Judge Higginbotham urged the committee to be more sensitive to the needs of minorities and women and the historic racism and sexism they have endured." Also in 1996, Higginbotham published the book *Shades of Freedom: Racial Politics and Presumptions of the American Legal Process,* and was awarded the prestigious Spingarn Medal by the NAACP.

In 1998, Justice Clarence Thomas was invited to speak at the National Bar Association (NBA) convention. The NBA is the largest organization of African American lawyers. Higginbotham, in an open letter to NBA members, criticized the appearance of Thomas at the convention. As reported by *The Savannah Morning News,* Higginbotham told NBA members that "it makes no more sense to invite Clarence Thomas than it would have for the National Bar Association to invite George Wallace for dinner the day after he stood in the schoolhouse door and shouted, 'Segregation today and segregation forever.'" He also wrote, "I can't believe that many organizations would be expected to invite someone as their major lecturer who has advocated diminution of that group's rights."

Higginbotham testified against the impeachment of President Clinton before the House Judiciary Committee in 1998. CNN reported that Higginbotham dismissed comparisons between the Clinton impeachment hearings and those that occurred during the Nixon administration, "There has never been. . .an impeachment proceeding on this minuscule level. . .Everyone talks about the Nixon experience, but that is as different, it's the difference between zero and infinity." He also argued that Clinton did not commit perjury, "Perjury has gradations. Some are serious, some are less. If the president broke the 55 mph speed limit and said under oath he was going 49, that would not be an impeachable high crime. And neither is this."

Shortly after testifying before the House Judiciary Committee, Higginbotham was hospitalized after suffering several strokes. Friends had been deeply concerned for his health. One friend, U.S. Court of Appeals Judge Nathaniel Jones, told the *Cincinnati Enquirer,* "We all advised him to slow down. He said that in all struggles for justice, someone must fall. He felt that he was in a struggle for justice, and if it were his fate to fall, so be it." Higginbotham died on December 14, 1998. Upon learning of his death, Harvard law professor Charles Ogletree remarked, "He was the epitome of the people's lawyer. Despite his individual merits and accomplishments, he never hesitated to lend a hand to the poor, the voiceless, the powerless and the downtrodden."

Sources

Chicago Tribune, February 16, 1992; February 19, 1992.

Cincinnati Enquirer, December 15, 1998.

Jet, October 16, 1995, p. 10; January 29, 1996, p. 6; December 16, 1996, p. 6.

New York Times, May 31, 1987, sec. 1, p. 44; December 15, 1989, p. B20; July 19, 1991, p. B7; February 14, 1992, p. D20; March 8, 1993, p. D8.

Philadelphia Inquirer, May 16, 1981, p. B1; October 20, 1981, p. B1; June 30, 1982, p. A3; August 25, 1982, p. B1; November 11, 1982, p. B3; November 12, 1982, p. C2; January 23, 1992, p. A19; October 27, 1992, p. A11; December 27, 1992, p. F1; January 25, 1993, p. A1; February 2, 1993, p. B1; May 27, 1993, p. G1; June 15, 1993, p. B5; December 18, 1993, p. D12.

The Savannah Morning News, July 31, 1998.

The Tech, February 14, 1995, pp. 1, 14.

Wall Street Journal, December 1, 1995, p. A14.

Other

Additional information for this profile was obtained from CNN.com; blackvoices.com; and http:\\www.undergroundrailroad.org\projects\news\052298.html.

—Amy Loerch Strumolo and David G. Oblender

Terry Hillard

1954—

Chicago police chief

When Terry Hillard became superintendent of Chicago's police force in 1998, he took over the public-safety department of the third-largest city in the United States. With the promotion, he also became the nation's highest-ranking African American law-enforcement officer. Hillard, however, was promoted to the superintendent's job amidst a time of turmoil and trouble. Charges of police brutality, corruption, and injudicious arrests had plagued the city in recent years, and he replaced an outgoing chief who was forced to step down after ethics questions were raised by the local media.

It was Hillard's quiet demeanor and spotless career record on the force that made him the mayor's top choice. "In the 1990s, a police superintendent in a big city must be able to juggle many responsibilities, not all of them directly related to fighting crime," remarked a *Chicago Tribune* report by Steve Mills and Andrew Martin. "The job often entails dealing with often-conflicting constituencies, including minority communities, the police union and City Hall. All can cut into a superintendent's popularity."

A Marine in Vietnam

Hillard was born in South Fulton, Tennessee, where his father was a cook for a railroad line, and the family eventually moved north to Chicago. After high school, he joined the Marines in 1963, and spent 13 months in Vietnam. When Hillard returned home, he planned to become a state police officer, but conceding to his mother's wishes—she wanted him to stay closer to home, since he applied and was accepted into the officer training program for the Chicago Police Department (CPD). After completing the course, Hillard's first assignment as a patrol officer was in a rough section of Chicago's South Side called East Chicago in 1968.

In 1975, Hillard was injured in the line of duty when he was struck by two bullets. The incident earned him the Superintendent's Award of Valor, the CPD's highest award for courage under fire. For many years, he served in the mayoral bodyguard detachments, and worked for Chicago's first female mayor, Jane Byrne, in the early 1980s, and for its popular African Ameri-

At a Glance . . .

Born c. 1944, in South Fulton, TN; son of a railroad cook; married to Dorothy Brown (a school counselor); children: one son, one daughter. *Military service:* Served in the U.S. Marine Corps beginning in 1963.

Career: Joined Chicago Police Department as patrol officer, 1968; wounded in the line of duty, 1975; served in the mayoral bodyguard contingent, 1980s; became district commander, then chief of detectives, 1995; named superintendent of police, 1998-.

Awards: Superintendent's Award of Valor, Chicago Police Department, 1975.

Addresses: *Office*—Chicago Police Department, 1121 S. State St.,Chicago, IL 60605.

can mayor, Harold Washington, who died in office in 1987. Hillard became district commander, and then the CPD's first African American chief of detectives.

Era of Ill Will

As he rose through the ranks Hillard, who still spoke with a Southern drawl, earned a reputation as a calm negotiator and fair supervisor. He emerged as an unlikely candidate, however, for the police superintendent's job when it suddenly became vacant at the end of 1997. The post is a high-profile one. The chief must often confront a barrage of media microphones and cameras during hastily called press conferences after a particularly heinous crime, or incident of police brutality. Moreover, the CPD itself was experiencing a troubled moment in its history. Its superintendent since 1992, Matt Rodriguez, had just resigned after a Chicago newspaper reported that he had maintained a friendship with a convicted felon. There had also been several incidents of police brutality and revelations of corruption among its ranks in recent months.

As a candidate for the post, Hillard had to fill out an extensive questionnaire, which ended with eight essay questions. One of the questions concerned community policing, and another offered a chance to speculate on the significant drop in crime in New York City in recent years. Hillard, to the surprise of some, was named superintendent in February of 1998 by Mayor Richard Daley, who admitted it had been a tough decision among a field filled with qualified candidates. In a *Chicago Tribune* account about the competition for

the job, a colleague "described Hillard as a firm but fair manager," noted Martin and Mills. "It's a joy to work for the guy," the source told the paper. "After he's told you you're wrong about something, that's it. You move on ... There's no finer gentleman." It seems Hillard's tranquil personality worked in his favor: two other leading candidates, deputy superintendent Charles Ramsey and Raymond Risley, who headed the CPD's organized crime division, "both favored more sweeping changes for the department than Hillard," the *Chicago Tribune* report observed.

Nation's Highest-Ranking Black Cop

Hillard became Chicago's first African American chief of police, heading a vital city department with 17,000 employees—among them 13,500 officers—and a budget of 923 million. Yet he also headed a force that is predominantly white—only 26 percent of the CPD's officers are African American, and just 12 percent are Latino. Overall, the force is responsible for maintaining order and solving crimes in a city that is almost evenly divided among whites, who predominantly live on the city's north side, and blacks and Hispanics, residents of its south and west sections. "Without a doubt, Hillard's job is one of the most difficult in city government," noted another *Chicago Tribune* article by Mills and reporter Todd Lighty. "He has more employees than any other city department head. And his job is such that the mistakes can be counted in human lives."

As the new superintendent, Hillard immediately began working to upgrade the CPD's recruiting and training programs for new officers. He also pledged to improve community relations. Among the new measures Hillard, he announced a plan to send the top brass—himself included—out of its South Loop headquarters more often and into the precincts in order to meet with patrol officers, and learn more about the concerns of the community.

The Harris Case

Some changes that Hillard made during his first year on the job were not widely accepted among the CPD's rank-and-file officers, however. One faction objected to a plan to install video cameras in patrol cars, and others voiced concern about a new policy to videotape murder confessions. Furthermore, Hillard's first year on the job was marked by criticism directed at the CPD for the handling of a terrible crime that received national media attention. During the summer of 1998, an 11-year-old girl named Ryan Harris was found murdered in a rough neighborhood of the city, and two boys, ages 7 and 8, were taken into custody as suspects. The arrests evoked an outcry of shock and disbelief, but the boys were released after it became apparent that detectives had little evidence to convict them.

Inside the department itself, more trouble surfaced for Hillard when a Chicago gang-unit officer was suspected of running a drug-trafficking ring. Then, on a single night in June of 1999, two unarmed African Americans were killed by Chicago police officers. One of the victims was a Northwestern University football player. A 26-year-old African American woman was shot by an officer while sitting in a car that had been pulled over. "What happened next isn't clear, but it's possible that the officer who shot [LaTanya] Haggerty mistook her cell phone for a pistol," noted *Newsweek*'s John McCormick. In the death of Bobby Russ, the Northwestern athlete, the officer broke Russ's car window and shoved his service revolver inside. Russ grabbed the revolver, and was shot during a struggle.

Acted Swiftly to Restore Faith

Public outcry against the CPD reached a crisis point over the next few days, with daily rallies outside City Hall during which community groups and minority activists denounced the CPD as a bastion of brutality and injustice. There were even accusations that Chicago's African American officers conducted themselves less honorably than their white counterparts. Hillard acted quickly to ease tensions, however. He reviewed the tapes made of the incidents, chose an African American prosecutor to handle the matter, and met with local ministers and African American media executives. "Something went very terribly wrong in both these incidents," *Newsweek* quoted Hillard as saying. "Mistakes were made." Calling for peace and calm, he spoke at community meetings during which angry residents jeered at him.

Over the course of that contentious summer of 1999, Hillard became frustrated when tensions over the matter had failed to subside. He felt that some in the community were attempting to use the uproar for their own political gain: "[They] don't want a thorough, impartial and just investigation," *Newsweek* quoted Hillard as saying about some of the CPD's most

vociferous critics. "[They] want these officers' heads." Both incidents prompted him to launch a series of new initiatives. "Hillard will draft reforms, including a review of police procedures by law professors," wrote McCormick in *Newsweek*. "He's also ordered his top brass to re-educate officers about the use of deadly force—and the need to respect every citizen." Hillard won praise from many corners for his cool-headed decisiveness. "The superintendent has responded quickly and has shown a willingness to answer the tough questions," one African American minister, Rev. James Meeks, told the *Chicago Tribune*'s Mills and Todd Lighty. "The problems of the Chicago Police Department did not start in one day. They cannot be fixed in one day."

Hillard, who makes $127,000 a year as Chicago's top cop, is married to a guidance counselor, Dorothy Brown Hillard. She is the sister of Jesse Brown, President Bill Clinton's onetime cabinet secretary for Veterans Affairs. Since the late 1970s, Hillard and his family have lived in Chicago's Chatham neighborhood. Chatham, located on the city's South Side, is also home to many prominent Chicagoans of color, such as former mayor Eugene Sawyer. It remains part of a tight-knit, extremely stable African American community inside what is called the city's Black Bungalow Belt. *Chicago Tribune* writer Patrick T. Reardon asked Hillard if he ever thought of moving elsewhere. "I'm perfectly satisfied with Chatham," Hillard told the newspaper. "That's where we raised our kids. Folks, when they move up in the world, they go from one house to another house. I just added on to my house."

Sources

Chicago Tribune, January 18, 1998; February 19, 1998; June 7, 1998; June 20, 1999.
New York Times, February 19, 1998.
Newsweek, July 5, 1999, pp. 26-27.

—Carol Brennan

Earle Hyman

1926—

Actor

In the United States, Earle Hyman is probably best known for his role as Russell Huxtable, the tall, kindly, and often wise father of Bill Cosby's character on *The Cosby Show*. However, among his fellow actors, his reputation rests upon a solid string of roles in classical theater, especially from the plays of William Shakespeare and Henrik Ibsen. Also, although few of Hyman's fans in the United States are aware of it, he is a popular and highly regarded actor in Norway, where he often performs roles in Norwegian.

Shakespearean Internship

Hyman has been playing roles in Shakespearean plays since 1951. Owen Dodson, a playwright and chair of the drama department at Howard University in Washington, D.C., was also a friend of Hyman's family. One day when Dodson was visiting, Hyman played a recording of actors reading selections from *Hamlet* for him. Three of the actors were well-known Shakespearean actors; the fourth voice was Hyman's recording of himself. Impressed, Dodson cast Hyman in the title role of a production of Hamlet at Howard in 1951. He was only 25-years-old at the time. The production was so well received that 500 people had to be turned away on the last night of the show.

Two years later in 1953, Hyman was cast as the lead in a New York production of another Shakespearean tragedy, *Othello*. As a result of that performance, he was invited to join a Shakespeare repertory company that was just being formed, the American Shakespeare Festival in Stratford, Connecticut. During five seasons with the company, Hyman performed a wide variety of Shakespearean roles.

Hyman is more than a Shakespearean actor, yet his experiences playing such a wide range of roles in so many Shakespearean plays in the first stage of his career were a significant part of his acting apprenticeship. His love of Shakespeare began when he was 11-years-old. Hyman's family had moved to Brooklyn from North Carolina during the Depression. However, like many African American children who lived in the North, he spent his summers down South. In an interview with Tony Brown for the *Knight-Ridder\Tribune News Service,* Hyman recalled that in the summer of 1937, the library in his parents' hometown of Warrenton, North Carolina, was opened to African Americans for the first time. He went in, and asked for the biggest book they had. The librarian gave him the complete works of Shakespeare. On summer afternoons, when there was nothing better to do, Hyman read Shakespeare. "I was too young to really understand it," he told Brown, "but it blew my mind." In 1993, over 45 years after the summer he discovered Shakespeare, Hyman returned to North Carolina to play the role of King Lear at the age of 66. He is the only African American actor to have played all four of the major Shakespearean tragic leads: Lear, Macbeth, Hamlet, and Othello.

Hyman's passion for the theater may have begun with Shakespeare, but it was the works of the 19th century Norwegian playwright, Henrik Ibsen, that had the

At a Glance . . .

Born October 11, 1926 in Rocky Mount, NC; son of Zachariah Hyman and Maria Lilly Hyman; moved to Brooklyn, NY at the age of six. *Education:* Studied acting at the American Theater Wing with Eva Le Gallienne and at the Actor's Studio.

Career: Was invited to join the American Negro Theater company in 1943; appeared as Rudolph in the American Negro Theater's performance of *Anna Lucasta* and travelled to London with this production, 1947; associated with the American Shakespeare Festival and played many roles including that of Othello, 1955-60; has played all of the major Shakespearean tragic leads: Hamlet, Othello, Macbeth, and King Lear; performed in *Driving Miss Daisy* both on Broadway and in Denmark and Sweden; acted frequently in Denmark and Sweden, including playing the lead in *The Emperor Jones* and Sam Semola in the premier of Athol Fugard's *Master Howard and the Boys* in Oslo; has appeared on numerous soap operas; played the role of Russell Huxtable on *The Cosby Show,*1984-92.

Honors: Nominated for a Tony award for his role in Edward Albee's *The Lady from Dubuque,* in 1979; won an ACE award for his work in a film production of *Long Day's Journey into Night,* 1983; won the Norwegian State Award for best actor for his role in *The Emperor Jones,* 1984; nominated for an Emmy for his role as Russell Huxtable on *The Cosby Show;* awarded the St. Olav Medal in Norway for his three decades of performing on the Norwegian stage, 1988.

Addresses: *Home*—Warrenton, NC. *Agent*—Henderson Hogan Talent Agency, 850 Seventh Avenue, New York, NY, 10019.

greatest impact on his career. The first play that Hyman saw was Ibsen's *The Ghosts.* When he was 13, his mother gave him a choice of going to see *The Wizard of Oz* at a local movie theater, or going to see a production of *The Ghosts* at the Brighton Beach Theater. He chose the play. It was that experience that inspired Hyman to become an actor. His teachers at Franklin K. Lane High School in Brooklyn encouraged his interest in the theatre. By the time he was 15, Hyman landed his first role when he performed in a radio series about African American history with actor

Paul Robeson. When he graduated from high school, Hyman was offered a prize to attend Columbia College and study in their drama school. However, he decided to try acting on a full-time basis.

Robeson and others asked Hyman to join a new company, The American Negro Theatre in Harlem. His third role with the company was the part of Rudolph in *Anna Lucasta.* The play became a solid hit, and eventually moved from Harlem to Broadway. When the cast traveled to London to perform the play, Hyman, then only 21-years-old, accompanied them. His role in Anna Lucasta firmly established his acting career.

A Passion for Ibsen and Norway

Hyman continued to be fascinated by the works of Ibsen. He began studying Norwegian, teaching himself how to read and write it so that he could read Ibsen in the original language. To learn more about his favorite playwright, Hyman decided to visit Norway in 1957. He contacted Ibsen's grandson and his wife, and arranged to visit them. On that visit, Ibsen's grandson introduced him to many people in the Norwegian theatre world, and Hyman fell in love with the landscape of Norway.

In 1962, when he was appearing in an American production of *Othello,* a friend contacted Hyman and asked him to consider playing Othello in a Norwegian production. He initially refused because he didn't feel that he had a command of the Norwegian language. However, he began reading the play in Norwegian during his tour, and, one day during rehearsal, his fellow actors fell silent. They told Hyman that he had just recited some of his lines in Norwegian. He contacted the Norwegian company, and told them he would perform as Othello.

For Hyman, the Norwegian production of *Othello* was the beginning of a long association with the Scandinavian theater, and with Norway as well. During the play's run, he fell in love with the actress who played Desdemona, and began a 26-year romance with her. He also began to be invited to audition for other roles in the Norwegian theater. Soon, Hyman had a thriving career on both sides of the Atlantic. He would often spend half a year performing in Norway, sometimes performing in English and sometimes in Norwegian, and then spend the rest of the year performing in the United States. He played the lead in Eugene O'Neill's *The Emperor Jones* at the Royal Theatre in Stockholm at the request of its artistic director, Ingmar Bergman. In the early 1990's, Hyman performed in *Driving Miss Daisy* in Danish, a language that is similar to Norwegian. In 1988, he read Ibsen onstage in Norwegian for the first time.

In recognition of his distinguished acting career on the

Norwegian stage, the king of Norway awarded Hyman with the St. Olav Medal in 1988. This is the highest civilian honor that a foreigner can be awarded in Norway. Hyman feels equally at home in both the United States and Norway. While he owns his family's old house in Warrenton, North Carolina, he also owns a house in a small village on the west coast of Norway, and has spoken of retiring there.

Hyman's command of the Norwegian language has opened the door to many roles, including roles that had not been written for African Americans. Like many actors of his era, Hyman's career has been played out against the backdrop of segregation and the civil rights movement in the United States. In the early stages of his career, he performed mostly with all-African American productions or in roles written exclusively for African American actors. Beginning in the late 1950s, theater companies in the United States began to experiment with non-traditional casting, in which actors are placed in roles according to their suitability for the role, without regard to race. When he was in rehearsal for the role of Colonel Pickering in a production of George Bernard Shaw's *Pygmalion* (a character that could not have been black historically), Hyman commented to a *New York Times* reporter that non-traditional casting was much more widely accepted in the European theater. For example, when he played the part of a Norwegian bishop in a play in Norway, no one was concerned that his race would interfere with the audience's experience of his interpretation of the part. Non-traditional casting occurred in the United States, but it continued to be a source of controversy. In the same article, Hyman stated, "I'm still saying that all roles should be made available to all actors of talent, regardless of race. Why should I be deprived of seeing a great black actress play Hedda Gabler?"

Starred as Russell Huxtable

While Hyman's major roles have been on the stage, he has also worked consistently in film and on television. He has appeared in hundreds of soap operas including *Love of Life,* and *As the World Turns.* He has played the role of Bill Cosby's father, Russell Huxtable, on *The Cosby Show* beginning in 1984, and was nominated for an Emmy. During one period, he was filming *The Cosby Show* during the day and then appearing in the two-person play, *Driving Miss Daisy,* in the evening.

While some people grow into their life's work or find it by accident, others like Hyman seem attracted to one field like a magnet from the very beginning. In an interview with David Black at the New School in New York, Hyman related the passion he feels for the theater. Of his career in theater, he remarked, "I cannot remember when I didn't want this life of illuminated emotion, this other world, this magic."

Sources

Books

Black, David. *The Magic of Theater,* Macmillan, 1993, pp. 159-175.
Hill, Errol. *Shakespeare in Sable,* University of Massachusetts Press, 1984.
Mapp, Edward. *Directory of Blacks in the Performing Arts,* Scarecrow Press, 1978.

Periodicals

Chicago Tribune, May 5, 1988, p. 17H; August 16, 1990, p. 15C.
Knight-Ridder\Tribune News Service, Sept 1, 1993, p. 1901K7115
New York Times, March 24, 1991, sec. 2, p. 5

Other

Additional information for this profile was obtained from Henderson Hogan Talent Agency.

—Rory Donnelly

Ronald Isley

1941—

Singer, composer

Singer\composer Ronald Isley has enjoyed a successful career in popular music for more than 40 years. As lead singer and composer for the Isley Brothers, Isley recorded a long string of hits including "Shout," "This Old Heart of Mine" and "It's Your Thing." A writer for *iMusic.com.* declared the Isley Brothers "a musical institution whose unmistakable sound has been the major influence for countless superstars of the '80s and '90s." Neil Strauss of the *New York Times* wrote that "In the mercurial world of pop music, surviving (while remaining relevant) can be a form of genius. This makes the Isley Brothers. . .as close to genius as any other pop act." Strauss added that "Ronald Isley is one of pop's most passionate and sensitive singers, wooing and seducing in a soft, liquid falsetto."

Isley was born on May 21, 1941 in Cincinnati, Ohio, the son of Kelly and Sallye Bernice Isley. As a teenager, Ronald and his brothers O'Kelly, Rudolph, and Vernon sang in Cincinnati area gospel choirs. In 1955, the brothers formed their own quartet. After the death of Vernon in a bicycle accident, the Isley brothers stopped performing for a year or so and then revived their act as a pop trio. The Isley Brothers moved to the New York City area in 1957 and made their first recording,

the doo-wop styled "The Cow Jumped Over the Moon," for the Teenage label. They also recorded a few singles for the Gone label. While their recordings didn't sell, the Isleys earned a reputation as exciting live performers in engagements at African American oriented venues such as the Apollo Theatre in Harlem and the Regal Theatre in Chicago. An appearance at Washington, D.C.'s Howard Theatre was attended by RCA Records producer Howard Bloom, who signed the brothers to a contract.

Scored R&B Hits

The Isley Brothers' first RCA release, "Turn to Me," went nowhere but their second release, "Shout," was a huge hit on the rhythm and blues chart in 1959. Written by Isley and his brothers, the song was inspired by a line in the Jackie Wilson song "Lonely Teardrops." The Isleys' version of "Shout" was only a minor hit on the pop charts, but a successful cover version by Joey Dee and the Starlighters in 1962 made the song familiar to a wider audience. The money brought in by "Shout" enabled the Isleys to move the rest of their family, including two younger brothers Ernie and Marvin, from Cincinnati to the New Jersey suburbs of New York City. "I was only seven years old when 'Shout' came out," Ernie Isley told Geoffrey Himes of the *Washington Post,* "but I remember it always got the audience up and dancing – and it still does. Everybody has an emotional connection to that song, because it contains everything rock 'n' roll is about – the energy, the freedom, the abandon."

After "Shout," the Isleys released several records that didn't make a dent on the charts. For a time, it seemed that the Isley Brothers were just another of the "one-hit wonders" that were so common in the music world of the late 1950s and early 1960s. The brothers left RCA for Atlantic Records, where they worked with the songwriting\producing team of Jerry Leiber and Mike Stoller. However, they still didn't find success. The situation improved when they moved to Wand Records in 1962. Producer Bert Berns had the Isley Brothers record a cover version of his own composition, "Twist and Shout," a song that had been recorded in the previous year by the Top Notes. A catchy blend of the raw energy of "Shout" with the Twist dance craze, "Twist and Shout" took the Isley Brothers back to the top of the R&B chart and was a much bigger hit on the pop chart than "Shout" had been. The song was also a hit in Britain, where a version was recorded by the Beatles. "I thought the Beatles version of 'T & S' kinda knocked us out. I liked their version," Ronald said in an interview with America Online.

Again, the Isley Brothers couldn't release a follow up hit to "Twist and Shout." In 1963, they left Wand for United Artists Records. After the failure of their initial United Artists single, "Tango," the Isleys were instructed by company executives to record a ridiculously exploitative song called "Surf and Shout" that also failed. Isley did not regard this early adversity as a negative experience. "[It was] a lot of fun. We learned something from every label we were on," he told America Online.

Founded a Record Label

In 1964 the Isley Brothers started their own label, T-Neck, taking the name from the family's adopted hometown of Teaneck, New Jersey. Ronald served as T-Neck's president, while his brothers Rudolph and O'Kelly were vice president and treasurer respectively. The Isley Brothers first T-Neck release, "Testify," featured the playing of a young and unknown guitarist named Jimi Hendrix. At the time, Hendrix was going by the name of Jimmy James and was part of the Isleys' touring band. When their T-Neck work quickly proved unprofitable, the Isley Brothers re-signed with Atlantic Records. However, they were dropped by the company a year later.

Seeing promise in the Isley Brothers, Motown Records president Berry Gordy signed them to his Tamla label. At Tamla, the Isleys worked with the song writing\producing trio of Holland, Dozier, and Holland. This trio was a major force behind a number of Motown sensations, including the Supremes. Although the Isleys' exuberant, gospel-tinged style didn't quite mesh with Motown's smooth style, the collaboration did produce a major hit, "This Old Heart of Mine," in 1966. The Isleys spent most of the late 1960s in Britain, where they were somewhat more popular than in the United States. The Isley Brothers had several hits in Britain, including "I Guess I'll Always Love You" and "Behind a Painted Smile," which were released on Tamla.

In 1969, the Isleys turned their attention back to the United States and revived their T-Neck label (in conjunction with Buddah Records) so that they would be able to record and produce their own material. When asked by America Online to name important influences on his music, Isley replied, "Several people; Clyde McFadder, Sam Cooke. . .Jackie Wilson, and the other would be Billy Ward of the Dominos." He added that his inspiration for lyrics comes "from experience. It's from the street."

Free to Experiment

The Isley Brothers' first T-Neck release, "It's Your Thing," soared to number two on the pop charts and earned a Grammy Award for best R&B vocal by a duo or group. Following the success of "It's Your Thing," the Isleys expanded the group to include younger brothers Ernie and Marvin and brother-in-law Chris Jasper. The younger members brought in a hard rock, guitar-based sound influenced by Jimi Hendrix.

By having their own record label, the Isley Brothers were free to experiment. In addition to their own songs, the Isleys recorded cover versions of material written by white singer\songwriters. Their recording of Stephen Stills' "Love the One You're With" was a hit in 1971. In 1974, the Isley Brothers reached number 16 on the British pop charts with a version of Seals and Crofts' "Summer Breeze." "We turned a lot of heads around in those days," Ernie Isley told Himes. "We started our own record label when Black acts didn't do that; we recorded songs by Stephen Stills, Bob Dylan, and Carole King when Black artists didn't do that; we played our own instruments when Black groups didn't do that. When you bought an Isley Brothers album, the people on the cover made all the sounds on the record inside."

After signing with Columbia Records, the Isley Brothers reached the height of their popularity during the 1970s. In addition to successful singles including "Who's That Lady?" in 1973 and "Fight the Power" in 1975, they had five platinum albums: *3 + 3* (1973), *The Heat is On* (1975), *Harvest for the World* (1976), *Go for Your Gun* (1977), and *Showdown* (1978). "While the band didn't get the massive publicity exposure of many rock and soul headliners, its exciting live performances and the quality of most of its recordings retained a strong hold on a large segment of the pop audience," wrote Irwin Stambler in *The Encyclopedia of Pop, Rock, and Soul.*

Success continued for the Isley Brothers into the early 1980s when they scored a top 40 pop single "Don't Say Goodnight" from the platinum selling album, *Go All the Way.* Their album, *Between the Sheets,* went gold in 1983. In 1984, the three younger members left the group to form Isley-Jasper-Isley. Ronald, Rudolph, and O'Kelly returned to being a trio and signed with Warner Bros. Records. Tragedy struck the Isleys when O'Kelly died of a heart attack just weeks after their first Warner Bros. album, *Masterpiece,* was released in 1986. The following year, Ronald and Rudolph recorded the album *Smooth Sailin',* which included the tribute song to O'Kelly, "Send a Message." The album also brought Ronald to the forefront as a solo artist.

On *Smooth Sailin',* Ronald worked closely with singer\composer\producer Angela Winbush. Winbush also collaborated on the Isley Brothers 1989 album *Spend the Night,* which was essentially a solo album for Ronald. The title cut from *Spend the Night* became a major R&B hit. In 1993, Ronald married Winbush. "We were friends first, then he became my manager. We developed a real strong relationship," Winbush told *Jet.*

In the 1990s, Rudolph Isley left performing to become a minister, and Ronald reformed the Isley Brothers with his younger brothers Ernie and Marvin. Their 1996 album, *Mission to Please,* gave the Isley Brothers their first gold record in more than a decade. Three songs on the album, including the hit single "Let's Lay Together," were produced and co-written by R. Kelly, who credits the Isley Brothers as a major influence on his musical style. Kelly happened to be working on an album of his own at the same time he was working with the Isley Brothers, and he asked Ronald to contribute vocals to the album's song "Low Down." He then cast Isley as the gangster-like character, Mr. Biggs, in the "Low Down" video. Isley said of Kelly to America Online, "He's like a son. We're best friends. We have so much to do futurally, that's covering music and movies."

Throughout most of his career, Isley has been plagued by poor financial management. In 1997, after being handed a 5 million bill for back taxes owed to the Internal Revenue Service, he declared bankruptcy. In February of 2000, after lengthy legal proceedings, Isley's assets, including royalties to his musical compositions, were purchased by financier David Pullman. Under the agreement, 15 and 20 year bonds backed by Isley's share of the royalty income would be sold by Pullman. At the end of the bonds' term, the royalty income will revert back to Isley or his heirs.

Isley, whose T-Neck label is now associated with Island Records, continues to perform with his brothers Ernie and Marvin. He often incorporates the Mr. Biggs character into stage shows. In a review of a performance at Washington, D.C.'s Constitution Hall, Esther Iverem of the *Washington Post* wrote, "Mr. Biggs is just an entertaining celluloid wrapping, one that gets mucked up as soon as Isley pours on his hot chocolate tenor and a falsetto that trails to a whisper. The show fused slick '90s marketing and '70 showmanship. . .Mr. Biggs is a powerful image that draws young fans attracted to wealth and power and older fans who simply like to see a man dressing sharp."

As he approaches 60 years of age, Isley shows no signs of slowing down. He told *iMusic.com* – "We have been very blessed with the opportunity of making music for many years but the truth is, we haven't even scratched the surface yet." That's great news for the many fans of the Isley Brothers in the United States and abroad.

Sources

Books

Hardy, Phil and Dave Laing. *The Faber Companion to 20th-Century Popular Music.* London: Faber and Faber, 1990.

Rees, Dafydd and Luke Crampton. *Encyclopedia of Rock Stars.* New York: DK Publishing, 1996.

Stambler, Irwin. *Encyclopedia of Pop, Rock and Soul.*

New York: St. Martin's, 1989.

Periodicals

Billboard, June 27, 1992, p. 13
Jet, May 23, 1994, p. 37; July 19, 1993, p. 38.
New York Times, July 29, 1996, p. C16
Washington Post, March 10, 1996, p. G1; September 20, 1996, p. N14; September 23, 1996, p. D7; July 30, 1999, p. N16; February 22, 2000, p. C1; February 24, 2000, p. C12.

Other

Additional information for this profile was obtained from iMusic Index (www.imusic.com), Rock and Roll Hall of Fame (www.rockhall.com), Yahoo! Music (http:\\musicfinder.yahoo.com), and America Online, Inc.

—Mary Kalfatovic

Fred James Jackson

1950—

Educator, poet, publisher

Fred James Jackson admits that he has taken "a lot of knocks" in life. Rather than allowing them to beat him down, he has formidably risen above adversity. Confident, articulate, and self-assured, he is clear about who he is and what he hopes to accomplish during his lifetime.

Born in High Point, North Carolina on June 11, 1950, Fred James Jackson was raised by a single mother. Perpetually battling with alcoholism, his mother shuffled herself and young son between many men and numerous homes. Jackson also witnessed his mother being abused by many of these men as well. A victim of her lifestyle, Jackson's mother died at the age of 36 when Jackson was only 11 years old. After stints in several foster homes and time spent with an abusive grandfather, Jackson found himself homeless by the age of 14.

With seemingly no escape from this bleak existence, Jackson happened to walk into the local YMCA one afternoon. As he recounted in an interview with *Contemporary Black Biography,* he found himself talking with Mr. Webb, a retired insurance executive who worked in the basket room. He explained his situation to Mr. Webb, including the fact that he did not even have 25 cents to his name. Mr. Webb immediately marched upstairs to the executive director's office, and when he returned Jackson found himself with room, board, and a job as assistant in the basket room.

While at the YMCA, Jackson's counselor, Mr. Thomas, befriended him and encouraged him to return to

school. At Thomas' insistence and with his financial assistance, Jackson entered the newly-formed Job Corps in 1966. Not only did the Job Corps symbolize, as he told *CBB,* "the first comfort zone" he had ever had, but it was also the first time that he heard himself referred to as "Jackson." He had previously thought his last name was Walker, his mother's maiden name. While in the Job Corps, Jackson learned his first trade, business and retailing, was introduced to tennis, and ran track. His track team, in fact, was so successful that they would have broken the NCAA record had they competed at the collegiate level. At the age of 17, Jackson joined the Army, earned the rank of drill sergeant, and was sent to Vietnam. As he told Bob Sylva of the *Sacramento Bee,* "The first home I ever had was in the Army." While serving in the Army, Jackson received four honorable discharges, numerous decorations, and a college degree.

Developed Creative Talents

Jackson remained in the Army until 1987. Towards the end of his military career, he began to focus more intensively on his creative talents, and in particular on singing and song-writing. While his life story may have been dark and difficult, Jackson worked hard to ensure that his life was not reflected in his art. Instead, he wrote about love. Recording under the name of Freddie James (there was already a performer by the name of Freddie Jackson), Jackson predicted in *The Observer* in 1986 that he "intended to challenge anybody up there who they [the music industry] say is Number 1."

At a Glance . . .

Born Fred James Jackson on June 11, 1950 in High Point, NC; mother Mary Jane Walker; divorced; children: Marrian Ann, Fred James Jr., Patrice M. *Education:* BA, Religious Education, Shreveport, 1977; attended, University of Maryland; certificate, Armed Forces Institute; attending, University of San Diego; *Military service:* United States Army, 1967-87.

Career: Veterans Affairs Officer, Boulder College, 1978-79; employment specialist PSE-3; procurement manager, McClellan Air Force Base Logistic Center, United States AirForce, 1975-87; executive director, The Community Drug Intervention Network Inc., 1987-92; procurement officer, United States Department of Agriculture, 1992-94; English teacher,department chair, Grant Joint Union School District, 1994-96; President, CEO, Black Rose Enterprise Publishing, 1986-; teacher, computer education\ business, Sacramento Unified School District\Hiram Johnson High School, 1995-; director, Hole in One Junior Gulf Club; recording artist under the name Freddie James.

Selected memberships: National Education Association, 1994-; California Teachers Association, 1994-; National Association of Black School Educators, 1995-; peer counseling leadership coordinator, tobacco drug and alcohol program coordinator, State of California, 1996-.

Selected awards: Vietnam Cross of Gallantry, 1969; two presidential citations, four honorable discharges; Senate Certificate of Recognition, State of California Assembly, 1996.

Addresses: *Office*—Black Rose Enterprise Publishing, PO Box 5283, Sacramento, CA 95817.

As he further explained, "I have that charisma in my voice, that draw, that sweetness, that romance that makes the ladies' toes tingle." Jackson's debut single was released in 1987. In addition to recording albums, he also composed the music for an anti-drug video entitled The Drug Busters.

As a single father of three children, including one suffering from cerebral palsy, parenting responsibilities eventually compelled Jackson to terminate his music career. He then turned to poetry writing, a natural extension of songwriting, as an outlet for his creative energies. In 1987 he founded Black Rose Enterprise, a publishing house dedicated to releasing his work. Since that time he has not only written and published numerous educational books, board games, and tapes for children, including *Soul Pha Bet A-Z, Catfish and Jabo,* and *Brain Fitness,* but he has also received three Pulitzer Prize nominations for his collections of poetry.

Self-described as the "Prince of Poetry," Jackson's work reveals a realistic and often harsh portrayal of the African American struggle for survival. For example, his volume entitled *They Call Me Names,* published in 1994, "has to do with a people," he told *The Observer,* "not so much what they call me, but who we are as a people." Another work, *Lighting – Master of the Blues,* has been described in *The Observer* as "an emotional travel through the life of a once renowned blues musician whose illiteracy caused him to fall from fame into obscurity." This book, Jackson told Stacy Bush of *The Observer,* was inspired by the neighborhood of his youth. "There were so many African Americans who had achieved great heights who were uneducated in terms of having the ability to read or write, but still obtained excellence in their particular area." In 1996, Jackson's work reached a mainstream audience when the J.C. Penney store in Florin, California displayed an exhibit of his works. Entitled "Poetry of a Man," the exhibit included both his poetry and his illustrations. As assistant store manager Eli Cain, Jr. explained to *The Observer,* "Mr. Jackson is a master craftsman . . .[He] has uniquely combined verse and art in a way that each supports itself. It's different, beautiful and very marketable."

Reinforced Commitment to Youth

While Jackson's journeys have taken him from the Army to the recording studio and printing press, his real calling, he believes, is to help the youth of his community. Possessing boundless energy, ideas, and ambitions, Jackson has channeled these powers into a variety of avenues aimed at instilling success in these children. As he recounted to *The Observer,* "Kids need to see success to be a success, they need to see it in their teachers, neighbors and in the community." Jackson himself wants to provide such a model as a way, he told *The Observer,* "of giving back to the people who helped me become a survivor." Towards this end, Jackson created the Community Drug Intervention Network in 1987. As he recounted to *CBB,* he wanted to "stop gang banging and focus on education." Through this network, Jackson offered self-esteem and motivational seminars for youths. Events such as the "Youth Slamma Jamma" basketball dunk and three-point shoot contest, featuring former Harlem Globetrotter Curly Neal, and a "Tribute to Jazz," which spotlighted talented young musicians, exemplified Jackson's diverse programming blending athletics and academics.

In 1994, after an 18-month stint as a procurement officer with the United States Department of Agriculture, Jackson took his efforts directly into the classroom and became a teacher. That he became a teacher is not surprising, for, as he told Sylva, "nobody cared about me. Then somebody did care. My teachers." Forever a drill sergeant, Jackson commands respect in the classroom. In addition to teaching business technology, computer applications, and physical education at Hiram W. Johnson High School in Sacramento, California, he has worked with at-risk children and those in in-house suspension programs.

Building upon the work he began with the Community Drug Intervention Network, Jackson founded the Hole-in-One Junior Golf Club in March of 1998. It is here that the force of Jackson's energies can be felt most directly. Jackson was exposed to golf as a child, earning extra money shining shoes and eventually caddying for golfers. He further refined his golf skills while in the Army. As its name suggests, the club strives to expose students to the game of golf. Club members view golf instructional videos, learn golf etiquette, and take practice swings at the Family Center driving range. Recruited while in elementary school, qualified students remain in the program through high school. In the spring of 2000, for instance, the club leadership selected 18 girls and 21 boys from the third grade, and there were 22 members enrolled at the high school level.

Despite its name, the Hole-in-One Club is targeted primarily at improving and maintaining strong academic standards and discipline for its participants. As stated in its promotional materials, the club's philosophy emphasizes that "success does not come by accident but by Preparation, Dedication, and Hard Work." Provided with peer tutoring, access to computerized remedial programs, and academic and social mentors and role models, members must maintain a 3.0 grade point average. The organization further promotes nonviolence and an anti-drug and alcohol policy. In an interview with Ariel Ruiz of *The Connection*, Jackson fully defined the mission of his club: "Ignorance is the enemy. And we are on a mission to reach out to kids and help them become successful in life . . .[F]rom golf, children learn the sport and the discipline to become better individuals." Ultimately, as Carla Rios commented, Jackson "not only visualizes the potential in young students but puts all of his effort in helping the students visualize it for themselves."

Utilized Own Past as Motivator

Clearly, it is not the game of golf per se that drives Jackson. In his interview with *CBB*, Jackson is poignantly clear as to the motivation behind his involvement in programs such as the Hole-in-One Club: "I am

led to do it, I am happy to do it. I come from it so I understand it, and I understand the kids. I was homeless, so I understand what it is like to be homeless. I was motherless so I understand what it is like to be motherless. I was fatherless so I understand what it is like to be fatherless. I slept on sidewalks so I understand it. I slept on porches where roaches and mice were crawling all around me, I understand it. I've had leeches, I've had boils, I've had tatter, I understand it. I've been in a foster home, I know all about that. I understand these kids . . .They say that the kid can't learn; well did you try to teach him? . . .My calling is to do what I do."

Jackson claims that it was anger that pulled him through the most debilitating times of his childhood. Anger, he told *CBB*, is a negative. Thus, "you've got to find something positive: being an achiever. Make those people who made you angry stand up and look at you in a positive way. Make that your footstool. I am always getting even with my grandfather, with my mom, with my stepdad . . . .I turned anger into a positive, into success . . .I've taken nothing and made something out of it." Such conversations lead Jackson to examine the meaning of success itself. As he remarked to *CBB*, "You have to come from a place to go to a place. Once you get there, that's success. Whatever destination you reach, wherever you stop, that's success. Because you didn't have it at the beginning. I've never forgotten where I came from."

Confident of where he is today, Jackson remains unsure of what the future may hold. As he knows so well from his singing and writing experiences, "It's about opportunities," he reminded *CBB*. "Somebody has to give you a break . . .If you get the right breaks, you are set for life." While some have suggested candidacies for state assembly or state senator, Jackson told *CBB* that he "won't know until it's time." He does dream about performing on stage with poet Maya Angelou, the person he reveres more than anyone else – and the national recognition such a spotlight would imply. Until then, Jackson told *CBB*, he will continue to "keep pushing these kids, keep doing what I am doing with the Hole-in-One, keep writing my books, and working on my cars, and taking care of my kids . . .It's all about the kids. It's not about me . . .I'm not looking for anything. Whatever comes, I'll share with those less fortunate than myself . . . .No big 'I's, not little 'you's. I'm just a man . . .The only thing in a name is what you want it to be. Fred James Jackson is just a name. It's my works that count."

Selected writings

Passion in Black, Black Rose Enterprise, 1992.
They Call Me Names, Black Rose Enterprise, 1994.
Lightning, Master of the Blues, Black Rose Enterprise, 1994.
One Race, Many Cultures 2, Black Rose Enterprise, 1996.

Sources

Periodicals

Observer, December 9-15, 1983, p. E-2; May 29-June 5, 1986, p. E-2; March 3-9, 1988, p. E-4; November 22-28, 1990, p. A-5; January 13- 19, 1994, p. B-1; October 6-12, 1994; May 11-17, 1995, p. E-2; April 24-30, 1997, p. A-5.

Sacramento Bee, November 4, 1999.
Sacramento Connection, Volume 1, No. 12, 1999.

Other

Additional information for this profile was obtained from an interview with *Contemporary Black Biography,* March 2000; and from promotional materials from the Hole-in-One Junior Golf Club.

—Lisa S. Weitzman

Millie Jackson

1944—

Rhythm and blues singer

Long before contemporary rap albums carried parental-advisory warnings, Millie Jackson's highly charged, sexually explicit soul records bore the admonishment "For Mature Audiences Only." Her mid-song, minutes-long tales of heartache and betrayal, usually delivered in rather frank language, gave Jackson a cult following for her originality, but also made her records all but unplayable on the radio. Despite these drawbacks, Jackson's popularity has endured well into a third decade, and music writers have deemed her the ultimate godmother to pop music's tough-talking rap divas of the 1990s.

Jackson was born in 1944 in Thompson, Georgia, and brought up in her grandparents' home. It was a devout household, and she attended church services as often as six days a week at times. When she was 15, she moved to New Jersey, where her father lived, and found work at Schrafft's, a famous New York City luncheon counter. She began her singing career one night on a dare at a Harlem nightclub, joining a band on stage at the urging of her friends. Her first paid engagement came in 1964 at a Hoboken, New Jersey venue; only in 1967 did she quit Schrafft's and embark on her first real concert tour. Life on the road proved to be difficult and unprofitable. Jackson returned to New York and took a clerical job in the garment district, although she continued to sing at night.

Single Parent

At this point in her life, Jackson became pregnant and married the father of her daughter. It was a short-lived union, however, and neither motherhood nor the romantic setback dampened her enthusiasm for performing. She cut her first single in 1970, and soon gained enough minor attention to win a record contract with Polydor, which released her debut, *Millie Jackson,* in 1972. The work offered standard soul fare, and a *Billboard* critic termed it "a top-drawer debut." Other reviewers compared her with Roberta Flack and Aretha Franklin, among others. During the first years of Jackson's career, record-company executives attempted to groom her as the next Diana Ross.

Two of Jackson's songs from the early 1970s climbed onto the Top Ten on the R&B charts. "Ask Me What You Want" and "My Man a Sweet Man." She had another hit with "Hurts So Good," a track that was included in the soundtrack to Cleopatra Jones, a blaxploitation film. Her most notable success came with the single "(If Loving You Is Wrong) I Don't Want to Be

At a Glance . . .

Born July 15, 1944, in Thompson, GA; married once, late 1960s; children: Neisha, Jerroll.

Career: Made professional debut in New Jersey nightclub, 1964; released self-titled debut, 1972; earned several gold records during the 1970s; wrote and starred in two Broadway musicals, late 1990s.

Awards: Nominated for Grammy Award as best female R&B vocalist, 1974, for" (If Loving You Is Wrong) I Don't Want to Be Right."

Addresses: *Office*—c\o BMG Records, 1540 Broadway, New York, NY10036.

Right," which earned her a Grammy nomination in the best female R&B vocalist category in 1974.

The Muscle Shoals Sound

Buoyed by this success, Jackson had enough leverage to convince her management company to let her co-produce some of her own tracks. The 1974 album, *Caught Up,* marked this new musical direction, as well as the start of collaborative efforts with a group of musicians from the famed Muscle Shoals Studios. Jackson's records became paeans to soured romance, mini-dramas about lust, infidelity, and betrayal that occurred mid-song. She had already done such monologues for several years during her live shows. "When I started singing, in order to be a good female vocalist you had to hit a higher note than the other female vocalists, and with this low voice of mine, there weren't too many high notes to hit," she told *Boston Globe* writer Jim Sullivan. "So I used to talk my way out of it and I found the audience liked me better talking than they did singing." Reviewers used the word "rap" to describe her style as early as 1976.

This approach became Jackson's signature style, and began earning her legions of devoted fans. Nearly all of her subsequent albums continued in this vein. Because Jackson's songs dealt with frank topics, and used words that were prohibited by Federal Communications Commission (FCC) guidelines, few of her songs received significant air time on the radio. Despite this drawback, several of Jackson's albums went on to earn her gold records, and she became known as the "Richard Pryor of Soul" for her free use of profanity. Even the usually recalcitrant legion of music critics seemed to appreciate Jackson's talents. In a 1978 review of Jackson's album, *Get It Out 'Cha System,* a *Billboard* review termed it

"ablaze with wit and wisdom, musical and lyrical."

Rejected Disco Slot

Jackson's stage shows became legendary events. She interacted with the audience, taunted the men, and brought fans into the act itself. When disco emerged as a credible new musical genre in the mid-1970s, critics began comparing a new star, Donna Summer, to Jackson, especially after Summer enjoyed great success with the hits "I Feel Love" and "Love to Love You Baby." The new, sexually charged atmosphere within music forced record company executives to reassess Jackson's talents, and the changing times also caused Jackson to re-evaluate her own career. "To be perfectly honest with you, I never took this serious until three years ago," she told *Washington Post* writer Jacqueline Trescott in 1980. "My contract was up; I renegotiated. And said, 'I am worth this much money? I better start taking it seriously.'"

Two successful live albums cogently showcased Jackson's unique stage presence and repudiated any efforts to peg her as an overproduced disco queen: *Live and Uncensored* from 1980, which included outtakes from shows at such venues as the Roxy in Los Angeles, and *Live and Outrageous,* released two years later. She continued to write, record, and produce new material every year or so, and even cut a duet with Elton John, "Act of War," that enjoyed modest chart success in Britain in 1985. In 1989, Jackson made her New York stage debut with a musical she co-wrote, *Young Man, Older Woman.* The musical played at the Beacon Theater, and toured elsewhere as well. It also provided the material for an album of the same name. *Young Man, Older Woman* was less a dramatic event than a nightclub act built around a romantic plot, one in which Jackson leaves her no-good husband for a younger man. The show garnered a positive review from the *New York Times*'s Neil Strauss, who compared her voice to that of Tina Turner's and asserted that the musical "proves that Ms. Jackson still has the strength, prurience, humor and taste for the extreme to hold her position as a big sister to most female rappers."

Jackson admitted elsewhere that the impetus for *Young Man, Older Woman* was drawn from real-life experiences, in some cases dating men more than 25 years her junior. She had never remarried after her first match ended in divorce, but did have a second child in the late 1970s. "Let's face it, when you reach my age and you haven't gotten married, chances are if you want to go anywhere, it may be that he is going to be younger," the 53-year-old singer told *Jet* in 1998. "[Men] my age are married, divorced or have so many hangups you don't want to be bothered with them anyway. If you're looking for an escort, he'll probably be younger. I have no problem with it."

Jackson followed the success of her play with *The*

Sequel—It Ain't Over!, which debuted at the Beacon in early 1997. The musical opens with Jackson's wedding to a younger man, a psychiatrist played by Douglas Knyght-Smith. The union quickly disintegrates over the course of several numbers that showcase Jackson's unique vocal talents. She still attracted a cult following, noted Lawrence Van Gelder of the *New York Times,* and still went off into her characteristic monologues during the songs—where "Jackson gives a display of the star power and showmanship that account for the excitement of the fans who turn out."

Jackson's 1999 release, *Between the Sheets,* was a compilation of her most memorable tracks, including "Hurts So Good" and "(If Loving You Is Wrong) I Don't Want to Be Right." "There's only one Millie Jackson, and she's here in all her fabulous glory," declared *Billboard* reviewer Michael Paoletta. For a performer who had never courted stardom, Jackson was undoubtedly pleased that she had achieved a place in music history. "This is an industry where you don't have ambitions," she told Trescott in the *Washington Post* interview in 1980. "The public will tell you where you are going for the next three or four years. You just say, I hope you will be nice and remember to take me somewhere."

Selected discography

Millie Jackson, Spring\Polydor, 1972.
It Hurts So Good, 1973.
Caught Up, 1974.
Soul Believer, 1974.
Still Caught Up, 1975.
Free and In Love, Spring\Polydor, 1976.
Best of Millie Jackson, 1976.
Lovingly Yours, 1977.
Get It Out 'Cha System, Spring\Polydor, 1978.

A Moment's Pleasure, 1979.
(With Isaac Hayes) *Royal Rappings,* 1979.
Live and Uncensored, 1980.
For Men Only, Spring\Polydor, 1980.
Just a Lil' Bit Country, 1981.
Live and Outrageous, 1982.
Hard Times, 1982.
E.S.P. (Extra Sexual Persuasion), 1984.
An Imitation of Love, 1986.
The Tide Is Turning, 1988.
Back to the S, 1989.
Young Man, Older Woman, 1992.
Totally Unrestricted! The Millie Jackson Anthology, Rhino, 1998.
Between the Sheets, Buddha\BMG, 1999.

Sources

Books

Guinness Encyclopedia of Popular Music, edited by Colin Larkin, Guinness Publishing, 1992, p. 1250.

Periodicals

Billboard, September 9, 1972; April 24, 1976; July 8, 1978; December 8, 1979; June 14, 1980; October 2, 1999, p. 30.
Boston Globe, June 24, 1980.
Jet, March 23, 1998, pp. 14-16.
New York Times, July 20, 1989, p. C19; January 16, 1995, p. C17; February 4, 1997.
Village Voice, January 6, 1998, p. 77.
Washington Post, March 8, 1980, p. B1.

—Carol Brennan

William J. Jefferson

1947—

Congressman

Climbing from a childhood during which he would rise hours before the sun to pick cotton, William Jefferson became Louisiana's first African American representative in the U.S. Congress since the days of Reconstruction in the nineteenth century. A staunch supporter of President Bill Clinton, he was among the most influential of the southern African American Democrats who entered Congress in the 1990s. Jefferson, a survivor of Louisiana's rough-and-tumble politics, ran for governor of the state in 1999. Although he was not elected, his prospects for higher office seemed bright as the new millennium dawned.

William Jennings Jefferson was born in Lake Providence, Louisiana, on March 14, 1947. Lake Providence is in East Carroll Parish, one of the poorest counties in the United States, and Jefferson, the sixth of ten children, grew up in dire poverty. "When I got there, it was already crowded," he told *Emerge* magazine. He was put to work picking cotton at the age of seven, getting up at 3:15 a.m. and often working until midafternoon for a daily wage of three dollars. His father was a handyman who only had a second grade education.

Attended Southern University

Jefferson's mother, though, placed a high value on education, serving for 12 years as president of the local Parent-Teachers' Association. Through her efforts, all 10 Jefferson children attended college. William (familiarly known as Bill) went to Southern University in Baton Rouge, Louisiana, majoring in English and political science and graduating in 1969. He was accepted immediately at Harvard Law School and made short work of that challenging program, receiving his degree in 1972.

After graduating from law school, Jefferson landed a position in eastern Louisiana as a law clerk for U.S. District Judge Alvin J. Rubin. He got his feet wet in politics as a legislative assistant to Democratic U.S. Senator J. Bennett Johnston. However, Jefferson returned to practicing law in 1976, and founded a new firm with several partners. The law firm of Jefferson, Bryan and Gray would become, in time, the largest African American law firm in the southern United States. In the 1970s, Jefferson also served in the U.S. Army Reserves and the Army's Judge Advocate Gen-

At a Glance . . .

Born March 14, 1947, in Lake Providence, LA; son of a handyman; married to Andrea. *Education:* Southern University, Baton Rouge, Louisiana, B.A., 1969; Harvard University, J.D., 1972; Georgetown University, LL.M., 1996. *Military service:* U.S. Army Reserves, 1969-78. Army Judge Advocate Corps, 1975. *Religion:* Baptist.

Career: United States Congressional Representative from Louisiana's Second District. Law clerk, U.S. District Judge Alvin Rubin, 1972-73; legislative aide, U.S. Senator Bennett Johnson, 1973-75; founding partner, law firm of Jefferson, Bryan and Gray, 1975-90; elected to Louisiana State Senate, 1979-90; elected to U.S. House of Representatives, 1990-; served on Ways and Means Committee.

Addresses: *Office*—240 Cannon House Office Building, Washington, DC20515.

eral's Corps.

As African American lawmakers began to make modest inroads into southern state legislatures in the 1970s, Jefferson gravitated back to the political arena. Elected to the Louisiana state senate in 1979, he twice won re-election to four-year terms, and rose to the chairmanship of the Senate's Governmental Affairs Committee. A resident of New Orleans, he twice ran for mayor in that city, losing both times but gaining wider name recognition. His chance for higher office came in 1990, when New Orleans's longtime U.S. House Representative, Lindy Boggs, decided to retire. Louisiana's Second District has boundaries close to those of the predominantly African American city of New Orleans.

Endorsed by New Orleans Mayor

Several of the most prominent names in African American Louisiana politics jumped into the race to succeed Boggs. Jefferson was endorsed by New Orleans mayor Sidney Barthelemy, but he faced staunch competition from Marc Morial, the son of New Orleans's first African American mayor, and later elected mayor of New Orleans himself. Jefferson led narrowly going into a November runoff election, and got his first taste of Louisiana-style campaigning when he was bruised by charges of having defaulted on mortgage loans; his campaign retaliated by publicizing the fact

that Morial was the father of an eight-year-old girl living in Africa's Ivory Coast. Jefferson narrowly won the runoff election, becoming Louisiana's first African American U.S. Representative since Reconstruction.

In Congress, Jefferson has had a notable career in several respects. He was named to a seat on the Ways and Means Committee, the tax-writing body that is probably the most powerful among the various House committees, and has used his position there to benefit African American-owned small businesses. He has taken the lead on the issue of so-called "environmental racism" (a hotly contested issue in Louisiana especially), successfully heading off the construction of a potentially hazardous plastics plant near an African American community. In recent years, Jefferson has raised his voice to protest the "digital divide," the inequity between higher- and lower-income communities in availability of computers and access to the Internet. He has introduced legislation providing for tax breaks that would enable low-income families to purchase computer equipment.

As significant as any of Jefferson's legislative activities, though, was the success he had in breaking into Washington's corridors of power in the 1990s, an era of Democratic control in the White House. Jefferson emerged in 1991 as a strong supporter of Arkansas Governor Bill Clinton in his run for the presidency, and continued to work closely with Clinton on various initiatives throughout the latter's tenure as President. A member of the moderate Democratic Leadership Council, he has avoided some of the government-activist stands taken by other African American Democrats in Congress, tending instead to favor partnerships between the public and private sectors in addressing social problems.

Ran for Governor

As a result of his work with the national Democratic party (he served as Louisiana co-chair for the 1988 and 1992 Democratic presidential campaigns), and of his election to represent the state's largest city, Jefferson's name recognition across Louisiana began to rise. His ambitions toward higher office became clear early on, as he twice considered running for governor (in 1991 and 1995), withdrawing both times, and contemplated a U.S. Senate run in 1996. In 1999, Jefferson jumped into the gubernatorial race once again, challenging incumbent Republican governor Mike Foster. Unlike the African American Democratic candidate who ran in 1995, Jefferson had the support of Louisiana's largely white-dominated Democratic organization.

Although Foster was tainted by the revelation that he had purchased voter mailing lists from Louisiana politician and former Ku Klux Klan leader David Duke, Jefferson largely avoided this negative issue in his own campaign, instead framing the choice in economic terms. "He's on the side of big business," Jefferson was quoted as saying in *Emerge.* "I'm on the side of working families and small entrepreneurs." Jefferson raised an impressive war chest of 2.2 million for the campaign, but his challenge to Foster was blunted by the presence of fringe candidates in the race, including one who went by the name of Messiah and spoke in tongues.

In the October 1999 election, Jefferson came out on the losing end of a 62 to 30 percent margin, with Louisiana's still heavily polarized electorate splitting largely along racial lines. However, the off-year election allowed Jefferson to keep his Congressional seat, and national observers were hardly discounting his future chances. The *Almanac of American Politics* noted that "one statewide campaign might lead to another, with better prospects for success." The father of five daughters, three of whom had already followed him to Harvard, Jefferson at the turn of the century seemed one of the brightest stars in African American politics.

Sources

Books

Barone, Michael, and Grant Ujifusa, *The Almanac of American Politics: 2000.* National Journal, 1999.

Henderson, Ashyia N., and Shirelle Phelps, eds., *Who's Who among African Americans.* 12th ed. Gale, 1999.

Periodicals

Black Enterprise, May 1997, p. 20.
Emerge, October 1999, p. 26.
Jet, October 18, 1999, p. 35.

Other

Additional information for this profile was obtained from http:\\www.house.gov\jefferson\ and http:\\www.nationaljournal.com (book purchase required)

—James M. Manheim

Henry A. Kimbro

1912–1999

Professional baseball player

Although some would say that the old Negro Leagues had no star comparable to the great Ty Cobb, many have always maintained that Cobb's match was Henry "Jumbo" Kimbro. He is often referred to as "the black Ty Cobb." Kimbro was a powerful center fielder with the Elite (pronounced "E-Light") Giants organization, which was based mostly in Baltimore. His career spanned 17 years, from 1937 to 1953. Had he not been considered too old at the time that baseball's color barrier fell in 1947, he undoubtedly would have been signed to the major leagues along with Jackie Robinson, John Wright, Roy Campanella, and others. It was his misfortune and major league baseball's great loss that Kimbro was born a few years too early and played out his career at a time when African American baseball players were relegated to the shadows of the Negro League.

Not "Evil" at All

Henry Allen Kimbro was born February 10, 1912 in Nashville, Tennessee. He grew up living on the outskirts of that city. His education ended after he finished elementary school because the high school he was supposed to attend was too far away. Because of his race, Kimbro was not allowed to attend the high school closer to his home. The fact that he had been effectively denied an education weighed heavily on Kimbro throughout his life. He was always very conscious of his inability to express himself well and, as a result, became a quiet loner. "That [lack of an education] had its effect on me," Kimbro told Brent Kelley in an interview for

the book, *Voices from the Negro Leagues.* "I couldn't say the things I wanted to say because I didn't go to school to learn to do that. It just tore me all to pieces. So I didn't talk too much. Somebody come and want to talk to me about something or other, and if he don't watch himself I'd be gone. I think that's where this 'evilness' come from." The "evil" Kimbro referred to was a label that he had been saddled with early in his baseball career. The combination of his brooding personality and explosive temper led people to consider him "evil." "There was so much I wanted to do and some things I couldn't do," Kimbro told Kelley. "That hurts you. It hurts real bad. People started calling me 'bad man' and 'evil' and all that kind of stuff and it just followed me around my whole baseball time and after that."

Joined the Elite Giants

Kimbro spent his childhood playing sandlot baseball in the many parks that occupied every corner of Nashville. As he grew older, Kimbro eventually played with a semi-pro team in Nashville, but resisted invitations to leave the city to play on other teams. When Kimbro was 24 years old, Jim Taylor, manager of the Chicago American Giants, persuaded him to travel through the South with the team. "I had never been no place," Kimbro recalled for Kelley, "so I said, 'yeah, I'll go.'" The following year, 1937, he began his professional baseball career by joining the Elite Giants organization. The team played in Columbus, Ohio, and then moved to Washington, D.C., for the 1938 season. In 1939,

At a Glance . . .

Born Henry Allen Kimbro, February 10, 1912 in Nashville, TN; died July 11, 1999, in Nashville, TN; married to Erbia Kimbro; children: Phillip, Larry, Harriet, Erbia Maria, Demetria.

Career: Professional baseball player in the Negro Leagues; Columbus Elite Giants,1937; Washington Elite Giants, 1938; Baltimore Elite Giants, 1939-49; New York Black Yankees, 1941; Baltimore Elite Giants, 1942-51; Birmingham Black Barons, 1952-53; retired as player, 1953; manager, Baltimore Elite Giants, c. 1950s; bought Bill's Cab Company, Nashville, c. 1944, served as owner\operator for 22 years; also owned a service station in Nashville for 22 years.

Awards: Member of All-Star East-West game, 1941, 1943, 1944, 1945, 1946, 1947;several times during the 1940s led the league in runs scored, doubles, triples; batting title (.346average) Cuban Winter League, 1947-48, and set league record with 104 hits; inducted into Wall of Fame, Milwaukee, 1998.

the team moved to Baltimore, where they remained until the Negro Leagues largely disbanded in the 1950s. Except for the year 1941, when he was traded to the New York Black Yankees, Kimbro played his entire career with the Elite Giants organization.

Kimbro was a stocky center fielder, 5'8" and 175 pounds. He threw right and batted left. James Riley described him in *The Biographical Encyclopedia of the Negro Baseball Leagues* as "a compact blend of speed and power." Kimbro was extremely fast on the basepaths, and was a very successful base-stealer. He had amazing strength in his upper body and was a powerful hitter. His shoulders were huge, a product, Kimbro always said, of swinging on ladders on the playground after school. He excelled in all aspects of the game. "A good defensive center fielder with great range and a good arm, he [Kimbro] was regarded as the best center fielder in the Negro National League in his prime," Riley wrote. "Henry Kimbro was so good in center field," observed Kelley, "that Wild Bill Wright was moved to right field, and Wright was a great center fielder himself and a great baseball player. But Kimbro was also a great ballplayer." As a fielder, Kimbro was exceptionally good at snagging fly balls. He was very fast and would run out into alleys to catch fly balls that seemed impossible to catch. "I was a pretty good fielder if the ball was hit in the air," Kimbro recalled for *Sports Illustrated* in 1992. "Because I was fast, wooooo, I

was fast." His weakness, however, was handling ground balls. Kimbro explained to *Sports Illustrated*, "I saw my best friend, a shortstop, lose two front teeth when the ball caught a bad hop. Fields in those days had rocks, gravel, all kind of stuff to make a ball kick up in your face. I got kind of ball shy. A grounder would come at me, and everyone would hold their breath."

A Powerful Hitter

Kimbro was also an incredible offensive player. Former teammate Frank Duncan, Jr., ranked Kimbro with greats Josh Gibson and Wild Bill Wright as one of the best pure, everyday hitters he had ever seen. Charlie Davis, a lefty who came to the Negro Leagues in 1950, also called Kimbro one of the great hitters. James "Jimmy" Dean, who pitched for the Philadelphia Stars between 1946 and 1949, was another who acknowledged Kimbro's excellent hitting ability. "Henry Kimbro was a hard man to pitch to. He could hit," Dean told Kelley. "He was a tough act to follow."

Kimbro's best seasons were from 1944 to 1947, although it must be said that he posted very good averages in the other years as well. Riley summarized Kimbro's achievements in those peak years in several offensive categories. "In 1944 he hit .329, led the league in stolen bases, and finished only one run behind league leaders Josh Gibson and Buck Leonard; in 1945 he hit .291 and tied with Cool Papa Bell for the league lead in at-bats; in 1946 he hit .371 and led the league in runs scored; in 1947 he hit .353 and led the league in runs scored, and tied for the league lead in doubles." Riley also noted that for three seasons between 1944 and 1947, Kimbro was among the top ten hitters in the league.

Kimbro was traditionally the leadoff batter. He almost always let the first pitch go by, and did not like to hit slow pitches. He also did not try to swing for home runs. "I didn't believe in that home run business," Kimbro told Kelley in 1994. "I liked to shoot that ball through that infield. I'd hit that ball between third base and shortstop–that was my spot." Although he was not considered a home-run hitter, Kimbro did hit one that was especially glorious, and for which he received no credit. Kimbro hit a towering home run out of Briggs Stadium–now Tiger Stadium–in Detroit. A sportswriter mistakenly credited the remarkable homer to Bill Hoskins, the left fielder who had batted after Kimbro. "I was really disgusted but I never did say anything about it. I just let it go," he said to Kelley. Fifty years later, the lack of credit for the home run still angered Kimbro. His amazement at this accomplishment had not dimmed with time. "I hit that ball out of Briggs Stadium! Out of Briggs Stadium. You know what size Briggs Stadium is–it's a mile high. I hit the ball out of the park over the right field roof," Kimbro told Kelley. *USA Today* finally made the feat official when it reported in 1997 that "Henry Kimbro. . .was the second player–black or white–to hit a ball out of Detroit's Tiger Stadium." Ted Williams was the first.

Major league baseball's color barrier, which did not fall until Jackie Robinson integrated the Brooklyn Dodgers in 1947, also prevented people from noticing Kimbro's greatness. At the age of 35, he was considered past his prime, too old to make the transition once the racial barrier fell. Yet in 1947 he hit .353, and .314 in 1948. During the 1949 and 1950 seasons, Kimbro hit .352 and .370 respectively.

Once the majors had been integrated, African American ballplayers were signed into the professional ranks in ever increasing numbers. With the prime talent siphoned out of the Negro Leagues, the quality of play fell dramatically and the Negro Leagues eventually disbanded. Kimbro played until 1953, and continued to post high batting averages. His career spanned 17 seasons, and he played in six Negro League All-Star East-West games.

After his retirement from baseball in 1953, Kimbro bought a new DeSoto and worked as a taxi driver for Bill's Cab Company in Nashville. In 1955, Kimbro bought the cab company, although he did not change the name. He also owned a service station in Nashville, and operated both businesses for 22 years. He kept working despite a heart attack and a stroke, maintaining between 13 and 15 cabs. A second stroke convinced Kimbro to retire, and he sold the business. He was well known and widely respected in his native Nashville, and made frequent appearances at Negro League reunions around the country. In 1998, Kimbro was honored as an inductee in the Yesterday's Negro League Baseball Players Wall of Fame, which is maintained by the Milwaukee Brewers ball club, and the County Stadium Wall of Fame. When Brent Kelley asked him if he would be a ballplayer again, Kimbro answered, "You mean if I could go back? Yeah. I loved to play baseball. I loved to play the game."

Kimbro passed away on July 11, 1999. His wife, Erbia,

sons Phillip and Larry, and daughters Erbia Maria Kimbro Drew, Harriet Kimbro Hamilton, and Demetria Kimbro survived him. "He lived a very good life and played against some of the top players of his day," said Larry Walker, owner of the Old Negro League Baseball Shop in Nashville, where Kimbro often spent time. "He's one of the greatest Negro League players that ever lived. He was a great man and a great player. We will all miss him," Walker told the *Nashville Tennessean*.

Sources

Books

Kelley, Brent. *Voices from the Negro Leagues*. Jefferson, NC: McFarland & Company, Inc., Publishers, 1998.
Riley, James A. *The Biographical Encyclopedia of the Negro Baseball Leagues*. New York: Carroll & Graf Publishers, Inc., 1994.

Periodicals

Maclean's, July 26, 1999, p.12.
Nashville Scene, August 2, 1999.
Nashville Tennessean, July 31, 1999.
New York Times, July 15, 1999, p.A20 (N).
Sports Illustrated, July 6, 1992, p.80; July 26, 1999, p.R1.
USA Today, May 20, 1997.

Other

Additional information for this profile was obtained from http:\\www.milwaukeebrewers.com\media\feat\fame72199.html1 1999; http:\\www.negroleaguebaseball.com\1999\July\Kimbro_obit.html 1999; and http:\\www.execpc.com\[]sshivers\1998inductees.html

—Ellen Dennis French

Barbara Lee

1946—

Congresswoman

"I want to continue fighting the good fight, which Ron has been so valiantly fighting for the last 30 years," said Barbara Lee when announcing her candidacy for the United States House of Representatives. The year was 1997, and "Ron" was Ron Dellums, a veteran Congressional representative from the Oakland, California area who epitomized a liberal California outlook on issues ranging from U.S. military intervention abroad to domestic antipoverty efforts. After a long political career with Dellums as her mentor, Lee assumed the mantle of his leadership when she won a special election to succeed him, and immediately created a stir by taking the same sorts of maverick stands on the issues that Dellums himself had been known for.

Barbara Lee was born July 16, 1946, in El Paso, Texas, a city with only a small African American population. Her father, a Korean War veteran, would later support her in her antiwar positions. In 1960, the family moved to the burgeoning San Fernando Valley in suburban Los Angeles, where Lee attended San Fernando High School. She immersed herself in music, and won two music achievement awards from the Rotary Club and the Bank of America. In 1967 Lee moved to the San Francisco Bay Area, which was the epicenter of the student activist movement that was transforming American values and behaviors.

Worked as Congressional Intern

Lee attended Mills College, a private school in Oakland that had long been known for inculcating questioning attitudes in its students. Graduating with a B.A. degree in 1973, she worked as a Congressional intern the following year under a program called Cal in the Capital, and landed in the office of Congressman Ron Dellums. Lee's experience with Dellums would shape her career: in an era when the attempt to combine politics and activism was much more commonly made, Lee had taken as a mentor the man who may have taken the combination farther than any other politician.

Emerging from the progressive and experiment-minded culture of Oakland and nearby Berkeley during the 1960s and 1970s, Congressman Dellums weathered successive national swings to the political left and right, eventually amassing considerable power by virtue of seniority. As chairman of the House Armed Services Committee until the 1994 Republican takeover of the

At a Glance . . .

Born July 16, 1946, in El Paso, TX; spent teenage years in San Fernando, CA. *Education:* Mills College, B.A., 1973; University of California at Berkeley, M.A. social work degree, 1975.

Career: United States Representative from California's Ninth District. Established community mental health center in Berkeley, mid-1970s; joined staff of Representative Ron Dellums, 1975; became chief of staff; member, California Assembly, 1990-96; member California State Senate, 1996-98; elected to U.S. House of Representatives, February, 1998, after Dellums endorsed her upon own retirement; re-elected November 1998; sole member of Congress to vote against authorizing Yugoslavia bombing, 1999; member, Banking & Financial Services and International Relations committees.

Addresses: *Office*—414 Cannon House Office Building, Washington, DC20515.

House, he was a thorn in the side of Defense Department budget-makers, often questioning the need for new offensive weapons systems and urging the diversion of funds instead to domestic concerns. Dellums's ongoing effort to convert aging Bay Area military bases to new, job-generating nonmilitary uses made an impression upon Lee when she joined his staff on a permanent basis.

Lee worked toward a graduate degree in social welfare at the University of California in Berkeley, using her limited spare time to create and nurture a community mental health center there. In 1975, she joined Dellums's staff, working for Dellums in both his Washington and Oakland offices for eleven years. Lee was also a small business owner in Oakland during this time, and raised her sons there. Eventually, she rose to the position of Senior Adviser and Chief of Staff.

Worked with California Republicans

Groomed for several years to be Dellums's successor when he finally decided to retire, Lee ran for and won election to the California Assembly in 1990, moving up to the California state senate in the elections of 1996. Despite her strongly liberal orientation, she worked successfully with California's Republican administration in those years, sponsoring 67 bills that

were signed into law by Republican Governor Pete Wilson. Lee focused on issues such as education, public safety, environmental protection, health, labor, and women's rights, and worked to promote links between California and African countries.

Dellums endorsed Lee in the special election that followed his retirement in February of 1998, and she went on to win the April election without a runoff, taking 67 percent of the vote. By a similar margin, she won election to a full term that November. Although Dellums's endorsement clearly played a crucial role, Lee tried to portray herself as something other than merely a Dellums clone. "Ron is not an anomaly in Oakland or San Francisco," she pointed out to *The Progressive.* "He comes out of a progressive tradition." The freethinking atmosphere of the Bay Area had in fact shaped Lee's thinking before she ever met Dellums, and other area figures continued to influence her.

Traveled to Cuba and Grenada

Two of these figures were Carlton Goodlet, an African American doctor from San Francisco, and Maudelle Shirek, Berkeley's vice mayor. Goodlet and Shirek steered Lee toward a pacifist and internationalist outlook after her election, encouraging her to travel to such officially disapproved states as Cuba (whose isolation through U.S. trade sanctions Lee deplored) and Grenada in the name of international understanding. The founder of a nonviolent conflict-resolution program in California schools, Lee sought to apply the lessons she had learned to international affairs. "Kids can't see us bombing, and then listen to use talking about getting guns out of the schools," she observed to *The Progressive.* "How can we tell them to solve problems without violence, if, in fact, we can't show an ability to solve problems without violence?"

Those positions were put to the test in some of the crucial House votes during Lee's first term. In December of 1998, Lee was one of five representatives in Congress to vote against authorization of President Clinton's renewed bombing of Iraq in the dispute that arose over United Nations weapons inspections. In March of 1999, as the U.S. and Europe became embroiled in the conflict in Kosovo, Lee took an even lonelier stand: she cast the sole vote against authorizing the bombing of Yugoslavia. "I was surprised," Lee admitted to *The Progressive.* "Being the only 'no' note is troubling. It's staggering. You wonder if there's something you've missed." Lee was heartened, however, by the support voiced privately by several of her colleagues, and vowed to continue her advocacy of peaceful solutions. "We have a chance to do something in the world," she said in the same interview. "But instead it's just bomb, bomb, bomb." The ideal of peace, it seemed, had found a spokesperson for the 21st century in Barbara Lee.

Sources

Books

Barone, Michael, and Grant Ujifusa, *Almanac of American Politics 2000,* National Journal, 1999.

Periodicals

The Progressive, May 1999, p. 10.
Los Angeles Times, April 8, 1998, p. 1.
Oakland Tribune, April 5, 1998.
San Francisco Chronicle, December 11, 1997; April 4, 1998, p. A22.

Other

Additional information for this profile was obtained from http:\\www.house.gov\lee\

—James M. Manheim

Samella Lewis

1924—

Artist, art historian, and educator

A creative and inspirational powerhouse who has touched the lives of countless African Americans involved with the visual arts, Samella Lewis has had a long and distinguished career. That career encompassed an astonishing range of creative activity: Lewis was an artist, an educator, a curator, a museum founder, an art historian, a textbook writer, an administrator, an editor, a filmmaker, and more. Overcoming pervasive racial discrimination in her earlier years, Lewis went on to become an extraordinarily influential figure in each of her many fields of endeavor.

Lewis was born Samella Sanders in New Orleans, Louisiana, on February 27, 1924. She was a high school honors student and entered Dillard University in New Orleans on a scholarship in 1941. Two years later she won another scholarship to the Hampton Institute in Virginia, this one in art. She graduated from Hampton with an art degree in 1945 and was immediately hired to teach there, which she did for two years. She decided to pursue advanced degrees in art history, receiving her M.A. from Ohio State University in 1948 and her Ph.D. three years later. During this busy time in her life, Lewis also married Paul Gad Lewis (a math and computer teacher), taught at Morgan State College, and began raising two children.

Shots Fired at House

Becoming art department chair at historically black Florida A&M University, Lewis inherited a program in dire financial straits. She managed to squeeze more money out of the school's president by promising to paint his portrait, and soon her department was flourishing, even attracting white students from nearby Florida State University. However, when Lewis emerged as a leader of the local branch of the National Association for the Advancement of Colored People (NAACP), she drew the wrath of the Ku Klux Klan, which fired shots through the windows of Lewis's house. The local police were unsympathetic to her situation.

One of Lewis's former teachers helped her find a teaching position in upstate New York, but these experiences deeply shaped her cultural attitudes. She became interested in art from outside the European sphere, and traveled to Taiwan and elsewhere in Asia during the early 1960s. Her study of Asian art drew her to California, where she became education coordinator of the Los Angeles County Museum of Art in 1968. Lewis clashed with administrators there, however. At one point, they even hired a private investigator to try to impugn her credentials. The museum eventually apologized to Lewis, but it had become clear to her that African Americans needed new institutions, institutions where their art and its connections to their culture and history could be displayed in a way uniquely their own.

While teaching at Scripps College, a prestigious private school in suburban Los Angeles, Lewis and artist Bernie Casey spent several thousand dollars of their own money to create Contemporary Crafts Gallery, later renamed simply The Gallery. The gallery served as a point of direct connection between African American

At a Glance . . .

Born February 27, 1924, in New Orleans, LA; married Paul G. Lewis in 1948; children: two sons. *Education:* Hampton Institute, Hampton, Virginia, B.S., 1945; Ohio State University, M.A., 1948; Ohio State University, Ph.D., 1951.

Career: Artist, art educator, writer, and filmmaker. Instructor, Hampton Institute,1946-47; associate professor, Morgan State University, 1948-53; professor and department chair, Florida A&M University, 1953-58; professor, State University of New York at Plattsburgh,1958-68; education coordinator, Los Angeles County Museum of Art, 1968-69; professor, Scripps College, 1970-84; founded the Museum of African American Art in Los Angeles, 1976; published textbook *Art: African American,* 1978.

Selected awards: Fulbright Fellowship, 1962; Ford Foundation Fellowship, 1965; Legend in Our Time Tribute, *Essence* Magazine, 1990; Getty Center for the History of Art and the Humanities Distinguished Scholar Award, 1996-97.

Addresses: *Agent*—Art Tradition, 5042 Wilshire Blvd., Suite 257, Los Angeles, CA 90036.

artists and the community, specializing in the distribution of inexpensive prints that would quickly bring art into the hands of ordinary people. The Gallery flourished, and Lewis remained there until 1979.

Founded Museum

In 1976, Lewis founded the Museum of African American Art in Los Angeles. As the staff's senior curator there until 1986, she organized numerous exhibitions and developed new ways of thinking about the relationship between museums and African American art. In an influential article, Lewis discussed the ideas of an "art of tradition," arguing that museums had a responsibility to explore the African and Afro-Caribbean roots of African American art, and an "art of inspiration" based upon the experiences of African Americans themselves.

Lewis also tried to document African American artists and their experiences in other ways. In the late 1960s, she began to make films about African American artists. Some of the films covered individual artists such

as John Outterbridge, Bernie Casey, and Richmond Barthé. Her first film, *The Black Artists,* was a more general history of African American art. *The Black Artists* was followed by a two-volume print work that Lewis edited with Elizabeth Waddy, *Black Artists on Art.* In 1978, she published the textbook *Art: African American.* This work, which went into a revised second edition in 1990, is still widely used in art history courses. Lewis also founded a scholarly journal, the *International Review of African American Art,* now under the aegis of her alma mater, Hampton University.

Central to Lewis's writings, and indeed to her educational efforts in general, was the idea that African American art should not strive toward a realm of refined expression separate from ordinary life, but rather should express the experiences of individuals and communities. As Lewis stated in *Art: African American,* "the artist is a community resource, valued and supported because he or she forsakes the 'ivory tower' and gets to the heart of community life." She drew on African attitudes toward the arts, which were directed toward the making of objects with important roles in community life.

Works Based on Own Childhood

Even if she had never realized any of her goals as an educator, writer, curator, and museum builder, Lewis would still be respected as a talented artist. In the 1940s and 1950s, she was known for realistic works that explored the experiences of African Americans in the South. Some of Lewis's earliest works were based on her own Louisiana childhood, and some of her works in the 1950s depicted the injustices routinely suffered by African Americans. Her later works were created in various media—drawings, sculptures, mixed-media works—and were often shaped by Lewis's explorations of the artistic cultures of the African diaspora. Especially in the years since her retirement, her work has been the subject of numerous exhibitions.

A teacher and inspiration to many African American creative figures, including the mixed-media artist Alison Saar, Lewis hardly slowed down upon her retirement from Scripps College in 1984. "Black women are nurturers," she told *Essence* in 1996. "We nurture our families by seriously listening to and seriously considering what they tell us. We also have an obligation to see that valuing and collecting our art is a significant aspect of nurturing. We must familiarize ourselves with our historical and contemporary art in order to understand and know ourselves." The degree to which Lewis herself has nurtured the development of African American art is incalculable.

Selected writings

Art: African American. Harcourt Brace Jovanovich,

1976.
The Art of Elizabeth Catlett. Museum of African American Art and Hancraft Studios, 1984.

Sources

Books

Heller, Jules, and Nancy G. Heller, *North American Women Artists of the Twentieth Century.* Garland, 1995.
Riggs, Thomas, ed., *St. James Guide to Black Artists.* St. James Press, 1997.

Smith, Jessie Carney, ed., *Notable Black American Women,* Book I. Gale, 1992.
Scanlon, Jennifer, and Sharon Cosner, *American Women Historians, 1700s–1990s: A Biographical Dictionary.* Greenwood Press, 1996.

Periodicals

Essence, July 1996, p. 64.

—James M. Manheim

Donnie McClurkin

1961—

Gospel vocalist and composer

One of gospel music's rising stars and most respected figures, Donnie McClurkin has devoted his musical life to gospel's original mission of providing help and hope to people in need. Forging a gospel style that is traditional in orientation but spiced with modern touches from such musical influences as Andrae Crouch and Take 6, McClurkin enjoyed strong sales with his 1996 debut album, *Donnie McClurkin,* and seemed poised for even wider success with the release of several new projects in the year 2000. Beyond his success in the musical arena, however, McClurkin has maintained an active career as a minister, remaining in direct contact with the audience to which he directs his music.

McClurkin was born in 1961, and raised in Amityville, New York, on Long Island outside of New York City. Both of McClurkin's parents were substance abusers, and his childhood was a difficult one, plagued by violence and abuse. Often trying to act as a peacemaker between his warring parents, he found a haven in his family church, the Gospel Tabernacle Assemblies of God, and made a commitment to the Christian religion when he was only nine years old. "The only way my mother could punish me was saying I couldn't go to church," McClurkin later recalled in a *Detroit Free Press* interview.

Mentored by Andrae Crouch

McClurkin's real spiritual awakening, however, came two years later when he encountered one of the great gospel singers of the modern era, Andrae Crouch. McClurkin's aunt, a backup singer for Crouch, had arranged a performance by Crouch at McClurkin's church. Crouch took an interest in the troubled youngster, encouraging him not only musically (McClurkin soon became a pianist with the church's youth choir) but also personally, corresponding with him and suggesting Scripture readings that might bring him comfort.

For McClurkin, the experience cemented a link in his mind between music and a more general effort to reach out to the afflicted. "Andrae fostered ministry, rather than fame," McClurkin explained to the online magazine *crosswalk.com.* "It was more ministry to him than anything else, not some glamorous career." McClurkin began to sing as a teenager, and with his four vocally talented sisters formed a group called the McClurkin Singers. As his vocal and compositional talents grew, however, McClurkin aimed not at the gospel spotlight, but at a different kind of ideal.

Forming a gospel ensemble called the New York Restoration Choir, McClurkin led the group in performances where gospel music could have a direct impact. The group appeared in prisons and sang on the street. The group recorded for the roots-oriented Savoy\Malaco labels. After telling members of the choir of a divinely inspired premonition that he would one day work with Detroit's renowned minister and gospel-singer Rev. Marvin Winans, McClurkin attended a seminar given by Winans in 1983. Winans likewise sensed a connection. "I don't even know what your

At a Glance . . .

Born in 1961 in Amityville, NY. *Religion:* Assemblies of God.

Career: Gospel vocalist. Formed group with sisters, the McClurkin Singers, late 1970s; formed and directed New York Restoration Choir, late 1970s; recorded with group forSavoy\Malaco label; attended gospel-music seminar given by Rev. Marvin Winans, 1983; became associate minister at Winans's Perfecting Church, Detroit, MI, 1989; led choirs inperformances at White House twice; recorded debut album *Donnie McClurkin,* 1996; recorded *The McClurkin Project* with sisters, 1999; recorded *Live in London &More,* 2000.

Addresses: *Label*—BMG Entertainment\Verity Records, 1540 Broadway, New York, NY 10019.

name is," he told McClurkin in recollections quoted in *crosswalk.com.* "I have nothing to offer you, but somehow we're going to work together." The prophecy took a while to come true. However, in 1989, McClurkin relocated to Detroit to join the staff of Winans's 2,000-member Perfecting Church as an associate minister.

Diagnosed with Leukemia

Nestled in the bosom of gospel music's foremost family, McClurkin seemed headed for a bright future as a performer. "I've been trained real well—having the Winans family at your disposal does that," McClurkin told the *Detroit Free Press.* Early in his career in Detroit, however, McClurkin was diagnosed with leukemia. The disease went into remission, thanks, McClurkin told *crosswalk.com,* to prayers from members of the Winans family. According to the *Free Press,* the disease left McClurkin's tenor voice permanently damaged. Doctors gave him a set of vocal exercises to perform in order to regain his strength. On his own web site's biography, McClurkin does not mention the illness.

McClurkin's career blossomed as he performed and led choirs within the Winans fold. He appeared at the White House during the presidencies of both George Bush and Bill Clinton, toured internationally, contributed backing vocals to a number of Winans recording projects, and wrote new music. He also cultivated a friendship with Demetrus Alexander, an executive at the Warner Alliance label. In October of 1996, McClurkin released his self-titled debut album.

McClurkin's debut album benefitted from production work by various top gospel performers, including Crouch, Mark Kibble of the a cappella group Take 6, and former CeCe Winans producer Cedric Caldwell. Effectively mixing traditional and contemporary styles, the album included several songs of McClurkin's own composition, a classical-styled version of the hymn "Holy, Holy, Holy," a Christianized Take 6 arrangement of the Pointer Sisters' rousing "Yes We Can Can," and Crouch's "We Expect You." McClurkin himself described his style as "eclectic" in conversation with *Billboard* magazine's Lisa Collins, and the unique musical assortment appealed to gospel fans. McClurkin's debut album remained in the Top Ten of Billboard's gospel sales chart for over two years.

Worked with Kelly Price

In 1999, McClurkin returned to the studio with his sisters to record The McClurkin Project for the Gospocentric label. The album showcased McClurkin's arranging skills with what the *Detroit Free Press* described as "tight, soaring harmony," and also featured McClurkin's own vocals on four tracks. In the spring of 2000, McClurkin's second solo release, *Live in London & More,* was slated for release on the Verity label, with guest appearances by Marvin Winans and Gladys Knight, and a songwriting contribution from R&B singer Kelly Price. Reportedly in negotiations with an Atlanta-based cable network for his own television show, McClurkin seemed to be a star on the rise.

McClurkin did not let his rising success distract him from the spiritual underpinnings of his musical career. Focusing his Perfecting Church ministry on families that, like his own, had suffered through destructive conflicts and sexual abuse, McClurkin laid plans to assume the pastorship of a church of his own. In the spring of 2000, he was conducting monthly services back in his home town of New York City, and hoped to conduct weekly services by the fall of 2000. With Psalm 118:17 as a credo ("I shall not die, but live and declare the works of the Lord"), McClurkin is a performer in touch with the spiritual roots of gospel music.

Selected discography

Donnie McClurkin, Warner Alliance, 1996.
The McClurkin Project, Gospocentric, 1999 (with sisters).
Live in London & More, Verity, 2000.

Sources

Periodicals

Billboard, January 29, 2000, p. 55.
Detroit Free Press, March 28, 1997, p. D1; January 9, 2000, p. E4.

Ebony, August 1998, p. 74.

Other

Additional information for this profile was obtained from http:\\www.allmusic.com; http:\\www.donnie mcclurkin.com; and http:\\www.music.crosswalk.com

—James M. Manheim

Gregory Meeks

1953—

Congressman

A skilled legislator and a conciliator by nature, Gregory Meeks has successfully struck a middle path between the ideological and entrepreneurial wings of the New York City Democratic Party's African American membership. To some, he represented a new style of political leadership that recognized the need for legislative nuts-and-bolts work without turning its back on the inspirational politics of the past. Elected to the United States Congress in 1998, Meeks represents one of the nation's largest and most durable middle-class African American communities.

Gregory Weldon Meeks had a long road to travel before reaching a position of political power and influence. The oldest of four children, he was born on September 25, 1953, and raised in public housing in New York's generally impoverished Harlem neighborhood. His father, a taxi driver, also worked as a handyman in the city's theater district from time to time, while his mother stayed home to raise her children when Gregory was young. After the children were old enough to fend for themselves, however, she returned to school and earned a college degree.

Meeks was one of those politicians who seemed born

to the profession, winning leadership positions in student government as early as junior high school. He graduated from Manhattan's Julia Richman High School in 1971. Completing his education without delay, he moved on to Long Island's Adelphi University, from which he graduated with a B.A. degree in 1975, and then to law school at Washington, D.C.'s Howard University. In the spring of 1978, not yet 25 years old, Gregory Meeks was a freshly minted lawyer.

Formed Community Organization

While he was away at school, Meeks's family had moved out of Harlem to the middle-class Rockaway section in the New York borough of Queens, and after receiving his degree he moved back home to join them. Meeks took a position as Assistant District Attorney in the Queens prosecutor's office, and got involved in politics at the most local, grassroots level: together with his community-minded mother, Meeks formed a neighborhood association devoted to such issues as street repair. That led to the founding of a political club, first called the Jesse L. Jackson Independent Democratic Club of the Rockaways, and later renamed the Thur-

At a Glance . . .

Born in New York, NY, on September 25, 1953; grew up in Harlem neighborhood; married, wife's name Simone-Marie, two daughters. *Education:* Graduated from Julia Richman High School, New York City; B.A., Adelphi University, Garden City, New York, 1975; J.D., Howard University, Washington, D.C., 1978. *Religion:* Baptist.

Career: United States Representative from New York's Sixth District. Assistant District Attorney, Queens, New York, 1978-84; staff attorney, New York State Commission on Investigations, 1984-85; Judge, New York State Workers' Compensation Board,1985-92; elected to New York State Assembly, 1992; won election to two more full two-year terms; elected to U.S. House in special election of February, 1998; member, Banking & Financial Services and International Relations committees.

Addresses: *Office*—1710 Longworth House Office Building,Washington, DC 20515.

good Marshall Regular Democratic Club. With black political influence on the rise in New York City, the club was an ideal springboard from which to launch a more substantial political career.

Through the 1980s, Meeks acquitted himself well in a series of public-sector legal jobs; he became a New York City drug prosecutor in 1980, assistant counsel to the New York State Investigations Commission in 1982 (where he worked to uncover the infiltration of organized crime into state government), and a state workers' compensation judge in 1985. He also established a law office of his own in 1984. Urged by friends in his political circle to run for office, Meeks jumped into a city council primary in 1991. He lost, but the exposure he gained helped him win election to the New York State Assembly the following year.

Meeks served three terms in the Assembly, winning kudos for his hard work on labor and transportation issues. Though he had sometimes backed insurgent candidates during his New York organizing days, in Albany, the state capital, he was a loyal follower of the Democratic Party. Another important result of Meeks's years in the state legislature was the contact he made with the most powerful black politician in Queens, the Rev. Floyd Flake. Flake, as the U.S. Representative from New York's Sixth District (including much of Queens), was an influential African Methodist Episco-

pal minister whose congregation had grown from a membership of 1,400 to over 11,000. He spearheaded economic development in his district, stimulating private-sector investment and the development of new housing.

Wins Flake's Endorsement

Flake retired from Congress in late 1997, pleading the need to spend more time attending to the affairs of his church (although he has also been urged to run for mayor of New York in 2001). The race to succeed him was intense, but Flake gave the nod to the newly married Meeks as his successor, and the area's Democratic party organization followed suit. Nevertheless, campaigning was intense in the months leading up to the special election in February of 1998. Three other major candidates faced off against Meeks for the job.

In typical fashion for New York City, the campaign turned into more of a brawl. One of Meeks's opponents raised the issue of Meeks having voted for an Assembly bill that would have given nonprofit status to a pro-pedophilia group called the North American Man-Boy Love Association, but Meeks countered that though he found the group's activities "deplorable and reprehensible," the bill had been crafted in such a way that the NAACP could likewise have been denied tax-exempt status without it. With the endorsement of the *New York Times,* which said that Meeks "seems most likely to thrive in the large and competitive arena of Congressional politics," Meeks won with an impressive 57 percent of the vote.

Attracted Diverse Support

Meeks's win attracted notice in part because of the diverse group of supporters he attracted to his corner; it included the Rev. Jesse Jackson and New York's fire-breathing and organizationally street-smart Rev. Al Sharpton, but also more moderate figures such as Flake and City Comptroller Alan Hevesi, who told the *Times* that Meeks was "very smart and extremely hardworking. He's also a guy who believes in working with all the communities," Hevesi said, predicting a successful future in Congress for Meeks.

Meeks, who had in fact touted himself as a "bridge builder" during the campaign, said upon his election that "[m]y role, as part of a new generation of African American leadership, is to take us to the new phase of the civil rights movement, that is, the economic development of our community." Inheriting Flake's seat on the House Banking Committee, he focused on bread-and-butter issues, winning a large grant for space technology classes at a local community college and bringing in 4 million to rebuild the Queens traffic artery Springfield Boulevard. Early in the year 2000, he found himself under pressure from both sides on the issue of normalizing trade relations with China, a possible boon to New York's economy but an unwelcome prospect for labor groups. Few doubted, though, that Meeks, fast becoming a seasoned politician, would surmount the problem and go on to win re-election in the fall.

Sources

Books

Barone, Michael, and Grant Ujifusa, *The Almanac of American Politics 2000,* National Journal, 1999.

Periodicals

Crain's New York Business, February 7, 2000, p. 6.
New York Times, January 10, 1998, p. B3; January 31, 1998, p. A14; February 1, 1998, p. A26; February 5, 1998, p. B5.

Other

Additional information for this profile was obtained from http:\\www.house.gov\meeks\

—James M. Manheim

Walter Mosley

1952—

Author

Walter Mosley has broken new ground as a mystery writer by incorporating issues of race into novels that stand on their own as gripping detective fiction. His novels are all written from an African American perspective. He has also branched out into the areas of science fiction and social commentary.

Critics have praised Mosley's writing for its realistic portrayal of street life in African American neighborhoods of post-World War II Los Angeles. Sara M. Lomax wrote in *American Visions* that Mosley has "a special talent for layering time and place with words and ideas." *Library Journal*'s review of *A Red Death* noted, "As before, Mosley's inclusion of life in Watts, contemporary social attitudes, and colloquial speech contribute to the excellence and authenticity of plot and character portrayal."

Much of Mosley's success has been due to the powerful recurring character of Ezekiel ("Easy") Rawlins, one of the most innovative private investigators to appear in fiction. Unlike many detectives who populate the pages of hard-boiled prose, Rawlins is a multidimensional character who stumbled into his sleuthing career as a means to pay mounting debts. Mosley has used Rawlins to expose the problems of getting by in a world where only a thin line lies between crime and business as usual. As Christopher Hitchens said in *Vanity Fair,* "Rawlins is more of a fixer than a hustler, a kind of accidental detective who gets pulled into cases because of his reluctantly acquired street smarts and savoir faire." D. J. R. Bruckner added in the *New York Times* that Easy Rawlins "is trapped into becoming a private detective, and the way he is trapped gives Mr. Mosley an opportunity to raise scores of moral questions in a novel of little more than 200 pages."

Walter Mosley was born in southeastern Los Angeles in 1952 and grew up in Watts and the Pico-Fairfax district. His father was an African American from the deep South, and his mother a white woman of Jewish descent whose family emigrated from Eastern Europe. This unique African American\Jewish heritage made prejudice a major topic in the household. An only child, Mosley grew up hearing about the woes of life for African Americans in the South, as well as the horrors of anti-Semitism across the Atlantic. However, he was also regaled by colorful accounts of partying and carrying on among his African American relatives, along with tales of czars in old Russia.

After earning a bachelor's degree at Johnson State

At a Glance . . .

Born January 12, 1952, in Los Angeles, CA; son of LeRoy (a school custodian) and Ella (a school personnel clerk) Mosley; married Joy Kellman (a dancer and choreographer), 1987. *Education:* Attended Goddard College, 1971; Johnson State College, B.A., 1977; attended writing program at City College of New York, 1985-89.

Career: Worked as a computer consultant for Mobil Oil, and as a computer programmer, potter, and caterer; became full-time writer, 1986-.

Awards: John Creasey Memorial Award and Shamus Award, both for outstanding mystery writing; *Devil in a Blue Dress* was nominated for an Edgar for best first novel by the Mystery Writers of America, 1990; winner of the Black Caucus of the American LibraryAssociation's Literary Award for *RL's Dream,* 1996; winner of the Annisfield-Wolf Book Award for *Always Outnumbered, Always Outgunned,* 1998; winner of the Trans-Africa International Literary Prize.

Member: TransAfrica; National Book Foundation; Poetry Society of America; Manhattan Theater Club.

Addresses: *Home*—New York City. *Publisher*—W. W.Norton & Co., Inc., 500 Fifth Ave., New York, NY 10110.

College in 1977, Mosley drifted for a number of years in various jobs, even working as a potter and caterer. He and Joy Kellman, a dancer and choreographer, moved to New York City in 1982 and were married in 1987. The parents of Kellman, who is white and Jewish, reportedly didn't speak to their daughter for five years after meeting Mosley.

Mosley settled down into a career as a computer programmer in the 1980s, but his work left him unfulfilled. Meanwhile, he read voraciously, including mysteries by Raymond Chandler, Dashiell Hammett, and Ross MacDonald and existential novels such as *The Stranger* by Albert Camus. This blend of suspense and philosophy served him well in the mysteries he would later write.

Novel Triggered Interest in Writing

According to a profile in *People* magazine, Mosley's decision to become a writer was strongly influenced by his reading of *The Color Purple* by Alice Walker. That book rekindled the youthful urge to write that he had lost and made him feel that he could create the same kind of prose. He began writing feverishly on nights, weekends, and whenever he could find time. Intent on devoting himself totally to his craft, Mosley quit his computer programming job in the mid-eighties and enrolled at the City College of New York to study with Frederic Tuten, head of the school's writing program. While in the program he also received instruction from writers William Matthews and Edna O'Brien.

In 1989 Mosley showed *Devil in a Blue Dress,* which he had first written as a screenplay, to his writing teacher. The teacher showed the book to his agent, who sold it to the W. W. Norton publishing company. When the novel came out in 1990, the *New York Times* said that it "marks the debut of a talented author." Rawlins's reappearance a year later in *A Red Death* caused Publishers Weekly to theorize that "Mosley . . . may well be in the process of creating a genre classic." *White Butterfly* was also greeted by critical acclaim, with *Cosmopolitan* saying that Mosley "brings it all so thoroughly, sizzlingly to life." The author's reputation soared when Bill Clinton said during his 1992 U.S. presidential campaign that Mosley was his favorite mystery writer.

Father's Background a Major Influence

Many characters in the Easy Rawlins novels are based on the experiences of Mosley's father, with similarities between LeRoy Mosley and Easy Rawlins especially apparent. After being treated like a hero abroad during World War II, LeRoy Mosley was dismayed to find that he was still a second class citizen back in the States. This disillusionment was also felt by veteran Easy Rawlins in *Devil in a Blue Dress.* However, the war made it clear to Rawlins that the white man was not much different from himself. Early in the novel, the character ruminates: "I had spent five years with white men, and women, from Africa to Italy, through Paris, and into the Fatherland itself. I ate with them and slept with them, and I killed enough blue-eyed young men to know that they were just as afraid to die as I was."

In a commentary in the *Los Angeles Times,* Mosley asserted that "black soldiers learned from World War II; they learned how to dream about freedom." LeRoy Mosley's dream of freedom took him to California, where endless jobs and opportunities were rumored to be waiting for everyone, including African Americans. In the *Los Angeles Times,* Mosley described the Los Angeles of Easy Rawlins as "a place where a black man can dream but he has to keep his wits about him. Easy lives among the immigrants from the western South. He dreams of owning property and standing on an equal footing with his white peers. Deep in his mind, he is indoctrinated with the terror of Southern racism. In his everyday life he faces the subtle, and not so subtle, inequalities of the American color line."

Racism an Ever-Present Theme

Similar to the canon of Chester Himes, an African American author who wrote Harlem-based crime novels in the 1940s and 1950s, Mosley's works have consistently addressed social and racial issues. Drawing on his father's life and his own as a close observer of the Watts riots during the 1960s, Mosley shows in his books how racism infects the lives of inner city African Americans. Double standards abound in *Devil in a Blue Dress,* in which a white man hires Rawlins to find a woman known to hang out in African American jazz clubs. Easy was chosen because he was African American and regarded as a bridge into a world where the white man dare not go. In *White Butterfly,* the police show a keen interest in the case of a murdered white cocktail waitress—after basically ignoring the murders of a series of black waitresses that occurred earlier.

Mosley has also tapped his African American\Jewish perspective to deal with Jewish suffering as perceived by African Americans. In *Devil in a Blue Dress,* two Jewish liquor store owners in the ghetto cause Easy Rawlins to remember when his unit broke open the gates of a Nazi extermination camp. This recollection leads to an understanding of similarities in the oppression suffered by African Americans in America and Jews abroad.

The author has provided a loud voice on racial strife in the real world as well. He was particularly angered over the racially motivated riots that occurred in Los Angeles in 1992. The rioting was triggered by the "not guilty" verdicts handed down in the first trial of four white Los Angeles police officers involved in the brutal beating African American motorist Rodney King. Mosley was outraged that racial tensions had led to blatant violence before people started to address the problems in urban African American communities. As he stated in an editorial in the *Los Angeles Times,* "The rioters sent out a message that is louder than a billion pleas over the past 400 years of beating, burning and death."

Moral Issues Raised Frequently

Mosley has found Greenwich Village, a noted haven for people in the arts, to be a good psychological base for him. "It's hard to be conspicuous here," he was quoted as saying in *Vanity Fair.* While he may not want be noticed, his writing has certainly put him on the literary map. Mosley is an important voice in a new brand of African American fiction that has spawned memorable characters and plots. As Charles Champlin wrote in the *Los Angeles Times Book Review,* "Mosley, who . . . knows Watts like an after-hours bartender, creates

characters—men, women and children—who are vivid, individual and as honest as home movies."

In 1994, Mosley published another installment in the Easy Rawlins series entitled *Black Betty.* The novel opens with Rawlins facing both the collapse of his real estate business, and the fact that his wife and daughter have walked out on him. In the midst of this turmoil, he is asked by a white private eye to find Elizabeth Eady, a seductive former housekeeper who is known as Black Betty. As Rawlins searches for Black Betty, he must also prevent his recently paroled friend, Mouse Alexander, from finding and exacting revenge on those who sent him to prison. Reviews of *Black Betty* were quite favorable. *Kirkus Reviews* called Black Betty, "Mosley's finest work yet," while a reviewer for *Publishers Weekly* praised the novel's "quietly emotive prose," and an ending that "fully satisfies." Barry Gifford, writing in the *New York Times Book Review,* remarked that "nobody will ever accuse Walter Mosley of lacking heart. . . .his words prowl around the page before they pounce, knocking you not so much upside the head as around the body, where you feel them the longest."

Departed From Easy Rawlins

Mosley's 1995 novel, *RL's Dream,* marked a departure from the Easy Rawlins mystery series. This novel tells the story of Atwater "Soupspoon" Wise, an aged and dying blues guitar player who is facing eviction from his New York apartment. He is soon befriended by an alcoholic white Southerner named Kiki Waters, who takes Wise into her home and cares for him. Wise longs to relive his glory days, and recalls to Waters about his struggles with racism and the time he played with a legendary Delta blues singer named Robert "RL" Johnson. As their friendship develops, the two share their individual stories, relive the pain of the past, and learn to heal their emotional wounds. Digby Diehl of *Playboy* noted that Mosley's mystery novels "don't prepare you for the emotional force of *RL's Dream.* Mosley mixes the nightmares of Soup's past with the immediate anguish of poverty, chemotherapy, and aging. The result is harsh, uplifting and unforgettable."

Following the release of *RL's Dream,* Mosley published another Easy Rawlins mystery, *A Little Yellow Dog,* in 1996. In the novel, Rawlins is working as a custodian at a junior high school. One of the teachers at the school, Idabell Holland, asks Rawlins to care for her little dog after Holland's husband allegedly threatens to kill it. After Rawlins and Holland have a brief romantic encounter, she is found murdered in the front seat of Rawlins's car. Holland's husband is also found murdered, and Rawlins discovers that he was part of a drug smuggling ring. Rawlins is suspected of the murders, and is forced to try to clear his name. *Kirkus Reviews* called the novel's plot "only average for this celebrated series." Bill Ott, writing for *Booklist,* praised *A Little*

Yellow Dog as "a superb novel in a superb series."

In 1997, Mosley published the novel *Gone Fishin'*. This novel is a prequel to the other Easy Rawlins novels, which take place during Rawlins's adult years. *Gone Fishin'* opens in 1939, when Rawlins and his friend, Mouse Alexander, are only 19-years-old. The novel does not have an intricate plot, but focuses primarily on Rawlins and Alexander as they come of age. Bill Kent of the *New York Times Book Review* remarked that *Gone Fishin'* will "disappoint anyone expecting another of his [Mosley's] atmospheric whodunits."

Always Outnumbered, Always Outgunned, which was published in late 1997, presented another departure from Mosley's Easy Rawlins series. The book consists of 14 stories which revolve around the character of Socrates Fortlow. Fortlow is an ex-convict who has been released from prison after serving 27 years for killing two acquaintances. He lives in an abandoned building in the Watts neighborhood of Los Angeles, and supports himself by delivering groceries for a supermarket. Throughout all 14 stories, Fortlow grapples with philosophical questions of morality in a world that is riddled with racism, crime, and poverty. Sven Birkerts, in a review of *Always Outnumbered, Always Outgunned* in the *New York Times Book Review,* remarked that the book delves into "the implications of moral action in a society that has lost all purchase on the spirit of the law." Birkerts also noted that the book's 14 stories "incorporate the Platonic dialogues as a kind of ghost melody; signature strains of the classic are vamped up in the rough demotic of present-day Watts." In 1998, actor Laurence Fishburne starred in a film version of *Always Outnumbered, Always Outgunned* on HBO.

Published First Science Fiction Novel

Mosley broke new ground in 1998 with the release of his first science fiction novel, *Blue Light*. Set in San Francisco during the 1960s, the plot focuses on a group of people who are struck by an extraterrestrial blue light. Some who are touched by the light die or go insane, while others are given supernatural abilities. Those with supernatural abilities are stalked by the Gray Man, an evil entity who seeks their destruction. Critical reviews of *Blue Light* were mixed. Patrick O'Kelley of *amazon.com* called the novel "somber and violent, bizarre and oddly reverent", but added that *Blue Light* marked "a promising new direction for Mosley." In the *New York Times Book Review,* Mel Watkins remarked that "for those readers accustomed to the gut-real encounters, sharp dialogue and quirky perceptions that enliven the first-person narrations of Mosley's Easy Rawlins mysteries. . .the surreal nature of *Blue Light* may be a disappointment."

Mosley published the novel, *Walkin' the Dog,* in late

1999. This novel signaled the return of Socrates Fortlow, the philosophical ex-convict that Mosley first introduced in *Always Outnumbered, Always Outgunned*. In *Walkin' the Dog,* Fortlow is faced with challenges such as being evicted from his home, avoiding confrontations with police, and caring for his two-legged dog, Killer. Although Fortlow is trying to live an honest life, he remains burdened by the sins of his past. Despite his difficult circumstances, he tries to face each day with determination and hope. *Walkin' the Dog* received generally favorable reviews. Writing for the *New York Times Book Review,* Adam Goodheart noted that "in prose as plain and gritty as asphalt, Mosley. . .adeptly builds a feeling of urgency and suspense around even seemingly ordinary episodes of his protagonist's life."

Voiced Social Concerns

In early 2000, Mosley published a social commentary entitled *Workin' the Chain Gang: Shaking Off the Dead Hand of History*. In this book, he challenges the American people to find imaginative and creative solutions to the political, social, racial, and economic problems within society. Among other things, he urges his readers to turn away from rampant consumerism and consumption, and cautions against overexposure to mass media. Mosley encourages readers to learn from the lessons and struggles of the African American experience, and envision a brighter future. Anthony O. Edmonds of the *Library Journal* called the book "a manifesto", and remarked that Mosley "offers little new or practical." In *Booklist,* Mary Carroll noted that "free market fanatics will hate this book", but believed that readers who are "receptive to a progressive critique of the religion of the market will value Mosley's creative contribution."

Walter Mosley has demonstrated a willingness to expand his horizons beyond the Easy Rawlins mystery series into the realms of science fiction and social commentary. He has actively used his popularity and influence to address the economic and social concerns of the day. As Emory Holmes II said in *Los Angeles Magazine,* Mosley has become "a rich and increasingly strident voice in publishing."

Selected writings

Devil in a Blue Dress, 1990.
A Red Death, 1991.
White Butterfly, 1992.
Black Betty, 1994.
RL's Dream, 1995.
A Little Yellow Dog, 1996.
Gone Fishin', 1997.
Always Outnumbered, Always Outgunned, 1997.
Blue Light, 1998.
Walkin' the Dog, 1999.
Workin' on the Chain Gang: Shaking Off the Dead

Hand of History, 2000.

Sources

American Visions, April\May 1992, pp. 32-34.
Booklist, May 1, 1996, p. 1469; January 1, 2000, p. 840.
California, August 1990, p. 115.
Cosmopolitan, July 1991, p. 28; July 1992, p. 30.
Detroit Free Press, November 17, 1991, p. 6.
Essence, January 1991, p. 32; October 1992, p. 50.
Kirkus Reviews, April 15, 1994; April 15, 1996.
Library Journal, June 1, 1991, p. 200; March 15, 1992, p. 68; February 1, 2000, p. 105.
Los Angeles Magazine, November 1998, p. 32.
Los Angeles Times, May 5, 1992, pp. B7, E1, E5; May 14, 1992, p. 6.
Los Angeles Times Book Review, July 14, 1991. pp. 1-2, 9.

New Statesman & Society, April 19, 1991, p. 37.
Newsweek, July 7, 1990, p. 65.
New York Times, September 4, 1990, pp. C13, C16.
New York Times Book Review, August 5, 1990, p. 29; June 5, 1994; January 26, 1997; November 15, 1998; November 7, 1999.
People, September 7, 1992, pp. 105-106.
Playboy, October 1995, p. 34.
Publishers Weekly, May 17, 1991, p. 57; April 25, 1994.
Vanity Fair, February 1993, pp. 46, 48, 50.

Other

Additional information for this profile was obtained from *amazon.com.*

—Ed Decker and David G. Oblender

Ronald Mutebi

1956—

King of Buganda

The life story of Ronald Muwenda Mutebi has sometimes been characterized as a reverse *Coming to America* tale, in reference to the 1988 Eddie Murphy film in which an African king undergoes drastic culture shock when he visits the West. The son of the deposed king of the Buganda, Uganda's largest ethnic group, Mutebi spent much of his life in England, and even worked as a window salesperson for a time. Mutebi returned to Uganda in 1987, and six years later was crowned the 36th Kabaka (king) of Buganda. The complex, tradition-rich ceremony marked the restoration of the ancient Ugandan kingdom 25 years after it and several others were technically abolished. Despite his years abroad and somewhat prosaic life, Mutebi asserted that he had always expected to fulfill his predestined duty. "Even though I had grown up in exile, I'd been brought up with the notion that I was my father's heir and that this role was something I would eventually do," he told Tim Carrington in a 1994 *Wall Street Journal* article.

An Ancient Line

Born in 1956, Mutebi is the son of Kabaka Sir Edward Mutesa, also known as King Freddy. The Bugandan royal house, which ruled over the 52 clans of the Bugandan people, enjoyed a tremendous position of power in Uganda. It was a rich, stable, and highly bureaucratized organization when the British arrived in the country in 1862 during the rule of Mutebi's great-grandfather. Sensing an opportunity to conquer a longtime rival, the neighboring Bunyoro kingdom, Mutebi's ancestor petitioned Britain's Queen Victoria for military help in order to subdue the Bunyoro. The clash would have a generations-long impact on Uganda. In 1893, Uganda was formally created as a British protectorate, and the Bugandan administrative system was implemented across the entire country. This led to lingering social and political resentment.

In 1953, a dispute arose between King Freddy and Uganda's British governor. The king was eventually ousted. "Exiled to England, King Freddy became a sportsman and a playboy, with a cool, classy presence reminiscent of Miles Davis," wrote *New York Times Magazine* writer Alex Shoumatoff. King Freddy returned two years later as a constitutional monarch, and when Uganda won its independence from the British Empire in 1962, Mutebi's father became the country's first president, a largely ceremonial post. The kingdom

At a Glance . . .

Born 1956 in Uganda; son of Kabaka Sir Edward Mutesa (King Freddy); married Sylvia Nagginda Luswata (a public relations specialist), August, 1999; children: Junju. *Education:* Attended Bradfield College, Cambridge University.

Career: Worked as a double-glazing salesperson and freelance writer in England in the 1970s and 1980s; returned to Uganda from exile, 1987; crowned 36th Kabaka (King) of Buganda, 1993-.

Addresses: *Office*—Royal Palace, Kampala, Uganda.

of Buganda itself, however, still enjoyed a large measure of autonomy. By this time, a young Ronald Mutebi had been sent to boarding school in England.

Fled Palace, Hailed a Cab

The new prime minister of Uganda, A. Milton Obote, was not of the Bugandan ethnic group, and a power struggle erupted between the Bugandan elite and the ruling government. In 1966, Uganda adopted a new constitution that abolished all tribal kingdoms. The conflict between the government and King Freddy escalated, and the royal Bugandan palace was stormed by soldiers led by Obote's army commander, General Idi Amin. Mutebi's father jumped over a palace wall, managed to find a taxicab, and made his way to England. Three years later, King Freddy died in a shabby London apartment, possibly poisoned by rivals. In 1971, Amin overthrew Obote in a military coup, and several years of dictatorship and murderous human-rights violations followed.

During this time, Mutebi studied at North London Polytechnic, then spent time at Bradfield College, part of the Cambridge university system. For a time, he even sold double thermopane windows door to door and, in the 1980s, occasionally contributed articles to a Nigerian magazine. Amin was overthrown in 1979, and Obote returned to power. However, he was ousted in a 1986 uprising led by Yoweri Museveni. The following year, Mutebi returned from his long exile and took up residence in a newly stabilized Uganda.

Restoration of Monarchy

Mutebi visited President Museveni in 1992, and urged restoration of the ancient Bugandan kingdom, at least in a ceremonial sense. Four other kingdoms were also allowed to resume leadership of their respective ethnic groups. Mutebi was crowned on July 31, 1993, in a lavish ceremony that re-created many of the traditional rites, except for an archaic practice of human sacrifice. He visited his father's preserved umbilical cord in a temple, touched the neck of a white cow with a ceremonial spear, and wore genuine leopard skin and shawls made from bark. The event was the focus of jubilant festivities throughout the Bugandan region of Uganda. Many exiles returned for the celebrations for the first time in a generation.

As a condition of his royal status, Mutebi is prohibited from becoming involved in political matters. His actual role is to utilize ethnic pride and a sense of destiny to shape Uganda's future. This includes using his position to generate support for various issues, such as halting the deforestation of Uganda and other environmental problems. "The more enlightened African governments in the 1990s have found, that rather than uproot ancient cultures, why not work hand in hand with them?" Mutebi explained to the *Wall Street Journal*'s Carrington. "A blending of ancient and modern is the only way Africa will progress."

An Opulent New Life

In Kampala, Uganda's capital city, Mutebi enjoys a much different life than the one he led in England. He has three palaces, and income from Bugandan lands ensures his financial security. One of his most important tasks is to settle clan disputes. Because there was no tribal leadership in Uganda for 30 years, Mutebi and other Ugandan monarchs were presented with a backlog of petitions.

Facing pressure to marry and produce an heir, Mutebi—already the parent of one son, whom he had fathered with a Rwandan woman—wed 35-year-old Sylvia Nagginda Luswata, a British-born Ugandan woman, in August of 1999. Luswata, who is not of the Bugandan ethnic group, had resided in the United States since her teens and was a graduate of New York University. She had worked for both the World Bank and the United Nations. The marriage of Mutebi and Luswata was marked by nationwide celebrations. Foreign correspondents in Kampala interviewed many Bugandans who were extremely optimistic about the continuation of the ancient royal line, which *New York Times* writer Ian Fisher described as "more than the usual cultural desire for an heir. It is rooted in the long troubles of Uganda and the desire of the people here to see the nation go on now that those troubles are gone."

Sources

Economist, December 19, 1998, p. 79.
New York Times, August 28, 1999.
New York Times Magazine, October 17, 1993, p. 24.
Time International, September 13, 1999, p. 41.
Wall Street Journal, December 19, 1994, pp. A1, A6.

—Carol Brennan

David Nakhid

1964—

Professional soccer player

Trinidadian soccer star David Nakhid played one season for the New England Revolution, one of the twelve teams of the Major League Soccer (MLS) organization. Nakhid's experience in North American soccer—which has yet to achieve the wild popularity that the sport enjoys in the rest of the world—was plagued by several difficulties, including a change in the team's coaching staff, a problematic losing streak, injuries, and a much-publicized incident in which a white teammate used a racial slur against Nakhid.

Nakhid was born in 1964 in the Republic of Trinidad and Tobago, two islands of the West Indies that lie just off the coast of Venezuela. It is a tropical, but highly modernized country where the majority of the population are descended from slaves brought to the Western hemisphere from Africa; English is the official language. A standout on the soccer field from an early age, Nakhid played for American University in Washington, D.C. during the mid-1980s, where he was an international-studies major. During his tenure, the team enjoyed several notable successes, and even made it to the National College Athletic Association's soccer championships during his junior year. In the 1985 finals, American University competed against the Uni-

versity of California at Los Angeles in a game that stretched into eight overtimes—the longest game in the history of collegiate soccer. Nakhid's team lost, 1-0.

An Overseas Veteran

After graduating from American University in 1986, Nakhid went on to spend eleven seasons playing for professional soccer teams in Europe and the Middle East. These included the Grasshoppers Zurich, a Swiss organization, a Greek team called PAOK, and Belgium's Waregem. He was also drafted by Al Ansar of Lebanon. As a member of the Grasshoppers, Nakhid was part of a team that took two national championships. During his stint with Waregem, he was twice voted Most Valuable Player. As a midfielder with Al Ansar, Nakhid and his team took three league championships. He also continued to play in Caribbean competitions. Nakhid was named Most Valuable Player at the Caribbean Shell Cup on three occasions. He was also given the honor of captaining the Trinidad and Tobago national team for the World Cup soccer championships in 1998.

The New England Revolution signed Nakhid, a mid-

At a Glance . . .

Born May 15, 1954, in Trinidad. *Education:* Earned degree in international studies from American University, 1986.

Career: Professional soccer player. Has played for Grasshoppers (Zurich, Switzerland),PAOK (Salonika, Greece), Waregem (Belgium), and Al Ansar (Lebanon); New England Revolution (a Major League Soccer organization team), Boston, MA, midfielder, 1998; also captain of Trinidad and Tobago national team.

Awards: Most Valuable Player, Caribbean Shell Cup, 1994, 1995, 1997.

Addresses: *Office*—Major League Soccer, 110 E. 42nd St., New York,NY 10017.

fielder, in February of 1998. As a member of the 12-team Major League Soccer organization, the Boston-based Revolution was part of a concerted effort to create a successful fan base for soccer among North Americans. However, as *New York Times* writer Kevin Baker noted a season later, "the fact remains that after four years of existence, M.L.S. is all but moribund, its attendance stagnant, its television ratings minuscule, its buzz inaudible."

Showed Early Promise

Nakhid had never played on a losing team until he arrived in Boston, and was predicted to become a key player who could help the Revolution advance to the M.L.S. playoffs. However, salary caps and an effort to keep the number of foreign players to a maximum of four per team hampered his job security from the start. Nakhid was the only player that season who was not signed to a guaranteed contract. The Revolution's coach, Thomas Rongen, was initially a great fan of Nakhid's, heralding him as one of the team's emerging standouts. However, problems surfaced early in the season. Nakhid sprained an ankle in a game against the Chicago Fire in June of 1998, which led to the Revolution's sixth straight loss. The losing streak demoralized Nakhid and his teammates.

Despite these difficulties, Nakhid remained optimistic. He planned to rehabilitate his ankle as quickly as possible, head back to the playing field, and help his team reverse their slide. "I still don't see anything real bad," Nakhid told the *Boston Globe*'s Jim Greenidge. "I'm still optimistic . . .. It has to start somewhere, and

I'm going to devote myself to seeing that we get back on track. I'm convinced we can still turn it around."

Encountered Prejudice

By August of 1998, the Revolution had lost an appalling nine games in a row. Moreover, some of Nakhid's teammates were angered when he requested some time off to play on the Caribbean All-Star team before the World Cup games—an honor he was virtually obliged to accept, since he was also captain of the Trinidad-Tobago team. The sniping reflected some internal problems and cultural differences within the world of international soccer. Some analysts claimed that players from the Caribbean were treated differently than European athletes, an accusation borne out by salary statistics—the predominantly black Caribbean soccer stars are the lowest-paid among the foreign players in the M.L.S. organization.

"It's like any other place in America," Nakhid told Frank Dell'Apa, another *Boston Globe* sportswriter. "We are seen as cheap labor. There is no way we will be paid as much as Europeans; even if they don't have comparable technical skills or production. It's something I disagree with." Moreover, players from the West Indies like Nakhid do not usually emerge as team leaders. "Caribbean players are seen as skill players," Nakhid told Dell'Apa. "It's the same situation as it used to be in the NBA, or the NFL, where the black quarterback was not considered to have the tactical brain for the position."

The situation within the Revolution continued to disintegrate. In late August of 1998, Rongen was replaced as the team's head coach. He later remarked said that some players had created problems on the team, but refused to name names. When the new coach, Walter Zenga, took over, Nakhid was not placed on the traveling team for the first game, and was benched during the next two. "Nakhid's situation is symptomatic of a team that has been fractured for many weeks," explained Dell'Apa, who argued that a particularly significant defeat for the Revolution in a game against Miami—the 3-2 loss probably killed their chances for a playoff spot—might have benefitted from Nakhid's skills had he been allowed to play more. Dell'Apa also noted that foreign players usually bear the brunt of the ill will when a soccer team is losing. Nakhid was pragmatic. "Someone was looking for a scapegoat, and maybe they found one," he told the *Boston Globe*.

Shocking Incident for M.L.S.

In October of 1998, during the final postseason practice for the Revolution, the tensions within the team erupted into violence. During an argument between Nakhid and a white teammate, Edwin Gorter, Gorter used a particularly ugly racial slur. Both men threw punches and had to be forcibly separated. The M.L.S. organization moved quickly to investigate the matter. Gorter was suspended for two games, ordered to make a public apology to Nakhid, and slapped with a $20,000 fine—the largest in M.L.S. history.

The money from Gorter's fine was used to pay for diversity training for all 12 teams in the league, as well as its front-office personnel. "Because MLS players come from a wide variety of environments, maybe they aren't sensitized to the results of what they say or do in this country," the League's commissioner, Douglas Logan, said, according to *Sports Illustrated*. "We bear the responsibility to educate people about that." *Boston Globe* writer Michael Holley, however, called the fine and forced apology pointless. "I would like to see the Revolution and the league set up a televised press conference in a section of Boston where Caribbean people live, maybe in Mattapan where Nakhid eats and gets his hair cut. Invite the community. Then ask Gorter to repeat what he said to Nakhid and ask him why he said it," Holley suggested.

Less than one month after the incident with Gorter, Nakhid was placed on waivers by the Revolution. The team's management claimed that the Revolution had to part with Nakhid because they were already over the four-man foreign player limit. Two other players who were playing for the Revolution on temporary work visas were also waived. Nakhid's experiences in North American soccer were not unusual. "Dispelling stereotypes is something I've had to do at university and in Europe," he had once said in the interview with Dell'Apa in the *Boston Globe*. "The only way to break it is to work hard."

Sources

Boston Globe, March 23, 1998, p. D7; June 18, 1998, p. F7; September 18, 1998, p. E2; October 11, 1998, p. C14; November 3, 1998, p. C4.
Fort Lauderdale Standard-Times, April 5, 1998.
New York Times, November 28, 1999.
Sports Illustrated, October 19, 1998, p. 23.

Other

Additional information for this profile was provided by the Major League Soccer website at http:\\www.mlsnet.com

—Carol Brennan

Louise Patterson

1901–1999

Cultural critic, activist

Before her death in 1999, Louise Thompson Patterson was the last surviving personality of the Harlem Renaissance. Although she was not actually one of the creative names associated with this flowering of African American culture in New York during the 1920s and 1930s, Patterson was a friend and confidant of many of the writers, musicians, and artists of the movement. She also played a key role in developing the movement's leftist political stance. An economist who worked for a variety of labor-friendly political organizations, Patterson was also attractive and vivacious, a popular hostess known for her ability to gather leading radical and creative minds at her Convent Avenue apartment for elegant dinners and raucous discussions.

Patterson was born Louise Alone Thompson in Chicago in 1901. Her family moved several times during her formative years, and they eventually settled in Oakland, California in 1919 after living in several western cities. In 1923, she became one of first African Americans to earn a degree from the University of California at Berkeley. A woman of any color with an economics degree from a prestigious school still faced discrimination in the job market, and Patterson was unable to find work. She moved to Chicago to pursue a graduate degree at the University of Chicago, but left school to become a teacher in the South. She took a job in Pine Bluff, Arkansas, in 1925, and was hired the following year at the Hampton Institute in Virginia.

Fired from Hampton

Patterson was already of a firm mind about certain issues, and she experienced problems with Hampton Institute's predominantly white administration. When students protested some rather demeaning official campus policies—such as a movie theater that was brightly lit to discourage necking, or a Hampton chorale's practice of serenading white visitors on Sundays with plantation songs—Patterson supported the demonstrators. She was frequently at odds with the school's administration, and was strongly encouraged to seek employment elsewhere.

In 1928, Patterson moved to New York after she had been awarded an Urban League fellowship to study at the New School for Social Research. She initially considered pursuing a career in social work as an excellent means of addressing social and economic injustice. However, Patterson quickly realized that the social welfare agencies of the day fostered a sense of

At a Glance . . .

Born September 9, 1901, in Chicago, IL; died August 27, 1999, in New York, NY; married Wallace Thurman (a writer; separated after six months and divorced) married William L. Patterson (a political activist), 1940; children: Mary Louise. *Education:* Earned degree (cum laude) from University of California at Berkeley, 1923; studied at the University of Chicago, c. 1924, and at the New School for Social Research, late 1920s.

Career: Worked for a Chicago firm, c. 1924; teacher in Pine Bluff, AR, 1925-26; Hampton Institute, Hampton, VA, 1926-27; affiliated with the Congregational Educational Society, New York City, 1930-33; worked for Langston Hughes and Zora Neale Hurston as an editorial secretary; National Committee for the Defense of Political Prisoners, assistant national secretary, 1933-34; International Workers' Order, organizer after 1934, and national recording secretary; affiliated with the Civil Rights Congress in the 1950s; co-founder of its Sojourners for Truth and Justice women's auxiliary.

Member: American Communist Party, Friends of the Soviet Union (secretary of Harlem chapter).

comedy written in a rural black dialect. After Hurston allegedly became jealous of Patterson, work on *Mule Bone* was discontinued. For the rest of her life, Patterson was forced to deny rumors that she and Hughes had been romantically involved.

During the Great Depression of the early 1930s, Patterson continued to become increasingly involved in the American Communist Party, which was thriving in Harlem at the time. With Augusta Savage, an artist, she founded the Vanguard, a leftist Harlem social club, and from their soirees formed the Harlem branch of a group known as the Friends of the Soviet Union. Patterson served as secretary of the local chapter for a time, and organized a much-publicized, months-long excursion of several prominent members of the Harlem Renaissance and other rising young African Americans to the Soviet Union at the invitation of a state-run film studio in Moscow. A film was planned, entitled *Black and White*, that would portray the historical and contemporary oppression of both African American and leftist movements in the United States. Langston Hughes accompanied Patterson as one of the 22 African Americans who sailed for the Soviet Union in June of 1932. When the group arrived in the Soviet Union, they were treated like royalty. "For all of us who experienced discrimination based on color in our own land, it was strange to find our color a badge of honor," Patterson wrote in an unpublished memoir, according to *New York Times Magazine* journalist Robert S. Boynton.

"Madame Moscow"

The film *Black and White* was never made. The film's German director spoke neither Russian nor English, and was rather surprised that none of the African Americans slated to star in the film could sing or dance well. In addition, a Russian screenwriter who knew little about African American culture or history wrote the script. Reasons for the project's cancellation were varied. Some claimed that the Soviet government had abandoned the film as part of a diplomatic-recognition deal with United States, "while Patterson's group insisted that the movie had simply fallen victim to its own best intentions," wrote Boynton, "a sentiment that earned her [Patterson] the sobriquet 'Madame Moscow.'"

During her time abroad, Patterson traveled through Central Asia, and eventually returned to the United States when her mother fell ill. After 1933, she worked for the National Committee for the Defense of Political Prisoners, serving as assistant national secretary. She also officially joined the Communist Party. The infamous Scottsboro trial of the early 1930s also rallied Patterson's organizational skills. In Alabama, nine African American youths from Scottsboro had been accused of sexually assaulting two white women on a train. All of the youths received death sentences or

dependency. At the same time, she was living in Harlem and meeting some of the more radical thinkers of the era. Patterson became a friend of William Patterson, an African American lawyer who had been part of the legal team on the infamous Sacco and Vanzetti case. Through the influence of people like William Patterson, her political convictions began to shift even more to the left.

Friend of Langston Hughes

For a brief time, Patterson was married to a Harlem Renaissance writer, Wallace Thurman, but the couple separated after only a few months. She lived in one of Harlem's affluent areas, and became friends with other figures associated with the burgeoning arts scene there, including the painter Aaron Douglas and his wife Alta. By 1930 Patterson had found work with the Congregational Educational Society, an organization that promoted better race relations through the growing organized labor movement. Patterson worked as an organizer for the CES, and also found work as an editorial secretary for Langston Hughes and Zora Neale Hurston when they were working on *Mule Bone*, a folk lengthy prison terms, despite dubious legal evidence against them. The Scottsboro case achieved tremendous notoriety, and was emblematic of the harsh, institutionalized injustices of the Deep South during that era. Patterson organized several Harlem events and a march on the nation's capital to protest the plight of the Scottsboro defendants.

Political Commitment Grew

By 1935 Patterson was working on behalf of a strong, organized group called the International Workers' Order, which had many chapters across the United States. The IWO was organized into chapters according to ethnicity, and offered low-cost insurance and other benefits to its members. The organization also fostered a political awareness through its newspapers and social halls. In 1938, Patterson and Langston Hughes founded the Harlem Suitcase Theatre. The tour company, funded by the IWO to provide a forum for African American playwrights, presented Hughes's *Don't You Want to Be Free?* as its debut performance.

Patterson married her longtime friend, William L. Patterson—by now one of the leaders of the American Communist Party—in 1940, and moved with him to Chicago. The couple worked for the IWO on the city's predominantly African American South Side. After the IWO was ordered to dissolve by a 1947 decree from the U.S. Attorney General, the couple devoted their energies to the founding of the Civil Rights Congress. In its decade-long existence, the CRC grew in strength to 10,000 members, and helped forced passage of some early, significant laws that protected civil rights in the years before the landmark Civil Rights Act of 1964. The CRC also worked to publicize cases of racial injustice in the South, defended Communists convicted

in the tense atmosphere of the McCarthy hearings and anti-Communist sentiment of the 1950s, and provided a training ground for many of the leaders of the civil-rights protests of the 1960s.

Patterson was active in the CRC's women's auxiliary, Sojourners for Truth and Justice, and continued to involve herself in political causes long after its dissolution. She even raised money for the defense fund of Communist Party member Angela Davis in the 1970s. Widowed in 1980, Patterson died in a New York nursing home in 1999. A daughter, Mary Louise Patterson, survived her. Langston Hughes's 1942 collection of poetry, *Shakespeare in Harlem,* is dedicated to her.

Sources

Books

Encyclopedia of the American Left, edited by Mari Jo Buhle, Paul Buhle, and Dan Georgakas, Garland Reference Library of the Social Sciences, Garland Publishing, 1990.
Facts on File Encyclopedia of Black Women in America, edited by Darlene Clark Hine, Facts on File, 1993, pp. 149-150.

Periodicals

Los Angeles Times, September 19, 1999, p. 2.
New York Times, September 2, 1999, p. C20.
New York Times Magazine, January 2, 2000.

—Carol Brennan

Walter Payton

1954–1999

Retired professional football player

One of the strongest and most talented men in football, Walter Payton could bench-press 390 pounds, leg-press more than 700 pounds, throw a football 60 yards, punt it 70 yards, kick 45-yard field goals, and walk the width of the field on his hands. It was this phenomenal combination of power and control that allowed Payton to play in every game except one during his 13 years of National Football League (NFL) competition.

Retiring after the 1987 season, Payton left behind 26 Chicago Bears team records and several NFL records. Ten years later, many of his records still stood, including most yards rushing in a career, most combined yards (rushing and receiving) in a career, most career touchdowns rushing, most 1,000-yard rushing seasons, most 100-yard rushing games in career, and most rushes in career. More than these individual achievements, however, his all-around team play—pass catching, blocking, personality, selflessness, and leadership—inspired his former coach Mike Ditka to call him, as quoted by Koslow, "the very best football player I've ever seen, period—at any position."

Walter Jerry Payton was born on July 25, 1954, in Columbia, Mississippi, "a kid's paradise" in his own words. Woods extended from one side of his house to the Pearl River. Several factories were on the other side. Both settings provided numerous opportunities for mischief with his older brother and sister, Eddie and Pamela. Early on, Payton used his natural running ability to avoid being caught by security guards while playing hide and seek at the nearby factories.

Hyperactive, prankish, and strong-willed, young Walter was often punished by his Baptist parents, Peter and Alyne. Payton later assessed his parents as firm but fair disciplinarians who instilled strong religious faith in their children. "My parents spent a lot of time with us and made us feel loved and wanted. I didn't care much about what went on around me, as long as I was in solid at home," he later recalled to Koslow.

Peter Payton worked at a factory that manufactured packs and parachutes for the U.S. government. By 1962, he had saved enough money to move his family to a new home with separate rooms for each child. It was located just one block from John J. Jefferson High School, the segregated school that all African American children attended from grades one through 12. Both parents instilled in their children an ideal of

At a Glance . . .

Born Walter Jerry Payton on July 25, 1954, in Columbia, MS; died November 1, 1999, in South Barrington, IL; son of Peter (a factory worker) and Alyne Payton; married Connie Norwood on July 7, 1976 (filed for divorce, 1994); children: Jarrett, Brittany; *Education:* Jackson State College (later Jackson State University), Jackson, MS, B.A., 1975. *Religion:* Baptist.

Career: Football halfback, punter, and placekicker, Jackson State College, 1971-74; halfback, Chicago Bears, 1975-87; part-owner, Payton-Coyne Racing Team; Walter Payton's Roundhouse, owner, 1996-99; Walter Payton Inc., owner and president,1979-99.

Selected awards: National Collegiate Athletic Association (NCAA) scoring leader,1973; Black All-American Team, 1973-74; NCAA Division II All-America Team, 1974;College All-Star Team, 1974; National Football Conference (NFC) rushing leader, 1976-80;National Football League (NFL) Pro Bowl, 1976-80 and 1983-86; NFL rushing leader and Most Valuable Player, 1977; United Press International (UPI) Athlete of the Year, 1977; Black Athlete of the Year, 1984; Professional Football Hall of Fame, inductee, 1993.

Member: Chicago Bears, board of directors; Walter Payton Foundation.

excellence, "never to settle for second best," as Payton later recalled.

Competed in High School

Taking his parents' principles to heart, Payton became a better-than-average student, though music took precedence over studies or sports. He was constantly drumming or tapping out a beat on anything in reach. Often he would dance or sing instead of doing his household chores, much to the dismay of his mother and siblings. "When you've got an angry brother and sister chasing you with a broom and a wet towel, well, you learn some good moves," he told a Football Hall of Fame audience at his 1993 induction.

In the ninth grade, Payton joined the track team as a long jumper and played drums in the school band. He consciously avoided the football team where his

brother, Eddie, was the star running back. Payton later claimed he did not want his mother having to worry about both of her sons being hurt. After Eddie Payton graduated, Jefferson High School's football coach asked Payton to try out for the team. Payton, then a sophomore, agreed only after being allowed to stay in the band as well. On his first high-school carry, he ran 65 yards for a touchdown. It was just a taste of things to come.

Jefferson merged with all-white Columbia High School in 1969, and Payton became the undisputed star of the newly integrated football team. Tommy Davis, Columbia's football coach, claimed that he could always count on Payton when the team needed to score. Payton's statistics proved that this was no exaggeration: he scored in every game during his junior and senior years. He was named to the all-conference team three years in a row. Payton also led the Little Dixie Conference in scoring during his senior year and made the all-state team. In addition to excelling at football, Payton averaged 18 points a game for Columbia's basketball team, leaped three-quarters of an inch short of 23 feet in the long jump, played some baseball, and continued to play drums in the school band.

Upon graduating, Payton followed his brother to nearby Jackson State College, soon starting alongside him in the team's backfield. Eddie Payton graduated after Payton's first year at college, however, and joined the NFL, allowing the younger Payton to become Jackson State's lone star. Payton was the team's halfback, punter, and place kicker, and he even passed on occasional option plays. Playing against other predominantly black schools, he ended his sophomore season as the nation's second leading scorer including the highest single-game total (46 points) in college history. The following year, 1973, he ran for 1,139 yards, led the country in scoring with 160 points, was voted the most valuable player in the conference, and was named to the Black All-America team.

Determined to become even better, Payton embarked on a new training program with his brother during the summer of 1973. The two Paytons sprinted up and down the sandbanks and steep levees alongside the Pearl River during the hottest part of the day. These workouts did more than just build up leg strength and endurance; the constantly shifting sand helped develop balance and the ability to better make a cut or abruptly change direction. Throughout the rest of his career, Payton would conduct similar workouts in comparable settings.

This grueling conditioning led to a successful senior year. Payton capped his college career by becoming the National Collegiate Athletic Association (NCAA) all-time leading scorer with 464 points. He was chosen to the Black All-America team again, made the NCAA Division II All-America team, and was named to the College All-Star team. About the only time he finished in second place was during a televised *Soul Train* dance contest. "He still swears that if he'd had a girl who could dance better, he could have won that contest," his coach Bob Hill told *Esquire* years later. Academically, Payton was an all-star as well, graduating in three-and- a-half years with his bachelor's degree in special education and beginning work on a master's degree. He studied hard, he later wrote in his autobiography *Sweetness,* "to help dispel the myth that athletes in general and black athletes in particular don't have to work to get their diplomas and that they don't learn anything anyway."

Payton also picked up the nickname "Sweetness" during his college years; it would stick with him throughout his career. Some claimed it was because of his sweet moves on the football field. Others attributed it to his sincerity, humble disposition, soft high-pitched voice, and concern for others. Raised a devout Baptist, he always led the team in its pre-game prayer.

The Chicago Bears chose Payton in the first round of the 1975 NFL draft, making him the fourth player picked overall. He demanded a signing bonus larger than that received four years earlier by Archie Manning, a quarterback from the University of Mississippi, a school formerly closed to African Americans. The Bears offered him 126,000, the highest amount ever paid to anyone from Mississippi.

The Bears were one of the NFL's more storied teams, counting many legendary names among their former players—Red Grange, Bronko Nagurski, Sid Luckman, Gale Sayers, and Dick Butkus. But these stars and those glory days were long gone—the franchise had not had a winning season since 1967. Payton's first season, 1975, was no exception. The team lost six of its first seven games. Payton was slowed by an ankle injury, missed the only game in his NFL career, and played sporadically in others. After healing, though, he gave the Chicago fans an inkling of his talent by leading the league in kickoff returns and finishing the season with 679 yards rushing, the most for any Bears runner since 1969.

The following summer, Connie Norwood, his fiancee, graduated from Jackson State. The two were married, and she became a settling influence in his life. That season he became the focal point of the Bears' offense, carrying the ball 311 times, the most in the league, and gaining 1,390 yards. An injury in the season's final game cost him a chance at the league rushing title, though he led the National Football Conference (NFC) in yards gained. His performance helped the Bears finish with seven victories and seven losses, their best season in eight years.

Most Valuable Player

At training camp in 1977, reporters noticed a different Payton. No longer open and seemingly carefree, he was silent, moody, and irritable. Once the season started, the reason became clear—he had been preparing himself for one of the greatest individual seasons in NFL history. Payton gained 160 yards in the season opener. The first 200-yard game in his career came in the seventh week. He ran for 275 yards in the tenth game, which broke O. J. Simpson's single-game rushing record. Many speculated he would break Simpson's season rushing record of 2,003 yards as well. He came close, but a freezing rain during the final game turned the field to ice, made footing a nightmare, and limited him to 47 yards.

Payton ended the 1977 season with 1,852 yards rushing, leading the NFL in yards gained and carries. The Bears finished 9-5 and qualified for the playoffs for the first time in 14 years. To nobody's surprise, Payton was voted the league's Most Valuable Player. At 23-years old, he was the youngest player to win the honor. Further accolades came from United Press International (UPI), which designated him its Athlete of the Year.

Fans from across the nation began to recognize Payton by his unique stutter step, running on his toes with short, stiff-legged strides. Although he could run 40 yards in 4.5 seconds, he was never a real breakaway threat, and was often caught from behind by opposing defenders. Compact instead of graceful, he preferred running up the middle or off tackle, surprising would-be tacklers with frequent sudden cutbacks and punishing them with a forearm, shoulder, or helmet. No other halfback combined Payton's speed, shiftiness, and brute power.

"I've never seen anybody who's more reluctant to get out of the way of a hit," his former coach Mike Ditka recalled in *Esquire.* "He really does look to punish the guy tackling him." No matter how hard he was tackled, Payton always would spring to his feet immediately and return to the huddle. He enjoyed blocking for other running backs or protecting his quarterback against blitzing linebackers seemingly as much as he loved running the ball. "That's what sets him head and shoulders above other running backs," Gale Sayers—also a legendary Bears running back—commented in *Esquire,* "the maximum effort he puts into the other phases of the game." After scoring a touchdown, Payton would hand the football to one of the Bears offensive linemen who blocked for him, explaining in Koslow's biography, *Walter Payton,* that "they're the ones who do all the work."

Became a Superstar

Before the 1978 season began, Payton signed contracts for the next three seasons reflecting his superstar status—400,000 for 1978, 425,000 for 1979, and 450,000 plus incentive bonuses for 1980. Clearly, the Bears were expecting big things from him and better days for the team. Under new coach Neill Armstrong, the Bears finished with a 7-9 record despite Payton's 1,395 yards, most in the NFC, and 50 pass receptions. Together with fullback Roland Harper's 992 yards, the two runners accounted for 72 percent of the Bears' offense.

The following year, Payton played with a painful pinched nerve in his shoulder but still amassed 1,610 yards, again leading the NFC. The Bears made the playoffs with a 10-6 record, but they were eliminated in the first round. He gained 1,460 yards in 1980 for an unprecedented fifth consecutive NFC rushing title, but the Bears fell to 7-9. The team continued its mediocre play the next year, finishing 6-10, and Payton, injured most of the season with cracked ribs and a sore shoulder, slipped to 1,222 yards, failing to win the NFC rushing title or make the Pro Bowl. Even so, he became the first player in NFL history to run for 1,000 yards six years in a row.

The Bears realized Payton's value, and signed him to a three-year contract worth 2 million. They also hired Mike Ditka as the new head coach. The 1982 season was tarnished by a player strike, however, and the Bears finished 3-6. The next season, with Jim McMahon installed at quarterback, they finished 8-8. Payton ran for 1,421 yards and caught 53 passes for 607 yards, personally accounting for 36 percent of the Bears' total yardage. After the season, Payton had arthroscopic surgery on both knees and renegotiated his contract. He received 240,000 a year for life, making him the highest-paid player in NFL history.

What Payton really wanted was to play for a Super Bowl champion. The 1984 Bears showed tremendous promise. Their defense was strong and the offensive line was able to open big holes for Payton and the other running backs, while effectively blocking for quarterback McMahon. Although the team finished 10-6, the season was highlighted by Payton breaking Jim Brown's 19-year NFL career rushing record of 12,312 yards on October 7. He finished the season with 1,684 yards and caught 45 passes to set a new Bears career receiving record.

In the divisional playoff game against the Washington Redskins, Payton ran for 104 yards, threw a 19-yard touchdown pass, and blocked with such ferocity that he knocked a defensive back out of the game. The Bears defeated Washington by a score of 23-19, but they were shut out by the San Francisco 49ers in the NFC title game the following week. Despite his 92 yards rushing and three pass receptions, Payton was despondent, calling it "the hardest thing I ever had to deal with."

Became a Super Bowl Champion

Payton and the rest of his teammates would have their revenge in 1985. Running up a 15-1 record with a devastating defense and a powerful offense, the Bears blasted through the regular season, strutting their superiority with an arrogant attitude and a music video entitled "The Super Bowl Shuffle." Payton enjoyed another excellent season, rushing for 1,551 yards.

Chicago won its two playoff games at home to earn the right to play the New England Patriots in Super Bowl XX. Like most of the Bears' regular season games, the result was never in doubt. Chicago crushed New England by a score of 46-10. Payton had his Super Bowl ring, but he seemed unhappy and moody in the locker room. Reporters speculated that he was upset because he had not scored a touchdown. They underestimated his competitive nature. "It wasn't the touchdown," he told *Esquire* months later. "The game was dull."

The 1986 Bears showed every sign of repeating as champions. They finished 14-2, while Payton displayed his usual form with 1,333 yards rushing and 37 pass receptions. The team stumbled in the playoffs, however, losing to Washington by a score of 27-13. The next season was marred by another player strike. Although the Bears and Payton played well enough to win 11 of their 15 games, they again lost to Washington in the playoffs. Payton was 33-years old, and the Bears had started to split his playing time with talented newcomer Neal Anderson. After 13 years, Payton decided it was time to retire while still on top of his game. He left behind 26 Chicago Bears team records and several NFL records: most rushes (3,838); most yards rushing (16,726); most combined (running and receiving) yards (21,736); most rushing touchdowns (110); most 1,000-yard seasons (10); and most 100-yard games (77) of any running back in history. Former teammate Dan Hampton accurately summed up Payton's career: "No one on this football team and no one in the NFL is actually in Walter Payton's league."

Following his retirement from the NFL, Payton began racing cars and boats while turning his financial attention full time to Walter Payton Inc., his personal company holding investments in real estate, timber, and restaurants. For many years, he worked to become the first African American to own an NFL franchise. He also devoted a great deal of time to various charities in the Chicago area and was on the Chicago Bears' board of directors. He was particularly involved with the Walter Payton Foundation, a children's charity founded by the Bears. On July 31, 1993, Payton was inducted into the Football Hall of Fame. His son, Jarrett, made the presentation, telling the assembled crowd: "Not only is my dad an exceptional athlete . . . he's my biggest role model and best friend. We do a lot of things together . . . I'm sure my sister will endorse this statement: we have a super dad."

Contracted a Deadly Disease

In February of 1999, Payton called a press conference and tearfully announced that he was suffering from a rare liver disease known as primary sclerosing cholangitis or PSC. The disease causes ducts that remove bile from the liver to become blocked. Bile backs up and permanently damages the liver. Payton told the press that he needed a liver transplant in order to save his life. Following the press conference Mike Singletary, Payton's close friend and former teammate, tried to remain positive. "As I look at Walter and the situation, I think this can be one of his finest hours," he told *People Weekly.* "I think there can be a great example out of this."

However, Payton received another devastating blow in May of 1999 when he learned that he had bile duct cancer. Because of the cancer, he was no longer eligible for a liver transplant. Although his fate was sealed, Payton faced the future with characteristic courage and dignity. On November 1, 1999, he died at his home in South Barrington, Illinois. Upon learning of Payton's death, NFL commissioner Paul Tagliabue told *People Weekly.* "The tremendous grace and dignity he displayed in his final months reminded us again why 'Sweetness' was the perfect nickname for Walter Payton." On November 6, 1999, fans, friends, loved ones, and former teammates attended a memorial service for Payton at Chicago's Soldier Field, the same field on which he had played so brilliantly. Rev. Jesse Jackson spoke at the service. As reported by the CNN.com, he told the assembled crowd "This light called Sweetness now belongs to heaven and to the ages."

Sources

Books

Koslow, Philip, *Walter Payton,* Chelsea House, 1995.
Payton, Walter, with Jenkins, Jerry B., *Sweetness,* Contemporary Books, 1978.

Periodicals

Chicago Tribune, September 2, 1979.
Esquire, October 1986, p. 91-97.
Jet, September 5, 1994, p. 48.
New York Times, January 4, 1985, p. 21.
Newsweek, December 5, 1977, p. 63.
People Weekly, November 15, 1999, p. 56-58.
Sport, December 1977 p. 57.
Sporting News, October 1, 1984, p. 2.
Sports Illustrated, August 16, 1982, p. 18.

Other

Additional information for this profile was obtained from CNN.com.

—James J. Podesta and David G. Oblender

Mekhi Phifer

1975—

Actor, rapper

Although he had no way of knowing it at the time, one of Mekhi Phifer's high school jobs would give him experience that he'd later apply in his career. Worn down by minimum-wage jobs, Phifer tried his hand as a street corner drug dealer—for exactly one day. However, he quickly realized that drug dealing was not his true calling. With no prior acting experience, director Spike Lee chose him to star as a drug dealer in his film *Clockers*. From there, Phifer went on to star in a slew of both moderately successful and critically acclaimed films.

Phifer was born in 1975, and raised in Harlem with his half brother. His mother, Rhoda, was a single mom and elementary school teacher. He never met his father. Phifer credits his mother constantly, applauding her for having the courage to raise him on her own. Although the family didn't have much money, he told *People,* "she always provided everything I needed." Phifer also remarked in *Essence,* "I know a lots of brothers just trying to do their thing and stay out of trouble. Thanks to my mom I didn't get caught up in the street nonsense."

Bad Career Choice

Phifer first tried his hand at acting at the age of seven. He played the Ghost of Christmas Present in a Harlem community center production of *A Christmas Carol.* Phifer studied hard in school, and was a good student. He also worked several after-school jobs that paid only minimum wage. At the age of 16, Phifer tried his hand

at dealing drugs. While peddling marijuana and crack cocaine on a Harlem street corner, he quickly realized that drug dealing was not the life for him. Phifer told *People,* "I was like, 'What am I doing out here? My mom raised me better than this.'" He went on to graduate from Lincoln Square Auxiliary Services High School in 1994, and was accepted into the State University of New York's electrical engineering program in New Paltz. A decision to accompany his cousin on a film casting call would change Phifer's life forever.

Phifer and his cousin attended an open casting call for the Spike Lee film, *Clockers.* Phifer showed up at the audition with a Woolworth's photo booth snapshot and no professional experience. Out of the 1,000 other hopefuls, and after ten callbacks, he landed a part in the film. "We got there and one of the casting associates pulled me aside and told me to come back, I was really excited," he told *Teen Magazine.* Phifer played the lead role of Strike, a moody 19-year-old crack dealer who is accused of a murder he may or may not have committed in the Brooklyn projects. Critics praised *Clockers* as one of Lee's strongest films, and lauded Phifer's performance. *Entertainment Weekly* wrote that the film was "a work of staggering intelligence and emotional force," and that Phifer played Strike "beautifully." *The New Republic* wrote that Phifer "plays Strike with a corkscrew ungainlyness that suggests both victim and rebel." Spike Lee told *People* magazine, "Mekhi definately knows who he is. He's very talented."

Phifer's role in *Clockers* earned the young actor a lot

At a Glance . . .

Born in 1975. *Education:* graduated from Lincoln Square Auxiliary Services high school, 1994.

Career: Actor; starred in the films: *Clockers,* 1995; *The Tuskegee Airmen,* 1995; *High School High,* 1996; *Soul Food,* 1997; *I Still Know What You Did Last Summer,* 1998; *A Lesson Before Dying,* 1999; *O,* 2000; *The Imposter,* 2000; released debut rap album, *New York Related: The HF Project,* 1999.

Member: Screen Actors Guild, 1995-.

Addresses: *Agent*—William Morris Agency, 151 El Camino Dr., BeverlyHills, CA 90212;

of attention, and more offers of acting roles. He landed a role in the critically acclaimed HBO movie *The Tuskegee Airmen,* which told the story of African American army fighter pilots who fought bravely in World War II. Phifer then starred with comedian Jon Lovitz in the comedy spoof *High School High.* The young actor made a favorable impression on the producer of *High School High,* David Zucker. Zucker told *People* that he enjoyed working with Phifer because, "He has no chip on his shoulder, no pretensions. He just knocked me over."

Teen Prince

In the popular music video for Brandy and Monica's "This Boy is Mine," Phifer made a cameo appearance as a man torn between the two pop music princesses. As a result of his appearance in the video, teen audiences throughout the world began to recognize his face. Phifer welcomed the attention, but wasn't entirely comfortable with the idea of being recognized when he went out. "I like it when people show me love," he told *Teen Magazine,* "but sometimes it's weird."

Phifer appeared in the moderately successful ensemble drama *Soul Food,* which was produced by R&B star Babyface. Phifer played Lem Davis, a volatile but good-natured ex-con who is married to the youngest daughter in a large and dynamic family. The family's willingness to gather for dinner each Sunday, through both good and bad times, is the glue which holds them together. *Soul Food* writer and director George Tillman Jr. told People, "He [Phifer] brings a natural aura to all the characters he plays. You can identify with him so much."

In 1998 Phifer starred in the horror film *I Still Know*

What You Did Last Summer, which was the sequel to the popular *I Know What You Did Last Summer.* Phifer played Tyrell Martin, the college boyfriend of Karla Wilson, who is played by Brandy Norwood. Martin and Wilson, along with their teenage friends, spend their Fourth of July weekend being chased and murdered by a fisherman with a bloody hook for a hand.

After his appearance in *I Still Know What You Did Last Summer,* Phifer took on a more serious role. In *A Lesson Before Dying,* a 1999 television movie based on the best-selling novel by Ernest J. Gaines, Phifer portrays Jefferson, a young African American man from a small town who is wrongly accused of killing a white shop owner. Jefferson is humiliated by whites during the trial, and his self-esteem is shattered. A local school teacher named Grant Wiggins, who is played by Don Cheadle, is sent to help restore the boy's dignity before he faces execution.

Returned to First Love

In 1998, Phifer started to expand his focus beyond acting. He released his debut rap album, *New York Related: The HF Project.* "I've been rhyming since I was 12 or 13," Phifer told *Teen Magazine.* "Music is my first love." He also became a partner in a management company that focused on launching new talent. In 2000, Phifer starred in a youthful adaptation of William Shakespeare's *Othello.* The film, which is called *O,* takes place in a modern-day wealthy prep school. He also starred with Gary Sinise in *The Imposter,* a film about aliens invading earth.

Phifer looks forward to eventually getting married and starting a family. Although he has little spare time, he won't spend it in acting class. Phifer laughs at the idea of being told to act like a fish, or to "sizzle like bacon." "I just want to study life," he told *People.* As an actor, Phifer plans to continue making films. However, he is willing to wait for quality roles. Phifer told *Jet,* "If I can't sit in the movie theater and chill and be proud, I don't need to be watching it—let alone starring in it."

Selected filmography

Clockers, 1995.
The Tuskegee Airmen, 1995.
High School High, 1996.
Soul Food, 1997.
I Still Know What You Did Last Summer, 1998.
A Lesson Before Dying, 1999.
O, 2000.
The Imposter, 2000.

Sources

Periodicals

Entertainment Weekly, September 25, 1995, p. 84.
Essence, January 1998, p.54.
Jet, June 21, 1999, p.25.
New Republic, October 2, 1995, p.38.
People Weekly, December 25, 1995, p. 124; November 23, 1998, p.107.
Teen Magazine, November 1997, p.46.

Other

Additional information for this profile was obtained from "Mekhi Phifer," *Internet Movie Database,* http:\\www.imdb.com (February 24, 2000); and " *Young Hollywood.com,* http:\\www.younghollywood.com (February 24, 2000).

—Brenna Sanchez

Norma Quarles

1936—

Journalist

Norma Quarles worked her way up through the ranks at NBC and CNN to become a respected journalist, but not until she'd tried careers as a boutique retail buyer and real estate broker. Once she made the jump to broadcasting, as a 36-year-old divorced mother of two, there was no looking back. After 21 years with NBC News and its affiliates, where she covered such nationally significant stories as the Bernhard Goetz shootings and the Baby M case, Quarles was inducted into the Hall of Fame of the National Association of Black Journalists. She then became a correspondent for CNN. Throughout her career, she's remained true to her multiracial roots, challenging stereotypes in the media and being respected for it.

Something of a Loner

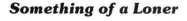

Born to Trinidadian parents in 1936, Quarles embodied the concept of the American melting pot, but was often ostracized for it. Even in the mixed community of New York City's South Bronx, Quarles—who is part Portuguese, English, Scottish, black, and Chinese—didn't fit in. "Back then," Quarles told Cosmopolitan, "people fell into one of two categories: black or white."

The neighborhood kids thought she was strange and made fun of her for not eating chitlins or collard greens. "So I never had many friends," she continued. "I was something of a loner." As an adult, Quarles vacationed in Cartegena, Colombia. Surrounded by multiracial people, who "looked just like me," she told Cosmopolitan, she felt like she belonged. "I've always known that I was different, but I never realized that it had such an effect on me."

With her exotic look, Quarles had a tough time fitting in even when she attended New York's Hunter College. She married an African American insurance executive at the age of 18 and moved to Chicago, where she started a family and became a dedicated mother. After spending years speaking in public at PTA meetings while her children were in school, Quarles had talent enough to audition and win a broadcasting position at a Chicago radio station, WSDM. The station had just changed its format to jazz, and featured female deejays. Because it was a small operation, Quarles was called on to be more than a pretty voice, and had to "do everything," she told Cosmopolitan, in addition to being on the air eight hours a day.

Her biggest struggle in Chicago had nothing to do with handling a challenging job. She felt that Chicago during the 1960s was steeped in racism. "They make no bones about the fact that they don't like you . . ." Quarles said in *Cosmopolitan*. With her family, Quarles moved into a primarily white middle-class neighborhood. Within a year, the entire neighborhood was African American. For the first time, her mixed background came into focus, and Quarles began to identify with one race. "When you're discriminated against for being black," she said in *Cosmopolitan*, "you know you're black." She had a tough time coming up with an answer to her children's question, "Mommy, why do people hate Negroes so much?"

A First for New York City

Following the breakup of her marriage, Quarles moved with her two children back to New York in 1966. As the civil rights movement progressed, there was more pressure in the media to integrate minorities into the workplace. There also was more pressure on minorities

in the media, because they were the trailblazing pioneers, setting the standards and shaping history. Quarles spent a year at a special training program at NBC. She then took jobs with NBC News affiliates in Chicago, Cleveland, and in New York City. It was while she was working as a reporter for WNBC-TV in New York City that she got her first big break. After substituting as a hostess for three weeks on a women's show, Quarles was offered the coanchor position on a 6 P.M. news program—it was the first coanchor spot to go to a woman in New York City.

Quarles received pressure from some African Americans for not being militant enough, but she reported news with a fair eye to both sides of the color line. When assigned a story about welfare mothers, Quarles focused on a white woman and her children. Back at the station, she was questioned by co-workers, who assumed the subject of her report would have been African American. "I fought that all the time," she told *Cosmopolitan*. However, Quarles saw her values as extending beyond mere color. "My values—kids, education, hard work—are neither black or white . . ." she said.

A Mother and Journalist

It was because of those values that Quarles opted to limit her career in many cases. Putting motherhood first, she never took a network assignment job that would involve national and international travel. Although it would have been a significant move up the ladder for her, both professionally and financially, Quarles always was clear that her responsibilities as a mother were her priority. She found a healthy balance between her career and raising her son and daughter.

Quarles may have passed up traveling assignment opportunities, but she still covered nationally significant news. She quickly earned high marks for her reporting skills, and gained respect in the industry. For her news stories on the film story "The Stripper," she was awarded a Sigma Delta Chi Deadline Club Award and a Front Page Award. For her "Urban Stories" series, she won an Emmy award. While working as an NBC New York correspondent, Quarles was assigned to cover such major headline stories as the Bernhard Goetz shooting and the Baby M case. She also was selected as a panelist on the League of Women Voters' vice presidential debate in 1984.

In 1988, after 21 years with NBC, Quarles left to join CNN. She continued her award-winning work there, being inducted into the Hall of Fame of the National Association of Black Journalists in 1990, and earning a CINE Golden Eagle in 1993. Also that year, she earned New York Association of Black Journalists Awards for a one-hour CNN special on race relations called "A House Divided," and also for a feature report, "The Delany Sisters." Quarles believes that her multiracial background and exotic look have helped her in her career, just not in obvious ways. "It's made me a broader person," she told *Cosmopolitan.* "I identify more with other people. I think I have fewer prejudices because of my background."

Sources

Books

Smith, Jessie Carney, editor, *Notable Black American Women,* Gale Research, 1992.
Henderson, Ashyia N., and Phelps, Shirelle, editors, *Who's Who Among African Americans, 12th Edition,* Gale Group, 1999.

Periodicals

Cosmopolitan, October 1986, p. 260.
Jet, April 30, 1990, p.12.

Other

Additional information for this profile was obtained from "Norma Quarles," *CNN Online,* http:\\ www.cnn.com (April 16, 2000).

—Brenna Sanchez

Glenn "Doc" Rivers

1961—

Professional basketball coach

Glenn "Doc" Rivers enjoyed an impressive 13-year career in the NBA. After his retirement from the NBA, he became a television analyst for Turner Sports. Although he lacked coaching experience, Rivers became the head coach of the Orlando Magic in 1999. Defying NBA analysts who said that the Magic were destined for a dismal season, the team fell just short of making the playoffs. Rivers's coaching style was cited as an important reason for the team's success.

Rivers was born on October 13, 1961, in Maywood, Illinois, and grew up in an athletic family. Although his father, Grady, was a policeman, both his uncle Jim Brewer and his cousin Byron Irvin played in the NBA. Rivers grew up in a tough section of Chicago, but was never tempted to get into trouble because he loved to play basketball at an early age. He was a passive student, until his studies coincided with his plans to be a basketball player. While in middle school, Rivers decided that he wanted to go to a high school that had a proud basketball tradition. He had to take an entrance exam to be accepted at Proviso East High School, and was forced to study for the first time in his life. The hard work paid off because Rivers achieved the second highest test score in the school. When he wasn't in school, Rivers was playing basketball. He was

forced to learn to contribute to his team in other ways besides scoring. He learned to play defense, box out, and move around to create space for himself. Slowly but surely, Rivers taught himself the game. As a freshman, he played so well that he was called up to the varsity team for the last part of the season. During the late 1970s, Rivers acquired his nickname during a summer basketball camp at Proviso East High School. Former Marquette coach, Rick Majerus, noticed that Rivers was wearing a Julius "Dr.J" Irving T-shirt, and called the young player "Doc".

Rose to NBA Stardom

Rivers became a McDonald's All-American player at Proviso, and was one of the most highly recruited players in the country. He enjoyed continued success both on the collegiate and international level. In the 1982 World Championship of Basketball, Rivers led the United States to the silver medal and was named the tournament's Most Valuable Player. After three years at Marquette University, Rivers left school early for the NBA draft. Like most athletes who leave school early, Rivers vowed to finish his education. However,

At a Glance . . .

Born on October 13, 1961, in Maywood, IL; son of Grady (a policeman) and Betty Rivers; married to Kris; children: Jeremiah, Callie, Austin, and Spencer; *Education:* Graduated from Marquette University, 1985.

Career: Drafted by the Atlanta Hawks, 1983; starting point guard for Atlanta, 1983-91; played for the Los Angeles Clippers, 1991-92; signed with the New York Knicks, 1992-94; played with the San Antonio Spurs, 1994-96; Turner Sports television analyst, 1996-99; headcoach of the Orlando Magic, 1999-.

Awards: McDonalds All-American, 1980; Tournament MVP of the World Championship of Basketball, 1982; set Atlanta Hawks single-season assist record (823),1986-87; NBA All Star, 1988; J. Walter Kennedy Basketball Citizenship Award, 1990.

Addresses: *Residence*—Orlando, FL; *Business*—The Orlando Magic, PO Box 76, Orlando, FL 32802-0076.

he fulfilled this promise. In 1985, Rivers earned a pre-law\political science degree from Marquette.

In the 1983 NBA draft, Rivers was selected by the Atlanta Hawks. After being selected in the second round of the draft, his first goal was to make the team. Once this was accomplished, he planned to eventually crack the starting lineup. Rivers accomplished these goals during his rookie season, and went on to become a mainstay with the Hawks. He spent eight years with the Hawks, setting team records for single-season assists (823 in 1986-87) and career assists (23,866).

Left Atlanta For Los Angeles

Following completion of the 1990-91 season, Rivers left Atlanta to play for the Los Angeles Clippers. With Rivers in the lineup, the Clippers made a rare appearance in the playoffs. After a year with the Clippers, he moved on to the New York Knicks. The coach of the Knicks, Pat Riley, brought Rivers to New York to help stabilize the team's talented, but inexperienced back-court. That season, Rivers led the Knicks to the best record in the Eastern Conference. The team cruised through the playoffs, and met the Chicago Bulls for the conference championship. The Knicks and the Bulls split the first four games, but New York lost the last two games. The Bulls won the series four games to two.

Although Rivers looked forward to leading the Knicks to an NBA championship, the rest of his career in New York was disappointing. During the middle of the 1993-94 season, he tore the anterior cruciate ligament in his left knee and was forced to sit out for the rest of the season. The Knicks went on to lose to the Bulls again in the playoffs. At the start of the 1994-95 season, rumors abounded that the veteran guard would be traded. At the time, Rivers told Curtis Bunn of the *New York Daily News* that he thought he would stay with the Knicks, "I watched us play for the championship and I know I could have helped us. I think I would have made the difference. So, why would you want to trade that guy? But, hey, I know as well as anyone that this is a business, so I'll treat it that way. But my energy and focus is on getting all the way back." In December of 1994, the Knicks released Rivers.

Despite his age and the fact that he had suffered a serious knee injury, Rivers believed that he was still capable of playing in the NBA. He received offers from six teams but, as he told *Jet,* his main goal was to play for a championship contender, "I asked myself, 'Why am I playing basketball?' And it is to try to win. So forget all the other things like the future of doing other things in Atlanta after the career is over. Right now, I'm a basketball player. I want to win a title." Rivers felt that the San Antonio Spurs offered the best opportunity to achieve this goal. The Spurs featured NBA star David Robinson, and had brought in Dennis Rodman to help with rebounding and defense. Rivers joined the Spurs in 1994. Although the team did well during the regular season, it consistently fell short in the playoffs. At the end of the 1995-96 season, Rivers announced his retirement after 13 seasons in the NBA.

Over the course of his NBA career, Rivers averaged 10.9 points, 5.7 assists, and 3.0 rebounds per game. More importantly, Rivers was considered a solid, unselfish leader. In his 13 NBA seasons, he led his teams to the playoffs 10 times. After the 1986-87 season, in which he averaged a double-double (12.8 points and 10.0 assists per game), he was selected to play in the 1988 All-Star Game. Rivers still shares the NBA single-game playoff record for most assists in one half with 15, which was achieved during a 1988 playoff game against the Boston Celtics.

A Short Retirement

Following his retirement in July of 1996, Rivers was immediately hired by Turner Sports to work as an on-camera NBA analyst. He also served as an analyst for the Spurs' local television broadcasts. Although he enjoyed his work on television, Rivers made it known that he wanted a position as an NBA coach or general manager. Two years into his broadcasting career, he was considered a prime candidate for an NBA coaching position. He was considered for the Washington Wizards head coaching vacancy and the Milwaukee Bucks general manager position, but finally accepted the head coaching job with the Orlando Magic in 1999. Rivers inked an 8 million guaranteed deal over four years.

The Magic was expected to be one of the worst teams in the NBA after trading four of its five starters. Most NBA analysts believed that adding a rookie coach to the mix would lead to a dismal season. However, under Rivers's guidance, the Magic played remarkably well. John Gabriel, the Orlando Magic general manager, commented on Rivers's first year as an NBA coach to Mike Wise of *The New York Times,* "Doc hasn't done this in a traditional fashion, letting players make a lot of mistakes and going away from the traditional NBA rotation of six or seven players. When he's wanted to overinstruct, yell or pull back the reins, he hasn't. The boundaries of that style are loose enough where guys are not inhibited. I thought this was a rebuilding year, but we didn't bottom out completely. Doc has been the glue in the process." Other analysts agreed that Rivers was working magic in Orlando. In an article for ESP-N.com, NBA coaching guru Jack Ramsey said, "Rivers' coaching job is the most unexpected and the most remarkable of the season." Although many scoffed at Rivers for giving up his secure and undemanding life as an analyst, he readily embraced the challenge of coaching an NBA team. In an interview with Phil Jasner of the *Philadelphia Daily News,* Rivers talked about his decision to become a coach in NBA, "This is what I wanted to do—there's no deeper answer. I understood where I was, in the TV booth, relaxed, enjoying my work, being told I was good at it. But it would have eaten away at me if I hadn't pursued this. It's a gamble, sure, but that's what life is about. I love being in the

fray. I actually feel better with the pressure, the competition. Watch me when we're doing shooting drills—if guys are fooling around . . . I tell them, in every competition there's a winner and a loser. Why not try to be a winner?"

Sources

Books

Rivers, Glenn "Doc" and Bruce Brooks. *Those Who Love the Game.* Henry Holt and Company: Newark, NJ. 1993.

Periodicals

Jet, January 16, 1995.
The New York Daily News, October 10, 1994.
The New York Times, January 9, 2000.
Philadelphia Daily News, January 14, 2000.

Other

Additional information for this profile was obtained at http:\\espn.go.com\nba\oneonone1230\index.html; and http:\\nba.com\Magic\bios\coach.html

—Michael J. Watkins

Dumas M. Siméus

1940—

Food company executive

Since he was a child, Dumas Siméus has worked to achieve his goals. When he bought a food company in 1996 and renamed it Siméus Foods International, he set a goal of having a billion-dollar company within five years. His company, which is a leading producer of custom food products for the restaurant industry, was on its way toward that goal with revenues of over 200 million in 1999. Siméus Foods International was ranked by *Black Enterprise* magazine in 1999 as the largest black-owned business in Texas and the 11th-largest in the nation. His company also ranks among the Top 100 food processors in the United States.

Set Goals at a Young Age

Born to livestock farmers in the village of Pont-Sondé, Haiti, Siméus was the oldest of 12 children. He recounted to the *Star Telegram* (Arlington, Texas) how, as an eight-year-old boy, he would stand on a dock in Haiti and watch the ships that were bound for France and the United States, "I wanted to go where they were going. I created a vision of being in one of those countries one day, of going to school, of becoming an entrepreneur." By listening to the "Voice of America" radio program, Siméus learned that the United States was a land of opportunity. He earned his high school diploma, and then worked for an American employee of the State Department in Haiti to earn the money he needed to emigrate. However, the house cleaning, irrigation projects, and many other jobs he undertook were not quite enough. Siméus' parents gave him the rest of what was needed by selling a small portion of their land and, in 1961, he moved to the United States.

Siméus found that the glowing reports of life in the United States that he'd heard on the radio program were not entirely true. Things were different in the United States from what he'd experienced in Haiti. "In Haiti, it was more of a caste system than anything else," he told *The Star Telegram*. "There, if you have an education, you're integrated into society. But the extent of the segregation in the United States shocked the hell out of me." Siméus attended Florida A& M for one semester. Segregation prevented him from enrolling at Louisiana State University, so he attended Southern University in Baton Rouge, Louisiana instead. Siméus eventually enrolled at Howard University in Washington, D.C., a school that traditionally welcomed African American and foreign students. While attending college, he also worked at a variety of jobs. When Siméus received his degree in electrical engineering, he received 27 job offers. He went to work as an electrical design engineer for Standard Oil, and then worked for Rockwell International. Five years after receiving his bachelor degree, Siméus worked on his MBA, receiving the degree from the University of Chicago. He then went on to work as vice president of international operations for Atari, Inc., a 2 billion video game and computer company, where he was responsible for 5,000 employees worldwide and over 1 billion in revenues. He also served as vice president of Latin American operations for Bendix Corporation, a 2.5 billion automotive parts manufacturer. Later, as CEO of Hartz Pet Food International, a 120 million subsidiary of Hartz Mountain Corporation, Siméus was

At a Glance . . .

Born in Pont-Sondé, Haiti, 1940; son of Mécène and Bonne Siméus, livestock farmers; married; children: four. *Education:* Howard University, Washington D.C., B.S., 1966; University of Chicago, Chicago, IL, MBA.

Career: Electrical design engineer, Standard Oil Corporation; Rockwell International; vice president of international operations, Atari, Inc.; vice president of Latin American operations Bendix Corporation; CEO, Hartz Pet Food International; Beatrice Foods 1984-90; president and COO, TLC Beatrice International Foods 1990-92; chairman and CEO, Siméus Foods International, Inc. 1996-.

Selected awards: "Mr. Leadership" award, Howard University; Southwest Area's Entrepreneur of the Year, 1999.

Member: Board of International Food service Manufacturers Association (IFMA); Chairman, Caribbean\ American Leadership Council; member Haitian\ American Business Development Council; National Organization for the Advancement of Haitians; Dallas Urban League, Inc.; DF\W Minority Business Development Council.

Addresses: *Office*—Siméus Foods International, Inc., 812 South 5th Avenue, Mansfield, TX 76063.

based in Paris and oversaw manufacturing and distribution operations in France, Belgium, England, and Germany.

Began Food Industry Career

Beatrice Foods was Siméus' entry into the food industry in 1984, and he was later put in charge of the Latin American division. He became president and chief operating officer for TLC Beatrice International Foods in 1990. In 1992, Siméus decided to realize a goal he had set long ago in Haiti of becoming an entrepreneur. He resigned from Beatrice and began to look for a company to buy. His friend, Don Lawhorne, chief executive of Mesbic Ventures Holding Co., a small-business investment firm in Dallas, Texas, invited Siméus to work out of his Dallas offices while he looked for the business he wanted. Siméus tried to buy Wise

Potato Chips but, as he told the *Star-Telegram*, "We spent about a year on it and tried very hard. I spent a lot of my money on legal fees, but they took another offer. When it didn't go through, I cried like a baby." He also experienced bigotry during business negotiations. Siméus recalled in a *Dallas Morning News* story that his negotiations with a private company went smoothly until the face-to-face meeting. "They see Dumas Siméus, black as charcoal," he said. While the owners "tried to be polite, a couple of them specifically said, 'You know, we spent 20 or 25 years trying to build this company, and we started it from scratch. We're well known in the community, and I don't think we can sell our company, regardless of the amount of money, to a black person.'"

In 1996 Siméus formed his holding company, Siméus Foods International, and then bought Portion-Trol Foods, renaming it after his holding company. He set up a deal with the previous owner, Flagstar Companies of Spartanburg, South Carolina, a large restaurant holding company, to buy 500 million in products from Siméus Foods over the next five years. Mesbic Ventures Holding Company helped finance the 55 million deal. The Mansfield, Texas, food processor already had a strong sales base with 24 years in operation supplying frozen processed foods to national restaurant chains. Siméus set to work immediately to expand the company's offerings from 27 to over 60 items. The company added customers and created a sales and marketing department.

In 1998, Siméus took the next step in his goal toward a billion-dollar business in five years when he purchased the Forest City, North Carolina roast beef and pork processing company of Fast Food Merchandisers. With this acquisition, Siméus added to his holdings a company with sales of 70 million and 350 employees. In 1999, sales exceeded 200 million. The company headquarters would remain in Mansfield, Texas. The company offerings included soups, gravies, sauces, salsas, steaks, roast beef, hamburger patties, sausages, pork products, chicken fried steak, breaded cheese sticks, spicy rice, frozen cookie dough and other products.

Siméus believes each employee is an important part of the organization, and refers to his over 700 employees as teammates. When he was honored as the Southwest Area's 1999 Entrepreneur of the Year in the wholesale\distribution category of a national competition sponsored by Ernst & Young, LLP, he gave credit to his teammates, "Although the award was presented in my name, it is shared with all of my teammates at SFI," he was quoted as saying in a company press release.

Business and Personal Goals

After learning of Siméus' ambitious five-year goal of a

creating a billion-dollar company, food industry experts believed that he would find it difficult to reach that goal because of the fierce competition within the food-processing industry. Never one to back down from a challenge, Siméus seems to relish challenge and told the *Star Telegram,* "It energizes me to be under the firing line all the time." He slightly reset his goal, which was to have a billion dollar company by 2001, five years from purchasing the company in 1996. His new goal is to reach 1 billion through internal growth and acquisitions by 2003. He also would like to return to the corporate culture that is found within a large company. "I want to go back to the culture I'm used to," Siméus told the *Star-Telegram.* "Reaching the billion-dollar mark will be some kind of milestone. It's not to make a whole lot of money, although that's part of it. It's the inner desire to be the best."

Siméus won't stop once he has reached his goal. On a more personal level, he has set another goal, "I wish to make a profound difference in the lives of those who are less fortunate than I am," he said in public relations literature from Siméus Foods International. He formed the Dumas M. Siméus Foundation, a nonprofit organization that supports efforts to distribute money and goods among poor Haitians living in the United States and Haiti, education and vocational training, and outreach efforts in communities surrounding the company

facilities in Mansfield, Texas and Forest City, North Carolina. Siméus has a long-term goal of building a hospital in his native Pont-Sondé, Haiti, where he has already made donations for building a church and feeding center. Siméus is fluent in French, Spanish, and English, and is also conversant in several other languages.

Sources

Periodicals

Star Telegram, March 14, 1999.

Other

Additional information for this profile was obtained from a public relations packet from Siméus Foods International; and from the Siméus Foods International web site at http:\\www.simeusfoods.com

—Sandy J. Stiefer

Norma Merrick Sklarek

1928—

Architect

Norma Merrick Sklarek became the first African American woman licensed as an architect in the United States when she passed the New York state examinations for her profession in 1954. In a career that spanned over 30 years, she designed several large-scale projects, including the American Embassy in Tokyo and a terminal at Los Angeles International Airport.

Sklarek was born in 1928 in Harlem to parents of West Indian heritage. The family moved to Crown Heights in Brooklyn when she was a child, and her father, Walter, would eventually earn his medical degree from Howard University during her early years. As a child, Sklarek exhibited obvious passion and talent for the visual arts: she sketched, painted furniture, and even drew murals. She was an only child, and received a rather inordinate amount of encouragement. "Although both my parents adored me, I did lots of things with my father that ordinarily girls did not do—like going fishing, painting the house, and doing carpentry work," she told Dorothy Ehrhart-Morrison in an interview for the book *No Mountain High Enough: Secrets of Successful African American Women.*

Decided on Architectural Career

Sklarek excelled in school, especially in the sciences, and attended primarily white high schools in the New York public school system during the 1930s and 1940s. As she contemplated college and her future direction, she realized that the professional career options open to women were rather limited. Sklarek knew that she was not very interested in becoming a teacher or a nurse. "My grades were such that I could consider any profession, but I had an interest in art, the sciences, and math," she recalled in the interview with Ehrhart-Morrison. "One day my father said to me, 'What about architecture?' I knew absolutely nothing about architecture, but it seemed to embody each of my interests, and I considered his suggestion." The fact that there were few African Americans in the profession failed to deter her.

Entering Barnard College, part of New York's Columbia University, Sklarek took one year of liberal-arts courses in preparation for applying to Columbia's rigorous architecture program. As a freshman at Columbia, she encountered some typical first-year difficul-

At a Glance . . .

Born April 15,1928, in New York, NY; daughter of walter Ernest (a physician) and Amelia Willoughby-Merrick; married in the early 1950s (divorced); married Rolf Sklarek (an architect; deceased, 1984); married Cornelius Welch (a physician), 1985; children: Gregory Ranson, David Rairweather, Susan. *Education:* Columbia University, B.Arch.,1950

Career: Worked for New York City government, early 1950s; licensed as an architect in New York state, 1954; worked for a private firm, New York City, 1954-55; Skidmore, Owens, Merrill (architects), New York City, architect, 1955-60; Gruen and associates (architects). Los Angeles, CA, began as architect, 1960, director of architecture, 1966-80; Weldon, Becket, and Associates, Santa Monica, CA project manager, 1980-85; Siegel, Sklarek, Diamond (architects), founding partner, 1985-89; Jerde Partnership, Venice, CA, prindipal, 1989-; has taught architecture at the City College of New York City and at the University of California at Los Angeles; commissioner on the California State Board of Architectural Examiners since 1970; University of Southern California Architects Guild, director, 1984-87.

Awards: Americans Institute of Architects, fellow, 1966

Member: American Institute of Architects (served as vice president of California chapter).

Addresses: *Office*–c/o The Jerde Partnership International, 913 Ocean front Walk, Venice, CA 90291

University School of Architecture. This was no small achievement, since only a certain number of female applicants were admitted into the program. She was, however, the youngest person in her class. After earning her degree in 1950, Skalrek applied for a job with 20 architectural firms, and was rejected each time. "I could never figure it out," she told Ehrhart-Morrison. "I don't know if the rejections were because I was a black person, because I was a young woman, or because of the economic recession at the time. Since I was turned down so many times in private industry, I went to work for the city of New York in a civil service job."

Not yet a licensed architect, Sklarek worked for the city's building department, but disliked the uncreative nature of the work. This experience motivated her to take the licensing examination for architects in New York state, a rigorous four-day test which few passed on the first try. Sklarek did pass on the first try and, in 1954, became one of a handful of African Americans in the profession. She was also the first African American woman to be licensed as an architect in the United States.

Dismayed by Negative Words

Sklarek quit her city job when she was hired at a private architectural firm. Initially, she was not given interesting assignments. For instance, she was responsible for designing all of the bathrooms in an office building. By this time, she had married and become the mother of two sons. Because it was the 1950s, an era preceding the enactment of equal employment opportunity laws, Sklarek faced many obstacles. On one occasion, she ran into some former colleagues from the municipal building department, who found it difficult to hide their astonishment when Sklarek told them about her new job. They told Sklarek that her former boss had written a harsh, unfavorable critique of her job performance. "He said that I was lazy, that I knew nothing about design and architecture, that I socialized, and that I was late every day," she recalled in *No Mountain High Enough*. Sklarek remembered that her present employers had asked, during her job interview, whether she had had any problems with her former boss, and she replied truthfully that she had not. "I guess [the interviewer] figured that nobody could be that bad," she told Ehrhart-Morrison, but the lesson was still a harsh one. "It taught me that it is possible to work next to somebody and not know that they hated you. It had to be personal. He was not a licensed architect, and I was a young kid—I looked like a teenager—and I was black and a licensed architect."

Sklarek spent a year with a small firm before being hired in 1955 by one of the country's preeminent architectural firms, Skidmore, Owens, Merrill. She spent five years there, and found that issues of race and gender seemed nonexistent in the workplace. Sklarek's responsibilities steadily increased, and she often

ties. "I had a hard time because everything was so different from high school," she recalled in *No Mountain High Enough*. "I was working extremely hard just to stay afloat, not getting As, but just trying to pass the course. I spent the summer deliberating whether or not to return to Columbia in the fall. I decided to stay. . . . My parents' only requirement was that I attend college near home. I wanted to go to Howard University in Washington, D.C., because I thought there was more social life at Howard, but my father wouldn't think of it."

Entered Columbia

Sklarek persevered, and was accepted to the Columbia

handled a large workload. Her personal life, however, suffered a setback with the end of her marriage. As a working mother, she often sought the help of two aunts to care for her young sons.

New Life in Los Angeles

Encouraged by her friends, Sklarek moved to California in 1960, and found work at another renowned firm, Gruen and Associates in Los Angeles. She was also licensed in architecture by the state of California in 1962. No other African American female would be licensed in architecture by the state of California for another 20 years. After six years at Gruen, Sklarek was named director of architecture, an executive position in which she supervised the work of several dozen architects. She was also named a fellow of the American Institute of Architects (AIA), becoming the first woman in the organization's Los Angeles chapter to achieve that honor.

Sklarek remained with Gruen until 1980, when she took a job with a Santa Monica architectural firm, Weldon, Becket, and Associates. Five years later, she co-founded Siegel, Sklarek, and Diamond, the largest architectural firm in the United States that was entirely owned by women. In 1989, she became a principal with the Jerde Partnership, yet another award-winning firm that is noted for its impressive design of public buildings. The Las Vegas Bellagio Hotel is one of the Jerde firm's best-known works. Sklarek's own notable designs include the American Embassy in Tokyo, Japan; Pacific Design Center in Los Angeles; Fox Plaza in San Francisco, and Terminal One of the Los Angeles International Airport.

Sklarek has taught architecture at both the City College of New York City and the University of California at Los Angeles. Active in the Los Angeles AIA chapter, she has also served as director for the University of Southern California Architects Guild. Since 1970, she has been a member of the commission of the California State Board of Architectural Examiners. After her second husband, architect Rolf Sklarek, passed away, Sklarek married physician Cornelius Welch in 1985, with whom she has a daughter, Susan. By the late 1990s, Sklarek was semi-retired and lived with her family in a home in Southern California, where she grows orchids and bromelia in her garden.

Sources

Books

Ehrhart-Morrison, Dorothy, *No Mountain High Enough: Secrets of Successful African American Women,* Conari Press, 1997.
Facts on File Encyclopedia of Black Women in America, edited by Darlene Clark Hine, Facts on File, 1993, p. 243.
Powerful Black Women, edited by Jessie Carney Smith, Visible Ink Press, 1996.

Periodicals

Cobblestone, August, 1988, p. 37.

—Carol Brennan

Kristoff St. John

1966—

Actor

Kristoff St. John is part of an ensemble cast of one of the most highly rated daytime dramas, *The Young and the Restless,* which airs weekdays on CBS. St. John plays Neil Winters, an advertising executive, husband, and father. An actor since his childhood days, St. John has appeared in a number of television films, sitcoms, and dramas, but over two million fans tune in daily to follow the story of the Winters quartet on *Y&R,* a show that has become the most-watched soap opera among African American viewers.

Born Christoff St. John in 1966 in New York City, the actor is the son of parents who were both experienced stage and screen performers. His father, Christopher, appeared in *Shaft,* the early 1970s Richard Roundtree film, and went on to a career as a director; mother Maria St. John was a graduate of London's Royal Academy of Dramatic Arts. St. John made his first television appearance at the age of seven in a show called *That's My Mama,* and in 1974 appeared in an episode of the popular ABC-TV sitcom *Happy Days.* He grew up in Bridgeport, Connecticut, and Los Angeles.

St. John's first feature film appearance was tearjerker boxing movie, *The Champ,* in 1979, for which he still used the original spelling of his name. He attended Calabasas and Nordhoff High Schools, and began studying acting in Los Angeles at several workshops, including the famed Actor's Studio. He continued to win steady work in television, playing a young Alex Haley in a 1979 miniseries, *Roots: The Next Generations,* as well as small-screen projects like *An Innocent Love* and *The Atlanta Child Murders.* In 1985, he appeared in NBC's *Charlie &Company* opposite comedian Flip Wilson and singer Gladys Knight. Over the next decade, he was frequently cast in guest appearances on top-rated shows like *Cosby, A Different World, Living Single, Family Matters,* and *Pensacola.* He was also offered recurring parts on *Hangin' with Mr. Cooper, Martin,* and *Diagnosis Murder.*

In 1989, St. John was cast as Adam Marshall in an NBC soap opera, *Generations.* He earned two Emmy nominations as best supporting actor for his work. That success helped him land the role of Neil Winters on another daytime drama, *The Young and the Restless,* early in 1991. Since 1989, *Y&R* has been the highest-rated daytime drama among African Americans, and his character was slated to become part of a quartet of black characters who would prove extremely popular with the *Y&R* following. With six permanent residents of Genoa City, the fictional Midwestern city in which the daytime drama is set, the actors are the largest contingent of African American characters in daytime drama.

St. John's Winters was, initially, the stereotypical nice guy—an ambitious young man who begins working in the mailroom of an advertising agency, and soon rises through the ranks to an executive level. "Neil is so agreeable," St. John told *Essence* writer Deborah Gregory back in 1995. "It's much more interesting for an actor to play a character who has a dark, angry or combative side." Winters soon meets Drucilla Barber, a character played by Victoria Rowell, who is both streetwise and beautiful; initially they do not seem a likely pair. "Wondering if those two were ever going to come together was a lot of fun," St. John told *Essence*'s Gregory. "At least now we are one of the few Black supercouples on the soaps with a continuous story line."

In the *Y&R* world, Drucilla has a sister, Olivia, played by Tonya Lee Williams. Her on-screen husband is another popular male actor, Shemar Moore. The quartet's racy romantic troubles provide the show's 2.3 million viewers with vicarious excitement. Moore plays Neil's formerly wild younger brother, Malcolm; the two had a troubled relationship growing up in Chicago, and Neil was dismayed when Malcolm arrived in Genoa City for a reconciliation. Drucilla, however, encouraged them to patch things up, and even helped Malcolm launch a lucrative career as a freelance photographer through her connections as a model.

Malcolm, true to Neil's presumptions about his brother's morals, soon found himself falling for Drucilla, who was now married to Neil. Malcolm visited her one day when she was sick and a double dose of cold medication had made her groggy; she embraced him, thinking it was Neil. Later, she became pregnant, and was unsure who the father of their child, Lily, really was. Meanwhile, Drucilla's sister, Olivia, lost her husband, and she and Malcolm became romantically involved. Yet Olivia—a doctor—harbored secret feelings for Neil. In time, Neil and Drucilla's marriage ended, and he became involved with Olivia. Throughout all these sibling and spousal conflicts, St. John's character has shed some of his nice-guy image, and speaks far more frankly.

"The four of us have a dynamic quality, we complement one another well," Tonya Lee Williams told *Jet*. "My and Victoria's characters are different, but together they spark. The same is true for Malcolm and Kristoff's characters. And the four of us together are buzzing." St. John consistently earns Daytime Emmy nominations as outstanding actor in a daytime drama series, but took the statue home only once, in 1992, for his Winters role. He is, however, a perennial winner in the same category for the NAACP Image Awards.

As a *Y&R* cast member, St. John has helped the daytime drama achieve impressive ratings numbers among African American viewers; the show is also popular with audiences in South Africa, Kenya, Jamaica, and other Caribbean nations. Some celebrities have even admitted their passion for tuning in to the travails of the Winters family, among them Aretha Franklin and Whoopi Goldberg.

St. John's decade-plus career in the daytime drama inspired him to create a web site, http:\\www.soap starworld.com, which features gossip and insider information on all the network soaps. The father of two, St. John is also the principal in his own production company, Moonboy, which in the early 1990s developed and directed a pilot that became the CBS Soap Break. The actor produced and hosted several of the episodes. Through Moonboy, St. John hopes to produce a screenplay that he wrote, *Café America.*

Sources

Ebony, October 1992, p. 50.

Essence, September 1995, p. 78.
Jet, April 6, 1998, pp. 53-54.

—Carol Brennan

Donna Summer

1948—

Singer

Like no other performer, Donna Summer personified the disco era during its zenith in the late 1970s. Working with a team of legendary European record producers, Summer wrote and recorded a string of hits that made her one of the most successful artists of the decade. She collected numerous gold records and awards during her prime, but her career was plagued by contractual and management problems during the 1980s.

Born in suburban Boston in 1948, LaDonna Andrea Gaines was one of seven siblings in a working-class household where church attendance and academic achievement were the rule. She began singing as a child in the gospel choir of her church, and was an especially devoted fan of gospel legend Mahalia Jackson. As a teenager, Summer sang in a Boston band called Crow, and shocked her family when she decided to move to New York City in order to find work on Broadway. At the age of 18, Summer auditioned for a role in the popular hippie musical *Hair.* She won a spot in the touring company for the show, and moved to Europe.

Stage Career in Europe

Summer spent the next several years overseas. She appeared in several German and Austrian stage productions, met and married a fellow performer, Helmut Sommer—from whom she took her eventual recording name—modeled, and occasionally worked as a backup singer for recording artists. During a 1973 Munich recording session with the band Blood, Sweat & Tears, Summer met producers Giorgio Moroder and Pete Bellotte, who were entranced by her voice. She accepted an invitation to work with them, and recorded "The Hostage," her debut single. "The Hostage "and two other recordings became minor hits in European dance clubs.

In 1975, Summer recorded a takeoff of a sexy, French hit from 1959, "Je T'Aime . . . Moi Non Plus." Her version of the song, entitled "Love to Love You Baby," featured a classic, speedy disco beat. The song was not a hit in Europe until Neil Bogart, an American record executive who had made a fortune with bubblegum pop records in the 1960s, suggested expanding the song to nearly 17 minutes in length. Summer was signed to Bogart's Casablanca Records, and the shortened version of the song reached No. 2 on the American charts by early 1976.

At a Glance . . .

Born LaDonna Andrea Gaines, December 31, 1948, in Dorchester, MA; married Helmut Sommer, (divorced, 1974); married Bruce Sudano, July 15, 1980; children: (second marriage) Amanda Grace.

Career: Appeared in stage productions of *Hair, Porgy & Bess,* and other American musicals in Germany and Austria, late 1960s, early 1970s; recorded "The Hostage" (European release only), 1973; recorded "Love to Love You Baby" and eponymous album, 1975; signed to Casablanca Records, 1975; achieved several Top Ten hits and gold records during the late 1970s; signed to Geffen Records, 1980, Epic Records, 1999-.

Awards: Best Original Song Oscar, Academy of Motion Picture Arts and Sciences, 1978, for "Last Dance" Best Female R&B Vocal Performance Grammy, National Academy of Recording Arts and Sciences, 1979, for "Last Dance", Best Female Rock Vocal Performance Grammy, 1980, for "Hot Stuff" Best Inspirational Performance Grammy, 1984, for "He's a Rebel," and 1985, for "Forgive Me;" (with Giorgio Moroder) Best Dance Recording Grammy, 1998, for "Carry On."

Addresses: *Office*—Epic Records, 550 Madison Ave., New York, NY 10022.

First Star of Disco Era

Summer has been called the first crossover artist in pop music history, an African American performer who began her recording career working in a genre that appealed to minorities—the denizens of the New York nightlife scene, in which African American, Latino, and gay culture thrived in its own unique mix. That underground popularity eventually attracted a more mainstream element. Record company executives began to realize that some of Summer's recordings that were marketed for the discotheque scene were selling briskly in mainstream record stores as well, even though they received no airplay on the radio.

The music industry journal *Billboard* created its disco chart in 1975. Summer soon began topping this chart, as well as the R&B and pop charts, with a string of hits. These hits included the 1976 releases *A Love Trilogy,* and the album *Four Seasons of Love.* The following year, she scored two more hits with the album *I Remember Yesterday,* and a double album, *Once Upon a Time.* All of these hits showcased Summer's

smooth, rich voice. One of Summer's greatest hits, "I Feel Love," was released in mid-1977 as a single from *I Remember Yesterday.* It would be the first hit to use what became known as the "galloping bass line," a pounding, 140-beat-per-minute rhythm created by a drum machine. Such production techniques were rapidly adopted as a standard in disco music. Summer would also be remembered as the first female recording artist to successfully incorporate synthesizers into her work.

A String of Hit Records

During the late 1970s, Summer kept a nearly nonstop schedule of recording and performing, even spending nearly two straight years on tour. She was one of the most popular recording artists of her day. Her concerts sold out regularly, fans mobbed her, and her record sales were astronomical. In 1978, Summer appeared in a dismal feature film that tried to capitalize on the disco craze, *Thank God It's Friday.* Despite the film's failure at the box office, one of the songs from the soundtrack, "Last Dance" became a number one hit and earned Summer a Grammy award and an Oscar for Best Original Song. A number of her other hits found their way onto her 1978 double live album, *Live and More,* which was recorded from a series of shows at the Universal Amphitheater near Los Angeles. This was followed by her double studio album *Bad Girls,* which was released in the spring of 1979. *Bad Girls* spent six weeks on the American album charts, and was the best-selling album by a female artist in 1979. It also earned Summer a Grammy award for Best Female Rock Vocal Performance.

Bad Girls would be one of the last records that Summer recorded for Casablanca. In late 1979, Casablanca released a compilation of Summer's hits entitled, *On the Radio—Greatest Hits, Volumes I and II.* One of the songs on the album, Summer's duet with Barbara Streisand entitled "No More Tears (Enough Is Enough)," topped the charts. In early 1980, Summer sued to be released from her contract with Casablanca, citing undue influence and fraud. Later that year, she became the first artist to sign with the Geffen label, which was founded by rising entertainment executive David Geffen. Elton John and John Lennon soon joined Summer on Geffen's roster.

Moved in a New Direction

The year 1980 was marked by other notable changes in Summer's life. She wed musician Bruce Sudano, whose Brooklyn Dreams band had backed her on some tours, and announced that she was a born-again Christian. Her debut album on Geffen, *The Wanderer,* reflected this new spirituality. The album reached No. 3 on *Billboard*'s charts, but its singles charted only in the 30s—a dismal showing compared to the string of gold records Summer had earned for her previous singles. The Wanderer was also the last album that Giorgio Moroder and Pete Bellotte produced for Summer.

In 1982, Summer teamed with producer Quincy Jones and released the album *Donna Summer.* One of the singles from the album, "Love Is in Control (Finger on the Trigger)," was a Top Ten hit. She also recorded a cover song with Jones entitled "State of Independence." Jones was also able to convince a roster of music legends—Michael Jackson, Lionel Richie, and Stevie Wonder among them—to sing backup on the album. Jones later remarked that this experience had inspired his production of "We Are the World," the 1984 Ethiopian famine-relief recording. Under the settlement terms of her lawsuit against Casablanca, Summer was required to record one more album for the label, which was now a part of Polygram Records. The title track of the album *She Works Hard for the Money,* climbed to No. 3 on the U.S. charts in 1983.

Became a Successful Painter

Summer tried unsuccessfully to be released from her recording contract with Geffen Records. Sales of her 1987 album, *All Systems Go,* were so poor that a planned North American concert tour was canceled. In the late 1980s, Summer turned to art as a means of creative expression. She began to paint large, Expressionist-style canvases, many of which sold for several thousands of dollars. In 1994, Summer moved to Nashville with her husband and young daughter. She recorded an album of Christmas carols with the Nashville Symphony, and continued to paint.

In 1997, Summer appeared alongside Gloria Estefan and Chaka Khan at a benefit concert, *Three Divas on Broadway.* Her career was also bolstered by a pop-culture revival of the disco era during the late 1990s. In early 1998, Summer appeared at Carnegie Hall for a concert to benefit the Gay Men's Health Crisis Center in New York. "After nearly two hours of mature ovations and controlled excitement. . .the remarkably well-behaved audience could no longer be contained,"

wrote Larry Flick in *Billboard.* "As she [Summer] began a salacious, guitar-drenched rendition of 'Hot Stuff,' fans rushed down the red carpeted aisles toward the stage."

By the end of the 1990s, Summer was signed to a recording contract with Epic Records. The company released yet another of her many best-selling anthologies, *VH1 Presents Donna Summer: Live & More—Encore!* She was also working on tracks for a planned musical autobiography, *Ordinary Girl.* "I think women have incredible powers," she told *Rolling Stone*'s Gina Zucker in 1999. "We can use both the intellectual side of the brain and the nurturing side, and we have to be proud of both."

Selected discography

Love to Love You, Baby, Oasis, 1975.
A Love Trilogy, Oasis, 1976.
Four Seasons of Love, Casablanca, 1976.
I Remember Yesterday, Casablanca, 1977.
Live and More, Casablanca, 1978.
Bad Girls, Casablanca, 1979.
On the Radio—Greatest Hits, Volumes I and II, Casablanca, 1979.
The Wanderer, Geffen, 1980.
Donna Summer, Geffen, 1982.
She Works Hard for the Money, Polygram, 1983.
All Systems Go, Geffen, 1987.
Another Place and Time, Atlantic, 1989.
Christmas Spirit, Mercury, 1994.
VH1 Presents Donna Summer: Live & More—Encore!, Epic, 1999.

Sources

Periodicals

Billboard, September 3, 1994, p. 21; March 16, 1998; June 12, 1999, p. 9.
Rolling Stone, August 5, 1999, p. 27.

—Carol Brennan

Lawrence Taylor

1959—

Former professional football player

During the 1980s, Lawrence Taylor was one of the NFL's most dominant players. As an extremely gifted linebacker, he led the New York Giants to two Super Bowl victories. Despite his accomplishments on the football field, Taylor was plagued by financial problems and an addiction to cocaine. However, these problems did not diminish his remarkable accomplishments in the NFL. In 1999, he was inducted into professional football's Hall of Fame.

Taylor was born on February 4, 1959 in Williamsburg, Virginia, one of Clarence and Iris Taylor's three sons. His father worked in the shipyards in Newport News, and his mother worked odd jobs to earn extra money for the family. Taylor grew up playing baseball and singing in the choir at his church. His first experience with football came during his sophomore year in high school. After almost quitting the team in his junior year, he found himself in the starting lineup midway through the season. During his senior season, Taylor became a star at defensive end and at the tight end position. Although he was not heavily recruited by universities with notable football programs, Taylor accepted a scholarship to the University of North Carolina after his graduation from high school in 1977.

In his first year at North Carolina, Taylor played exclusively on special teams. The team compiled an 8-3-1 record in the Atlantic Coast Conference (ACC). Off the field, Taylor was called "The Monster" because of his reputation for wild behavior. During his sophomore year, he was hampered by injuries and finished the season with only eight tackles. Taylor told Michael Shapiro of the *New York Times* about his attitude in college, "It was party time in college. I was bad. I used to go downtown and get into fights all the time. I was trying to be a hoodlum in college, going to frat houses and destroying everything. I had a reputation in Chapel Hill that nobody messed with L.T. I kind of liked that[00fe]Then I learned another way to get respect from people. That's what it's all about, getting respect." He soon discovered that it was more important to earn respect on the football field rather than for his outlandish behavior off the field. As a junior, Taylor was a key part of a team that finished 8-3-1 and made an appearance in the Gator Bowl. The Tarheels defeated Michigan, 17-15, and Taylor made the play of the game by sacking Michigan quarterback John Wangler to stop a key drive. He finished the year with 80 solo tackles and five sacks.

At a Glance . . .

Born Lawrence Julius Taylor, February 4, 1959, in Williamsburg, VA; son of Clarence and Iris Taylor. *Education:* attended the University of North Carolina.

Career: Played football at the University of North Carolina, 1977-80; drafted second overall by the New York Giants, 1981; starting linebacker for the New York Giants, 1981-92; retired from the NFL, 1993.

Awards: First team All-American and the Atlantic Coast Conference Player of the Year,1980; NFL Rookie of the Year, 1981; Pro Bowl selection, 1981-90; NFL Defensive Player of the Year, 1981, 1982, 1986; NFL's Most Valuable Player, 1986; member of the NFL'sAll 1980's team, 1990; named to NFL's 75th Anniversary Team, 1994; elected on the first ballot to the NFL's Hall of Fame, 1999.

Addresses: *Home*—Upper Saddle River, NJ; *Business* —c\o The Pro Football Hall of Fame, 2121 George Halas Drive NW, Canton, OH 44708.

During Taylor's final season at North Carolina in 1980, the team won its first seven games enroute to an 11-1 record. The Tarheels won the ACC title, and Taylor was named a first team All-American and the ACC Player of the Year. Taylor racked up 55 solo tackles and 16 sacks. After playing in the East-West Shrine Game, Taylor withdrew from North Carolina to prepare for the NFL draft.

Became a First-Round Draft Choice

On April 28, 1981, Taylor was the second player picked in the first round by the New York Giants. The Giants general manager, George Young, told Michael Katz of the *New York Times* about the decision to draft Taylor, "It was not a difficult decision to make. You can't pass up a guy who you think will be a Pro Bowler for ten years. You can't tell yourself that you need help at another position." Taylor joined a team that already had a solid linebacking core. The Giants signed the rookie to a big contract, and changed their whole defensive scheme to accommodate a player who had never played a single down in the NFL. Taylor quickly dispelled any doubts about his abilities with his dominating play during his first practice as a Giant. In his first season, the Giants made the playoffs for the first time in 18 years and won their wildcard playoff game

against the Philadelphia Eagles. Taylor led the team with 133 tackles and 9.5 sacks. He was named Rookie of the Year, Defensive Player of the Year, and was a unanimous choice for the All-Pro team.

Taylor's second NFL season got off to a rocky start. He injured his foot during the preseason, and then the NFL players went on strike. After the players strike was resolved, Taylor regained his form and was named to the Pro Bowl for the second straight year. He was again named the NFL's Defensive Player of the Year. After such an impressive second season, Taylor held out for more money before his third season. He missed most of the preseason, and returned only after the Giants management promised to talk about a new contract after the season. Late in 1983, Taylor signed a deal with the New Jersey Generals of the now-defunct United States Football League (USFL). The Giants were forced to buy out Taylor's USFL contract and offer their star linebacker a substantial raise, or risk having him bolt to the rival league. During the mid-1980s, the Giants steadily improved as Taylor became the most dominant player in the game. Following the 1985 season, he gained notoriety for a different reason. Sportscaster Howard Cosell broke the story that Taylor was addicted to cocaine and had spent time in a rehabilitation center. Taylor confirmed the rumors, but then refused to speak to the media about the subject.

Named Most Valuable Player

In 1986, the Giants defense led the team on a 12 game winning streak and a first-place finish in the NFC East. In the first round of the playoffs, the Giants crushed the San Francisco 49ers by a score of 49-3, and then blanked the Washington Redskins, 17-0. The Giants went on to face the AFC-champion Denver Broncos in the Super Bowl. During the second half, the Giants blew the game open and cruised to a 39-20 victory and the NFL Championship. In 1986, Taylor had set a Giants record by compiling 105 tackles, 20 1\2 sacks, and three forced fumbles. Those efforts earned him a unanimous selection as the NFL's Most Valuable Player, a spot on the All-NFL team, and a sixth consecutive start in the Pro Bowl. Despite these achievements, Taylor told Frank Litsky of the *New York Times* that his years as a football player were taking their toll, "I'm a guy who's starting to get old, not as old as some but a lot older than others. I'm a lot slower than I used to be. I get tired easier . . . It's not distressing. I compensate with other things. I'm a little smarter than I used to be. I try to use that to my advantage."

After their Super Bowl victory, the Giants and their star linebacker seemed to go downhill. Taylor was hampered throughout most of the 1987 season by a hamstring injury. The NFL also experienced labor problems. Players were locked out, and two games were staffed by replacement players. The Giants finished the season with a disappointing 6-9 record. In 1988, Taylor was suspended for the first four games of the season when he tested positive for cocaine. After serving his suspension, Taylor returned to the lineup. However, the Giants missed the playoffs for the second year in a row. The team made the playoffs in 1989, but lost at home in the first round.

Twilight of a Sterling Career

After three sub-par seasons, Taylor started the 1990 season by holding out for most of training camp. Five days before the Giants first regular season game, he signed a new contract and recorded five sacks in limited action during the season opener. The Giants went on to post an excellent 13-3 record. In the playoffs, the Giants routed the Chicago Bears, and then defeated the San Francisco 49ers to advance to Super Bowl XXV against the Buffalo Bills. The Giants completed their season with a stunning 20-19 championship victory over the favored Bills.

Coach Bill Parcells left the Giants following the 1990 season, and the team experienced a decline. Taylor had made up his mind to retire at the end of the 1992 season, but missed the last six weeks of the season with an Achilles tendon injury. He came back for one more season in 1993, and led his team to an 11-5 record and a playoff berth. Although the Giants lost to the 49ers in the playoffs, Taylor's list of accomplishments were notable. Over a 13-year career, Taylor recorded 132 1\2 sacks, and was a unanimous choice for the NFL's All-1980's team. He was also selected for the NFL's 75th Anniversary Team. Following the 1993 season, Taylor announced his retirement from the NFL.

A Long Strange Trip

After retiring from the NFL, Taylor started his own company, All Pro Products, Inc. The company went public at 5 a share, and financial observers watched in amazement as the company tripled in value during the first month of its existence. The stock price went up to 15.50 a share, but it turned out that the unbelievable growth of All Pro Products was illusory. The Securities and Exchange Commission found that two traders had manipulated the price of the stock, which skyrocketed despite the fact that the company lost over 900,000. In the end, Taylor lost several hundred thousand dollars and the company's stock, which was once valued at 10.8 million, was worth only pennies. Despite these financial struggles, Taylor stayed in the limelight by appearing in Wrestlemania XI. Taylor and several other NFL stars performed in a much-hyped bout with World Wrestling Federation bad-guy, Bam Bam Bigelow.

Unfortunately, Taylor's life seemed to spiral out of control. In May of 1996, Taylor was in Myrtle Beach,

South Carolina for a celebrity golf tournament when he was arrested for trying to buy 100 worth of crack cocaine from an undercover police officer. Taylor received 60 hours of community service, checked into another rehab center, and was made to undergo random drug tests. He also received three summons for traffic violations, pleaded guilty to filing a false income tax return, and was questioned by a state-grand jury about his ties to organized crime. In an article by New York Times reporter Mike Freeman, Taylor was quoted as saying, "My whole life seems like it's in the toilet. Well, it's going to be in the toilet now . . . I ought to kill myself."

In May of 1998, Taylor was arrested for failing to pay child support. He was released after spending 12 hours in jail and paying 4,429 in back child support. In addition to paying 12,000 a year for the care of his daughter, Wendy, Taylor paid 50,000 a year to his former wife Deborah and their three children, and another 12,000 a year to a fifth child. All of these support payments could not be maintained on Taylor's 50,000 to 100,000 yearly income. His lawyer, Michael T. Melani, told David M. Herszenhorn of the *New York Times,* "His current financial situation has deteriorated substantially since his days as a football player. We will be making a request to reduce (his support payments) to a sum that he could afford. He's struggling and he's doing everything he can to take care of his obligations. Like everybody else, he was very embarrassed." Along with these financial problems, Taylor was arrested in St. Petersburg, Florida at a charity golf tournament for trying to buy 50 of crack cocaine from an undercover police officer. Although Taylor insisted that he was framed, he entered a drug rehabilitation center and declared bankruptcy to prevent foreclosure on his mansion in Upper Saddle River, NJ.

In the midst of his financial and legal troubles, Taylor was listed among the 76 candidates eligible for the NFL Hall of Fame. It was feared that many voters would overlook the accomplishments of his stellar NFL career and reject him because of his personal problems. However, Taylor was voted into the Hall of Fame in January of 1999. In a 1994 article in the *New York Times,* Taylor's former coach Bill Parcells summed up Taylor's career, "This sounds corny, but I think he was the consummate team player. He was very easy to coach because all you had to do was show him where the competition was. He wasn't selfish statistically. If we didn't win, he felt like he had failed no matter what he did. When people talk about who was the best outside linebacker, they're not going to put him in a group with seven or eight others. The bus station is full of guys who were going to be the next Lawrence Taylor."

Sources

Books

Hershberg, Dan. *Lawrence Taylor.* Chelsea House Publishers: Philadelphia, PA. 1998

Periodicals

New York Times, December 21, 1981; January 4, 1987; January 23, 1994; May 14, 1998; October 25, 1998.

—Michael J. Watkins

Derrick Thomas

1967–2000

Professional football player

Possessing tremendous speed and agility, Derrick Thomas was a linebacker who struck fear in the hearts of opposing NFL quarterbacks. A perennial selection to the Pro Bowl, he enjoyed ten stellar seasons with the Kansas City Chiefs. Tragically, Thomas was paralyzed in a car accident near Kansas City, Missouri on January 23, 2000. While recovering in a hospital in Miami, Florida, he developed a blood clot and suffered cardio-respiratory arrest. He died on February 8, 2000.

Thomas was born on January 1, 1967 in Miami, Florida, and would become one of the most dominating defensive players in the history of the National Football League (NFL). In 1972 when Thomas was five his father, who was a pilot in the Air Force, was shot down over Vietnam while flying a B-52 bomber. Thomas's father declared missing in action, and then declared legally dead in 1980. Thomas was raised in South Miami by his mother, Edith Morgan, and her foster mother Annie Adams. He grew up in the inner city and, as a child, had several run-ins with the police. At the age of 14, Thomas was arrested for burglary and sent to the Dade Marine Institute, a boot camp pro-

gram which served as a last option for young offenders before sending them to prison. It was there that Thomas turned his life around. He returned to South Miami High School and excelled on the football field as a running back, tight end, and linebacker. Thomas told Jeffry Flanagan of the *Kansas City Star* about his transformation from troubled youth to football standout, "I stopped running with the wrong people. Instead of sitting around and throwing rocks at cars and buses, and trying to figure out what place to rob, I put all my energy into football."

Committed to Football

After earning all-league honors at South Miami High School, Thomas earned a scholarship to the University of Alabama and proceeded to dominate the Southeast Conference. During his junior year with the Crimson Tide, Thomas recorded 67 tackles and a school-record 18 sacks. As a senior at Alabama, he won the Butkus Award as the country's top linebacker and was named an All-American. He set school records with 52 sacks and 74 tackles for a loss over the course of his career as a collegian. In 1989, Thomas was drafted fourth overall

At a Glance . . .

Born Derrick Vincent Thomas, January 1, 1967, in Miami, FL; died February 8, 2000, in Miami, FL; son of Robert Thomas (an Air Force captain) and Edith Morgan; children: Burgandie, Derrick Jr., Derrion, Derrius, Robert, Micayla, and Alexis; *Education:* University of Alabama, attended.

Career: Played running back, tight end, and linebacker at South Miami High School,1983; starred at linebacker at the University of Alabama, 1984-88; linebacker with the Kansas City Chiefs, 1989-99.

Member: Third and Long Foundation, founder, 1990.

Awards: All-American and Butkus Award winner, 1988; Defensive Rookie of the Year, Mack Lee Hill Award winner, 1989; named to the Pro Bowl 1989-97; set NFL single-game sack record (7), 1990; Chiefs MVP, 1991, 1994; NFL Man of the Year, 1993; won Byron-"Whizzer" White Humanitarian Award, 1995; holds Chiefs career record for sacks(126.5), safeties (3), and fumble recoveries (19).

by the Kansas City Chiefs after Troy Aikman, Tony Mandarich, and Barry Sanders. As a rookie, he announced his arrival in the NFL by rolling up 10 sacks and 55 quarterback pressures. Thomas went on to earn the Defensive Rookie of the Year Award from the Associated Press. He also started in the Pro Bowl and won the Mack Lee Hill Award, which is awarded to the Chiefs' best rookie.

In his second season with the Chiefs, Thomas set the NFL single-game sack record against the Seattle Seahawks, sacking quarterback Dave Krieg seven times and forcing two fumbles. He accomplished this feat on Veteran's Day after watching four Air Force jets fly over the stadium during a pre-game ceremony. Thomas started in his second Pro Bowl after leading the NFL with 20 sacks. His 20 quarterback sacks in 1990 established a new Chiefs record and was the fifth-highest total in league history. He also forced six fumbles and made 63 tackles over the course of the 1990 season. Off the field, Thomas established his own charitable organization, the Third and Long Foundation. The foundation started out as a way to raise money for poor kids. However, with Thomas's active participation, it focused more intently on encouraging children to read and pursue their educational goals.

Came of Age in the NFL

In 1991, Thomas earned his third consecutive trip to the Pro Bowl. He was also named the Chiefs' Most Valuable Player (MVP) on the strength of a 13.5-sack, 79-tackle season. The following year brought another invitation to the Pro Bowl as Thomas led the team with 67 tackles, 14.5 sacks, eight forced fumbles, and one touchdown.

In 1993, Thomas was named the NFL Man of the Year for his efforts both on the field and with the Third and Long Foundation. In addition to establishing his charity as a force in the Kansas City area, he led the Chiefs to the AFC Championship game. Thomas also became further identified with the cause of Vietnam veterans after giving the keynote speech at Memorial Day services in front of the Vietnam Veterans Monument. He received the Veterans of Foreign Wars Hall of Fame Award for his work on behalf of soldiers stationed overseas. He was also designated by former President George Bush as the "832nd Point of Light" for his charity work in and around Kansas City.

Thomas followed a strong 1993 campaign with perhaps his best season as a professional. Besides earning a sixth straight trip to the Pro Bowl, Thomas was named the Chiefs MVP for the second time. In only his sixth season, he became the team's all-time sack leader with 72.5 sacks, including the 11 he racked up over the course of the 1994 season. Always known as a fierce pass-rusher, Thomas was now receiving recognition for his overall game. Then-coach of the Oakland Raiders, Art Shell, commented on Thomas's skills to Flanagan of the *Kansas City Star,* "Everybody knows what he can do in rushing the passer. Now, he's stopping the run, too. He's the complete package. Almost unstoppable." Along with his usual eye-popping sack totals, Thomas also recorded a career-high 86 tackles with six forced fumbles.

The following two years were typically outstanding. Thomas made two more trips to the Pro Bowl—extending his Chiefs record for Pro Bowl appearances. In 1995, Thomas was again recognized for his charitable work when he received the Byron "Whizzer" White Humanitarian Award. After eight years in the NFL, the injury bug finally bit Thomas. Before the 1997 season, he hurt his left triceps tendon during the pre-season and missed four games. Thomas was forced to play out the rest of the season with an arm brace, which limited his effectiveness. He was also switched to a new linebacker position, but still managed to record 9.5 sacks and 55 tackles. Despite a less than stellar season, Thomas earned a spot on his ninth straight Pro Bowl team. In 1998, Thomas started ten of the season's 16 games. After recording six sacks to start the season, he tallied only six more for the rest of the season. Thomas's frustration boiled over during a nationally televised game against the Chiefs' archrival, the Denver Broncos. Late in the game, with Kansas City losing badly, Thomas was penalized three times for personal fouls in one defensive series. Thomas was suspended for a week, and Chiefs' coach Marty Schottenheimer resigned after the season when it became clear that he had lost control of the team.

A Tragic End

During the 1999 season, Thomas was used mostly as a pass-rusher. He compiled only seven sacks, and the Chiefs season ended without a playoff appearance. Despite his team's absence from post-season play, Thomas was still interested in professional football. He had planned to fly from Kansas City to St. Louis to watch the St. Louis Rams play in the NFC Championship Game against the Tampa Bay Buccaneers on January 23, 2000. The roads in Kansas City were icy as the city was experiencing its first snowstorm of the year. Thomas was hurrying through traffic in his Chevrolet Suburban on his way to the airport when his vehicle hit a patch of ice and flipped over several times. Thomas and a friend were thrown from the vehicle. Thomas was paralyzed and his friend and business partner, Michael Tellis, died instantly. A third passenger, who was wearing a seat belt, was uninjured.

The following day, Thomas was transferred from a Kansas City hospital to Jackson Memorial Hospital in Miami, Florida to have an operation on his shattered spine. Everything seemed to be going well for Thomas, who was in extraordinary physical condition, and he was looking forward to a successful rehabilitation. On the morning of February 8, 2000, Thomas went into cardio-respiratory arrest and died. Dr. Barth Green, a neurosurgeon at Jackson Memorial Hospital told *ESPN*, "A certain percentage of people with paralysis suffer from blood clots. Sometimes you can see them and sometimes they're hidden in the deeper veins of the body. And that's what happened to Derrick." The blood clot occurred in his pulmonary artery and deprived Thomas of blood and oxygen, which triggered the cardio-respiratory arrest.

The news of Thomas's death devastated the Kansas City community and the sports world in general. Carl Peterson, the Kansas City Chiefs president and general manager told the *New York Times'* Thomas George, "We would see his heart grow over the next 11 years, and he always went back and kept in touch with the people who touched his life. Derrick came to the heartland of America, and it was here that he gave his heart." At a memorial service at the Chiefs Arrowhead Stadium, 22,750 fans viewed the body of their fallen hero and a B-2 Stealth bomber flew over the site to honor Thomas. Although his career was cut short, he had established Chiefs' records in Pro Bowl appearances (9), sacks (126.5), safeties (3), forced fumbles (45), and fumble recoveries (18). In an obituary published in *The Dallas Morning News,* NFL Players Association executive director Gene Upshaw expressed his thoughts about the life of Derrick Thomas, "I never looked at Derrick Thomas as a football player. I looked at Derrick Thomas as one of the finer people that I had ever been around and as a friend. The thing I'll always remember about Derrick is his smile, that's one thing I'll never get out of my mind. Derrick will hang over this stadium forever."

Sources

Periodicals

Dallas Morning News, February 9, 2000.
Kansas City Star, February 8, 2000.
New York Times, February 16, 2000.

Other

Additional information for this profile was obtained from
http:\\www.kcchiefs.com\latest\mainnews.asp?storyID=1304&cat=1
http:\\www.kcchiefs.com\rosters_stats\player.asp
http:\\espn.go.com\nfl\news\2000\0208\343189.html

—Michael J. Watkins

Tina Thompson

1975—

Professional basketball player

Tina Thompson, All-Star forward for the Houston Comets, has developed a large fan base as much for her play as for her personality. She has played for the WNBA since she was chosen as the league's first overall pick in the 1997 inaugural draft. She has been an integral part of the Comets' "Big Three," sharing the spotlight with Cynthia Cooper and Sheryl Swoopes. With the Big Three, the Comets have been a formidable force in the league and have won three consecutive WNBA titles. Thompson was a WNBA All-Star in 1997 and 1998. While she plans to eventually go to law school and become a judge, she also plans to play for a while. "If my body holds up, and I'm physically and mentally fit, I'll be playing for a while," Thompson told fans at a WNBA online interactive chat.

Played Ball With the Boys

Thompson was born in Los Angeles, California on February 10, 1975. The family had five children including Thompson; she grew up with two brothers and two sisters. She seemed destined for a life in basketball. By the time she reached sixth grade, Thompson was already one of the tallest children in her class, standing 5'11" tall. Her brother, Tommy, and his friends played basketball at the recreation center near their home and she would tag along. Although they would not let her play with them inside the center, she managed to find games outside. Thompson related in a WNBA web site feature, "A lot of the boys there didn't like the fact that a girl was playing basketball, 'their' sport. They were actually rather cruel." But as her game developed and those boys saw that she had developed a nice outside shot, Thompson gained some respect and was eventually invited inside to play.

Thompson attended Inglewood Morningside High School in the early 1990s and continued playing basketball, joining her father and brother at the playgrounds. She also played on the school team. Thompson earned a reputation for toughness and shooting, and scored over 1,500 points. She played volleyball too, but was eventually kicked off the team for shooting baskets with the volleyballs.

Thompson entered the University of Southern California in 1993 and majored in sociology. She earned good grades, and was named PAC-10 Freshman of the

At a Glance . . .

Born February 10, 1975, in Los Angeles, CA; *Education:* University of Southern California, B.S. in sociology, 1997.

Career: Starred at Inglewood Morningside High School in Los Angeles, California; played for the University of Southern California, 1993-97; drafted in the first round by the Houston Comets, May 1997, first pick in inaugural WNBA draft; forward for the Houston Comets, 1997-.

Awards: Named PAC-10 Freshman of the Year, 1994; PAC-10 second-leading rebounder and third-leading scorer, 1997; AP All-America second team, Kodak District All-America Team, 1996-97; All PAC-10 First Team, 1996-97; named to All-WNBA First Team, 1997; named to All-WNBA First Team, 1998; voted a West team starter in WNBAfirst-ever All-Star Game, 1999.

Addresses: *Office*—Houston Comets, Two Greenway Plaza, Suite 400, Houston, TX 77046-3865.

Year in 1994. By the time Thompson graduated from college in 1997, she was the PAC-10 conference's third leading career rebounder with 1,168 rebounds, and its second leading scorer with 2,248 points. She planned to attend law school, and eventually become a judge. However, the Women's National Basketball League (WNBA) was formed, and Thompson was picked first by the Houston Comets in the inaugural draft. She said in a WNBA online chat, "For me, it was the most unbelievable experience of my life. Being a part of history, the first ever to be picked for the WNBA, is something I will never live down… . It is the highlight of my career." In her first game with the Comets, Thompson reacted like most athletes would in a new situation. She said in her online chat, "The most…nervous I felt was the first game. We played in Cleveland, and they were picked to be number one in the East. It was a big game. We played very well, shot very well and we killed them. That was the most exciting day, because we weren't expected to be a good team. Winning that game was a real motivation for us."

Solid Professional Play

Thompson established herself as a valuable player during her first year. She led the Comets in rebounds in 1997 with 6.6 rebounds per game, good for seventh place overall in the WNBA. Thompson also led the

team in blocked shots, averaging one per game and ranking sixth in the league. She was ranked second on the Comets that year in scoring, three-point percentage, and was ranked third in free-throw percentage. Thompson recorded a WNBA career-high 24 points and nine rebounds against the Cleveland Rockers on July 29, 1997, and was named to the 1997 All-WNBA First Team. In 1998 she was ranked second on the Comets in free-throw percentage, three-pointers, and third in scoring and three-point percentage. Thompson's solid performances contributed to three consecutive WNBA championships for the Houston Comets in 1997, 1998, and 1999.

In 1997, Kellogg USA became the official cereal sponsor of the WNBA. To show its support, the company created limited-edition series of Special K cereal boxes honoring the WNBA. The first series was an inaugural season-themed multi-pack of Kellogg's cereals, where five league players were featured. When the Houston Comets won the 1997 WNBA Championship, the Special K boxes featured Tina Thompson along with teammates Cynthia Cooper and Sheryl Swoopes. The Comets became the first women's sports team to appear on a box of Kellogg's cereal.

While Thompson established herself as a solid player, teammates Sheryl Swoopes and Cynthia Cooper, already known for their play in the American Basketball League (ABL), received a lot of the attention. Instead of craving the spotlight, Thompson focused on developing her game. Thompson and her teammates received a great deal of press about their offensive play, but their defensive abilities were often overlooked. Thompson proved to be a solid defensive player. Houston Comets coach Van Chancellor said in a WNBA web site feature, "It's a shame, but Tina never gets enough credit for her defense. She is the best post defender in this league, and often she sacrifices offense because she has to work so hard against the bigger opponents on defense." Thompson replied, "I love playing defense because it is a symbol of hard work and hustle. I don't mind playing against bigger players or getting physical, I do it because it helps us win games." Thompson's defensive prowess has allowed teammates Swoopes and Cooper to excel offensively. Cooper said, "Sheryl [Swoopes] and I do a lot of scoring but Tina helps make it possible with all the little things she does, from screening, to hitting threes to grabbing rebounds. She is a big part of everything that happens for us."

Won Third Consecutive Championship

Thompson's play during the 1999 season was solid as well. She was voted a West team starter in the WNBA's first-ever All Star Game that summer. She led her team in rebounds, scored a game-high 26 points and grabbed nine rebounds in a July game against the Cleveland Rockers, and scored 22 points and a game-high 12 rebounds in June against the Orlando Miracle.

Thompson also reached career highs in points, free throws, and steals. She helped to lead the Comets to their third-straight WNBA championship in 1999, despite the team's difficulties with injuries and the death of teammate Kim Perrot, who died of lung cancer in August.

Although she is serious about playing basketball, Thompson also has fun. Like many athletes, Thompson has certain rituals before a game. She has lunch at approximately the same time, takes a nap, puts on her "lucky" and traditional red lipstick, and puts on her uniform in a certain order. She also has a shooting ritual before warming up. She has become known for wearing deep red lipstick during games, a ritual she began in college. Thompson told *Sports Illustrated for Kids,* "Before a game during my freshman year in college, I left on my lipstick. I played great. I thought, 'It's the lipstick.' I've worn it ever since."

When not playing basketball, Thompson loves to read books and go shopping. Her favorite book is *I Know Why The Caged Bird Sings* by Maya Angelou. She cites her parents and older brother as her role models.

While Thompson has said that she has always admired former Lakers star Magic Johnson, she modeled her game after her brother. Thompson is grateful for here success. She told a fan in a WNBA email reply, "I've been put in a very blessed situation and I am not going to take it for granted at all."

Sources

Periodicals

Sports Illustrated for Kids, July 1997.

Other

Additional material for this profile was obtained from the WNBA and Comets web sites at http:\\www.wnba.com;
and http:\\www.wnba.com\comets

—Sandy J. Stiefer

Ivan van Sertima

1935—

Historian

A mild-mannered scholar of British-Caribbean background, Ivan van Sertima unleashed a revolution in the popular historical imagination with his 1977 book *They Came Before Columbus: The African Presence in Ancient America.* In that book, van Sertima argued that explorers from the great cultures of ancient Egypt had traveled to the Western Hemisphere and deeply influenced pre-Columbian cultures there, in contrast with other possible early visitors such as the Vikings, who left few cultural traces of their presence. Along with van Sertima's later work exploring other facets of African influence in ancient cultures, the book stands at the center of efforts to develop African-centered models of primary and secondary education. However, the validity of van Sertima's research has often been questioned by scholars from the mainstream of academic anthropology.

Ivan Gladstone van Sertima was born in Kitty Village in Guyana, a small country on South America's Caribbean coast, on January 26, 1935. Guyana was then a colony of Great Britain, and van Sertima retained British citizenship even after embarking on his scholarly career in the United States. Van Sertima's father, Frank Obermuller, was a trade union leader. Van Sertima completed primary and secondary schooling in Guyana. In 1956, he landed a job as a broadcaster and writer with the government information service in Guyana's capital city of Georgetown. The following year, he published a book of poetry entitled *River and the Wall.*

Published Book of Poetry

River and the Wall was published in Guyana, but the book attracted attention in England as well, and van Sertima moved there in November of 1959. He began work on a degree in African languages and literature at the London School of Oriental and African Studies. Along the way, he learned to speak Swahili and Hungarian fluently.

During the 1960s, however, van Sertima's creative efforts were widely diffused through many different endeavors. He did broadcasts about literature for the BBC, wrote poetry, worked on a novel called *Blackhouse* that was filmed under the title of *The Black Prince,* compiled a dictionary of legal terms in Swahili, and embarked upon his career as a scholar with a series of essays on Caribbean literature. He received his B.A. degree, with honors, in 1969 from the London School of Oriental and African Studies.

Following graduation from college, van Sertima briefly resumed his broadcasting career. However, in 1970, he took time off to visit the United States for the first time. While there, he made two crucial intellectual discoveries. The first was a monumental historical work of the 1920s, Leo Wiener's *Africa and the Discovery of America.* The book was an example of the "diffusionist" school of thinking which held that cultural traits in general, and in this case African traits in particular, tended to migrate around the globe rather than springing up separately and spontaneously in different cul-

At a Glance . . .

Born January 26, 1935, in Kitty Village, British Guyana; married Maria Nagy, October 24, 1964; children: Lawrence Josef. *Education:* London School of Oriental and African Studies, London, England, B.A. with honors, 1969; Rutgers University, M.A., 1977.

Career: Scholar, critic, educator, and poet. Press and broadcasting officer, Government Information Office, Georgetown, Guyana, 1956-59; freelance broadcaster and writer, London, England, 1959-69; broadcaster, Central Office of Information, London, 1969-70; instructor, Rutgers University, 1970-72; assistant professor, Rutgers, 1972-79; wrote best-selling book, *They Came Before Columbus,* 1977; associate professor of African studies, 1979-; numerous other writings; has edited many books on African civilizations and their influence.

Awards: Nominator, Nobel Prize in Literature, 1976-80; Clarence L. Holte Prize, Twenty-First Century Foundation, 1981.

Addresses: *Office*—Department of African Studies, Rutgers University, New Brunswick, NJ 08094.

tures. The second was the widely reported discovery of a group of large heads of African appearance, created by the Olmec culture of Central America in, it was then thought, the eighth or seventh century B.C.

Theorized African Voyages to Americas

Enrolling in a master's program at Rutgers University in New Jersey, van Sertima was hired there as an instructor in 1970 in the school's new African Studies department. He has continued to teach there ever since, winning promotions to assistant professor in 1972 and associate professor in 1979, the latter coming after he received his M.A. degree. The bulk of van Sertima's time in the 1970s, however, was occupied with the writing of *They Came Before Columbus,* a massive work whose evidence for the pre-Columbian African discovery of the New World encompassed many historical subjects and fields of knowledge.

Van Sertima's central argument was that the Nubian rulers of ancient Egypt organized expeditions for the gathering of natural resources. One of these expeditions crossed the Atlantic Ocean and landed on the Caribbean coast. The Olmecs, predecessors to the Maya and the other great cultures of Central America, created their large ceremonial heads in depiction and in honor of these African invaders. Van Sertima supported his thesis with other claims of African influence on New World cultures, involving the presence of certain cultivated crops, including cotton, and of Egyptian practices such as pyramid-building and mummification of the dead.

They Came Before Columbus, which was published in 1977 on the heels of Alex Haley's massive best-seller *Roots,* was hugely successful, not only among African American readers, but with the American public in general. The Book-of-the-Month Club made it a featured selection, and van Sertima became a widely sought-after lecturer. Van Sertima, quoted in the volume *Caribbean Writers,* pointed to some of the reasons for the book's resonance: "Many people feel a certain kind of happiness when they read my book. A certain kind of shadow lifts. The psyche of blacks is raised. No man who believes his history began with slavery can be a healthy man. If you lift that shadow, you help repair that damage." Van Sertima's work began to be featured in university African Studies courses, as well as African-centered curricula that were beginning to emerge in urban elementary and high schools.

Disputed Critics' Arguments

However, the academic community has not been kind to van Sertima's work. The criticism began with a *New York Times* review of *They Came Before Columbus,* in which British scholar Glyn Daniel referred to the book as "ignorant rubbish." Van Sertima, according to *Caribbean Writers,* rejoined that Daniel was "a man impervious to original thought." A lengthy review of van Sertima's claims in a 1997 issue of the journal, *Current Anthropology,* took issue with almost all of them. The review asserted that the features of the Olmec heads were only superficially African, and pointed out that the period of Egyptian pyramid-building did not coincide with the one during which van Sertima's voyages were alleged to have taken place. It also faulted van Sertima, who is not an anthropologist or archaeologist, for ignoring the work of Central American researchers, and noted that no actual artifacts of African presence have been found in the New World. The authors of this critique also turned van Sertima's cultural outlook on its head, accusing him of disparaging the achievements of Native American cultures.

Van Sertima has defended his claims, but declined to respond to the 1997 article. However, he has compiled an impressive record of publications since *They Came Before Columbus,* editing works that investigated ancient Egyptian culture generally and focusing on its effects on the rest of the ancient world. Among these works are *The African Presence in Early Europe* (1985) and *The Golden Age of the Moor* (1991). Van Sertima is the founder of the *Journal of African Civilizations,* a monograph series on African subjects, and served as a nominator for the Nobel Prize committee during the late 1970s. He is also a recipient of the Clarence L. Holte Prize of the Twenty-First Century Foundation.

Selected writings

River and the Wall, 1958.
Caribbean Writers: Critical Essays, 1968.
Swahili Dictionary of Legal Terms, 1968.
They Came Before Columbus: The African Presence in Ancient America, 1977.
Blacks in Science: Ancient and Modern, 1983 (editor).
Black Women in Antiquity, 1984 (editor).
Egypt Revisited, 1985 (editor).
The African Presence in Early Europe, 1985 (editor).
The African Presence in Early Asia, 1985 (editor, with Runoko Rashidi).
Great African Thinkers, Volume I: Cheiki Anta Diop, 1986 (editor).
Great Black Leaders, Ancient and Modern, 1988 (editor).
The Golden Age of the Moor, 1991 (editor).
Egypt: Child of Africa, 1994 (editor).
Journal of African Civilizations, ongoing (editor).

Sources

Books

Contemporary Authors, volume 104, Gale, 1982; New Revision Series, volume 42, Gale, 1994.
Herdeck, Donald E., *Caribbean Writers: A Bio-Bibliographical-Critical Encyclopedia,* Three Continents Press, 1979.
Murphy, Rosalie, ed., *Contemporary Poets,* first ed., St. James, 1970.
The Schomburg Center Guide to Black Literature, Gale, 1996.

Periodicals

Current Anthropology, June 1997, p. 419.
New York Times, March 13, 1977.

—James M. Manheim

Bob Watson

1946—

Baseball administrator

A star baseball player for the Houston Astros during the 1970s, Bob Watson moved into administration after his playing career ended and notched a series of "firsts." He was baseball's first African American assistant general manager, first African American general manager, and first African American to lead his team to a World Series victory, taking over the helm of the New York Yankees organization and leading the team to baseball's championship in 1996. Watson has been conscious of his position as a role model, and has lamented the lack of opportunities available to African Americans at the highest levels of major league baseball. "I am really tired of being the first of anything in baseball," he told the *New York Times*. "I'd like to see all those firsts turned into second, third, fourth, and fifth."

Robert Jose Watson was born in Los Angeles on April 10, 1946, and was raised by his grandparents in the city's South Central neighborhood. Powerfully built and athletic from his early days, he had what it took to stand up to the area's tough characters. "Growing up, I was always one of the strongest kids in my neighborhood," he recalled in an interview with *Texas Monthly*. "[O]n two occasions, when I was put in threatening situations, I, unfortunately, did hurt some guys. So I

worked hard to stay on an even keel."

Endured Southern Segregation

Nicknamed "Bull" for his six-foot-two-inch, 215-pound stature, Watson briefly attended Los Angeles Harbor College, but turned to baseball when he was signed by the Houston Astros organization in 1965. He was only 18-years-old at the time. Even though he progressed quickly in the minor leagues, Watson's years with the Astros' predominantly southern farm system were difficult ones because he faced the brunt of racial segregation. Playing in Cocoa, Florida and Salisbury, North Carolina, he was unable to find an apartment complex that would accept African American tenants, and ended up virtually homeless.

"It was total culture shock for a kid from L.A.," Watson told *Texas Monthly*. "Emotionally, I definitely wasn't ready for it." A restaurant in Salisbury gave away free Salisbury steaks to players who hit home runs, but although Watson hit them frequently, the restaurant refused to serve him. In 1969, Watson had reached his breaking point. By then he was part of the Astros lineup, but was briefly sent down to the team's Savan-

At a Glance . . .

Born on April 10, 1946, in Los Angeles, CA; married in 1968, wife's name Carol; children, Keith and Kelley. *Education:* Attended Los Angeles Harbor College. *Military service:* U.S. Marine Corps, 1966-71. *Religion:* Non-denominational.

Career: Professional baseball administrator; signed by Houston Astros organization,1965. Played with several southern minor-league teams and with the Astros, late 1960s; played outfield and first base for the Astros, 1969-79; set several team records with Astros; traded to Boston Red Sox, 1979; played for the New York Yankees, 1980; played in World Series with Yankees, 1981; traded to Atlanta Braves, 1984; batting coach, Oakland Athletics, 1984-88; assistant general manager, Houston Astros, 1988-93; general manager, Houston Astros, 1993-95; general manager, New York Yankees, 1995-97; part of group that tried to buy Oakland Athletics,1999.

Awards: Named to National League All-Star team, 1973 and 1975.

Addresses: *Office*—Former General Manager, New York Yankees, Yankee Stadium 161 St. and River Ave., Bronx, NY 10451.

nah, Georgia farm club. Unable to find a hotel that would admit him, Watson decided to quit baseball and boarded a flight back home to Los Angeles. However, the plane stopped over in Houston, where the Astros' assistant general manager met him at the airport to deliver the news that he had been recalled to the major leagues.

Although he broke into major league baseball as a catcher, Watson played that position in only ten games. He switched to the outfield, and moved to first base in 1975. Watson remained with the Astros until 1979 and was a consistently strong hitter. He batted over .300 in six of his 11 seasons in the Astros' starting lineup, and reached a career high batting average of .324 in 1975. That year, and also in 1973, Watson was named to the National League All-Star team. In both 1976 and 1977, he batted in more than 100 runs. He also scored the one millionth run in major-league history in 1976. A fierce competitor, Watson once broke the jaw of an opposing shortstop when he ran into him to break up a double play. After setting several team records, he was traded from the Astros to

the Boston Red Sox in 1979.

Appeared in 1981 World Series

A natural for the American League's designated hitter role (whereby a player can bat in place of the pitcher but does not play defense), Watson enjoyed strong seasons during the latter years of his career. He signed with the New York Yankees in 1980, and was a member of the Yankees team that lost to the Los Angeles Dodgers in the 1981 World Series. Watson led the Yankees to victory in the first game of the World Series with a three-run home run. Following the 1984 season, which he spent with the Atlanta Braves, Watson retired from baseball with a lifetime batting average of .295.

Watson moved into management, spending four years as a hitting coach with the Oakland Athletics. He moved back to Houston to take a job as assistant general manager with the Astros in 1988, becoming baseball's first African American assistant general manager. By accepting the position, Watson took a pay cut from 120,000 to 40,000 per year. However, he believed that the job was an important stepping stone to more important positions.

Watson performed well in the Astros front office, and engineered several key trades. When the team's new owner, Drayton McLane Jr., fired several top Astros officials, Watson was named general manager in 1993. By assuming this important role, he became major-league baseball's first African American general manager. "I would have to say it's a very important step for baseball, a very important step for the Houston Astros and a very important step for Bob Watson," Watson told *Sports Illustrated.*

One of Watson's goals as general manager was to lead the Astros to their first World Series appearance. He nearly succeeded, as the team enjoyed two consecutive second-place finishes in the National League. Although confident and qualified after a lifetime in baseball, "I still felt this huge pressure to be a role model for other blacks," Watson told *Texas Monthly.* The Astros performed well under Watson's leadership, but his stress level increased as rumors circulated that the Astros were going to be sold to a new owner.

Led Yankees to Championship

In 1996, Watson accepted a management job with the New York Yankees. His two-year contract reportedly paid 350,000 a year. The decision to leave Houston for New York was a difficult one, and any stress Watson experienced in Houston increased exponentially in New York because he had to work with the Yankees' temperamental owner George Steinbrenner. Known for micromanaging the Yankees' affairs, Steinbrenner had run through a rapid succession of 14 general managers and had fired and rehired the same team manager, Billy Martin, five times. Additional stress was placed on Watson by medical problems, including the surgical removal of a cancerous prostate gland.

Watson achieved a lifelong dream when the Yankees won the World Series championship in 1996, the team's first series appearance in 16 years. Many observers commented on how distinctly the team had been stamped with Watson's personality, and on the cohesiveness and organization with which the Yankees operated. However, when the injury-plagued Yankees failed to repeat as world champions in 1997, conflict flared between Watson and Steinbrenner. Watson exhibited the depth of his frustration during several substantial interviews, and finally left the Yankees in February of 1998. Doctors had also cautioned him to cut back on his punishing work schedule.

For the first time in over 30 years, Watson was out of baseball. With money in the bank and a strong enthusiasm for fishing, he found ways to pass the time. However, he interviewed for several general manager positions and joined a group of investors seeking to buy the Oakland Athletics, which would have made him the first African American owner of a major-league team. Although the deal fell through, few doubted that Watson would return to baseball and continue opening doors for African Americans who have given so much to America's national pastime.

Sources

Books

Watson, Bob, *Survive to Win,* Thomas Nelson, 1997.

Periodicals

Knight-Ridder\Tribune News Service, April 12, 1997.
Jet, February 23, 1998, p. 47.
New York Times, April 29, 1997, p. C3; April 27, 1999, p. D3.
Sporting News, February 9, 1998, p. 50; October 18, 1999, p. 56.
Sports Illustrated, October 18, 1993, p. 74.
Texas Monthly, April 1997, p. 48.

—James M. Manheim

Joe Williams

1918–1999

Singer

His name is not as well known to the general public as those of jazz legends like Louis Armstrong, Duke Ellington, or Ella Fitzgerald, but Joe Williams is nevertheless counted among the masters of jazz and blues singing; he has, in fact, earned the title "Emperor of the Blues." His singing style, which he developed over a long and consistently successful career, contributed to the success of the Count Basie Orchestra and influenced the style of many younger singers.

Joseph Goreed was born in the small farming town of Cordele, Georgia, on December 12, 1918. His father, Willie Goreed, vanished when Williams was very young. His mother, Anne Beatrice Gilbert, who was no older than 18 when she gave birth to her only child, provided a strong emotional bond until her death in 1968.

Soon after Williams was born, his mother moved them in with his grandparents, who had enough money to support an extended family. During this time, Anne Gilbert was saving up for a move to Chicago, Illinois. Once she had made the move—alone—she began saving the money that she earned cooking for wealthier white Chicagoans so that her family could join her. By the time Williams was four, he and his grandmother and his aunt were on a train to Chicago, where they would live for many years.

Probably most important to Williams's later life was the music scene—fueled largely by African American musicians—that thrived in Chicago in the early 1920s. Years later, he recalled going to the Vendome Theatre with his mother to hear Louis Armstrong play his trumpet. Chicago also offered a host of radio stations that featured the then rebellious sound of jazz, exposing Williams to the styling of Duke Ellington, Ethel Waters, Cab Calloway, Joe Turner, and others. By his early teens, he had already taught himself to play piano and had formed a quartet, known as the Jubilee Boys, that sang at church functions.

In his mid-teens, Williams began singing solo at formal events with local bands. The most that he ever took home was five dollars a night, but that was enough to convince his family that he could make a living at it. At the age of 16, Williams dropped out of school. After a family conference, the name "Williams" was chosen as a better last name for a singer, and he began marketing himself in earnest to Chicago clubs and bands. His first job was a kind of compromise—not unusual for a young singer—at a club called Kitty Davis's. Hired to

At a Glance . . .

Born Joseph Goreed, December 12, 1918, in Cordele, GA; raised in Chicago, IL; changed surname to Williams, c. 1934; died March 29, 1999, in Las Vegas, NV; son of Willie Goreed (believed to be a farm laborer) and Anne Beatrice Gilbert (a cook); married Wilma Cole, 1942 (divorced, 1946); married Anne Kirksey, 1946 (divorced, c. 1950); married Lemma Reid, 1951 (divorced, 1964); married Jillean Milne Hughes-D'Aeth, 1965; children: (third marriage) JoAnn, Joe, Jr.

Career: Began singing in his early teens with church quartet the Jubilee Boys; solo singer for Chicago bands during the early 1930s; sang and toured with several different bands,including Jimmie Noone, 1938-39, Les Hite, 1939-40, Coleman Hawkins, 1941, Lionel Hampton, 1942-43, Andy Kirk, 1946-47, and Red Saunders, 1951-53; sang with the Count Basie Orchestra, 1954-1961, toured Europe in the late 1950s; began solo career, 1961; recording artistand singer on soundtracks for films, including *Jamboree,* 1957 (with the Count BasieOrchestra), *Cinderfella,* 1960 (with the Count Basie Orchestra), and *The Moonshine War,* 1969, *Sharky's Machine,* 1981, *City Heat,* 1984, *All of Me,* 1984; played the role of Grandpa Al on *The Cosby Show,* 1980s.

Selected awards: Grammy Awards for *I Just Want to Sing,* 1985, and *Ballad and Blues Master,* 1992; Ebony Lifetime Achievement Award, 1993; performed at the WhiteHouse for President Bill Clinton, 1993; Jazz Vocalist Award, Los Angeles Jazz Society, 1997;inducted into the International Jazz Hall of Fame, 1997.

Les Hite band, which accompanied the likes of Louis Armstrong and Fats Waller. One year later, he went on a larger tour with the band of saxophonist Coleman Hawkins.

Williams quickly attracted the interest of jazz great Lionel Hampton. In 1942, Hampton hired Williams both for the band's home performances at the Tic Toc Club in Boston and for their cross-country tours. His work with Hampton ended when the band's regular male singer was able to return. By that time, Williams was able to resume his burgeoning career in Chicago.

Experienced Personal Upheaval

Williams's first marriage—to Wilma Cole in 1942—set in motion a pattern of marital difficulties that he wouldn't be able to break until the 1960s. The emotional relationship quickly became painful for both partners, although the union remained legal until 1946. That same year, he married Anne Kirksey, with whom he also had a briefly happy relationship; they separated in 1948 and divorced in the early 1950s. It was during his second marriage that Williams experienced his one serious bout with depression. Following a nervous breakdown in the spring of 1947, he spent a year in Elgin State Hospital, where he received now controversial "treatments" such as electroshock therapy.

Williams's marriage to Lemma Reid, which survived from 1951 until 1964, produced two children, JoAnn and Joe Jr. The union wasn't, however, any more resilient than the first two had been: Lemma returned to her mother's home in Cincinnati soon after JoAnn's birth. Williams met Jillean Milne Hughes-D'Aeth, an Englishwoman, in 1957. After their first meeting, Williams and Hughes-D'Aeth did not see each other again until two years later, when the Basie band was touring in England. Before Williams left Europe, he knew that he was in love. In May of 1960, he and Hughes-D'Aeth rented a New York apartment together. The two were married on January 7, 1965.

Basie and Beyond

In the early 1950s, Chicago disc jockey Daddy-O Daily secured for Williams an opportunity to sing with the band of one of the most powerful band leaders of the era—Count Basie. After the gigs, Williams returned to his floating solo career style, but by 1954 Basie wanted him on contract. Williams would stay with the "Basie machine" until 1961, making New York his home base and securing the best exposure a blues singer could have. National tours were interspersed with long spells in a number of America's musical capitals, when the band would play at one club for three or four weeks at a time. After 1955, the band stopped every year at the Newport Jazz Festival, one of the biggest events on the

clean the bathrooms, Williams was allowed to sing with the band in the evening and keep the tips, which would sometimes amount to 20 dollars a night.

Toured the U.S. With Big Bands

Williams's first professional break came in 1938 when clarinet and saxophone master Jimmie Noone invited him to sing with his band. Less than a year later, the young singer was earning a reputation at Chicago dance halls and on a national radio station that broadcast his voice from Massachusetts to California. Williams toured the Midwest in 1939 and 1940 with the jazz calender. The years 1956, 1957, and 1959 also found the Basie band touring Europe, where the popularity of jazz had skyrocketed.

Williams developed his essential repertoire while he was with Basie, including standards such as "Every Day (I Have the Blues)," "Five O'Clock in the Morning," "Roll 'em Pete," "Teach Me Tonight," "My Baby Upsets Me," and "The Comeback." The recordings that he made with the Basie band cemented his popularity, selling briskly in record shops and earning airplay at major radio stations across the country. In 1955, Williams won *Down Beat* magazine's New Star Award. That same year, he won *Down Beat*'s international critics' poll for Best New Male Singer, as well as their readers' poll for Best Male Band Singer—citations he would continue to accumulate throughout his career.

Despite his tremendous success with Count Basie, Williams eventually began to feel that his position with the Basie band was limiting his potential as an artist. By 1960, he was planning the beginnings of a solo career that would allow him to pursue a broader range of material in blues and jazz. Initially, Basie's manager, Willard Alexander, set Williams up with a group of strong musicians and a tour schedule that would take him across the United States during a six month period. The bookings increased; Williams toured for almost all of 1961. By the late 1960s, he was on the road performing between 30 and 40 weeks each year.

Williams continued to produce albums and received overwhelmingly positive reviews for both his recordings and his performances. Even after his 70th birthday in 1988, Williams continued touring and recording. He was particularly sought after to sing at tributes to his peers, including Sarah Vaughan, Ella Fitzgerald, and Louis Armstrong. As always, Williams's performances received glowing reviews in magazines and newspapers; a New Yorker interviewer described a 1986 performance: "Williams has an enormous bass-baritone. It is lilting and flexible. It moves swiftly and lightly from a low C to a pure falsetto. It moves through glottal stops and yodels and delicate growls, through arching blue notes and vibratos that barely stir the air."

Received Numerous Accolaides

In addition to his music career, Williams acted in several films. At the request of his friend and devoted fan, Bill Cosby, he played the role of Claire Huxtable's father on the popular 1980s sitcom *The Cosby Show*. Williams also lent his velvety baritone voice to film soundtracks, including *Jamboree, Cinderfella, The Moonshine War, Sharky's Machine, City Heat,* and *All of Me.* He performed at the White House for President Bill Clinton in 1993, and appeared at the Kennedy Center Honors in Washington D.C. during the 1990s. He also released the albums *Jump for Joy* (1993), *Here's to*

Life (1994), and *Feel the Spirit* (1995).

Williams was the recipient of many accolades and awards. In 1983, he had his star placed beside Count Basie's on the "Gallery of Stars"sidewalk in Hollywood. In 1985, Williams received a Grammy Award for Best Jazz Vocalist for the album *I Just Want to Sing.* He earned a second Grammy Award for his release *Ballad and Blues Master* in 1992, and was honored by the Johnson Publishing Company with its prestigious Ebony Lifetime Achievement Award in 1993. In 1997, he was presented with the Jazz Vocalist Award from the Los Angeles Jazz Society. That same year, Williams was inducted into the International Jazz Hall of Fame.

After complaining of respiratory problems, Williams was admitted to a hospital in Las Vegas in March of 1999. One week later, he called his wife to ask her to pick him up from the hospital. However, Williams had wandered away before she arrived. John Levy, his manager, told *Jet* that "Joe was disoriented. The medication caused him not to have it all together. . . .His conversation was wild and rambling. I knew something was wrong. He wasn't of his right mind. He never would have walked out of that hospital." After walking for nearly two miles, Williams collapsed and died a few blocks from his home.

Although Williams enjoyed a remarkable and varied career, he never achieved the same status as some white vocalists. As he remarked in an interview with the *Los Angeles Times,* "There's a reason for that. You can't put down a people on one hand and treat them as romantic heroes on the other, can you? How can you do that and still keep up with the status quo? A friend of mine once said that hate is too important an emotion to waste on someone you don't like."

Selected discography

A Man Ain't Supposed to Cry, Roulette, 1957.
Memories Ad-lib, Roulette, 1958.
Joe Williams Sings About You, Roulette, 1959.
A Swingin' Night at Birdland—Joe Williams Live, Roulette, 1962.
Joe Williams at Newport '63, Victor, 1963.
The Heart and the Soul of Joe Williams, Sheba, 1971.
Joe Williams With Love, Temponic, 1972.
Joe Williams Live, Fantasy, 1973.
Big Man, the Legend of John Henry, Fantasy, 1975.
Prez and Joe, GNPS\Crescendo, 1979.
Then and Now, Bosco, 1984.
every night: Live at Vine St., Verve\PolyGram, 1987.
The Overwhelming Joe Williams, RCA, 1988.
Ballad and Blues Master, Verve\PolyGram, 1992.
Joe Williams: A Song Is Born, VIEW, 1992.
Jump for Joy, Bluebird\RCA, 1993.
Here's to Life, Telarc, 1994.

Feel the Spirit, Telarc, 1995.

Sources

Books

Grouse, Leslie, *Everyday: The Story of Joe Williams,* Quartet, 1984.

Periodicals

Entertainment Weekly, November 20, 1992.
Jet, September 9, 1985; April 19, 1999.
Los Angeles Times, June 14, 1991.
New Yorker, October 27, 1986.
New York Times, June 22, 1989; June 27, 1991.
Washington Post, October 16, 1991.

—Ondine E. Le Blanc and David G. Oblender

Sherley Anne Williams

1944–1999

Author, poet, educator

The road from impoverished migrant worker to celebrated author, poet, and professor may sound like a difficult one. However, Sherley Anne Williams traveled that road with wit, humility and relative ease. Her natural talent for writing and passion for the topics she wrote about created a life many African American children only dreamed about. "For a black child, horizons were very limited," Williams recalled to Mona Gable of the *Los Angeles Times Magazine*. "Things would open up a tiny bit, but we would say, 'Don't hope to hard.' There was no way I could have predicted that any of this would happen to me."

Born to a migrant worker and his wife and raised in the housing projects of Fresno, California, Williams described her childhood to Gable as, "the most deprived, provincial kind of existence you can think of." When she was eight years old, Williams's father died of tuberculosis. His death left the family more destitute than before. "I was not very outgoing or self-confident as a kid," she admitted Gable. "Even in a poverty-stricken environment, we were enormously poor. And I have always felt that very much."

Lost in Books

In an effort to cope with poverty and loneliness, Williams found solace in books, a practice that was discouraged by her mother. "I think she felt reading wasn't a skill I needed to the excess I was taking it," she recalled to Gable, "and that it would put ideas in my head beyond the possibility of them being fulfilled, so I

would be really dissatisfied with my lot in life." While most people she had grown up with were dropping out of school, Williams proved to be a bright and able student. An eighth grade science teacher recognized her potential and insisted that she enroll in college prep courses. Although she was eager to learn in high school, Williams was still uncertain about her future and feared that she would spend the rest of her life working in the same cotton and fruit fields as her parents. "I was really full of inarticulate longings I didn't know how to express," she told Gable. "I remember walking the shelves in the library one day, trying to see if I could tell by the title of the books if they were about black people, because I was too embarrassed to ask the librarian. I mean, what if there were no books? So by that, I came upon Richard Wright's *Black Boy* and Eartha Kitt's *Thursday's Child*. It was largely through these autobiographies I was able to take heart in my life."

As a high school student, Williams realized she had a passion for language and writing and was encouraged to apply to college. As a freshman at Fresno State University, she discovered the writings of Langston Hughes and Sterling Brown. "They were the earliest influences on my work," Williams told Gable. "I was totally captivated by their language, their speech and their character because I've always liked the way black people talk. So I wanted to work with that in writing."

Beginning the Writer's Life

Eager to distance herself from the cotton fields and fruit

Born Sherley Anne Williams August 25, 1944 in Fresno, CA; died July 6, 1999 in San Diego, CA; daughter of Jessee Winson Williams and Lelia Maria (Siler) Williams; children: John Malcolm. *Education:* Fresno State College (now California State University, Fresno), B.A., 1966; Fisk University, 1966; Howard University, 1966-67; Brown University, M.A., 1972.

Career: Fresno State College (California State University, Fresno), co-director of tutorial program, 1965-66; Miles College, Atlanta, Georgia, administrative internal assistant top resident, 1967-68; California State University, Fresno, lecturer in ethnic studies, 1969-70; Federal City College, Washington, DC, consultant in curriculum development and community educator, 1970-72; California State University, Fresno, associate professor of English, 1972-73; *Ours to Make,* television show, 1973; University of California, San Diego, Afro-American literature department, assistant professor, 1973-76, associate professor and department chairperson, 1976-82, professor, 1982-99; *The Sherley Williams Special,* television show, 1977; Letters from a New England Negro, full-length drama, produced 1982; Fulbright lecturer, University of Ghana, 1984.

Awards: National Book Award and Pulitzer Prize nominations, *The Peacock Poems,* 1975; National Book Award nomination, *Some One Sweet Angel Chile,* 1982; Emmy Award, 1982; *Dessa Rose* named notable book by *New York Times,* 1986; American Library Association Caldecott Award, Coretta Scott King Book Award, *Working Cotton,* 1992.

orchards of the San Joaquin Valley, Williams headed east for graduate school, first to Fisk University in Nashville, then Howard University in Washington, DC. She transferred to Brown University, where she received her master's degree in American literature in 1972. That same year, she went to work as an associate professor of English at her alma mater, Fresno State College, which had been renamed California State University, Fresno.

Williams also published her first book in 1972, *Give Birth to Brightness: A Thematic Study in Neo-Black Literature.* A collection of essays on contemporary African American fiction, the book was generally well received. "Miss Williams has written a readable and

informative survey of black literature," Mel Watkins wrote in the *New York Times.* "In using both her knowledge of Western literature and her understanding of black life, she provides insight into the sadly neglected area of reversed values that plays such a significant role in much of black literature."

In 1973, Williams became an assistant professor of Afro-American literature at the University of California, San Diego. She was the first African American woman to be hired in that department. Two years later Williams published her first book of poetry, *the Peacock Poems,* which was nominated for a Pulitzer Prize and a National Book Award. Her second volume of poetry, *Some One Sweet Angel Chile* was also a National Book Award nominee and a television performance of those poems earned Williams an Emmy Award.

Dessa Rose

Although Williams was a successful poet, her true passion was fiction writing. While still a student at Brown, Williams discovered an essay by African American activist Angela Davis. The essay revolved around the true story of a pregnant African American woman who helped lead a slave revolt in North Carolina in 1829. The woman was sentenced to death, but was allowed to live until her baby was born. Williams traced the story back to its original source, American Negro Slave Revolts, which was written by Marxist historian Herbert Aptheker. In that same book, she discovered the story of a white woman who gave refuge to runaway slaves on her North Carolina farm. What would have happened, Williams wondered, if these two women had met?

For the next 15 years, Williams pondered that question. In 1982, she sat down to write her first novel based on her discoveries, *Dessa Rose.* Williams felt that the true story of a slave woman hadn't been told before, and she was eager to develop the character. "As I began to explore that character more," she told Cheryll Greene of *Essence,* "I could see other issues that were worth talking about, such as some positive possibilities for relations among black men and women. People were working actively for survival in ways that perhaps didn't make the history books, but that were real nonetheless."

Dessa Rose was published in 1986 to a chorus of positive reviews. David Bradley of the *New York Times* described the novel as, "artistically brilliant, emotionally affecting and totally unforgettable." His colleague, Christopher Lehmann-Haupt, in a separate review, wrote that Williams, "breathed wonderful life into the bare bones of the past. And thus does she resolve more issues than are dreamed of in most history textbooks." *Dessa Rose,* Cheryll Greene of *Essence* wrote, "is one of those books that opens a window onto our souls, changing the way we see ourselves and our possibilities."

A movie based on *Dessa Rose* never materialized, although a deal had been struck and Williams was hired to write the screenplay. Instead, Williams returned to the classroom and began devoting her time to writing children's books. Her first children's novel, *Working Cotton,* was based on her childhood in the cotton fields. The book received a American Library Association Caldecott Award, a Coretta Scott King Book Award, and was listed among the best books of 1992 by *Parents* magazine. Her second book for children, *Girls Together,* was published in 1999, just a few months before Williams's death from cancer on July 6. At the time of her death, she was working on a sequel to *Dessa Rose.*

"Writing for me is really a process of saying, 'Here, read this,'" Williams described to Claudia Tate, the editor of *Black Women Writers.* "It reinforces the fact that I'm in touch with somebody other than my own mind. . . . I always wrote with the idea of being published, not to just slip it away in a shoebox somewhere. I do believe that writing is about communication." To that end, Williams succeeded in communicating on a variety of levels. She willingly shared the story of her own life, a life built on hope, hard work and talent.

Selected writings

Give Birth to Brightness: A Thematic Study in Neo-Black Literature, Dial, 1972.
The Peacock Poems, Wesleyan University Press, 1975.
Some One Sweet Angel Chile, Morrow, 1982.
Dessa Rose, Morrow, 1986.
Working Cotton, Harcourt, 1992.
Girls Together, Harcourt, 1999.

Sources

Books

Mitchell, Angelyn, editor, *Within the Circle: An Anthology of African-American Literary Criticism from the Harlem Renaissance to the Present,* Duke University Press, 1994.
Tate, Claudia, editor, *Black Women Writers at Work,* Continuum, 1983.
Williams, Sherley Anne, *Give Birth to Brightness: A Thematic Study in Neo-Black Literature,* Dial, 1972.

Periodicals

Essence, December 1986, p. 34.
Independent (London), September 3, 1999, p. 6.
Los Angeles Times, August 8, 1986, p. V-1; July 11, 1999, p. 2.
Los Angeles Times Magazine, December 7, 1986, p. 22.
New York Times, July 8, 1972, p. A-23; July 12, 1986, p. A-12; July 14, 1999, p. A-21.
New Yorker, September 8, 1986, p. 136.
Publishers Weekly, July 26, 1999, p. 26.

—Brian Escamilla

Deborah C. Wright

1958—

Bank president

The appointment of Deborah C. Wright in 1999 to head the largest African American-owned bank in the United States was met with a bit of industry skepticism, for the Harvard-educated executive had virtually no commercial banking experience. Yet Wright was chosen as the new chief executive officer of Carver Federal Savings Bank for her talents in coalition-building among business, government, and community leaders. It was hoped that Wright could help the Harlem-based bank emerge as a leader in what many viewed as a second renaissance for this troubled section of New York City. *New York Times* writer Elisabeth Bumiller described her as "part of a new generation of black professionals who went to Ivy League colleges and worked at the elite financial institutions of New York."

Born in the late 1950s, Wright spent her early youth in Bennetsville, South Carolina. She is descended from four generations of Baptist ministers—from her great-grandfather to her brother. Bennetsville's Shiloh Baptist Church had been founded by her grandfather, and her own father, Harry was a leading civil-rights figure in his community during her childhood. An aunt, Marian Wright Edelman, was the first African American woman to be admitted to the bar of the state of Mississippi. Edelman also founded the Children's Defense Fund, an influential lobbying group aimed at improving the lives of American children from impoverished neighborhoods, during the 1970s.

Integrated Public Pool

Wright grew up during the civil rights era. In South Carolina, she and her brother and sister attended an elementary school where they were the sole African American students. "It was intense," she told Bumiller in the *New York Times*. "I felt pretty much just ignored." With her siblings and father, Wright arrived one day at Bennetsville's all-white public swimming pool as part of the Reverend's plan to integrate it. When the Wrights moved to Dallas, Texas, they once again encountered racist attitudes, especially when court-ordered busing forced the area's public schools to integrate.

Despite the hardships, Wright did well in school, and emerged as a natural leader. She discovered that, among her high-achieving peers in student government, prejudices about skin color were less obvious. Wright made a surprising choice for college, rejecting

At a Glance . . .

Born c. 1958, in Bennetsville, SC; daughter of Harry C. Wright (a Baptist minister). *Education:* Earned degree from Radcliffe College; earned joint degree from Harvard University School of Business and Harvard University School of Law, 1984. *Politics:* Democrat. *Religion:* Baptist.

Career: First Boston Bank, associate in corporate finance, 1984-87; New York City Partnership (business advocacy group), New York, director of marketing, 1987-92; named to Housing Authority Board, New York City, by Mayor David Dinkins, 1992-94; named-commissioner for Housing Preservation and Development by Mayor Rudolph W. Giuliani, 1994; Upper Manhattan Empowerment Zone Development Corporation, director, 1996-99; Carver Bancorp, New York City, chief executive officer, 1999-.

Addresses: *Office*—Carver Bancorp, 75 W. 125th St., New York, NY10027-4512.

Atlanta's prestigious all-black women's college, Spelman College, in favor of Radcliffe, which is part of the Harvard University system.

Earned Graduate Degree from Harvard

Both Edelman and other women in her family were Spelman alumnae, but Wright was adamant about seeking out a different kind of college experience. "My father tried to convince me not to go, because he thought I was going to be disillusioned," she told Bumiller, and admitted that he was correct, in a way. As Wright explained in the *New York Times* interview, she expected that such a rarefied, intellectual place would be free from the racist attitudes that had marked her youth in the American South, "but you just had a constant feeling of being unwanted," she told Bumiller. Still, Wright excelled at Radcliffe, and was accepted to a prestigious graduate-school program at Harvard. In 1984, she was one of just 11 students to earn a joint M.B.A. and law degree.

Wright was hired by First Boston Bank as an associate in corporate finance. For a time, she entertained dreams of becoming the first African American woman to be offered a partnership at a large Wall Street investment firm. Her aunt and other family members, however, felt that such a career was a disservice to her

heritage, and there was much family pressure on Wright to enter public service instead. When she quit First Boston after three years, she was earning 135,000 a year, but she admitted to a certain degree of disenchantment with the job. "It was a really bewildering time," Wright told Bumiller in the *New York Times,* "because I had never been in a position where I didn't achieve what I set out to. I was not connected in any way, not to the work, not to the people."

Became a City Commissioner

In 1987, Wright took a pay cut of nearly 100,000 a year to work for a business advocacy group, the New York City Partnership, as director of marketing for a building project in Harlem. Five years later, she was named to the Housing Authority Board of New York City by Mayor David Dinkins. In 1994, Wright was promoted to commissioner for Housing, Preservation and Development by Dinkins's successor, Rudolph W. Giuliani. She then moved on to become the director of the Upper Manhattan Empowerment Zone Development Corporation, a post that would give her tremendous experience in bringing together community, civic, and private-sector interests to revitalize blighted urban areas.

Empowerment zones, which were created during the first Clinton administration, were specially-designated urban neighborhoods that were given federal funds and tax incentives toward the creation of programs for new businesses, job training, and home ownership. The idea had stalled in Congress before an influential Democratic congressman from Harlem, Charles B. Rangel, rescued it. The part of New York City that included his district became one of the nine federal empowerment zones created in 1994.

Wright was the only person that both Rangel and New York state governor, George Pataki, could agree upon for the job. She oversaw a budget of 550 million, which was earmarked for improving the economic health of the area. At the time, Harlem had an unemployment rate of 19 percent, few large businesses, and a high number of high school dropouts. "This isn't a job," Wright told Bumiller in the *New York Times.* "It really is an emotional undertaking. It's such a wound in the psyche of the African-American public to see this place that was such a mecca be on its back, and knowing that the answers are not really brain surgery."

A New Optimism in Harlem

Wright's job as head of the Upper Manhattan Empowerment Zone Development presented tremendous challenges. She maintained a somewhat uneasy alliance with Rangel and his office, but she soon became known as Harlem's unofficial finance minister. "When people need things these days in Harlem, they go to Ms. Wright," declared Bumiller in the *New York Times*. Under Wright's leadership, funds were appropriated for a major retail and entertainment complex, Harlem U.S.A., that would include a Gap and a Disney store. The first major chain supermarket in several years also opened in Harlem during Wright's tenure. However, not all residents were pleased with the changes taking place in Harlem. "Not surprisingly, she has set off neighborhood criticism that she is turning Harlem over to outside white businesses," explained Bumiller.

In the spring of 1999, Wright was tapped to become CEO of Carver Bancorp, the parent company for Carver Federal Savings Bank, and the largest African American-owned financial institution in the United States. Carver Federal Savings Bank is also the sole African American-owned bank in the state of New York. Founded in 1948, Carver had suffered some heavy losses, and Wright's predecessor had been fired as a result. Although Carver had 420 million in assets, it lost 5 million in one quarter during 1998, a state of affairs tied to the purchase of a new computer system and chargeoffs in Carver's consumer loan portfolio. While searching for a new CEO, Carver rejected a merger attempt by another large minority-owned institution, Boston Bank of Commerce.

A 21st-Century CEO

Wright was heralded as the perfect combination of talents for Carver's particular situation. The head of the CEO search team, interim president David R. Jones, told *Black Enterprise* writers Kimberly L. Seals and Eric L. Smith that choosing Wright was not difficult, despite the lack of banking experience on her resume. "We were looking for someone to take Carver into the next century," Jones said. ". . .We needed someone that could assemble a team of high-class, young African American talent." Another supporter of the appointment was Richard D. Parsons, president of the Time Warner media empire. Wright's new employer, Parsons told *New York Times* reporter Terry Pristin, "is

known as a safe place to put your money. But in terms of putting something back into the community, it didn't do such a wonderful job. She [Wright] understands how this bank can use its depositors' funds to help re-energize the community where those depositors live."

Wright immediately began a program to revitalize Carver's balance sheet and make it a key player in the rising economic fortunes of Harlem. Generally, banks in impoverished neighborhoods rarely offer the array of services that financial institutions in other communities do. However, Wright planned to make the seven Carver branch offices a more vital part of the community's economy. She hoped to improve Carver's rate of small-business loans, begin offering insurance and investment advice, and even introduce such conveniences as electronic banking and debit cards. "We should also be able to increase other services that our community uses on a regular basis, like check-cashing and money-wiring capabilities," Wright told Seals and Smith in the *Black Enterprise* article.

Wright lives in Greenwich Village, a rather long commute to her Carver office on W. 125th St. Her father is pastor of Cornerstone Baptist Church in the Crown Heights section of Brooklyn, where, after Sunday services, many members of the congregation—either depositors or investors with Carver—complain to her about the bank itself or the price of its shares. "If we can't exploit the growth in our own backyard, it's hard to move beyond it," Wright told *Crain's New York Business*. "Our strategy is to focus our people on our core businesses and buy talent from others for services in which we can't compete."

Sources

Black Enterprise, July, 1999, pp. 24.
Crain's New York Business, July 12, 1999, p. 3.
New York Times, March 28, 1997; April 13, 1999, p. B8.
U.S. Banker, June, 1999.

—Carol Brennan

Albert R. Wynn

1951—

Congressman

The perfect representative of the new breed of black politician that came to power in the 1990s, Albert R. Wynn is competent, a master of policy nuts and bolts, often described as a "team player." Preferring legislative give-and-take to impassioned speechmaking, he has emerged as a champion of the black entrepreneur, and has proven adept at defending the interests of that group in the sometimes hostile atmosphere fomented by the conservative Congresses of the 1990s. Wynn, representing Maryland's Fourth District in Congress, speaks for the heartland of America's black middle class—the suburban counties just to the east of Washington, D.C.

Wynn was born in Philadelphia on September 10, 1951, but grew up "inside the Beltway"—in the zone enclosed by Washington, D.C.'s freeway ring that is home to tens of thousands of U.S. government employees and to an African American population that in recent years has flourished economically in comparison with those in many other parts of the country. He was raised largely in Glenarden, Maryland after spending his first-grade year in North Carolina. In those years, schools in Maryland's Prince George's County were still racially segregated, and Wynn attended all-black schools through the eighth grade.

Excelled at Debate

The following year, integration came to suburban Washington, and Wynn was sent to a junior high school in nearby Landover Hills. He was one of several dozen black students in an otherwise all-white environment, but he flourished academically and became involved in extracurricular activities, playing trombone in the band and becoming a star debater. Even at this early age Wynn's political skills showed through: he emerged as something of an unofficial spokesman for the school's African American student body.

Graduating from DuVal High School in Lanham, Maryland, Wynn attended the University of Pittsburgh on an unusual scholarship—one for debate. Graduating with a science degree in 1973, he studied Public Administration at Washington's Howard University for a year, and then switched to law, moving across town to the top-flight program at Georgetown University. He earned his degree there in 1977.

Wynn would form his own law firm, Albert R. Wynn and Associates, in 1982, but by that time he had already taken several steps up the Maryland political ladder. Fresh out of law school he became the Executive Director of the Prince George's County Consumer Protection Division, holding that post until 1981. In the same year that he opened his law firm, he ran for and won election as a Democrat to the Maryland House of Delegates (the lower body of the state legislature), displacing the white representatives who had held power in the increasingly minority-dominated district.

Faced Competition from Thirteen Democrats

In 1987, Wynn moved up to the Maryland State Senate. He served as Deputy Majority Whip (a party leadership post within the Democratic senate delegation), and won re-election to a second four-year term in 1990. In the wake of the 1990 U.S. census, the boundaries of Maryland's congressional districts were redrawn, and the 58 percent black population of the new Fourth District, which included Prince George's County, offered an opportunity that was spotted by numerous local politicians: no fewer than thirteen Democrats, along with seven Republicans, threw their hats into the ring for the seat.

In the summer primary, Wynn eked out a victory by only two percentage points over another local office-holder; in this heavily Democratic district, the win virtually guaranteed that he would coast to election in the fall. Nevertheless, Wynn campaigned vigorously. A large, genial man, he enjoys pressing the flesh, although, as he told the *Washington Post*, "I see a lot of old friends this way I haven't seen in years, people from high school. Sometimes I see law school classmates. Then I feel embarrassed. They're going to downtown law firms, and their classmate is standing on a corner."

Winning the fall election by a landslide, Wynn set about addressing the concerns of the African American businesspeople and government employees who made up his constituency. He campaigned against racial discrimination within several large federal bureaucracies, including the National Institutes of Health, the Library of Congress, and the Voice of America shortwave radio office. However, Wynn, a member of the moderate Democratic Leadership Council that has tried to direct the Democratic Party away from big-government solutions to social problems, also looked to small businesses as potential saviors of foundering urban communities.

Hoped to Track Business Loans

"I want to develop incentives geared . . . toward small business and to take a look at their regulatory burden," Wynn told *Fortune*. "You talk to small business guys and they say, 'We're inundated with paperwork.'" Early in his congressional career, Wynn pushed for a small-business counterpart to the Home Mortgage Disclosure Act, which required banks and other mortgage lenders to keep track of how many loans they were offering in minority communities. Although that bill had led to the revelation of substantial patterns of discrimination, Wynn's bill went nowhere after the Republican House takeover in 1994.

Nevertheless, Wynn continued to push for the interests of small businesses. At the grassroots level, he sponsors a yearly job fair in his district, bringing more than 200 employers together with thousands of job-seekers. He has worked to increase the percentage of federal contracting directed toward small businesses from 20 to 23 percent, and has tried to restrict the process of "bundling," or grouping contracts together, that often puts federal work out of the reach of smaller firms. The Small Business Administration rewarded Wynn's efforts with a leadership award.

Wynn coasted to re-election every two years, despite the efforts of a 1996 opponent who claimed that he would pose naked for *Playgirl* magazine if voters moved over to his corner. Wynn found some of his initiatives stymied by the conservatives who controlled the House in the late 1990s. But he demonstrated an ability to work with members across the aisle, forging a Commerce Committee subcommittee compromise with a Republican counterpart that simplified the complaint process for those seeking redress from the federal Equal Employment Opportunity Commission. A close associate not only of President Clinton, but also of Maryland Governor Parris Glendenning, Wynn was accumulating political favors and learning to travel easily in the halls of power as the 2000 elections approached, although he was rocked by accusations of delinquent child-support payments in late 1999. He seemed a potential candidate for higher office in the coming years.

Sources

Books

Barone, Michael, and Grant Ujifusa, *Almanac of American Politics 2000,* National Journal, 1999.

Periodicals

Black Enterprise, October 1994, p. 24.
Emerge, November 1997, p. 26.
Entrepreneur, April 1997, p. 102.
Fortune, January 25, 1993, p. 99.
Washington Post, October 25, 1992, p. B3; October 11, 1998, p. B10; December 9, 1999, p. B4.

Other

Additional information was obtained from http:\\www.house.gov\wynn\

—James M. Manheim

Cumulative Nationality Index

Volume numbers appear in **bold.**

Cumulative Occupation Index

Volume numbers appear in **bold**.

Art and design

Allen, Tina **22**
Andrews, Benny **22**
Andrews, Bert **13**
Armstrong, Robb **15**
Bailey, Radcliffe **19**
Bailey, Xenobia **11**
Barboza, Anthony **10**
Barnes, Ernie **16**
Barthe, Richmond **15**
Basquiat, Jean-Michel **5**
Bearden, Romare **2**
Biggers, John **20**
Brandon, Barbara **3**
Brown, Donald **19**
Burke, Selma **16**
Burroughs, Margaret Taylor **9**
Camp, Kimberly **19**
Campbell, E. Simms **13**
Catlett, Elizabeth **2**
Chase-Riboud, Barbara **20**
Cowans, Adger W. **20**
Delaney, Beauford **19**
Douglas, Aaron **7**
Driskell, David C. **7**
Edwards, Melvin **22**
Ewing, Patrick A.**17**
Feelings, Tom **11**
Gantt, Harvey **1**
Gilliam, Sam **16**
Golden, Thelma **10**
Guyton, Tyree **9**
Harkless, Necia Desiree **19**
Harrington, Oliver W. **9**
Hayden, Palmer **13**
Hope, John **8**
Hudson, Cheryl **15**
Hudson, Wade **15**
Hunt, Richard **6**
Hutson, Jean Blackwell **16**
John, Daymond **23**
Johnson, William Henry **3**
Jones, Lois Mailou **13**
Kitt, Sandra **23**
Lawrence, Jacob **4**
Lee, Annie Francis **22**
Lee-Smith, Hughie **5, 22**
Lewis, Edmonia **10**
Lewis, Samella **25**
McGee, Charles **10**
Mitchell, Corinne **8**
Morrison, Keith **13**

Moutoussamy-Ashe, Jeanne **7**
N'Namdi, George R. **17**
Pierre, Andre **17**
Pinkney, Jerry **15**
Pippin, Horace **9**
Porter, James A. **11**
Ringgold, Faith **4**
Saar, Alison **16**
Saint James, Synthia **12**
Sanders, Joseph R., Jr. **11**
Savage, Augusta **12**
Serrano, Andres **3**
Shabazz, Attallah **6**
Simpson, Lorna **4**
Sklarek, Norma Merrick **25**
Sleet, Moneta, Jr. **5**
Tanner, Henry Ossawa **1**
Thomas, Alma **14**
Tolliver, William **9**
VanDerZee, James **6**
Walker, A'lelia **14**
Walker, Kara **16**
Wells, James Lesesne **10**
Williams, Billy Dee **8**
Williams, O. S. **13**
Williams, Paul R. **9**
Williams, William T. **11**
Woodruff, Hale **9**

Business

Abdul-Jabbar, Kareem **8**
Ailey, Alvin **8**
Al-Amin, Jamil Abdullah **6**
Alexander, Archie Alphonso **14**
Allen, Byron **24**
Amos, Wally **9**
Avant, Clarence **19**
Baker, Dusty **8**
Baker, Ella **5**
Baker, Gwendolyn Calvert **9**
Banks, Jeffrey **17**
Banks, William **11**
Barden, Don H. **9, 20**
Barrett, Andrew C. **12**
Bennett, Lerone, Jr. **5**
Bing, Dave **3**
Borders, James **9**
Boston, Kelvin E. **25**
Boston, Lloyd **24**
Boyd, John W., Jr. **20**
Boyd, T. B., III **6**
Brimmer, Andrew F. **2**

Brown, Les **5**
Brown, Marie Dutton **12**
Brunson, Dorothy **1**
Burrell, Thomas J. **21**
Burroughs, Margaret Taylor **9**
Busby, Jheryl **3**
Cain, Herman **15**
CasSelle, Malcolm **11**
Chamberlain, Wilt **18**
Chapman, Jr., Nathan A. **21**
Chappell, Emma **18**
Chenault, Kenneth I. **4**
Clark, Celeste **15**
Clark, Patrick **14**
Clay, William Lacy **8**
Clayton, Xernona **3**
Cobbs, Price M. **9**
Colbert, Virgis William **17**
Coleman, Donald A. **24**
Connerly, Ward **14**
Conyers, Nathan G. **24**
Cornelius, Don **4**
Cosby, Bill **7**
Cottrell, Comer **11**
Daniels-Carter, Valerie **23**
Davis, Ed **24**
de Passe, Suzanne **25**
Delany, Bessie **12**
Delany, Sadie **12**
Divine, Father **7**
Dre, Dr. **14**
Driver, David E. **11**
Ducksworth, Marilyn **12**
Edelin, Ramona Hoage **19**
Edmonds, Tracey **16**
Elder, Lee **6**
Ellington, E. David **11**
Evans, Darryl **22**
Evers, Myrlie **8**
Farmer, Forest J. **1**
Farr, Mel Sr. **24**
Farrakhan, Louis **15**
Fauntroy, Walter E. **11**
Fletcher, Alphonse, Jr. **16**
Franklin, Hardy R. **9**
Friday, Jeff **24**
Fudge, Ann **11**
Fuller, S. B. **13**
Gaston, Arthur G. **4**
Gibson, Kenneth Allen **6**
Goldsberry, Ronald **18**
Gordon, Pamela **17**

Thomas, Clarence **2**
Thomas, Franklin A. **5**
Tubbs Jones, Stephaie **24**
Vanzant, Iyanla **17**
Wagner, Annice **22**
Washington, Harold **6**
Wilder, L. Douglas **3**
Wilkins, Roger **2**
Williams, Evelyn **10**
Williams, Gregory **11**
Williams, Patricia J. **11**
Williams, Willie L. **4**
Wright, Bruce McMarion **3**
Wynn, Albert **25**

Military
Abacha, Sani **11**
Adams Early, Charity **13**
Alexander, Margaret Walker **22**
Babangida, Ibrahim **4**
Bolden, Charles F., Jr. **7**
Brown, Erroll M. **23**
Brown, Jesse **6**
Bullard, Eugene **12**
Cadoria, Sherian Grace **14**
Chissano, Joaquim **7**
Christophe, Henri **9**
Conté, Lansana **7**
Davis, Benjamin O., Jr. **2**
Davis, Benjamin O., Sr. **4**
Europe, James Reese **10**
Eyadéma, Gnassingbé **7**
Flipper, Henry O. **3**
Gravely, Samuel L., Jr. **5**
Gregory, Frederick D. **8**
Habré, Hissène **6**
Habyarimana, Juvenal **8**
Harris, Marcelite Jordan **16**
Jackson, Fred James **25**
James, Daniel, Jr. **16**
Johnson, Hazel **22**
Kerekou, Ahmed (Mathieu) **1**
Lawrence, Robert H., Jr. **16**
Nyanda, Siphiwe **21**
Obasanjo, Olusegun **5, 22**
Phelps, Shirelle **22**
Powell, Colin **1**
Pratt, Geronimo **18**
Rawlings, Jerry **9**
Reason, J. Paul **19**
Stanford, John **20**
Staupers, Mabel K. **7**
Stokes, Louis **3**
Touré, Amadou Toumani **18**
Vieira, Joao **14**
Von Lipsey, Roderick K. **11**
Watkins, Perry **12**
West, Togo, D., Jr. **16**

Music
Adams, Oleta **18**
Adams, Yolanda **17**
Albright, Gerald **23**
Anderson, Marian **2**
Armstrong, Louis **2**
Armstrong, Vanessa Bell **24**
Ashford, Nickolas **21**
Austin, Patti **24**
Avant, Clarence **19**
Ayers, Roy **16**
Badu, Erykah **22**
Baker, Anita **21**
Baker, Josephine **3**
Basie, Count **23**
Bassey, Shirley **25**

Bechet, Sidney **18**
Belafonte, Harry **4**
Belle, Regina **1**
Beverly, Frankie **25**
Blige, Mary J. **20**
Bonga, Kuenda **13**
Brandy **14**
Braxton, Toni **15**
Brooks, Avery **9**
Brown, Charles **23**
Brown, Foxy **25**
Bumbry, Grace **5**
Busby, Jheryl **3**
Caesar, Shirley **19**
Calloway, Cab **1**
Campbell, Tisha **8**
Carroll, Diahann **9**
Carter, Betty **19**
Carter, Regina **23**
Charlemagne, Manno **11**
Charles, Ray **16**
Cheatham, Doc **17**
Chuck D **9**
Clark-Sheard, Karen **22**
Cleveland, James **19**
Clinton, George **9**
Cole, Nat King **17**
Cole, Natalie Maria **17**
Collins, Albert **12**
Coltrane, John **19**
Combs, Sean "Puffy" **17**
Cooke, Sam **17**
Count Basie **23**
Crawford, Randy **19**
Crothers, Scatman **19**
Crouch, Stanley **11**
Crowder, Henry **16**
Davis, Anthony **11**
Davis, Miles **4**
Davis, Sammy, Jr. **18**
de Passe, Suzanne **25**
Dixon, Willie **4**
Donegan, Dorothy **19**
Dorsey, Thomas **15**
Downing, Will **19**
Dr. Dre **10**
Dre, Dr. **14**
Duke, George **21**
Dupri, Jermaine **13**
Edmonds, Kenneth "Babyface" **10**
Edmonds, Tracey **16**
Ellington, Duke **5**
Eubanks, Kevin **15**
Europe, James Reese **10**
Evans, Faith **22**
Evora, Cesaria **12**
Fats Domino **20**
Fela **1**
Fitzgerald, Ella **8, 18**
Flack, Roberta **19**
Foxx, Jamie **15**
Franklin, Aretha **11**
Franklin, Kirk **15**
Gaye, Marvin **2**
Gibson, Althea **8**
Gillespie, Dizzy **1**
Gordon, Dexter **25**
Gordy, Berry, Jr. **1**
Graves, Denyce **19**
Gray, F. Gary **14**
Green, Al **13**
Hailey, JoJo **22**
Hailey, K-Ci **22**
Hammer, M. C. **20**
Hammond, Fred **23**

Hampton, Lionel **17**
Hancock, Herbie **20**
Handy, W. C. **8**
Harrell, Andre **9**
Hathaway, Donny **18**
Hawkins, Coleman **9**
Hawkins, Erskine **14**
Hawkins, Tramaine **16**
Hayes, Isaac **20**
Hayes, Roland **4**
Hendricks, Barbara **3**
Hendrix, Jimi **10**
Hill, Lauryn **20**
Hinderas, Natalie **5**
Holiday, Billie **1**
Horne, Lena **5**
House, Son **8**
Houston, Cissy **20**
Houston, Whitney **7**
Howlin' Wolf **9**
Humphrey, Bobbi **20**
Hyman, Phyllis **19**
Ice Cube **8**
Ice-T **6**
Isley, Ronald **25**
Jackson, Fred James **25**
Jackson, George **19**
Jackson, Isaiah **3**
Jackson, Janet **6**
Jackson, Mahalia **5**
Jackson, Michael **19**
Jackson, Millie **25**
James, Etta **13**
James, Rick **17**
Jarreau, Al **21**
Jean, Wyclef **20**
Jean-Baptiste, Marianne **17**
Jenkins, Ella **15**
Jimmy Jam **13**
Johnson, Beverly **2**
Johnson, James Weldon **5**
Johnson, Robert **2**
Jones, Bobby **20**
Jones, Elvin **14**
Jones, Quincy **8**
Joplin, Scott **6**
Jordan, Montell **23**
Joyner, Matilda Sissieretta **15**
Joyner, Tom **19**
Kelly, R. **18**
Kendricks, Eddie **22**
Khan, Chaka **12**
King, B. B. **7**
King, Coretta Scott **3**
Kitt, Eartha **16**
Knight, Gladys **16**
Knight, Suge **11**
Kravitz, Lenny **10**
L.L. Cool J **16**
LaBelle, Patti **13**
León, Tania **13**
Lester, Julius **9**
Levert, Gerald **22**
Lewis, Terry **13**
Lincoln, Abbey **3**
Little Richard **15**
Love, Darlene **23**
Lover, Ed **10**
Lymon, Frankie **22**
Madhubuti, Haki R. **7**
Makeba, Miriam **2**
Marley, Bob **5**
Marrow, Queen Esther **24**
Marsalis, Wynton **16**
Mase **24**

Irving, Larry, Jr. **12**
Jackson, Shirley Ann **12**
Jawara, Sir Dawda Kairaba **11**
Jemison, Mae C. **1**
Jenifer, Franklyn G. **2**
Johnson, Eddie Bernice **8**
Julian, Percy Lavon **6**
Just, Ernest Everett **3**
Kountz, Samuel L. **10**
Latimer, Lewis H. **4**
Lawless, Theodore K. **8**
Lawrence, Robert H., Jr. **16**
Leffall, LaSalle, Jr. **3**
Lewis, Delano **7**
Logan, Onnie Lee **14**
Lyttle, Hulda Margaret **14**
Manley, Audrey Forbes **16**
Massey, Walter E. **5**
Mboup, Souleymane **10**
McCoy, Elijah **8**
McNair, Ronald **3**
Morgan, Garrett **1**
O'Leary, Hazel **6**
Person, Waverly **9**
Pitt, David Thomas **10**
Poussaint, Alvin F. **5**
Prothrow-Stith, Deborah **10**
Quarterman, Lloyd Albert **4**
Riley, Helen Caldwell Day **13**
Robeson, Eslanda Goode **13**
Robinson, Rachel **16**
Roker, Al **12**
Samara, Noah **15**
Satcher, David **7**
Shabazz, Betty **7**
Sinkford, Jeanne C. **13**
Staples, Brent **8**
Staupers, Mabel K. **7**
Sullivan, Louis **8**
Terrell, Dorothy A. **24**
Thomas, Vivien **9**
Tyson, Neil de Grasse **15**
Washington, Patrice Clarke **12**
Watkins, Levi, Jr. **9**
Welsing, Frances Cress **5**
Williams, Daniel Hale **2**
Williams, O. S. **13**
Woods, Granville T. **5**
Wright, Louis Tompkins **4**

Social issues
Aaron, Hank **5**
Abbott, Diane **9**
Abdul-Jabbar, Kareem **8**
Abernathy, Ralph David **1**
Abu-Jamal, Mumia **15**
Achebe, Chinua **6**
Adams, Sheila J. **25**
Agyeman, Jaramogi Abebe **10**
Al-Amin, Jamil Abdullah **6**
Alexander, Sadie Tanner Mossell **22**
Ali, Muhammad, **2, 16**
Allen, Ethel D. **13**
Andrews, Benny **22**
Angelou, Maya **1**
Annan, Kofi Atta **15**
Anthony, Wendell **25**
Archer, Dennis **7**
Aristide, Jean-Bertrand **6**
Asante, Molefi Kete **3**
Ashe, Arthur **1, 18**
Auguste, Rose-Anne **13**
Azikiwe, Nnamdi **13**
Baisden, Michael **25**
Baker, Ella **5**

Baker, Gwendolyn Calvert **9**
Baker, Houston A., Jr. **6**
Baker, Josephine **3**
Baker, Thurbert **22**
Baldwin, James **1**
Baraka, Amiri **1**
Bates, Daisy **13**
Beals, Melba Patillo **15**
Belafonte, Harry **4**
Bell, Derrick **6**
Bell, Ralph S. **5**
Bennett, Lerone, Jr. **5**
Berry, Bertice **8**
Berry, Mary Frances **7**
Bethune, Mary McLeod **4**
Biko, Steven **4**
Blackwell, Unita **17**
Bolin, Jane **22**
Bond, Julian **2**
Bonga, Kuenda **13**
Bosley, Freeman, Jr. **7**
Boyd, John W., Jr. **20**
Boyd, T. B., III **6**
Boykin, Keith **14**
Braun, Carol Moseley **4**
Brooke, Edward **8**
Brown, Elaine **8**
Brown, Jesse **6**
Brown, Jim **11**
Brown, Lee P. **1**
Brown, Les **5**
Brown, Tony **3**
Brown, Zora Kramer **12**
Bryant, Wayne R. **6**
Bullock, Steve **22**
Bunche, Ralph J. **5**
Burroughs, Margaret Taylor **9**
Butler, Paul D. **17**
Butts, Calvin O., III **9**
Campbell, Bebe Moore **6, 24**
Canada, Geoffrey **23**
Carmichael, Stokely **5**
Carter, Mandy **11**
Carter, Stephen L. **4**
Cary, Lorene **3**
Chavis, Benjamin **6**
Chideya, Farai **14**
Childress, Alice **15**
Chissano, Joaquim **7**
Christophe, Henri **9**
Chuck D **9**
Clark, Joe **1**
Clark, Kenneth B. **5**
Clark, Septima **7**
Clay, William Lacy **8**
Claytor, Helen **14**
Cleaver, Eldridge **5**
Clements, George **2**
Cobbs, Price M. **9**
Cole, Johnnetta B. **5**
Collins, Barbara-Rose **7**
Comer, James P. **6**
Cone, James H. **3**
Connerly, Ward **14**
Conté, Lansana **7**
Conyers, John, Jr. **4**
Cook, Toni **23**
Cooper, Anna Julia **20**
Cooper, Edward S. **6**
Cosby, Bill **7**
Cosby, Camille **14**
Cose, Ellis **5**
Crockett, George, Jr. **10**
Crouch, Stanley **11**
Cummings, Elijah E. **24**

Cunningham, Evelyn **23**
da Silva, Benedita **5**
Dash, Julie **4**
Davis, Angela **5**
Davis, Danny K. **24**
Davis, Ossie **5**
Dee, Ruby **8**
Dellums, Ronald **2**
Dickerson, Ernest **6**
Diop, Cheikh Anta **4**
Divine, Father **7**
Dixon, Margaret **14**
Dodson, Howard, Jr. **7**
Dove, Rita **6**
Drew, Charles Richard **7**
Du Bois, W. E. B. **3**
DuBois, Shirley Graham **21**
Dunham, Katherine **4**
Early, Gerald **15**
Edelin, Ramona Hoage **19**
Edelman, Marian Wright **5**
Edley, Christopher **2**
Edwards, Harry **2**
Elder, Larry **25**
Elder, Lee **6**
Elders, Joycelyn **6**
Ellison, Ralph **7**
Esposito, Giancarlo **9**
Espy, Mike **6**
Europe, James Reese **10**
Evers, Medgar **3**
Evers, Myrlie **8**
Farmer, James **2**
Farrakhan, Louis **15**
Fauntroy, Walter E. **11**
Fauset, Jessie **7**
Fela **1**
Fields, C. Virginia **25**
Foreman, George **15**
Forman, James **7**
Fortune, T. Thomas **6**
Franklin, Hardy R. **9**
Franklin, John Hope **5**
Franklin, Robert M. **13**
Frazier, E. Franklin **10**
Fulani, Lenora **11**
Fuller, Charles **8**
Gaines, Ernest J. **7**
Garvey, Marcus **1**
Gates, Henry Louis, Jr. **3**
Gayle, Helene D. **3**
Gibson, Kenneth Allen **6**
Gibson, William F. **6**
Gist, Carole **1**
Goldberg, Whoopi **4**
Golden, Marita **19**
Gomez-Preston, Cheryl **9**
Gossett, Louis, Jr. **7**
Graham, Lawrence Otis **12**
Gregory, Dick **1**
Grier, Roosevelt **13**
Griffith, Mark Winston **8**
Grimké, Archibald H. **9**
Guinier, Lani **7**
Guy, Rosa **5**
Guy-Sheftall, Beverly **13**
Hale, Lorraine **8**
Haley, Alex **4**
Hall, Elliott S. **24**
Hamblin, Ken **10**
Hamer, Fannie Lou **6**
Hampton, Fred **18**
Hampton, Henry **6**
Hani, Chris **6**
Hansberry, Lorraine **6**

Shaw, Bernard **2**
Simpson, Carole **6**
Simpson, O. J. **15**
Sinbad **1, 16**
Smiley, Tavis **20**
Smith, Barbara **11**
Smith, Roger Guenveur **12**
Smith, Will **8, 18**
St. Jacques, Raymond **8**
St. John, Kristoff **25**
Stewart, Alison **13**
Stokes, Carl B. **10**
Stone, Chuck **9**
Tate, Larenz **15**
Taylor, Meshach **4**
Taylor, Regina **9**
Thigpen, Lynne **17**
Townsend, Robert **4, 23**
Tucker, Chris **13, 23**
Tyson, Cicely **7**
Uggams, Leslie **23**
Underwood, Blair **7**
Usher **23**
Van Peebles, Mario **2**
Van Peebles, Melvin **7**
Vereen, Ben **4**
Warfield, Marsha **2**
Warner, Malcolm-Jamal **22**
Warwick, Dionne **18**
Washington, Denzel **1, 16**
Wattleton, Faye **9**
Watts, Rolonda **9**
Wayans, Damon **8**
Wayans, Keenen Ivory **18**
Weathers, Carl **10**
Whitfield, Lynn **1, 18**
Wilkins, Roger **2**
Williams, Billy Dee **8**
Williams, Montel **4**
Williams, Samm-Art **21**
Williams, Vanessa **4, 17**
Williamson, Mykelti **22**
Wilson, Flip **21**
Winfield, Paul **2**
Winfrey, Oprah **2, 15**
Yoba, Malik **11**

Theater
Ailey, Alvin **8**
Allen, Debbie **13**
Amos, John **8**
Andrews, Bert **13**
Angelou, Maya **1**
Arkadie, Kevin **17**
Armstrong, Vanessa Bell **24**
Baraka, Amiri 1
Bassett, Angela **6, 23**
Beaton, Norman **14**
Belafonte, Harry **4**
Borders, James **9**
Brooks, Avery **9**
Calloway, Cab **14**
Campbell, Naomi **1**
Campbell, Tisha **8**
Carroll, Diahann **9**
Cheadle, Don **19**
Childress, Alice **15**
Clarke, Hope **14**
Cleage, Pearl **17**
Curtis-Hall, Vondie **17**
Davis, Ossie **5**
Davis, Sammy, Jr. **18**
Dee, Ruby **8**
Devine, Loretta **24**
Diggs, Taye **25**

Duke, Bill **3**
Dunham, Katherine **4**
Dutton, Charles S. **4, 22**
Esposito, Giancarlo **9**
Europe, James Reese **10**
Fishburne, Larry **4**
Freeman, Al, Jr. **11**
Freeman, Morgan **2, 20**
Fuller, Charles **8**
Glover, Danny **1, 24**
Glover, Savion **14**
Goldberg, Whoopi **4**
Gordone, Charles **15**
Gossett, Louis, Jr. **7**
Graves, Denyce **19**
Grier, Pam **9**
Guillaume, Robert **3**
Gunn, Moses **10**
Guy, Jasmine **2**
Hansberry, Lorraine **6**
Harris, Robin **7**
Hemsley, Sherman **19**
Holland, Endesha Ida Mae **3**
Horne, Lena **5**
Hyman, Earle **25**
Hyman, Phyllis **19**
Ingram, Rex **5**
Jackson, Millie **25**
Jackson, Samuel L. **8, 19**
Jamison, Judith **7**
Jean-Baptiste, Marianne **17**
Jones, James Earl **3**
Joyner, Matilda Sissieretta **15**
King, Yolanda **6**
Kitt, Eartha **16**
Kotto, Yaphet **7**
La Salle, Eriq **12**
Lee, Canada **8**
Lemmons, Kasi **20**
Leon, Kenny **10**
Lincoln, Abbey **3**
Lindo, Delroy **18**
Mabley, Jackie "Moms" **15**
Marrow, Queen Esther **24**
McDaniel, Hattie **5**
McDonald, Audra **20**
McKee, Lonette **12**
McQueen, Butterfly **6**
Mills, Florence **22**
Mitchell, Brian Stokes **21**
Moore, Melba **21**
Moses, Gilbert **12**
Moss, Carlton **17**
Moten, Etta **18**
Muse, Clarence Edouard **21**
Nicholas, Fayard **20**
Nicholas, Harold **20**
Norman, Maidie **20**
Payne, Allen **13**
Powell, Maxine **8**
Primus, Pearl **6**
Ralph, Sheryl Lee **18**
Randle, Theresa **16**
Rashad, Phylicia **21**
Reese, Della **6, 20**
Rhames, Ving **14**
Richards, Lloyd **2**
Robeson, Paul **2**
Rolle, Esther **13, 21**
Rollins, Howard E., Jr. **16**
Rotimi, Ola **1**
Schultz, Michael A. **6**
Shabazz, Attallah **6**
Shange, Ntozake **8**
Smith, Anna Deavere **6**

Smith, Roger Guenveur **12**
Snipes, Wesley **3, 24**
Soyinka, Wole **4**
St. Jacques, Raymond **8**
Taylor, Meshach **4**
Taylor, Regina **9**
Thigpen, Lynne **17**
Thompson, Tazewell **13**
Thurman, Wallace **16**
Townsend, Robert **4, 23**
Tyson, Cicely **7**
Uggams, Leslie **23**
Underwood, Blair **7**
Van Peebles, Melvin **7**
Vance, Courtney B. **15**
Vereen, Ben **4**
Walcott, Derek **5**
Washington, Denzel **1, 16**
Washington, Fredi **10**
Waters, Ethel **7**
Whitaker, Forest **2**
Whitfield, Lynn **18**
Williams, Bert **18**
Williams, Billy Dee **8**
Williams, Samm-Art **21**
Williams, Vanessa L. **4, 17**
Williamson, Mykelti **22**
Wilson, August **7**
Winfield, Paul **2**
Wolfe, George C. **6**
Woodard, Alfre **9**

Writing
Abu-Jamal, Mumia **15**
Achebe, Chinua **6**
Al-Amin, Jamil Abdullah **6**
Alexander, Margaret Walker **22**
Andrews, Raymond **4**
Angelou, Maya **1, 15**
Ansa, Tina McElroy **14**
Aristide, Jean-Bertrand **6**
Arkadie, Kevin **17**
Asante, Molefi Kete **3**
Ashe, Arthur **1, 18**
Ashley-Ward, Amelia **23**
Azikiwe, Nnamdi **13**
Baisden, Michael **25**
Baker, Houston A., Jr. **6**
Baldwin, James **1**
Bambara, Toni Cade **10**
Baraka, Amiri **1**
Beals, Melba Patillo **15**
Bell, Derrick **6**
Bennett, Lerone, Jr. **5**
Berry, Mary Frances **7**
Bluitt, Juliann S. **14**
Bontemps, Arna **8**
Booker, Simeon **23**
Borders, James **9**
Boston, Lloyd **24**
Bradley, Ed **2**
Brimmer, Andrew F. **2**
Briscoe, Connie **15**
Brooks, Gwendolyn **1**
Brown, Elaine **8**
Brown, Les **5**
Brown, Marie Dutton **12**
Brown, Sterling **10**
Brown, Tony **3**
Brown, Wesley **23**
Bullins, Ed **25**
Bunche, Ralph J. **5**
Burroughs, Margaret Taylor **9**
Butler, Octavia **8**
Campbell, Bebe Moore **6, 24**

Cumulative Subject Index

Volume numbers appear in **bold**.

Davis, Benjamin O., Jr. **2**
Flipper, Henry O. **3**

West Side Preparatory School
Collins, Marva **3**

White House Conference on Civil Rights
Randolph, A. Philip **3**

Whitney Museum of American Art
Golden, Thelma **10**

WHO
See Women Helping Offenders

"Why Are You on This Planet?"
Yoba, Malik **11**

William Morris Talent Agency
Amos, Wally **9**

WillieWear Ltd.
Smith, Willi **8**

Wilmington 10
Chavis, Benjamin **6**

WOMAD
See World of Music, Arts, and Dance

Women Helping Offenders (WHO)
Holland, Endesha Ida Mae **3**

Women's Auxiliary Army Corps
See Women's Army Corp

Women's Army Corps (WAC)
Adams Early, Charity **13**
Cadoria, Sherian Grace **14**

Women's issues
Allen, Ethel D. **13**
Angelou, Maya **1, 15**
Baker, Ella **5**
Berry, Mary Frances **7**
Brown, Elaine **8**
Campbell, Bebe Moore **6, 24**
Cannon, Katie **10**
Charles, Mary Eugenia **10**
Christian-Green, Donna M. **17**
Clark, Septima **7**
Cole, Johnnetta B. **5**
Cooper, Anna Julia **20**
Cunningham, Evelyn **23**
Dash, Julie **4**
Davis, Angela **5**
Edelman, Marian Wright **5**
Elders, Joycelyn **6**
Fauset, Jessie **7**
Giddings, Paula **11**
Goldberg, Whoopi **4**
Grimké, Archibald H. **9**
Guy-Sheftall, Beverly **13**
Hale, Clara **16**
Hale, Lorraine **8**
Hamer, Fannie Lou **6**
Harper, Frances Ellen Watkins **11**
Harris, Alice **7**
Harris, Leslie **6**
Harris, Patricia Roberts **2**
Height, Dorothy I. **2, 23**
Hernandez, Aileen Clarke **13**
Hill, Anita **5**
Hine, Darlene Clark **24**

Holland, Endesha Ida Mae **3**
hooks, bell **5**
Jackson, Alexine Clement **22**
Joe, Yolanda **21**
Jordan, Barbara **4**
Jordan, June **7**
Lampkin, Daisy **19**
Larsen, Nella **10**
Lorde, Audre **6**
Marshall, Paule **7**
McCabe, Jewell Jackson **10**
McMillan, Terry **4, 17**
Meek, Carrie **6**
Millender-McDonald, Juanita **21**
Mongella, Gertrude **11**
Morrison, Toni **2, 15**
Naylor, Gloria **10**
Nelson, Jill **6**
Nichols, Nichelle **11**
Norman, Pat **10**
Norton, Eleanor Holmes **7**
Painter, Nell Irvin **24**
Parker, Pat **19**
Rawlings, Nana Konadu Agyeman **13**
Ringgold, Faith **4**
Shange, Ntozake **8**
Simpson, Carole **6**
Smith, Jane E. **24**
Terrell, Mary Church **9**
Tubman, Harriet **9**
Vanzant, Iyanla **17**
Walker, Alice **1**
Walker, Maggie Lena **17**
Wallace, Michele Faith **13**
Waters, Maxine **3**
Wattleton, Faye **9**
Winfrey, Oprah **2, 15**

Women's National Basketball Association (WNBA)
Cooper, Cynthia **17**
Edwards, Teresa **14**
Griffith, Yolanda **25**
Holdsclaw, Chamique **24**
Leslie, Lisa **16**
McCray, Nikki **18**
Peck, Carolyn **23**
Perrot, Kim **23**
Swoopes, Sheryl **12**
Thompson, Tina **25**

Women's Strike for Peace
King, Coretta Scott **3**

Worker's Party (Brazil)
da Silva, Benedita **5**

Workplace equity
Hill, Anita **5**
Clark, Septima **7**
Nelson, Jill **6**
Simpson, Carole **6**

Works Progress Administration (WPA)
Alexander, Margaret Walker **22**
Baker, Ella **5**
Douglas, Aaron **7**
Dunham, Katherine **4**
Lawrence, Jacob **4**
Lee-Smith, Hughie **5, 22**
Wright, Richard **5**

World African Hebrew Israelite Community

Ben-Israel, Ben Ami **11**

World beat
Belafonte, Harry **4**
Fela **1**
N'Dour, Youssou **1**
Ongala, Remmy **9**

World Bank
Soglo, Nicéphore **15**

World Boxing Association (WBA)
Whitaker, Pernell **10**

World Boxing Council (WBF)
Whitaker, Pernell **10**

World Council of Churches (WCC)
Mays, Benjamin E. **7**
Tutu, Desmond **6**

World Cup
Milla, Roger **2**
Pelé **7**

World hunger
Belafonte, Harry **4**
Iman **4**
Jones, Quincy **8**
Leland, Mickey **2**
Masire, Quett **5**
Obasanjo, Olusegun **5**

World of Music, Arts, and Dance (WOMAD)
Ongala, Remmy **9**

WPA
See Works Progress Administration

WRL
See War Resister's League

Xerox Corp.
Rand, A. Barry **6**

Yab Yum Entertainment
Edmonds, Tracey **16**

Yale Child Study Center
Comer, James P. **6**

Yale Repertory Theater
Dutton, Charles S. **4, 22**
Richards, Lloyd **2**
Wilson, August **7**

Yale School of Drama
Dutton, Charles S. **4, 22**
Richards, Lloyd **2**

YMCA
See Young Men's Christian Associations

Yoruban folklore
Soyinka, Wole **4**
Vanzant, Iyanla **17**

Young Men's Christian Association (YMCA)
Butts, Calvin O., III **9**
Goode, Mal **13**

Cumulative Name Index

Volume numbers appear in **bold.**

Hayden, Robert Earl 1913-1980 **12**
Hayes, Isaac 1942— **20**
Hayes, James C. 1946— **10**
Hayes, Roland 1887-1977 **4**
Haynes, George Edmund 1880-1960 **8**
Haynes, Marques 1926— **22**
Haywood, Margaret A. 1912— **24**
Heard, Gar 1948— **25**
Hedgeman, Anna Arnold 1899-1990 **22**
Hedgeman, Peyton Cole
  See Hayden, Palmer
Height, Dorothy I(rene) 1912— **2, 23**
Hemphill, Essex 1957— **10**
Hemsley, Sherman 1938— **19**
Henderson, Gordon 1957— **5**
Henderson, Natalie Leota
  See Hinderas, Natalie
Henderson, Wade 1944(?)— **14**
Hendricks, Barbara 1948— **3**
Hendrix, James Marshall
  See Hendrix, Jimi
Hendrix, Jimi 1942-1970 **10**
Hendrix, Johnny Allen
  See Hendrix, Jimi
Henry, Aaron Edd 1922-1997 **19**
Henry, Lenny 1958— **9**
Henson, Matthew (Alexander) 1866-1955 **2**
Herenton, Willie W. 1940— **24**
Herman, Alexis Margaret 1947— **15**
Hernandez, Aileen Clarke 1926— **13**
Hickman, Fred(erick Douglass) 1951— **11**
Higginbotham, A(loysius) Leon, Jr. 1928-1998 **13, 25**
Hightower, Dennis F(owler) 1941— **13**
Hill, Anita (Faye) 1956— **5**
Hill, Beatrice
  See Moore, Melba
Hill, Bonnie Guiton 1941— **20**
Hill, Calvin 1947— **19**
Hill, Grant (Henry) 1972— **13**
Hill, Janet 1947— **19**
Hill, Jesse, Jr. 1927— **13**
Hill, Lauryn 1975(?)— **20**
Hill, Oliver W. 1907— **24**
Hill, Tamia
  See Tamia
Hillard, Terry 1954— **25**
Hilliard, David 1942— **7**
Hilliard, Earl F. 1942— **24**
Himes, Chester 1909-1984 **8**
Hinderas, Natalie 1927-1987 **5**
Hine, Darlene Clark 1947— **24**
Hines, Gregory (Oliver) 1946— **1**
Hinton, William Augustus 1883-1959 **8**
Holder, Eric H., Jr. 1951(?)— **9**
Holdsclaw, Chamique 1977— **24**
Holiday, Billie 1915-1959 **1**
Holland, Endesha Ida Mae 1944— **3**
Holland, Robert, Jr. 1940— **11**
Holmes, Larry 1949— **20**
Holte, Patricia Louise
  See LaBelle, Patti
Holyfield, Evander 1962— **6**
Hooks, Benjamin L(awson) 1925— **2**
hooks, bell 1952— **5**
Hope, John 1868-1936 **8**
Horne, Lena (Mary Calhoun) 1917— **5**
Hounsou, Djimon 1964— **19**
Houphouët-Boigny, Félix 1905— **4**
Houphouët, Dia
  See Houphouët-Boigny, Félix
House, Eddie James, Jr.
  See House, Son
House, Eugene

See House, Son
House, Son 1902-1988 **8**
Houston, Charles Hamilton 1895-1950 **4**
Houston, Cissy 19(?)(?)— **20**
Houston, Whitney 1963— **7**
Howard, Corinne
  See Mitchell, Corinne
Howard, Desmond Kevin 1970— **16**
Howard, Juwan Antonio 1973— **15**
Howlin' Wolf 1910-1976 **9**
Hrabowski, Freeman A., III 1950— **22**
Hudlin, Reginald 1962(?)— **9**
Hudlin, Warrington, Jr. 1953(?)— **9**
Hudson, Cheryl 19(?)(?)— **15**
Hudson, Wade 1946— **15**
Huggins, Larry 1950— **21**
Hughes, (James Mercer) Langston 1902-1967 **4**
Hughes, Albert 1972— **7**
Hughes, Allen 1972— **7**
Hughley, Darryl Lynn 1964— **23**
Humphrey, Bobbi 1950— **20**
Humphries, Frederick 1935— **20**
Hunt, Richard (Howard) 1935— **6**
Hunter, Billy 1943— **22**
Hunter, Charlayne
  See Hunter-Gault, Charlayne
Hunter-Gault, Charlayne 1942— **6**
Hunter, George William
  See Hunter, Billy
Hurston, Zora Neale 1891-1960 **3**
Hutchinson, Earl Ofari 1945— **24**
Hutson, Jean Blackwell 1914— **16**
Hyman, Earle 1926— **25**
Hyman, Phyllis 1949(?)-1995 **19**
Ice Cube 1969(?)— **8**
Ice-T 1958(?)— **6**
Iceberg Slim 1918-1992 **11**
Iman 1955— **4**
Ingraham, Hubert A. 1947— **19**
Ingram, Rex 1895-1969 **5**
Innis, Roy (Emile Alfredo) 1934— **5**
Irving, Clarence (Larry) 1955— **12**
Isley, Ronald 1941— **25**
Iverson, Allen 1975— **24**
Jackson, Alexine Clement 1936— **22**
Jackson, Fred James 1950— **25**
Jackson, George 1960(?)— **19**
Jackson, George Lester 1941-1971 **14**
Jackson, Isaiah (Allen) 1945— **3**
Jackson, Janet 1966— **6**
Jackson, Jesse 1941— **1**
Jackson, Jesse Louis, Jr. 1965— **14**
Jackson Lee, Sheila 1950— **20**
Jackson, Mahalia 1911-1972 **5**
Jackson, Mannie 1939— **14**
Jackson, Maynard (Holbrook, Jr.) 1938— **2**
Jackson, Michael Joseph 1958— **19**
Jackson, Millie 1944— **25**
Jackson, O'Shea
  See Ice Cube
Jackson, Reginald Martinez 1946— **15**
Jackson, Samuel L. 1948— **8, 19**
Jackson, Sheneska 1970(?)— **18**
Jackson, Shirley Ann 1946— **12**
Jacob, John E(dward) 1934— **2**
Jagan, Cheddi 1918-1997 **16**
Jakes, Thomas "T.D." 1957— **17**
Jam, Jimmy
  See Jimmy Jam
James, Daniel "Chappie", Jr. 1920-1978 **16**
James, Etta 1938— **13**
James, Juanita (Therese) 1952— **13**

James, Sharpe 1936— **23**
Jamison, Judith 1943— **7**
Jammeh, Yahya 1965— **23**
Jarreau, Al 1940— **21**
Jarvis, Charlene Drew 1941— **21**
Jawara, Sir Dawda Kairaba 1924— **11**
Jean, Wyclef 1970— **20**
Jean-Baptiste, Marianne 1967(?)— **17**
Jefferson, William J. 1947— **25**
Jeffries, Leonard 1937— **8**
Jemison, Mae C. 1957— **1**
Jenifer, Franklyn G(reen) 1939— **2**
Jenkins, Beverly 1951— **14**
Jenkins, Ella (Louise) 1924— **15**
Jimmy Jam 1959— **13**
Joe, Yolanda 19(?)(?)— **21**
John, Daymond 1969(?)— **23**
Johnson, "Magic"
  See Johnson, Earvin "Magic"
Johnson, Ben 1961— **1**
Johnson, Beverly 1952— **2**
Johnson, Carol Diann
  See Carroll, Diahann
Johnson, Caryn E.
  See Goldberg, Whoopi
Johnson, Charles 1948— **1**
Johnson, Charles Spurgeon 1893-1956 **12**
Johnson, Charles Arthur
  See St. Jacques, Raymond
Johnson, Earvin "Magic" 1959— **3**
Johnson, Eddie Bernice 1935— **8**
Johnson, Hazel 1927— **22**
Johnson, Jack 1878-1946 **8**
Johnson, James William
  See Johnson, James Weldon
Johnson, James Weldon 1871-1938 **5**
Johnson, John Arthur
  See Johnson, Jack
Johnson, John H(arold) 1918— **3**
Johnson Jr., Harvey 1947(?)— **24**
Johnson, Marguerite
  See Angelou, Maya
Johnson, Michael (Duane) 1967— **13**
Johnson, Norma L. Holloway 1932— **17**
Johnson, Robert L. 1946(?)— **3**
Johnson, Robert T. 1948— **17**
Johnson, Robert 1911-1938 **2**
Johnson, Virginia (Alma Fairfax) 1950— **9**
Johnson, William Henry 1901-1970 **3**
Johnson-Brown, Hazel W.
  See, Johnson, Hazel
Jones, Bill T. 1952— **1**
Jones, Bobby 1939(?)— **20**
Jones, Carl 1955(?)— **7**
Jones, Cobi N'Gai 1970— **18**
Jones, Elaine R. 1944— **7**
Jones, Elvin 1927— **14**
Jones, Ingrid Saunders 1945— **18**
Jones, James Earl 1931— **3**
Jones, Le Roi
  See Baraka, Amiri
Jones, Lillie Mae
  See Carter, Betty
Jones, Lois Mailou 1905— **13**
Jones, Marion 1975— **21**
Jones, Quincy (Delight) 1933— **8**
Jones, Roy Jr. 1969— **22**
Jones, Ruth Lee
  See Washington, Dinah
Jones, Sissieretta
  See Joyner, Matilda Sissieretta
Jones, Star(let Marie) 1962(?)— **10**
Joplin, Scott 1868-1917 **6**
Jordan, Barbara (Charline) 1936— **4**
Jordan, June 1936— **7**

Seale, Robert George
  See Seale, Bobby
Sears-Collins, Leah J(eanette) 1955— **5**
  See Williams, Billy Dee
Selassie, Haile
  See Haile Selassie
Sembène, Ousmane 1923— **13**
Senghor, Léopold Sédar 1906— **12**
Sengstacke, John Herman Henry 1912-1997 **18**
Serrano, Andres 1951(?)— **3**
Shabazz, Attallah 1958— **6**
Shabazz, Betty 1936— **7**
Shakur, Assata 1947— **6**
Shakur, Tupac Amaru 1971-1996 **14**
Shange, Ntozake 1948— **8**
Sharpton, Al 1954— **21**
Shaw, Bernard 1940— **2**
Sheffey, Asa Bundy
  See Hayden, Robert Earl
Sheffield, Gary Antonian 1968— **16**
Shell, Art(hur, Jr.) 1946— **1**
Sherrod, Clayton 1944— **17**
Shipp, E. R. 1955— **15**
Sifford, Charlie (Luther) 1922— **4**
Silas, Paul 1943— **24**
Siméus, Dumas M. 1940— **25**
Simmons, Russell 1957(?)— **1**
Simmons, Ruth J. 1945— **13**
Simone, Nina 1933— **15**
Simpson, Carole 1940— **6**
Simpson, Lorna 1960— **4**
Simpson, O. J. 1947— **15**
Simpson, Valerie 1946— **21**
Sinbad 1957(?)— **1, 16**
Singletary, Michael
  See Singletary, Mike
Singletary, Mike 1958— **4**
Singleton, John 1968— **2**
Sinkford, Jeanne C. 1933— **13**
Sister Souljah 1964— **11**
Sisulu, Sheila Violet Makate 1948(?)— **24**
Sklarek, Norma Merrick 1928— **25**
Slater, Rodney Earl 1955— **15**
Sleet, Moneta (J.), Jr. 1926— **5**
Smaltz, Audrey 1937(?)— **12**
Smiley, Tavis 1964— **20**
Smith, Anna Deavere 1950— **6**
Smith, Arthur Lee, Jr.
  See Asante, Molefi Kete
Smith, Barbara 1949(?)— **11**
Smith, Bessie 1894-1937 **3**
Smith, Clarence O. 1933— **21**
Smith, Emmitt (III) 1969— **7**
Smith, Jane E. 1946— **24**
Smith, Jennifer 1947— **21**
Smith, John L. 1938— **22**
Smith, Joshua (Isaac) 1941— **10**
Smith, Orlando
  See Smith, Tubby
Smith, Roger Guenveur 1960— **12**
Smith, Tubby 1951— **18**
Smith, Walker, Jr.
  See Robinson, Sugar Ray
Smith, Will 1968— **8, 18**
Smith, Willi (Donnell) 1948-1987 **8**
Sneed, Paula A. 1947— **18**
Snipes, Wesley 1962— **3, 24**
Soglo, Nicéphore 1935— **15**
Somé, Malidoma Patrice 1956— **10**
Sosa, Sammy 1968— **21**
Sowell, Thomas 1930— **2**
Soyinka, (Akinwande Olu)Wole 1934— **4**
Spaulding, Charles Clinton 1874-1952 **9**

Spikes, Dolores Margaret Richard 1936— **18**
Sprewell, Latrell 1970— **23**
St. Jacques, Raymond 1930-1990 **8**
St. John, Kristoff 1966— **25**
Stallings, George A(ugustus), Jr. 1948— **6**
Stanford, John 1938— **20**
Stanton, Robert 1940— **20**
Staples, Brent 1951— **8**
Staupers, Mabel K(eaton) 1890-1989 **7**
Steele, Claude Mason 1946— **13**
Steele, Shelby 1946— **13**
Stephens, Charlotte Andrews 1854-1951 **14**
Stevens, Yvette
  See Khan, Chaka
Steward, Emanuel 1944— **18**
Stewart, Alison 1966(?)— **13**
Stewart, Kordell 1972— **21**
Stewart, Paul Wilbur 1925— **12**
Stokes, Carl B(urton) 1927— **10**
Stokes, Louis 1925— **3**
Stone, Charles Sumner, Jr.
  See Stone, Chuck
Stone, Chuck 1924— **9**
Stone, Toni 1921-1996 **15**
Stout, Juanita Kidd 1919-1998 **24**
Strawberry, Darryl 1962— **22**
Street, John F. 1943(?)— **24**
Stringer, C. Vivian 1948— **13**
Sudarkasa, Niara 1938— **4**
Sullivan, Leon H(oward) 1922— **3**
Sullivan, Louis (Wade) 1933— **8**
Summer, Donna 1948— **25**
Sweat, Keith 1961(?)— **19**
Swoopes, Sheryl Denise 1971— **12**
Swygert, H. Patrick 1943— **22**
Sykes, Roosevelt 1906-1984 **20**
Tafari Makonnen
  See Haile Selassie
Tamia 1975— **24**
Tanner, Henry Ossawa 1859-1937 **1**
Tate, Eleanora E. 1948— **20**
Tate, Larenz 1975— **15**
Taulbert, Clifton Lemoure 1945— **19**
Taylor, Billy 1921— **23**
Taylor, Charles 1948— **20**
Taylor, John (David Beckett) 1952— **16**
Taylor, Kristin Clark 1959— **8**
Taylor, Lawrence 1959— **25**
Taylor, Meshach 1947(?)— **4**
Taylor, Regina 1959— **9**
Taylor, Susan L. 1946— **10**
Taylor, Susie King 1848-1912 **13**
Terrell, Dorothy A. 1945— **24**
Terrell, Mary (Elizabeth) Church 1863-1954 **9**
The Artist
  See Prince
"The Goat"
  See Manigault, Earl "The Goat"
Thigpen, Lynne 19(?)(?)— **17**
Thomas, Alma Woodsey 1891-1978 **14**
Thomas, Clarence 1948— **2**
Thomas, Derrick 1967-2000 **25**
Thomas, Frank Edward, Jr. 1968— **12**
Thomas, Franklin A(ugustine) 1934— **5**
Thomas, Isiah (Lord III) 1961— **7**
Thomas, Rufus 1917— **20**
Thomas, Vivien (T.) 1910-1985 **9**
Thompson, Tazewell (Alfred, Jr.) 1954— **13**
Thompson, Tina 1975— **25**
Thugwane, Josia 1971— **21**
Thurman, Howard 1900-1981 **3**

Thurman, Wallace Henry 1902-1934 **16**
Till, Emmett (Louis) 1941-1955 **7**
Tillman, George, Jr. 1968— **20**
Tolliver, William (Mack) 1951— **9**
Toomer, Jean 1894-1967 **6**
Toomer, Nathan Pinchback
  See Toomer, Jean
Tosh, Peter 1944-1987 **9**
Touré, Amadou Toumani 1948?— **18**
Touré, Sekou 1922-1984 **6**
Towns, Edolphus 1934— **19**
Townsend, Robert 1957— **4**
Townsend, Robert 1957— **23**
Tribble, Isreal, Jr. 1940— **8**
Trotter, (William) Monroe 1872-1934 **9**
Trouillot, Ertha Pascal
  See Pascal-Trouillot, Ertha
Tubbs Jones, Stephanie 1949— **24**
Tubman, Harriet 1820(?)-1913 **9**
Tucker, C. DeLores 1927— **12**
Tucker, Chris 1973(?)— **13, 23**
Tucker, Cynthia (Anne) 1955— **15**
Tucker, Rosina Budd Harvey Corrothers 1881-1987 **14**
Ture, Kwame
  See Carmichael, Stokely
Turnbull, Walter 1944— **13**
Turner, Henry McNeal 1834-1915 **5**
Turner, Tina 1939— **6**
Tutu, Desmond (Mpilo) 1931— **6**
Tyree, Omar Rashad 1969— **21**
Tyson, Cicely 1933— **7**
Tyson, Neil de Grasse 1958— **15**
Uggams, Leslie 1943— **23**
Underwood, Blair 1964— **7**
Unseld, Wes 1946— **23**
Upshaw, Eugene, Jr. 1945— **18**
Usry, James L. 1922— **23**
Utendahl, John 1956— **23**
Van Peebles, Melvin 1932— **7**
Van Peebles, Mario (Cain) 1957(?)— **2**
van Sertima, Ivan 1935— **25**
Vance, Courtney B. 1960— **15**
VanDerZee, James (Augustus Joseph) 1886-1983 **6**
Vandross, Luther 1951— **13**
Vann, Harold Moore
  See Muhammad, Khallid Abdul
Vanzant, Iyanla 1953— **17**
Vaughan, Sarah (Lois) 1924-1990 **13**
Vaughn, Mo 1967— **16**
Vereen, Ben(jamin Augustus) 1946— **4**
Vieira, Joao 1939— **14**
Vincent, Marjorie Judith 1965(?)— **2**
Von Lipsey, Roderick 1959— **11**
wa Ngengi, Kamau
  See Kenyatta, Jomo
Waddles, Charleszetta (Mother) 1912— **10**
Waddles, Mother
  See Waddles, Charleszetta (Mother)
Wagner, Annice 1937— **22**
Walcott, Derek (Alton) 1930— **5**
Walcott, Louis Eugene 1933— **2, 15**
  See Farrakhan, Louis
Walker, Albertina 1929— **10**
Walker, Alice (Malsenior) 1944— **1**
Walker, Cedric "Ricky" 1953— **19**
Walker, Herschel (Junior) 1962— **1**
Walker, Kara 1969— **16**
Walker, Madame C. J. 1867-1919 **7**
Walker, Maggie Lena 1867(?)-1934 **17**
Walker, Nellie Marian
  See Larsen, Nella
Walker, T. J. 1961(?)— **7**